Patrizia Di Bello teaches History and Thec
of London. She is the author of *Women's Ai*
(2007), and the editor, with Gabriel Koureas,
currently working on photography and sculpt

Colette Wilson is Lecturer in French Studies ai
at the Institute of Germanic and Romance Stu ... the
research seminar 'Photography: Theory, Practice, Debate'. She is the author of *Paris and the Commune 1871–1878: The Politics of Forgetting* (2007). Her current research focuses on French representations of Egypt.

Shamoon Zamir is Associate Professor of Literature and Visual Studies at New York University Abu Dhabi. He has taught at the University of Chicago, York University and the University of London. He is the author of *Dark Voices: W.E.B. Du Bois and American Thought* (1995) and has recently completed a study of the photography of Edward S. Curtis.

THE

FROM TALBOT TO RUSCHA

PHOTO

AND BEYOND

BOOK

EDITED BY **PATRIZIA DI BELLO, COLETTE WILSON AND SHAMOON ZAMIR**

Routledge
Taylor & Francis Group
LONDON AND NEW YORK

First published 2012 by I.B. Tauris

Published 2020 by Routledge
2 Park Square, Milton Park, Abingdon, Oxon OX14 4RN
605 Third Avenue, New York, NY 10017

Routledge is an imprint of the Taylor & Francis Group, an informa business

A full CIP record for this book is available from the British Library
A full CIP record is available from the Library of Congress

Library of Congress Catalog Card Number: available

ISBN 13: 978-1-8488-5615-8 (hbk)
ISBN 13: 978-1-8488-5616-5 (pbk)

CONTENTS

NOTES ON CONTRIBUTORS

David Campany is a writer, curator and Reader in Photography at the University of Westminster. His books include *Art and Photography* (2003), *Photography and Cinema* (2008), *ANONYMES: Unnamed America in Photography and Film* (Le Bal/Steidl, 2010) and *Jeff Wall: Picture for Women* (Afterall/MIT Press, 2011).

Patrizia Di Bello lectures on the History and Theory of Photography in the Department of the History of Art and Screen Media at Birkbeck College, University of London. Her publications include *Women's Albums and Photography in Victorian Britain: Ladies, Mothers and Flirts* (2007); and *Art, History and the Senses: 1830 to the Present* (2010), ed. with Gabriel Koureas.

David Evans lectures on the History and Theory of Photography at The Arts University College at Bournemouth. Publications include *John Heartfield: AIZ / VI 1930-38* (1992), *Appropriation* (2009) and *Critical Dictionary* (2011).

Mick Gidley is Emeritus Professor of American Literature and Culture at the University of Leeds. Alongside articles and books on literary and cultural history, including *Views of American Landscapes* (co-ed., 1989; 2007), his publications on photographic themes include *Photography and the USA* (2011), such collections as *American Photographs in Europe* (co-ed., 1994) and *Writing with Light* (ed., 2011), and three books on Curtis, most recently *Edward S. Curtis and the North American Indian Project in the Field* (2003; 2010).

Gabriel Koureas is Lecturer at Birkbeck College, University of London. His monograph *Memory, Masculinity and National identity in British Visual Culture, 1914–1930*, was published in 2007. Other publications include '"Desiring Skin": Eugenics, Trauma and Acting Out of Masculinities in British Inter-war Visual Culture', in Brauer and Cullen (eds), *Art Sex and Eugenics: Corpus Delecti* (2008); and 'Visualising an Open Wound: Nicosia, a Divided City in an Expanded Europe', in Martin (ed.), *City in Art* (2007).

Paul Melo e Castro is Leverhulme Early Career Fellow in the Department of Spanish, Portuguese and Latin American Studies at the University of Leeds. His Ph.D., completed in 2008, focused on the representation of Lisbon in the 1960s in the novel, the film and the photobook.

Annebella Pollen is Lecturer in the History of Art and Design and former Research Fellow for the project 'Methodological Innovations: Using Mass Observation' at the University of Brighton. Her AHRC-funded Ph.D. thesis 'Identity, Memory, Compassion and Competition: Mass-Participation Photography and Everyday Life' was completed in 2010. Previous publications on the subject of popular photography include 'Polyfoto of an Unknown Woman' (2008), available online at www.unknownsitter.com, and 'Sweet Nothings: Suggestive Brighton Postcard Inscriptions', *Photography and Culture* 2(1) (2009).

Graham Smith is Professor Emeritus in Art History at the University of St Andrews and a Fellow of the Royal Society of Edinburgh. He has been editor of the international quarterly *History of Photography* since 2001. His most recent publications include '*Light that Dances in the Mind*' (2007), 'Talbot's Epigraph to *The Pencil of Nature*', *History of Photography* (2010) and 'Time and Memory in Talbot's Calotypes of Oxford and Hill and Adamson's of St Andrews', in Jan Baetens, Alexander Streitberger and Hilde Van Gelder (eds), *Time and Photography* (2010).

Ian Walker is Reader in the History of Photography and Programme Leader for the MA/MFA Documentary Photography at the University of Wales, Newport. He has written widely on photography and, in the past few years, his research has focused on the relationship between documentary photography and Surrealism. He has published two books: *City Gorged with Dreams: Surrealism and Documentary Photography in Interwar Paris* (2002) and *So Exotic, So Homemade: Surrealism, Englishness and Documentary Photography* (2007). He is now working on a collaborative book on Czech Surrealist photography.

Liz Wells edited *The Photography Reader*, 2003 and *Photography: A Critical Introduction*, 2009, 4th edn; she is co-editor of *Photographies* (Routledge Journals). Publications on photography and the land include *Land Matters: Landscape Photography, Culture and Identity* (2011). She is Professor in Photographic Culture, Faculty of Arts, University of Plymouth. She teaches on the MA in Photography and the Book and convenes the research group for Land/Water and the Visual Arts, within the University's Research Centre for Media, Art and Design.

Colette Wilson lectures at the Institute of Germanic and Romance Studies, where she directs the MA in Cultural Memory and the seminar series 'Photography: Theory, Practice, and Debate'. Her recent publications include: *Paris and the Commune 1871–78: The Politics of Forgetting* (2007), and a specially edited number of the *Journal of Romance Studies* entitled 'The Well-travelled Lens: Studies in Photography and Cultural Encounter, Memory and Identity' 8(1) (2008).

Shamoon Zamir is Associate Professor of Literature and Visual Studies at New York University Abu Dhabi. He has recently completed a study of Edward Curtis and his photobook *The North American Indian*. His previous publications include *Dark Voices: W.E.B. Du Bois and American Thought* (1995) and the edited volumes *The Unruly Garden: Robert Duncan and Eric Mottram, Letters and Essays* (2007, with A. Evans), and *The Cambridge Companion to W.E.B. Du Bois* (2008).

PICTURE CREDITS

Chapter 2

All figures: William Henry Fox Talbot, *Sun Pictures in Scotland* (London: John Murray, 1845), courtesy of the Harry Ransom Center, the University of Texas at Austin.

Chapter 3

All figures: Edward S. Curtis *The North American Indian*, 20 vols and 20 loose-leaf portfolios (Cambridge, MA: The University Press [Vols 1–5] and Norwood, MA: The Plimpton Press [Vols 6–20], 1907–30), courtesy of the Guildhall Library, City of London. Photographs by Shamoon Zamir.

Chapter 4

All photographs by Emil Otto Hoppé, courtesy of the E.O. Hoppé Trust, Curatorial Assistance, Pasadena, CA.

Figure 1: Emil Otto Hoppé, portrait of George Bernard Shaw, 1933.

Figures 2a, 4 and 5: Emil Otto Hoppé, from *Romantic America* (New York: B. Westermann, 1927).

Figure 2b and 3: Emil Otto Hoppé, from *Picturesque Great Britain* (Berlin: Ernst Wasmuth, 1926).

Chapter 5

Figure 1: Walker Evans, 'Main Street Looking North From Courthouse Square', *Fortune* (May 1948). Photograph by Polly Braden.

Figures 2, 3 and 4: Walker Evans, 'Homes of Americans', *Fortune* (May 1946). Photograph by Polly Braden.

Figure 5: Walker Evans, 'Labor Anonymous', *Fortune* (November 1946). Photograph by Polly Braden.

Chapter 6

All figures: *The Sculptures of Picasso, with Photographs by Brassaï*, with an essay by Daniel Henry Kahnweiler (London: Rodney Phillips & Co, 1949), © Estate Brassaï – RMN, Réunion des musées nationaux and © Succession Picasso/DACS, London 2010. Photographs by Polly Braden.

Chapter 7

Figure 1a: Williams, Arizona, 1992. Photograph by Ian Walker.

Figure 1b: Ed Ruscha, '*Mobil*, Williams, Arizona' and '*Standard*, Williams, Arizona', from *Twentysix Gasoline Stations* (Alhambra, CA: The Cunningham Press, 1962), © Ed Ruscha, courtesy the artist and Gagosian Gallery.

Figure 2a: Ed Ruscha, 'Hands Flipping Pages', 1963, © Ed Ruscha, courtesy the artist and Gagosian Gallery.

Figure 2b: Ed Ruscha, '*Standard*, Amarillo, Texas', from *Twentysix Gasoline Stations*, 1962, © Ed Ruscha, courtesy the artist and Gagosian Gallery.

Figure 3a: Ed Ruscha, *Standard Station, Amarillo, Texas*, 1963, © Ed Ruscha, courtesy the artist and Gagosian Gallery.

Figure 3b: Seven copies of *Twentysix Gasoline Stations* in the exhibition *In Visible Light*, Museum of Modern Art, Oxford, 1997. Photograph by Ian Walker.

Figure 4a: Ed Ruscha, contact sheet for *Twentysix Gasoline Stations*, 1962, © Ed Ruscha, courtesy the artist and Gagosian Gallery.

Figure 4b: Title page of the copy of *Twentysix Gasoline Stations* in the collection of the Library of the University of Wales, Newport. Photograph by Ian Walker.

Chapter 9

All figures: Search 88, *One Day for Life: Photographs by the People of Britain, Taken on a Single Day* (London: Bantam Press, 1987), © Search 88 Cancer Trust. Photographs by Polly Braden.

Chapter 10

Figure 1: Heiner Müller and Sibylle Bergemann, *Ein Gespenst verlässt Europa* (Cologne: Kiepenheuer & Witsch, 1990), © Sibylle Bergemann and © 1990 Verlag Kiepenheuer & Witsch, GmbH & Co. KG, Cologne. Photographs by Polly Braden.

Figure 2: Bertolt Brecht, *Kriegsfibel* (Berlin: Eulenspiegel Verlag, 1955), courtesy Das Neue Verlag GmbH, Akademie der Künste, Berlin, Bertolt-Brecht-Archiv, BBA B9. Photographs by Polly Braden.

Figure 3: Original dust jacket of Bertolt Brecht, *Kriegsfibel* (Berlin: Eulenspiegel Verlag, 1955), courtesy Das Neue Verlag GmbH, Akademie der Künste, Berlin, Bertolt-Brecht-Archiv, BBA B9.

Figure 4: Left: 'Am Tage der Saarrückgliederung' (Day of the Return of the Saar), *Adolf Hitler: Bilder aus dem Leben des Führers* (Altona-Bahrenfeld: Cigaretten-Bilderdienst, 1936), courtesy David Evans. Right: Bertolt Brecht, *War Primer* (London: Libris, 1998), courtesy Libris. Photographs by Polly Braden.

Chapter 11

All figures: Carlos Freire and Robert Solé, *Alexandrie l'Égyptienne* (Paris: Stock, 1998), courtesy Carlos Freire. Photographs by Polly Braden.

Chapter 12

All figures: Eduardo Gageiro, *Lisboa no Cais da Memória 1957–1974* (Lisbon, 2003), courtesy Eduardo Gageiro. Photographs by Polly Braden.

Chapter 13

Figures 1, 2 and 3: Orhan Pamuk, *Istanbul, Hatiralar Ve Sehir*, with photographs by Ara Güler (Istanbul: YKY, 2003), courtesy Ara Güler and Orhan Pamuk. Photographs by Polly Braden.

Figure 4: Ara Güler and Orhan Pamuk, *Ara Güler's Istanbul* (London: Thames & Hudson, 2009), courtesy Ara Güler and Orhan Pamuk. Photographs by Polly Braden.

ACKNOWLEDGEMENTS

For their contribution to the development of The Photobook project, we would like to thank the Arts and Humanities Research Council, who provided funding for The Photobook workshops and conference, and for the illustrations in this book; Birkbeck College, who hosted workshops and conference, and Liz Drew for her technical and moral support; Gerry Badger, for speaking at the conference; Caroline Blinder and Susan Butler for their contributions to the workshops; Naomi Segal and the Institute for Germanic and Romance Studies for their support in the early stages on this project; Polly Braden for photographing our photobooks; Philippa Brewster for her support at I.B.Tauris.

INTRODUCTION

Patrizia Di Bello and Shamoon Zamir

Ever since the publication of Henry Fox Talbot's *Pencil of Nature* (1844–46) as a series of six fascicles, the home of the photograph has been the book as much as the gallery wall. It could even be argued that the book is the first and proper home of the photographic image from which it moved out to take up residence in the fine art gallery and the modern museum in the early twentieth century – just as the proper home of vernacular or private photography is the album or scrapbook. Despite this fact, histories of photography have not generally accorded the photobook a place of central importance, if they have paid it any attention at all; accounts have been organized more often around trajectories of technological developments, national histories, genres, iconic images, or the landmark bodies of work by individual photographers as auteurs.[1] Recent years, however, have witnessed a growing interest in the photobook, and this interest among both scholars and collectors is widespread enough to justify speaking of an emergent intellectual and cultural moment which is moving us to new levels of integrated understanding beyond the more scattered studies which have come before.

The ensemble of essays gathered here presents close readings of individual photobooks, from the early days of photography to the present, as well as some analysis of examples at the 'prismatic fringes' of the genre – magazines, catalogues, biographies.[2] Despite its wide temporal and formal scope, however, and despite its chronological organization, the collection does not attempt a history or a theorizing of genre. Motivated by the emergent scholarly interest in the photobook and in image and text interactions, the contributors are primarily preoccupied with developing ways of reading the photograph in the book. Understanding how meanings are shaped by an image's interactions with another, or its place in a group or sequence, or through its dialectical coexistence with text is the foundation upon which histories as well as aesthetic and cultural conceptualizations of genre must be built up if they are to prove durable, even in their inevitable partiality.

As Sergei Eisenstein noted in his seminal 1939 essay on the principle of montage in film, literature and art, the juxtaposition of two separate elements 'resembles a creation – rather than a sum of its parts – from the circumstance that in every such juxtaposition the result is qualitatively distinguishable from each component element reviewed separately'. Juxtaposition engenders 'a "third something"' which is 'not fixed or ready-made, but arises – is born' because it demands that 'the emotions and mind of the spectator' or reader not remain passive but become actively engaged in the creative process. Most importantly perhaps, Eisenstein's exploration of combinatory forms in a variety of arts leads him to an expanded understanding of the meaning of 'image' in art. For Eisenstein, montage exists not 'as something unrelated, but as a given particular representation of the general theme that in equal measure penetrates all the shot pieces'. The discussion here bears on film but applies equally to painting or literature. For Eisenstein:

> The juxtaposition of these partial details in a given montage construction calls to life and forces into the light that general quality in which each detail has participated and which binds together all the details into a whole, namely, into the generalized image, wherein the creator, followed by the spectator, experiences the theme.

It is the combination of individual images, visual only or visual and verbal, that constitutes the proper work of art, the creation of a larger and more complete 'image', or what Eisenstein calls an 'image of the theme itself'.[3]

If there is one thing which unites the essays in this volume, it is the exploration of the experience of the combinatory effect or aspect which Eisenstein refers to as a 'third something'. Not all the contributions are focused on art in Eisenstein's sense of the term; some examine works which occupy the boundary between art and social science, or between art and social documentary, and others deal with popular or 'coffee-table' work in which the combinatory form may foster a cultural or ideological conservatism. But in every photobook examined, the photograph is the primary vehicle of expression and communication, or it stands in equal, if sometimes conflicted, partnership with the written word. We take much of our intellectual and methodological impetus from Carol Armstrong's proposal that 'the irreducibility of the particular example' requires us to construct and refine practices of reading 'more than the articulation of a structure of knowledge'.[4]

Armstrong's analysis of the nineteenth-century British photobook has, perhaps more than any other scholarly work before it, provided an exemplary demonstration through detailed case studies of the importance of the photobook to histories of photography. *The Open Book: A History of the Photographic Book from 1878 to the Present*, an exhibition at the International Center of Photography in New York (June–September 2005),[5] picked up where Armstrong's study left off. While the exhibition recognized the role of the book within the histories of photography and exemplified the increasingly common practice in museums and galleries of displaying photobooks as part of photographic exhibitions (the Canon gallery at the Victoria and Albert Museum in London does so regularly), it also paradoxically brought into focus the potentially unbridgeable division between the gallery and the book, since the display of book covers or a single open page behind glass only made evident the impossibility of engaging with the haptic and visual experience of the book as material object. The only work in English to attempt a broad overview across time and national spaces is Martin Parr and Gerry Badger's two-volume *The Photobook: A History* (2004 and 2006). No work on the subject could hope to be fully inclusive, and there are obvious omissions and some contentious emphases in Parr and Badger's account; but it remains the most comprehensive survey of the field available. As Parr acknowledges, even at the start of the twenty-first century 'there is no scholarly consensus as to exactly what books are out there, and no comprehensive listing of the world's most important photographic books'. As a consequence, 'in terms of researching the history of photography, the photobook is the final frontier of the undiscovered'.[6]

If this claim is largely uncontentious, the attempt to define what exactly a photobook is brings us into more difficult and resistant critical terrain. Parr and Badger propose two key criteria as a means of imposing some degree of order on the overwhelming scale and diversity of the materials potentially available for inclusion in a history such as theirs and of making the delimited material manageable for critical investigation. They argue that for a book containing photographs to be considered as a photobook, it must present something more than a mere collection of images; it must demonstrate intention and coherence in design, whether this refers to the agency of the photographer-auteur, of an editor, or possibly even of an editorial team. The photobook has a 'particular subject – a specific theme' and what matters most is how the images work together: 'the sum, by definition, is greater than the part'.[7]

Almost all of the contributions in the present volume accept a relatively high level of intention or coherence in design in more or less these terms in their readings of individual works. More problematic is Parr and Badger's definition of the photobook as 'a book – with or without text – where the work's primary message is carried by photographs'.[8] Such an attempt to grant primacy to the image, and to relegate the text to a supportive or enhancing role, quickly unravels in the face of too many of the examples which Parr and Badger themselves include in their history. Do the 31 photographs by Walker Evans in the original edition of *Let Us Now Praise Famous Men* (1941) really carry the 'work's primary message' more than the hundreds of pages of brilliant and infuriating text by James Agee? Can we really speak of the 20 volumes and 20 portfolios of Edward S. Curtis's *The North American Indian* (1907–30) as a photobook as Parr and Badger mean it without also acknowledging that it is also probably the largest ethnography ever assembled? And even if we accept that today Dorothea Lange's images are better known than the sociological text which Paul Taylor wrote for their collaboration on *American Exodus* (1939), it would be a mistake to ignore the fact that Lange and Taylor saw the meanings of the work resting squarely and equally 'upon a tripod of photographs, captions, and text'.[9] Evans and Agee, and Curtis equally did not prioritize the image over the text when speaking of their own work. Photographs and text always interact, even if the text is mostly elsewhere, as in Talbot's *Sun Pictures in Scotland*, or the photographs have been lost, as in Alexander Honory's *The Lost Pictures*, 'the ultimate photobook' at the end of Parr and Badger's survey.[10] In the photobook, then, photographs certainly move beyond the role of illustrations or transmitters of evidence to claim an active role in generating an independent meaning grounded in the unique ontology of their visual form. But at the same time, they do not transcend the texts that accompany them; rather, image and text work within a dialectical relationship.

Most of the contributions to the present volume treat the relationship of image and text as an important concern and this reflects the growing critical interest in image-text interactions which has developed roughly alongside the interest in the forms and history of the photobook.[11] But what unites all the contributions here is that each of them examines works in which the photograph is integral and essential, and not merely supplemental, to the work's meanings. Chapters on publications at the fringes of the photobook, such as Walker Evans's pages for *Fortune* magazine, and Orhan Pamuk's *Istanbul: Memories of a City*, a lengthy autobiographical text which incorporates a number of small, poor-quality black and white photographs from a variety of sources, bring into focus the way in which attempts to delimit definitions too narrowly may foreclose the possibilities of a new history before it has been written. The fact that a work such as *The North American Indian* is today valued above all for its photogravures than for its ethnographic text may tell us more about the ways in which photographic history and the interests of collectors and dealers have evolved over the years than about the work itself or the historical and cultural specificity of its meanings. If we come to the photobook only or largely through models of visual analysis derived from earlier forms of photographic history or criticism, or through museum practices and art world economics, then it may be that we will close down the new perspectives and insights which a history of photography seen through the lens of the photobook promises before these have been properly opened up.

Photobooks which combine images and texts tend also to be products of collaborative authorship. Several books considered in this volume are the result of a partnership, which is not to say a relationship of exact equality, between a photographer and a writer. This is so in Carlos Freire's *Alexandrie l'Égyptienne* with accompanying text by Robert Solé, and in *Ein Gespenst verlässt Europa* (*A Spectre is Leaving Europe*) by the writer Heiner Müller and the photographer Sibylle Bergemann. In Curtis's *The North American Indian* the text was the creation of a team of ethnographers, informants and editors, including the photographer himself. With E.O. Hoppé we have a photographer turned sole author – though as Mick Gidley shows here, the photographer was only one factor in the making of the photobooks he authored. Indeed, an analysis of Hoppé's autobiography shows that 'Hoppé' was a narrative construction as much as an individual, and his photobooks must be seen as codifications, however partial, of specific cultural moments as much as works by him. In other books, such as Bertolt Brecht's *War Primer* or Orhan Pamuk's *Istanbul*, the work of the writer is primary: the photographs have been appropriated or borrowed but used against or independently of the intentions of the photographer or photographers who made them. Talbot's *Sun Pictures in Scotland*, our point of departure, offers perhaps the most elusive example of the collaboration between photographer and writer, and between image and text. As Talbot himself explains, all his images are 'scenes connected with the life and writings of Sir Walter Scott'.[12] The relevant texts from the works of Scott do not accompany the images but the assumption of a familiarity on the part of the intended nineteenth-century viewer makes them everywhere present in Talbot's anthology. Scott's embedded presence not only inspires but in a sense legitimates and co-authors *Sun Pictures*.

Co-authorship, however, does not pertain only to the combining of image and text. *The Sculptures of Picasso* is Brassaï's creation but it exists only to record the 'authorship' of another artist working in a different medium. We can thus come to Brassaï's book because we are engaged by his work as a photographer or because we want a record of Picasso's creativity. Authorship can be more diffuse still in other types of photobooks. *One Day for Life* is a collection of photographs created and submitted by the 'general public' as a form of collective self-representation but the final shape of the book results from decisions made by an editorial team. Walker Evans's magazine work also involves the editorial recycling of vernacular photography. And in exhibition catalogues and gallery publications the process of editorial selection is very often supplemented by co-authored essays and descriptive entries for individual images.

While the movement from Talbot to Ed Ruscha and beyond could be read as signalling an alternative historical project stretching from the Victorian era to the present, this is not our intended scope and ambition. The concern of our collection is more properly with the contrasts, commonalities and dialogues between a variety of practices, forms and thematics which have shaped this trajectory. In this respect, Talbot's *Sun Pictures in Scotland* (1845) and Ruscha's *Twentysix Gasoline Stations* (1962), read in juxtaposition to each other and through the commentaries of Graham Smith and Ian Walker, do not so much suggest a historical narrative as a set of preoccupations and strategies which have been worked through and explored diversely within this history, and which in turn provide the organizing matrix which underpins the conversations between the essays collected here.

The two works by Talbot and Ruscha would appear at first to have little in common. Talbot's is an exemplary embodiment of a Victorian aestheticism, expensively produced and inviting both haptic and visual indulgence; Ruscha's now landmark photographic contribution to late twentieth-century conceptual art is a small and cheaply produced paperback which blurs the boundary between high art and vernacular forms, and seems to celebrate its own physical fragility and therefore potential disposability. Talbot's images find their inspiration in the life and literary works of Walter Scott, while Ruscha's images of near-identical gasoline stations strung out along the much-mythologized Route 66 are largely unencumbered by textual frames and seem determined in their serial banality to undermine the activity of aesthetic contemplation. However, these differences are best grasped not as polar oppositions which can only be resolved by being separated out along a developmental or progressively organized art historical narrative, but as the terms of a single dialectic which has, in varying forms, determined the shape and direction of this narrative at various moments.

If the differences between *Sun Pictures* and *Twentysix Gasoline Stations* come as no real surprise, what is more striking perhaps are the shared preoccupations and continuities which connect the two works. Both are concerned with the relations between place, history and nationhood. Both explore, whether romantically or ironically, places which have become weighted with cultural memory and myth – what Pierre Nora has termed 'lieux de mémoire' (sites of memory).[13] In this sense, both carry a sense of something that is passing, even if the sense of melancholy is more ambiguously given in Ruscha. Both are also books of travel, the photobook not merely as a record but also in some way an enactment of journeying, and kinds of autobiography or memoir by indirection. These similarities and continuities, as much as the differences between the two works, help us bring into focus the cultural work undertaken by photobooks from the nineteenth century to the present day.

The subject matter of the photobooks considered and the avenues of investigation pursued in this collection are diverse. There is, then, no single theme – no one 'image of the theme itself' in Eisenstein's words – which governs all the essays. That said, a concern with the relationship of place and memory, and with the photobook as a vehicle for memorializing this relationship is a preoccupation which unites almost all the contributions. In addition to Talbot and Ruscha, this preoccupation is evident in the representations of the city in Colette Wilson's chapter on *Alexandrie l'Égyptienne* (1998), Paul Castro's on *Lisboa no Cais da Memória* (2003) and Gabriel Koureas's on *Istanbul: Memories of a City* (2005). It is there equally, if sometimes indirectly, in the considerations of the collective and individual representations of nation and national history (Annebella Pollen, David Campany and David Evans), of national landscape (Liz Wells), of the photographer as international citizen and traveller (Mick Gidley), and of the culturally dispossessed (Shamoon Zamir).

If the essays in this volume share certain cultural concerns, they tend to investigate them by grappling, in one way or another, with the problems of form: for example, the relationship of image and text; the quality of image reproduction; the dialogue between traditional art forms and photography; the appropriation and redeployment of existing imagery; the movement through the photobook as a translation of the experience of the street. Ethical, political and cultural concerns are by no means of secondary concern here but these are approached firstly through an analysis of aesthetic practice rather than through a methodology which privileges the social construction of visual meaning over the aesthetic. Such an approach requires at least some knowledge of the relationship of the forms of the photobook to the general history of the printing and reproduction of photographs in books or magazines.

The 'plates' in Fox Talbot's *Sun Pictures* were produced with the first negative-positive photographic system, which allowed the photographer to produce from each negative a potentially infinite number of prints on-paper that could be bound or hand-tipped in the pages of books and albums. As Armstrong argues, Talbot's photography was developed for the book, and books are intrinsic to the medium of photography. The new medium of photography was, then, always intended to become the content of an older one, the book.

The textual minimalism of *Sun Pictures* might now seem a pioneering example of the use of photographs to construct rather than illustrate a narrative. However, this image-led mode of book production was not a novelty introduced by photography. Many illustrated books and publications in the early nineteenth century began as collections of images rather than as texts in search of illustrations. These images were produced by engravers, who enjoyed a higher cultural and financial status than the 'letterpress' printers who produced text using moveable type. It was only towards the end of the process of making the plates that poems or other short texts were sourced or commissioned, often at short notice and paid by the line, to 'illustrate' the images.[14] What photography introduced was the possibility of bypassing the work of skilled artists, draughtsmen and engravers, enabling one process to produce and reproduce images ready for binding between pages of text.

It was only later in the nineteenth century, with the development of wood-engravings that could be printed at the same time and on the same page as text, that the relationship between image and text reversed into the one we assume today when we speak of 'illustration': optional images commissioned to embellish and somehow 'match' a pre-existing text, to which they have a conceptually subservient relation. But this privileging of text over image, of the image being required to match a text identified as the primary moment of ideation and creativity, was not always followed. Images remained primary in commercially produced albums and 'gift', 'picture' or 'drawing-room' books, precursors of today's coffee-table books. Hand-tipped plates – engravings, lithographs or photographs – continued to be used as a sign of high production values and cultural prestige in more expensive publications. Photographs added market value as a 'novelty', but also acquired a new authority as images invested with a documentary or evidentiary power by their indexicality,[15] especially in books with a claim to scientific or experiential veracity such as the international geographical series Orbis Terrarum, discussed in Gidley's chapter on Hoppé. The development of the half-tone system at the end of the century finally permitted photographs to be reproduced photomechanically (in continuous tone and without being manually turned into an engraving) at the same time and on the same page as text, via the same printing method. This fostered a closer relationship between photographs and texts, as they now interacted on the same footing and could nestle together on the same page, rather than being separated by the gulf, cultural as well as technical, of plate and letterpress. It also made it easier to have more than one image printed on the same page, for the verso and the recto of two pages to be combined into a 'double-page spread' of text and images, or for a photograph to 'bleed' across the gutter.

If the half-tone process helped to consolidate the conventions of mass-marketed illustrated books and magazines still familiar today, it also enabled more creative and exploratory work with the photographic image itself, as demonstrated by the experimentation of avant-garde artists in Europe and Russia in the 1920s and 1930s. Montage as a new organizing principle by which images could convey a narrative and carry meaning spread rapidly from the avant-garde to the wider field of 'modern' design and advertising, whether for commercial products or political propaganda.[16]

Photographs invaded the page not only of books, but also of magazines and newspapers, where some of the more interesting experimentation on the layout and sequencing of photographs took place, as discussed in David Campany's chapter on Walker Evans. In his *War Primer*, by contrast, Brecht extracts press photographs from their original mass media contexts and combines them with short poetic texts into 'photoepigrams', thus subverting the meaning of the original photograph to produce his own critique of fascism and war, a practice of appropriation examined by David Evans.

Walter Benjamin argued that text can be mobilized to rescue photographs from 'modish commerce' and give them a revolutionary political role to play.[17] If this describes Brecht's strategies, a similar impetus could arguably be said to have motivated conceptual artists such as Ruscha in their embrace of plain, factual photographs and inexpensively produced books as an alternative to an art system geared towards the production of fetishized, expensive, one-off objects traded like any other commodity. As Lucy Lippard notes, the fetishized art object 'dematerialized' into performance, happenings and conceptual events, only to rematerialize in the form of photographs,[18] often disseminated through low-production-values photocopies and cheaply printed booklets.[19] Ultimately, however, 'modish commerce' wins: *Twentysix Gasoline Stations* is now a highly collectable item, having gone through a complex material and conceptual journey here explored by Ian Walker.

Thanks to the developments in printing technology, almost all the photobooks examined in this collection are, or were at the time of their original publication, inexpensive items. Talbot, of course, worked before the cost of printing had been reduced by the half-tone process. Curtis, on the other hand, working during the first three decades of the twentieth century, specifically chose photogravure, the most expensive mode of photographic reproduction, rather than the half-tone process, ostensibly more suited to the requirements of salvage ethnography. As discussed in Zamir's chapter, what Curtis and his team produced was a book which did not resemble either the illustrated works of social science contemporaneous with it, or the social documentaries which appeared either at the same time as Curtis was at work or in the years immediately following the completion of his project. The contrast between the high production values of Talbot and Curtis on one hand and the more modest works considered in this volume on the other gives us a better grasp of the myriad ways by which meanings are generated in the photobook.

During the first half of the twentieth century, photographic prints were rarely collected by art museums. For individual photographers, producing books was, therefore, a good way to sell photographs and perhaps rescue them from the ephemeral realm of magazines and newspapers, and to establish the photographer as an author/artist in his or her own right. Brassaï, for example, began to photograph Picasso's sculptures for *Minotaure*, the French Surrealist magazine, where they featured in its first edition in 1933. This work continued and was eventually published in *The Sculptures of Picasso*, the focus of Patrizia Di Bello's chapter, an example of the post-war ideals of making high art available to a broader audience via photographically illustrated art-books.

With the widespread arrival of the photograph in the gallery and the museum after the Second World War and the institutional and commercial confirmation of the medium as an art form, the popularity of the photobook did not decline but rather the genre was transformed and developed. One manifestation of this change was the exhibition catalogue. While crucial in establishing photographers as artists worthy of being collected for posterity, exhibitions remain ephemeral events needing to be memorialized. Liz Wells explores this paradox in her chapter on exhibition catalogues, booklets or monographs. The catalogue is an ambiguous kind of photobook, on the one hand merely the record of an event of relatively limited duration and on the other an object or work in its own right, sometimes even the occasion for the exhibition in the first place.

The photobook's complex relationship to the exhibition, whether as a systematic record of an event, as an informal souvenir or as the product the exhibition is marketing, is not only visual but also tactile. More so than prints, the photobook is available for the public to hold, leaf through, buy, take home and collect. As Parr highlights, 'beautiful to open and pleasurable to leaf through', photobooks speak of a tactile engagement with images beyond the visual, for which there is no equivalent in the gallery space.[20] A concern with the physicality of the photobook thus also informs nearly all of the chapters.

Today computers, e-book readers and iPads seem to promise the final dematerialization of the book in favour of fragmented flows of digital texts and images flickering on different screens. Arguably, however, such technologies have revitalized the production and dissemination of paper-based photobooks. In a more general sense, the photobook's latest dis-incarnation into data to be re-materialized by means of a variety of devices – all imbued with their specific tactile pleasures and frustrations – is but the latest demonstration of the nature of both photographs and books as 'multiple instance or type artwork',[21] which are more akin to plays, songs or scripts than a unique or 'ontologically singular' artwork such as a painting.[22] In the same way that a book can be published as different editions, each subtly but significantly different, a photograph can exist in a variety of instances: as an ephemeral image in a magazine; as a fine archival print in a museum; as a postcard in a personal collection; and as pages in different books. This is one of the material and conceptual knots touched upon by Koureas as he compares reproductions of Ara Güler's photographs of Istanbul in Pamuk's inexpensive paperback with the same images in the more expensive photobook *Ara Güler's Istanbul* (2009). The medium of the book has meaning of and in itself.[23] It can declare 'prestigious photobook' even in advance of the material produced and selected, as in *One Day For Life*. It can suggest 'utilitarian brochure' even when it has come to be seen as a key example of conceptual art, as in the case of *Twentysix Gasoline Stations*, copies of which were recently still catalogued in libraries under 'transportation' or sold by second-hand dealers as trade booklets.

Cheaply printed or expensively produced, photobooks are not just for looking; they 'function in a direct and private interaction with the reader and they only come alive when they are used, touched, handled, manipulated'.[24] This is a key material characteristic in Paul Castro's analysis of the photobook as open to 'tactical' reading. Using Michel de Certeau's conceptual framework to analyse the street and movement through the city, Castro's chapter allows us to see how the photobook can constitute a 'strategy' deployed to guide and inform our journey through a narrative – in this case, one that also embodies the photographer's tactical journeys through the city of Lisbon, and through his own archive of images, to create and make public political narratives that run counter to official governmental strategies.[25] Like de Certeau's city stroller or *Lisboa*'s photographer, the reader can move tactically through the book to suit individual whims and needs running counter to the order imposed by its design, thus subverting the official strategy or sequential narrative of the book.

Pictures in books always have the potential to be read independently of the narrative constructed by the text and sequence. The reader/viewer is richly rewarded when opening the book at random, flicking the pages backwards from the end, or stopping to look at individual pages in no particular sequence. Photographs disrupt the flow of written words and invade 'the structure of literacy'.[26] At any moment, we might be touched by a photograph's 'punctum' in a way totally unrelated to the 'studium' or subject matter or 'strategy' of the book as a whole – setting us off on an involuntary train of Proustian reminiscences and sensations.[27] Like the children looking at picturebooks discussed by Walter Benjamin,[28] we step into a photobook as a space which is both imaginary and given 'real' authority by photography. We can move through it according to unsystematic, momentary 'tactics' developed on the spur of the moment and by our own fantasy. Our reading of a photobook might be tactical, disrupting or subverting the book's sequential development, but as we close the book, all the photographs leap 'back in again so there should be no disorder', as in Hans Christian Andersen's tale of a magic picturebook in which 'everything was alive' and came out of the page.[29] Unlike photographs in shoeboxes, photo-wallets, or folders of j-pegs, photographs in a book go back to a stable order. The bound format holds the photographs securely and maintains equilibrium between order and disorder, sequence and random looks, stability and instability, memory and change. Photobooks can reward 'library-desk' study and 'coffee-table' perusal.[30] A photobook is, in other words, defined by how it is experienced as much as by how it is made.

This experience must be grasped not just in its mental but also in its sensuous and haptic dimensions. Constance Classen argues that 'we live in a society of the image ... in which, while there may be many representations of touch, there is often nothing actually there to feel'. Advertising, television and the Internet 'are designed to be consumed by the eyes and the ears' and 'the endless appeal to the sense of touch one finds in contemporary visual imagery, unaccompanied as it is by actual tactile gratification, may have helped make touch the hungriest sense of postmodernity'.[31] Books, on the other hand, 'are eminently tactile objects. They can be held, carried, opened and closed, rifled, piled, or even placed on one's head to improve posture'.[32] This might help explain the contemporary interest in photobooks. Placed in a photobook, photographs no longer just represent a world out there, a distant referent rendered permanently visible by being photographed yet remaining untouchable, but become a part of an object available to our sense of touch – no longer invisible windows through which we can see our cultural Others or our fellow citizens, cities we may or may not have visited, famous works of art and sights that are no longer available, but objects of an opaque materiality which lead us to a multisensorial experience.

Our own emphasis on the haptic experience of the photobook is no doubt determined in large part by the lack of what Classen refers to as 'tactile gratification' in modern-day cultures, of the West at least. But it is worth remembering that the photograph itself, from the very moment of its first emergence, has been perceived as the agent of a radical dematerialization. As early as 1859, the American Oliver Wendell Holmes proclaimed the cultural changes wrought by the photograph in just such terms:

> Form is henceforth divorced from matter. In fact, matter as a visible object is of no use any longer, except as the mould on which form is shaped. Give us a few negatives of a thing worth seeing, taken from different points of view, and that is all we want of it.

Holmes's rhetoric carries a sense of self-conscious exaggeration alongside a first flush of excitement, but his characterization of the photograph as a 'universal currency' or as 'bank notes' was perhaps more prescient than he realized.[33] The attraction of the stereoscope or stereograph (with which Holmes's essay is primarily concerned and a version of which he invented) lay precisely in restoring through the effect of three-dimensionality a sense of greater materiality than the flat two-dimensional photograph, a cultural desire which lives on in three-dimensional cinema and television.

Our intent is not to fetishize the photobook or to divert its cultural energies into a new aestheticism. The experience of the hand working in partnership with the eye returns us to the content proper of the book; it does not substitute for it. Brassaï's photographs of Picasso's sculptures reproduce the distance from the work of art in a gallery, the injunction against touching, and at the same time bring us to a level of tactile and visual intimacy unavailable inside the exhibition space. The opulence of image and book production in *The North American Indian* may appear at first to be at odds with the self-declared documentary intent of the project, a transformation of the dispossessed cultural Other not only into a museum relic but an *objet d'art* for the viewer's detached contemplation. But, as Zamir argues, it is the very aesthetic and material dimensions of Curtis's work which can bring us to surprising ethical engagements.

The contributors each treat the relationship between aesthetics and ethics or politics in different ways. Wilson locates the engagements with Alexandria of Carlos Freire and Robert Solé in a tradition of orientalism, although here we are dealing with a Brazilian photographer who has made France his home and a Francophone Egyptian. By contrast, Koureas takes Orhan Pamuk's autobiographical text on Istanbul as a form of what may be called self-orientalizing, a sort of counter-strategy within the traditions of orientalism. If Brecht's *War Primer* and Eduardo Gageiro's Lisbon photographs present us with perhaps the most direct engagement with the politics of the photographic image, David Evans's treatment of Sibylle Bergemann's images from the German Democratic Republic suggests an altogether more ambiguous and indirect critical response to state ideology.

This introduction does not by any means exhaust the themes and avenues of investigation pursued by the essays in this volume but it does provide a good indication of some of the main currents of cultural thought which weave in and out of the essays and which help organize them into a dialogic whole. The scholarly interests of the contributors to this volume are located across the fields of visual arts, literature and cultural studies and some are practising photographers. It was a set of common interests which extend across these fields that brought the contributors together but it was also a sustained dialogue between us that helped consolidate and further develop these common interests. The present collection is, in fact, the product of an almost year-long conversation. This took the form of a series of monthly workshops, generously funded by the Arts and Humanities Research Council of England, which stretched across the 2008–9 academic year and which culminated in a two-day conference hosted by Birkbeck College at the University of London.[34]

Notes

1 The following offer representative examples: Beaumont Newhall, *The History of Photography: From 1839 to the Present Day* (New York: The Museum of Modern Art, 1949, and subsequent editions); Helmut Gernsheim, *A Concise History of Photography* (London: Thames and Hudson, 1965 and subsequent editions); Naomi Rosenblum, *A World History of Photography* (New York: Abbeville Press, 1984 and subsequent editions); Jean-Claude Lemagny and André Rouillé (eds), *A History of Photography*, trans. Janet Lloyd (1986; Cambridge: Cambridge University Press, 1987); Michel Frizot (ed.), *The New History of Photography*, trans. Susan Bennett et al. (1994; Cologne: Könemann, 1998).

2 '[C]ertainly periodicals can form the prismatic fringes of a library'; Walter Benjamin, 'Unpacking my Library: A Talk about Book Collecting' (1931) in *Illuminations*, ed. Hannah Arendt and trans. Harry Zhon (Bungay, Suffolk: Fontana/Collins, 1983), pp. 59–67 (p. 66).

3 Sergei Eisenstein, 'Word and Image' (1939), in Eisenstein, *The Film Sense*, ed. and trans. Jay Leyda (London: Faber and Faber, 1968), pp. 17, 34, 19.

4 Carol Armstrong, *Scenes in a Library: Reading the Photograph in the Book, 1843–1875* (Cambridge, MA: MIT, 1998), pp. 7, 6.

5 Andrew Roth, *The Open Book: A History of the Photographic Book from 1878 to the Present* (Göteborg: Hasselblad Center, 2004).
6 Martin Parr, 'Preface', in Parr and Gerry Badger, *The Photobook: A History*, 2 vols (London: Phaidon, 2004, 2006), vol. 1, pp. 5, 4.
7 Parr and Badger, *The Photobook* 1, p. 7.
8 Parr and Badger, *The Photobook* 1, p. 6.
9 Dorothea Lange and Paul Taylor, *American Exodus: A Record of Human Erosion* (New York: Reynal and Hitchcock, 1939), p. 6.
10 'In his charming volume, Honory provides mnemonics in the form of words for each lost picture, opposite where the photograph itself might have been reproduced' (Parr and Badger, *The Photobook* 2, p. 326).
11 See, for example, Jefferson Hunter, *Image and Word: The Interaction of Twentieth-Century Photographs and Texts* (Cambridge: Harvard University Press, 1987); Clive Scott, *The Spoken Image: Photography and Language* (London: Reaktion, 1999); Alex Hughes and Andrea Noble (eds), *Phototextualities: Intersections of Photography and Narrative* (Albuquerque: University of New Mexico Press, 2003); and Mick Gidley (ed.), *Writing with Light; Words and Photographs in American Texts* (Oxford: Peter Lang, 2010). The relation of image and text is, of course, also a major concern of Armstrong's *Scenes in a Library*.
12 From a pre-publication announcement circulated in June 1845.
13 Pierre Nora (ed.), *Les Lieux de mémoire* (Paris: Gallimard, 1984–93), vol. 2, *La Nation, I* (1986), pp. vii–x.
14 Michael Twyman, *Printing 1770–1970: An Illustrated History of Its Development and Uses in England* (1970; London: The British Library, 1998); Patrizia Di Bello, 'Albums as Printed Media', in *Women's Albums and Photography in Victorian England: Ladies, Mothers and Flirts* (Aldershot, UK and Burlington, VT: Ashgate, 2007), pp. 42–8.
15 See Lucien Goldschmidt and Weston J. Naef, *The Truthful Lens: A Survey of the Photographically Illustrated Book 1844–1914* (New York: Grolier Club, 1980).
16 See, for example, Margarita Tupitsyn and Christina Kiaer, *Rodchenko and Popova: Defining Constructivism* (London: Tate, 2009); Maud Lavin and Matthew Teitelbaum, *Montage and Modern Life* (Cambridge, MA and London: MIT, 1992); Stephen Bury (ed.), *Breaking the Rules: The Printed Face of the European Avant Garde 1900–1937* (London: The British Library, 2007).
17 Walter Benjamin, 'The Author as Producer' (1934), trans. Edmund Jephcott, in Michael W. Jennings, Brigit Doherty and Thomas Y. Levin (eds), *The Work of Art in the Age of its Technological Reproducibility and Other Writings on Media* (Cambridge, MA and London: The Belknap Press of Harvard University Press, 2008), pp. 79–95.
18 Lucy Lippard, *Six Years: The Dematerialization of the Art Object from 1966 to 1972* (New York and London: Praeger/Studio Vista, 1973); see especially the 'Postface', pp. 263–4.
19 Robe Perrée, *Cover to Cover: The Artist's Book in Perspective* (Rotterdam: NAi Publishers, 2002).
20 Parr and Badger, *The Photobook* 1, p. 4. See also Elizabeth Edwards and Janice Hart (eds), *Photographs, Objects, Histories: On the Materiality of Images* (London and New York: Routledge, 2004).
21 Noël Carroll, *A Philosophy of Mass Art* (Oxford: Clarendon Press, 1998), p. 211.

22 Peter D. McDonald, 'Ideas of the Book and Histories of Literature: After Theory?', *PMLA* 21:1 (2006), pp. 214–28 (p. 223).

23 Donald F. McKenzie, '"What's Past Is Prologue": The Bibliographical Society and History of the Book', in *Making Meaning: 'Printers of the Mind' and Other Essays* (Amherst: University of Massachusetts Press, 2002), pp. 259–75.

24 Pavel Büchler, 'The Pages', in *Books: Turning Over the Pages* (Cambridge: Kettle's Yard Gallery, 1986), n.p.

25 The photobook as a metaphor for the city street has also been explored in the exhibition *Few Are Chosen: Street Photography and the Book, 1936–1966* at the Metropolitan Museum of Art, New York, November 2004–March 2005.

26 Martha Langford, *Suspended Conversations: The Afterlife of Memory in Photographic Albums* (Montreal and Kingston: McGill-Queen University Press, 2001), p. 125.

27 The terms are coined and used by Roland Barthes throughout his *Camera Lucida: Reflections on Photography*, trans. Richard Howard (London: Cape, 1982).

28 Walter Benjamin, 'A Glimpse into the World of Children's Books', trans. Rodney Livingstone, in *The Work of Art in the Age of its Technological Reproducibility* (1926), pp. 226–35.

29 Benjamin, 'Children's Books', p. 226.

30 For a discussion of the different postures and locations of reading (at a desk, in bed, etc.) see Michael Hatt, '"The Book Beautiful": Reading, Vision, and the Homosexual Imagination in Late Victorian Britain', in Luisa Calé and Patrizia Di Bello (eds), *Illustrations, Optics and Objects in Nineteenth-Century Literary and Visual Cultures* (Basingstoke: Palgrave Macmillan, 2010), pp. 167–84.

31 Constance Classen, 'Fingerprints: Writing about Touch', in Classen (ed.), *The Book of Touch* (Oxford and New York: Berg, 2005), pp. 1–12 (p. 2).

32 Classen, 'Fingerprints', p. 7.

33 Oliver Wendell Holmes, 'The Stereoscope and the Stereograph' (1859), in Alan Trachtenberg (ed.), *Classic Essays on Photography* (New Haven: Leete's Island Books, 1980), pp. 80, 81.

34 'The Photobook' conference was held on 3–4 April 2009.

H. FOX TALBOT'S 'SCOTCH VIEWS' FOR *SUN PICTURES IN SCOTLAND* (1845)

For Larry J. Schaaf

Graham Smith

> 'Vows and pilgrimages are not peculiar to the religious enthusiast.'
> Samuel Rogers, *The Pleasures of Memory*

> 'The magnifying glass of memory brings high relief.'
> Marcel Proust, *À la recherche du temps perdu*

In October 1844 William Henry Fox Talbot, the inventor of negative-positive paper photography, travelled to Scotland in order to take pictures for a 'photographic work called Sun Pictures in Scotland'.[1] Talbot initiated this project three months after publishing the first fascicle of *The Pencil of Nature*, and bound volumes of *Sun Pictures in Scotland* were distributed to subscribers in July 1845, a month after the fourth fascicle of *The Pencil* appeared.[2] Despite being contemporaneous with *The Pencil*, *Sun Pictures* has a discrete identity and possesses a distinct visual and conceptual coherence. This unitary character is due to the fact that its plates are all of 'scenes connected with the life and writings of Sir Walter Scott'.[3]

Sun Pictures was a timely book, for it coincided with the apotheosis of Scott that occurred after his death in September 1832. Indeed, there appears to have been an element of opportunism in Talbot's decision to produce the book: by linking photography to Scott, he evidently hoped to promote his own invention. *Sun Pictures* was also in accord with contemporary interest in the history, landscape and buildings of Scotland. In reality, these elements are interwoven, for the heightened interest in Scotland was stimulated in large part by the writings of the 'Wizard of the North'.[4]

My study begins by exploring the role played by Scott's poetry and novels in the lives of Talbot and his family. The second section begins with an account of Talbot's tour of Scotland. Next it recounts the production of *Sun Pictures* after Talbot's return to England, drawing on letters written by his mother, who played an important role in bringing the book to fruition. This section ends with a summary of the contents of the book. The third part of my study focuses upon the heritage of Scott as it came to be embodied in sites associated with him and with his work, in travel writings inspired by his poetry and novels and by prints, drawings and paintings depicting the landscapes and monuments described in them. Most particularly, it considers links between Talbot's photographs and these traditions.

Talbot and Scott

> I have just finished the Lady of the Lake. – I read all the notes. I have also read these plays of Shakespeare. John. Richard 2^d^. Henry 4th & I am now reading Henry 5th. I have nearly finished it.

These lines occur in a letter Talbot wrote to his mother in 1813.[5] Talbot was evidently precocious, for he was writing from school at Harrow and was barely thirteen at the time. 'The Lady of the Lake' is, of course, Scott's hugely popular poem set in Scotland during the first half of the fifteenth century, which had been published three years before.

Thirteen years later Talbot quoted from *The Lady of the Lake* to evoke the beauty of the island of Corfu.[6] 'It is a lovely wilderness,' he observed, 'quite unlike any other place I have seen, and one thinks as one rambles thro' it, what a Paradise it *might* be'. Next he transcribed eight lines from stanza fifteen of *The Lady of the Lake*, in which the mysterious hunter, James Fitz-James, looked out over Loch Katrine. Talbot closed this quotation by attaching to it a fragment from the first lines of the sixteenth stanza: 'Blithe were it *then* to wander here! / But *now*! …'.

Talbot's knowledge of Scott was not restricted to *The Lady of the Lake*. Writing from Cambridge in 1819, he volunteered that he had read *The Bride of Lammermoor* and liked it very much.[7] Some months later, he asked his mother whether she had read *Ivanhoe*, observing: 'I have no time to read it now & have merely gazed upon the outside. By the report of all who read it, it is very good'.[8] References to Scott's novels continue during the 1820s, appearing repeatedly in Talbot's correspondence with his mother. In 1828, for instance, he wrote: 'I liked Walter Scott's 2^d^ series of the Canongate "*the fair maid of Perth*" so much that I procured the 1st

series. There are two very good stories in it'.[9] Other titles mentioned in this correspondence are *Peveril of the Peak*, *Quentin Durward*, *Woodstock*, *Anne of Geierstein* and *Waverley*.[10]

Scott's novels also occupied an important place in the social life of Talbot's family. 'We had *tableaux* again last Tuesday,' reported Talbot's half-sister Horatia in a letter of 1830. 'They made me act *Rowena* in the last scene in *Ivanhoe* & Lady Dudley was Rebecca in a beautiful oriental dress'.[11] Two years later Lady Elisabeth mentioned a mysterious 'Box', which Queen Consort Adelaide had sent to Caroline: it displayed '*tableaux* of all the Waverley Novels ..., ending with a Pageant including the Tomb & all the Chara[c]-ters'.[12] Scott even played a role in Talbot's courtship of Constance Mundy, for she mentioned *The Abbot* in three letters written before their marriage.[13]

It is difficult today to comprehend the extent of Scott's fame during the nineteenth century.[14] For Thomas Carlyle, 'the Author of *Waverley* was like some living mythological personage and ranked among the chief wonders of the world'.[15] Likewise, the catalogue of the Edinburgh Centenary Exhibition of 1871 compared Scott's significance for Scotland to that of Dante in Florence, and, in the same year, *The Illustrated London News* pronounced him 'the greatest original author of the nineteenth century', equal in stature to Homer and Shakespeare. The huge number of works of art inspired by Scott's writings is another indicator of his fame.[16]

October 1844 to July 1845

From 26 September to 2 October 1844 Talbot was in York attending a meeting of the British Association for the Advancement of Science. After this gathering, he journeyed north to Durham and Newcastle, continuing on to the Scottish Borders. He spent a week in the Borders, visiting the abbeys at Kelso, Dryburgh, Melrose and Jedburgh. From Jedburgh he wrote to Constance: 'Extremely dark weather both yesterday and today has prevented me from making any views of the ruined Abbey here'.[17] Talbot arrived in Edinburgh on 10 October and took rooms at Rampling's Hotel in Waterloo Place. Two days later he travelled to Glasgow, continuing south to Hamilton and Lanark before returning to the capital. On 18 October he left Edinburgh once more, journeying to Stirling and Callander, from which he made an excursion to Loch Katrine, the setting of *The Lady of the Lake*. He returned to Edinburgh on 22 October and began his homeward journey the next day. On the way south he revisited Melrose Abbey and went to Abbotsford, Scott's home, where he signed the visitors' book.[18] From Kelso he made another pilgrimage to Dryburgh Abbey, Scott's burial place, and then set out for Carlisle, before crossing the country once more to arrive in York on 29 October.[19]

When Talbot returned to Wiltshire, his mother took a forceful role in the production of the volume resulting from her son's tour, and several letters attest to the businesslike nature of her interventions. In the first of these, Lady Elisabeth expressed concern over the fact that Sir David Brewster had shown Henry's 'Scotch views' to Lord and Lady Kinnaird and urged her son not to allow the photographs to be exhibited further before the book was distributed.[20] Lady Elisabeth also reminded him of the need to produce a prospectus announcing the publication by subscription of the volume of 'Scotch views'.[21] In other letters she expressed concern that purchasers of the book would not understand the revolutionary character of Henry's 'representations'.[22] It was she who compiled the list of subscribers.

The volumes sent to subscribers contained a title page, a list of plates and 23 photographs. Inserted into each copy was also a 'Notice to the Reader', which announced: 'The plates of the present work are impressed by the agency of Light alone. They are the sun-pictures themselves, and not, as some persons have imagined, engravings in imitation'. Except for the title itself, the title page of *Sun Pictures* is identical to that in the first fascicle of *The Pencil*, displaying as its epigraph the same lines from Virgil's *Georgics* (3.291–2):

> Juvat ire jugis qua nulla priorum
> Castaliam molli devertitur orbita clivo.[23]

These lines celebrate the invention of photography, while also drawing attention to the difficulties Talbot overcame before he achieved success, but in *Sun Pictures* the motto can also be read literally, for Talbot's itinerary in Scotland took him to remote parts of the country. Except for brief observations in the captions to two of the plates, *Sun Pictures* contains no text. Of the 23 plates in the book, 13 are mounted individually on the pages. These compare in size with those in *The Pencil*. The remaining views are smaller and are mounted two to a page. Four repeat large plates, having been 'taken in duplicate as a necessary precaution'.[24] Taking into account the text of the pre-publication announcement, it is clear that Talbot intended his views to comprise a visual anthology of subjects connected with Scott.

Sites of Memory

> In our travels through Scotland I have mentioned many scenes, which were ennobled by being called the retreats of William Wallace. … These traditional anecdotes, whether true, or fabled, add grandeur to a scene.[25]

In this passage William Gilpin articulates the notion of the picturesque landscape or landscape of memory, using sites connected with the hero of Scotland's War of Independence. If Scott were to be substituted for Wallace, this text could provide an epigraph for *Sun Pictures*, for the buildings and landscapes represented in it were likewise enhanced by association with the 'Wizard of the North'. In fact, a passage from William Scrope's *Days and Nights of Salmon Fishing in the Tweed* explicitly links the notion of landscape of association to Scott by focusing upon the role his writings played in animating the scenery of the Borders:

> My first visit to the Tweed was before the Minstrel of the Forth had sung those strains which enchanted the world, and attracted people of all ranks to this land of romance. The scenery therefore at that time, unassisted by story, lost its chief interest; yet was it all lovely in its native charms. All these outward pictures he might see and feel: but he could see no farther: the lore had not spread its witchery over the scene – the legends slept in oblivion.[26]

In practice, the 'lore' contained in Scott's writings not only spread its 'witchery' over the Borders but also extended over other landscapes and buildings in Scotland, creating sites replete with association – what Pierre Nora has termed 'lieux de mémoire'.[27]

Heriot's Hospital

The first plate in *Sun Pictures* shows Heriot's Hospital, a seventeenth-century structure that was once attributed to Inigo Jones. Situated on the south side of Edinburgh, Heriot's was a prominent feature of the nineteenth-century city, as can be seen from a panorama that J.M.W. Turner made in 1831 as a frontispiece to Robert Cadell's *Poetical Works of Sir Walter Scott*.[28] In 1834, during his last visit to Scotland, Turner sketched Heriot's Hospital from the grounds, and Gerald Finley has suggested that these drawings may have been intended as studies for an illustration for Scott's novel *The Fortunes of Nigel*.[29] It is clear that Heriot's was already an important element in the iconography of Scott when Talbot visited Edinburgh in October 1844.

The foundation had been established in 1624 with a bequest from George Heriot, who had accumulated a huge fortune as jeweller and goldsmith to James VI and I. As 'Jingling Geordie', Heriot is one of the principal characters in *The Fortunes of Nigel*, where he promises: 'And for the wealth God has sent me, it shall not want inheritors while there are orphan lads in Auld Reekie'.[30] Scott also treated Heriot in his introduction, explaining how he came to '[make] free with the name of a person who has left the most magnificent proofs of his benevolence and charity that the capital of Scotland has to display'.[31] He also discussed Heriot's in his *Provincial Antiquities and Picturesque Scenery of Scotland*, describing it as 'one of the proudest ornaments of Edinburgh'.[32]

Talbot's photograph shows the southwest corner and south (back) elevation of Heriot's Hospital, focusing upon the corner blocks and the tracery windows of the foundation's chapel. Talbot's carefully composed picture expresses the solidity and permanence of Heriot's building, qualities appropriate to the donor and to his foundation, and complements the spirit of his benefaction. It is also a nice visual expression of Scott's admiration for Heriot and opens *Sun Pictures* with gravitas.

The Scott Monument

Situated on the south side of Princes Street, George Meikle Kemp's Scott Monument, the second plate in *Sun Pictures*, is situated 200 metres from the site of Rampling's Hotel, where Talbot stayed in October 1844. Talbot's photograph shows the north and west sides of this Victorian Gothic structure, 'as it appeared when nearly finished, in October 1844'. The view is to the southeast, and it is possible to make out the arches of North Bridge, the viaduct connecting the Old and New towns. Katherine Peveraro has proposed that the photograph was taken from a window of the Royal Hotel, at 53 Princes Street, and this is supported by the angle and direction of Talbot's view.[33]

Talbot referred to his photograph in the letter, mentioned at the beginning of this paper, to John Murray. 'It will be curious,' he wrote, 'to compare my 2^{d} plate, the Monument to Walter Scott at Edinburgh, with the view of the same contained in your copy of Mr Hill's splendid work. My view was taken much nearer, and therefore the details of architecture are more discernable'.[34]

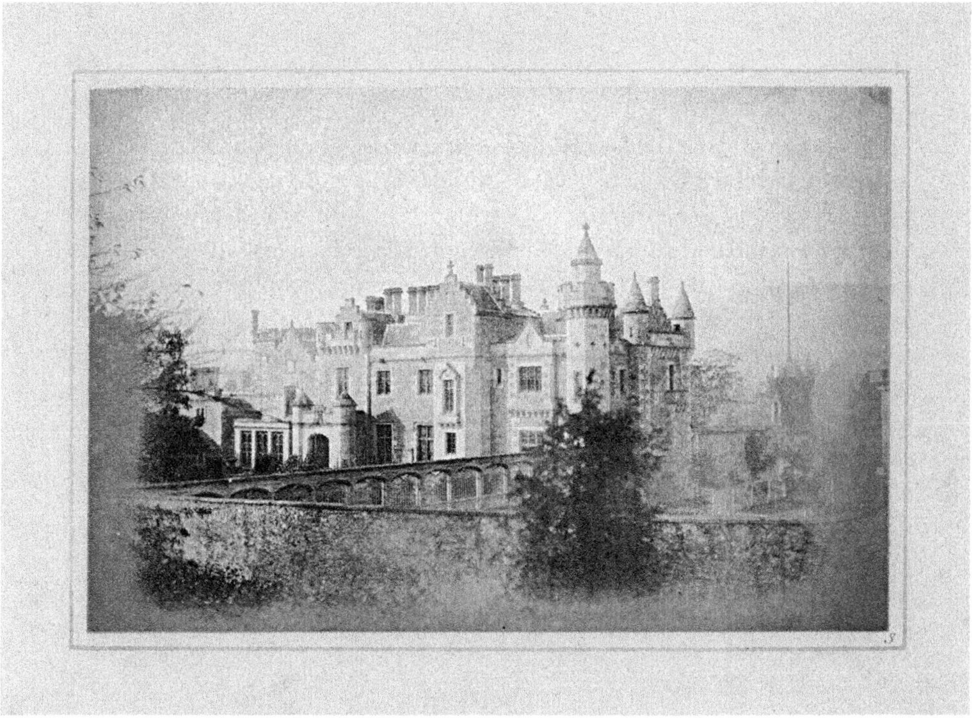

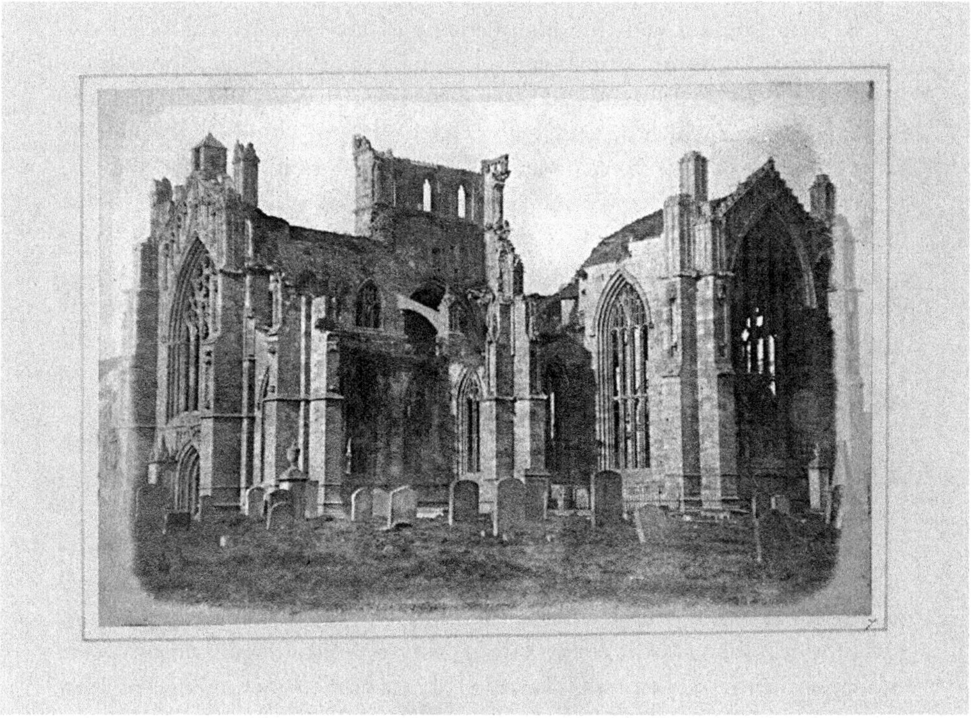

1a. William Henry Fox Talbot, 'Abbotsford', salt print from a calotype negative, in *Sun Pictures in Scotland* (London, 1845).

1b. William Henry Fox Talbot, 'Melrose Abbey', salt print from a calotype negative, in *Sun Pictures in Scotland* (London, 1845).

The photograph may be linked to observations Talbot made in *The Pencil* in his commentary to plate XVII: 'Those amateurs especially … who find the rules of *perspective* difficult to learn and to apply – and who moreover have the misfortune to be lazy – prefer to use a method which dispenses with all that trouble'. 'And,' he continued, 'even accomplished artists now avail themselves of an invention which delineates in a few moments the almost endless details of Gothic architecture which a whole day would hardly suffice to draw correctly in the ordinary manner'. When he composed this text, Talbot may have had in mind a photograph he had taken in 1843 showing one of the towers of Orleans Cathedral, but his plate of the Scott Monument, with its finials and buttresses, validates this claim equally well. The second plate is therefore a testimonial to Talbot's invention, in addition to providing an authoritative record of the memorial to Scott at a particular moment in time.

Abbotsford

In 1811, in keeping with the requirements of his appointment as Sheriff-Depute of Selkirkshire, Scott bought a farm in the Borders overlooking the River Tweed.[35] This property had a farmhouse, which Scott transformed into Abbotsford – and which he would later characterize as 'a kind of Conundrum Castle' and a 'romance in Architecture … a sort of vision'.[36]

Abbotsford must have reminded Talbot of Lacock Abbey, his own 'house in the country',[37] for Lacock is precisely what Abbotsford pretends to be – a medieval building converted for modern habitation.[38] Talbot always considered the accurate representation of architecture to be one of the 'applications' of his invention. In 'Some Account of the Art of Photogenic Drawing', for instance, the paper he read to the Royal Society in London in January 1839, he recalled: 'In the summer of 1835 I made … a great number of representations of my house in the country, which is well suited to the purpose, from its ancient and remarkable architecture. And this building I believe to be the first that was ever yet known *to have drawn its own picture*'.[39] Six years later, commenting on plate fifteen in *The Pencil* – 'One of a series of views representing the Author's country seat in Wiltshire' – he referred to this paper and to 'these curious self-representations'. In the light of this background, Abbotsford's pictures of itself have multiple functions: they are at once authentic 'self-representations' of Scott's home – metonymies of Scott himself – and demonstrations of what Talbot considered to be one of the principal applications of his invention.

Talbot made four negatives at Abbotsford. The first of these is a general view from the east, looking over the wall that encloses the southeast side of the property (Figure 1a). The second was taken from outside the entrance gate, looking into the forecourt. The third shows the turreted entrance and provides a good sense of the eclectic nature of the building. Also part of this group is a photograph of an effigy of Maida, Scott's favourite dog. This memorial is just visible in the second and third views.[40] Talbot suspended some drapery behind the effigy in order to concentrate on the sculpture. In addition, he transcribed the Latin encircling the base of the sculpture, indicating that the inscription was 'nearly as follows': 'Maidae marmorea dormis sub imagine Maida / Ante fores domini sit tibi terra levis'. In fact, it reads 'Maidae marmorea dormis sub imagine Maida / Ad januam domini sit tibi terra levis', which John Gibson Lockhart, Scott's biographer and son-in-law, translated as 'Beneath the sculptured form which late you wore, / Sleep soundly, Maida, at your master's door'.[41]

Abbotsford became a monument to the author and a secular pilgrimage site, one that was visited by a host of travellers during Scott's lifetime.[42] On Scott's death the painter David Wilkie asked: 'Why might not Abbotsford be made the Blenheim of literature?'[43] Abbotsford continues to attract thousands of visitors each year and is ultimately the most personal of Scott's memorials. But the monument to Maida is in some respects the most personal memorial of all, for it too is a metonymy for Scott, recalling his love of his dogs and alluding to one of his most endearing characteristics.

Melrose Abbey

Melrose Abbey is a different kind of monument – one in which 'memory crystallizes and secretes itself' (Figure 1b).[44] Melrose embraces five centuries of the religious history of Scotland, extending from its foundation in the twelfth century to its dissolution in the sixteenth century, but it is also a monument to Scotland, for it was there that the heart of Robert the Bruce found its resting place. Melrose Abbey is, in essence, a palimpsest representing successive periods in the history of Scotland.

Crystallized in Melrose are also memories emanating from Scott's 'Romance of Border Chivalry', *The Lay of the Last Minstrel*.[45] This poem concerns a Border feud in the sixteenth century, as it was recounted by a harper who had been given shelter by Anne, Duchess of Buccleuch and Monmouth, at Newark Castle, near Selkirk. The 'last minstrel' sang a ballad concerning the duchess's ancestor, Lady Buccleuch of Branksome Hall. In an effort to put a stop to a courtship that had developed between her daughter and Lord Cranstoun, the duchess resorts to necromancy, sending Sir William of Deloraine to Melrose Abbey to 'win the treasure of the tomb' occupied by 'the wondrous Michael Scott; a Wizard of ... dreaded fame' (2.138–9).

Scott famously began the second canto with a description of Melrose Abbey as it appeared by moonlight when Deloraine approached it:

If thou would'st view fair Melrose aright,
Go visit it by the pale moonlight;
For the gay beams of lightsome day
Gild, but to flout, the ruins grey.
When the broken arches are black in night,
And each shafted oriel glimmers white;
When the cold light's uncertain shower
Streams on the ruin'd central tower;
When buttress and buttress, alternately,
Seem framed of ebon and ivory;
When silver edges the imagery,
And the scrolls that teach thee to live and die;
When distant Tweed is heard to rave,
And the owlet to hoot o'er the dead man's grave,
Then go – but go alone the while –
Then view St. David's ruin'd pile;
And, home returning, soothly swear,
Was never scene so sad and fair!

Deloraine entered the church by 'a steel-clench'd postern door' (2.95), which may be the door into the south transept that appears in Talbot's photographs. Scott then described the great east window (2.113–28) before recounting how Deloraine and a monk opened the wizard's tomb and took from him 'his Book of Might' (2.217).

When Harriet Beecher Stowe visited Melrose in the 1850s, she employed a striking photographic metaphor to characterize Scott's description of the abbey:

> We went into a minute examination with our guide ... who seemed to have a full sense of its peculiar beauties. I must say here, Walter Scott's description in the Lay of the Last Minstrel is as perfect in most details as if it had been written by an architect as well as a poet – it is a kind of glorified daguerreotype.[46]

Talbot's photographs, like that of the Scott Monument, attest once more to the capacity of photography to record the myriad details of Gothic architecture. They are also linked to a long tradition of images of ruins, a tradition discussed by Rose Macaulay in *Pleasure of Ruins*, a book designed 'to explore the various kinds of pleasure given to various people at various epochs by the spectacle of ruined buildings.[47] Talbot's photographs offer many of the forms of 'ruin-pleasure' discussed by Macaulay, but they also possess the particular dimension of depicting Roman Catholic remains in post-Reformation Scotland. As such, they attest to what Samuel Johnson termed 'proof of the waste of reformation'.[48] They also display a quality that Talbot considered intrinsic to photography – the capacity to suggest the passage of time. Talbot was enchanted by the power of photography to preserve historic monuments and, by revealing the marks that give such buildings the patina of time, to open windows into the past. Moreover, he relished the possibilities photographs offered to connect emotionally with ancient sites. In this respect he shared Johnson's view that contemplation of the past was an elevating activity. 'Whatever withdraws us from the power of our senses; whatever makes the past, the distant, or the future predominate over the present,' pronounced Johnson, 'advances us in the dignity of thinking beings'.[49]

Loch Katrine

Scott's greatest success as a poet came in 1810 with the publication of *The Lady of the Lake*. This poem is set in the fifteenth century and revolves around a conflict between James V and the clan Douglas. Having been banished by the king, James of Douglas and his daughter, Ellen, had been given sanctuary on an island on Loch Katrine in the Trossachs. This island, known now as Ellen's Isle, formed a natural paradise. In the first canto, which contains vivid descriptions of the scenery of the region, a lone huntsman finds himself at Loch Katrine. Calling himself James Fitz-James, he meets Ellen on the shore of the loch, and she leads him to shelter on the island. Fitz-James falls in love with Ellen but discovers she already has two suitors. In the final canto Ellen presents herself at the royal court at Stirling and pleads for her father's pardon. There she discovers that Fitz-James is James V, and, as a result of her intervention, Douglas and the king are reconciled.

The Lady of the Lake sold 25,000 copies in eight months, breaking all previous records for the sale of poetry.[50] Readers were transfixed by the poem's narrative and enchanted by the scenery it described, and hordes of sightseers descended upon Loch Katrine to experience the magic for themselves. In essence, *The Lady of the Lake* became to Loch Katrine and the Trossachs what *The Lay of the Last Minstrel* was to Melrose Abbey and the Borders.

In 'Malise's Journey to the Trossacks [*sic*]', published in an Edinburgh weekly in 1811, James Hogg, the Ettrick Shepherd, poked fun at this phenomenon:

> Mr Scott has superseded the possibility of ever more pleasing, by a second description of the Trossacks, but in so doing he has certainly added to the pleasure arising from a view of them. Whoever goes to survey the Trossacks, let him have the 11th, 12th, and 13th divisions of the first canto of the *Lady of the Lake* in his heart; a little Highland whisky in his head; and then he shall see the most wonderful scene that nature ever produced. ... The fancy must be aroused, and the imagination and spirits exhilarated in order that he may enjoy these romantic scenes and groves of wonder with the proper zest.[51]

A painting of the 1820s in the National Gallery of Scotland provides a visual counterpart to this phenomenon.[52] This picture, by John Knox, depicts the east end of Loch Katrine and shows Ben Venue in the background. There are boats and fishermen on the loch, and a horse and cart carrying travellers approaches. On an outcrop on the left side of the painting three travellers appear to be waiting to board a vessel that will take them to picnic on Ellen's Isle. In the meantime a highlander plays the bagpipes to establish an appropriate mood for this pilgrimage. On a promontory overlooking the loch is a hut to shelter travellers and enable them comfortably to enjoy views of Loch Katrine.

Talbot's mental image of Loch Katrine was formed early, as we have seen, but it must have remained vivid from subsequent readings of the poem. It is tempting to think that Talbot had a copy of *The Lady of the Lake* with him and that, like Orville Dewey, an American who visited the Trossachs in 1833,[53] he may have read the poem the night before setting out from Callander. Certainly he had approached Loch Katrine with anticipation and may have felt something like Maria Edgeworth's excitement when she arrived there in 1823:

> Here we are! I can hardly believe we are really at the place we have so long wished to see: we have really been on Loch Katrine. We were fortunate in the day; it was neither too hot, nor too cold, nor too windy, nor too anything.[54]

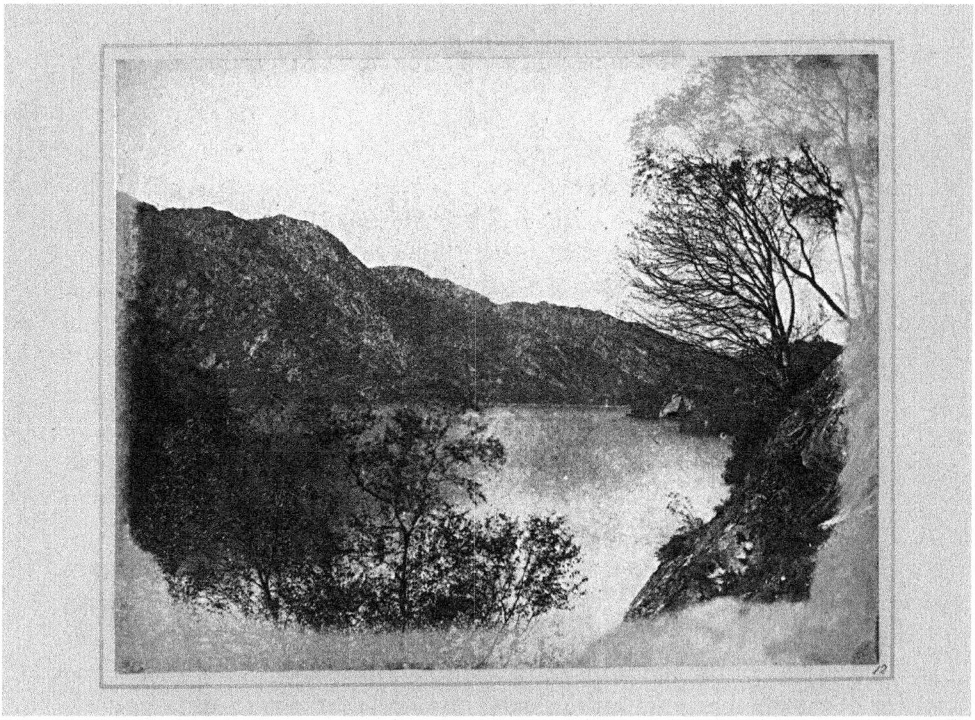

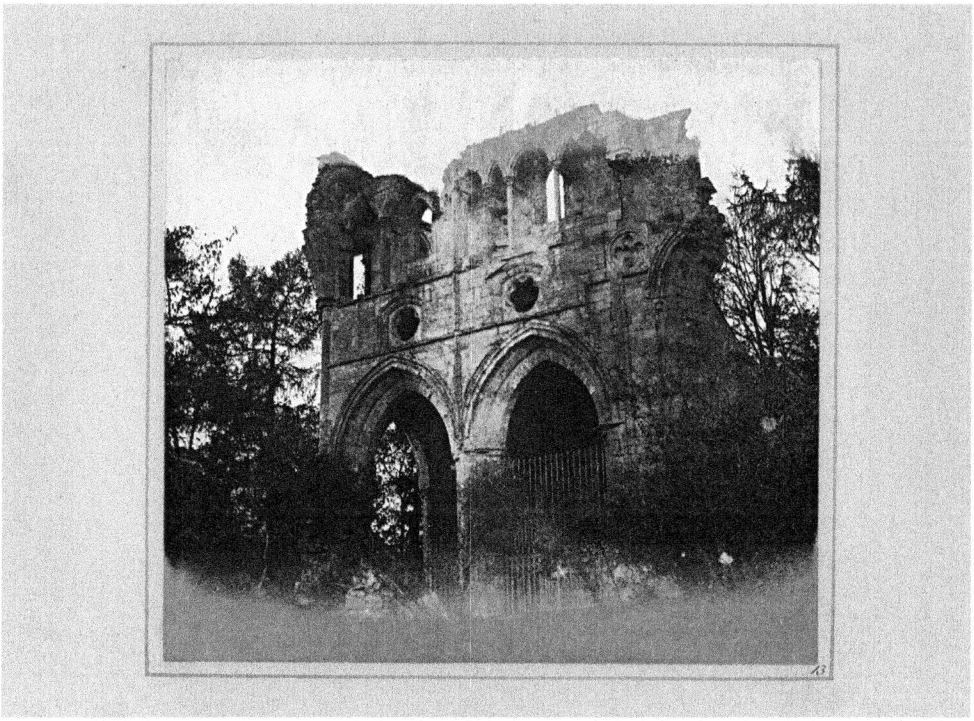

2a. William Henry Fox Talbot, 'Loch Katrine', salt print from a calotype negative, in *Sun Pictures in Scotland* (London, 1845).

2b. William Henry Fox Talbot, 'The Tomb of Sir Walter Scott, in Dryburgh Abbey', salt print from a calotype negative, in *Sun Pictures in Scotland* (London, 1845).

As Gillen D'Arcy Wood has suggested, it is also possible that the act of photographing Loch Katrine may have acquired a self-referential quality for Talbot, reminding him of when, in October 1833, he attempted to make *camera lucida* sketches at Lake Como.[55]

For Talbot, Scott's verse must also have been overlaid with impressions derived from other writings and from images, most particularly the compositions Turner produced for *The Poetical Works of Sir Walter Scott*.[56] These came to complement and even to supersede the verbal images generated by Scott's writings, for they engendered their own traditions. It may also be the case that the very idea of a photographically illustrated book inspired by the life and writings of Scott was prompted by the success of Turner's illustrations.

D'Arcy Wood criticizes the 'unromantic clarity' of Talbot's photographs of Loch Katrine and concludes that Talbot's 'denuded landscape images dissolve the Romantic aura of Scott mythology, giving us the Highlands as the "real"'.[57] The mundane does indeed intrude upon the poetic in the first of the photographs, but the second picture is characterized by a velvety amorphousness that engenders a mood of romance. Furthermore, Talbot's third plate (Figure 2a) provides a visual equivalent to lines in the first canto describing James Fitz-James's first view of Loch Katrine – while also evoking the sublime, primordial nature of the Trossachs:

> And thus an airy point he won,
> Where, gleaming with the setting sun,
> One burnished sheet of living gold,
> Loch Katrine lay beneath him rolled,
> In all her length far winding lay,
> With promontory, creek, and bay,
> And islands that, empurpled bright,
> Floated amid the livelier light,
> And mountains that like giants stand
> To sentinel enchanted land.
> High on the south, huge Benvenue
> Down to the lake in masses threw
> Crags, knolls, and mounds, confusedly hurled,
> The fragments of an earlier world;
> A wildering forest feathered o'er
> His ruined sides and summit hoar.[58]

The epidermis of memory, like that of individuals, may be renewed, and so sites like Loch Katrine came to be inscribed afresh by artists and writers who reflected upon the imagery generated by Scott's poetry. If Turner's vision of Loch Katrine and the Trossachs impressed itself upon the text of 'The Lady of the Lake', in the second half of the nineteenth century George Washington Wilson and others introduced new images that came to coexist with the earlier ones.

Dryburgh Abbey

Situated about three miles from Melrose, Dryburgh Abbey – the last large plate in *Sun Pictures* – was established in 1150 and was destroyed in 1322 by the army of Edward II. The abbey was rebuilt during the fifteenth century, but its life as a monastic community ended with the Scottish Reformation. The 11th Earl of Buchan bought the ruins in 1786 and was buried in the sacristy in 1829. Scott was interred in the north transept three years later.[59]

Talbot framed his photograph to focus upon the north transept, isolating the surviving bays and their ruinous clerestory (Figure 2b). Trees frame this detail so that it appears to be returning to nature. Only the barrier closing the right arch indicates that this space houses something portentous. In essence, this fragment is isolated to become a 'natural' monument to Scott, like something in Francesco Colonna's *Hypnerotomachia Poliphili*. The memorial function is also indicated by Talbot's caption – 'The Tomb of Sir Walter Scott, in Dryburgh Abbey'. At the same time, this plate is linked visually and thematically to those of Abbotsford, Melrose Abbey and the Scott Monument, and so 'Scott's' architecture forms a connective thread linking the beginning, middle and end of *Sun Pictures*.

Conclusion

It was stated early in this paper that Talbot's photographs for *Sun Pictures* constitute an anthology of views associated with Walter Scott. This has been borne out by examination of those 'realms of memory'. It has also become apparent that many of Scott's sites embody multiple histories, some of which are not connected directly with him. In short, Talbot's photographs record complex, multi-faceted sites of memory. These views are unified, however, by the fact that all of them had been inscribed by Scott in some fashion. If much of Europe had been 'Byronised' during the first decades of the nineteenth century, Scotland in the same period had been 'Scottified'.[60] Consequently, Talbot could reasonably have assumed that his subscribers would be able to conjure up passages from Scott when they leafed through their copies of *Sun Pictures*. In essence, he could expect his subscribers to be informed by what Henry James in 1871 would term 'latent preparedness'.[61] But the plates in *Sun Pictures* also function as practical demonstrations of the new art of photography. Like his plates in *The Pencil of Nature*, Talbot's photographs for *Sun Pictures* illustrate the qualities and applications of his 'royal road to *Drawing*'.[62]

Notes

1 Henry Fox Talbot to the publisher John Murray (16 May 1846). See Larry J. Schaaf, Talbot Correspondence Project, De Montfort University (hereafter TCP), 9887.
2 H. Fox Talbot, *Sun Pictures in Scotland* (London, 1845). For the dates of the fascicles of *The Pencil of Nature*, see Larry J. Schaaf, *H. Fox Talbot's* The Pencil of Nature, *Anniversary Facsimile*, Introductory Volume (New York: Hans P. Kraus, Jr, 1989), p. 9. Earlier publications on *Sun Pictures* include Hans P. Kraus Jr, *Sun Pictures Catalogue One: Early British Photographs on Paper* (New York: Hans P. Kraus, Jr, n.d.), cat. no. 12, and my 'William Henry Fox Talbot's Views of Loch Katrine', *Bulletin – Museums of Art and Archaeology University of Michigan* 7 (1984–5), pp. 48–77. These reproduce all the plates in *Sun Pictures*.
3 From a pre-publication announcement put out in June.
4 See James Holloway and Lindsey Errington, *The Discovery of Scotland: The Appreciation of Scottish Scenery through Two Centuries of Painting* (Edinburgh: National Gallery of Scotland, 1978).
5 TCP, Talbot to Elisabeth Feilding (5 March 1813), 589.
6 TCP, Talbot to Elisabeth Feilding (7 May 1826), 1430.
7 TCP, Talbot to Elisabeth Feilding (10 August 1819), 853.
8 TCP, Talbot to Elisabeth Feilding (26 December 1819), 858.
9 TCP, Talbot to Elisabeth Feilding (29 October 1828), 1732.
10 TCP, Elisabeth Feilding to Talbot (28 February 1823), 1038; Elisabeth Feilding to Talbot (10 December 1823), 1135; Talbot to Elisabeth Feilding (29 June 1826), 1451; Talbot to Elisabeth Feilding (7 September 1829), 1854; Constance Talbot to Talbot (n.d.), 339.
11 TCP, Henrietta Horatia Maria Gaisford to Talbot (2 December 1830), 2094.
12 TCP, Lady Elisabeth to Talbot (1 November 1832), 2454.
13 TCP, Constance Mundy to Talbot (30 October 1832), 2447; (5 November 1832), 2458; (7 November 1832), 2461.
14 See Ian Duncan, *Scott's Shadow: The Novel in Romantic Edinburgh* (Princeton: Princeton University Press, 2007).
15 See Catherine Gordon, 'The Illustration of Sir Walter Scott: Nineteenth-Century Enthusiasm and Adaptation', *Journal of the Warburg and Courtauld Institutes* 34 (1971), p. 297.

16 Gordon, 'The Illustration of Sir Walter Scott,' p. 297.
17 TCP, Talbot to Constance Talbot (9 October 1844), 5096.
18 Hans P. Kraus, Jr., *Sun Pictures: Catalogue Seventeen* (*William Henry Fox Talbot: Selections from a Private Collection*), text by Larry J. Schaaf (New York: Hans P. Kraus Inc., 2007), p. 36.
19 My account of Talbot's itinerary is derived in part from Katherine Peveraro, 'Views of the North: Visions of Scotland from Talbot, Turner and Scott', M.Litt. thesis, University of St Andrews (2004), pp. 23–8. Peveraro draws on a record of expenses kept by Nicolaas Henneman (Fox Talbot Museum, Lacock, doc. no. 24508).
20 TCP, Elisabeth Feilding to Talbot (25 April 1845), 5239.
21 TCP, Talbot to Elisabeth Feilding (30 May 1845), 5265.
22 TCP, Elisabeth Feilding to Talbot (29 July 1845), 5339.
23 *Virgil. Eclogues, Georgics, Aeneid 1–6*, trans. H. Rushton Fairclough, rev. G.P. Goold (Cambridge, MA, and London: Harvard University Press, 1999), p. 197. Rushton translates this passage: 'Joyous it is to roam o'er heights, where no forerunner's track turns by a gentle slope down to Castalia'. See also my 'Talbot's Epigraph in *The Pencil of Nature*', *History of Photography* 34(1) (2010), pp. 90–5.
24 W.H.F. Talbot, 'The Traveller's Camera', *The Literary Gazette and Journal of Belles Lettres, Science and Art* 1871 (1852), p. 876.
25 William Gilpin, *Observations, relative chiefly to picturesque beauty, made in the year 1776, On several Parts of Great Britain; particularly the High-Lands of Scotland*, vol. 2 (London: R. Blamire, 1789), p. 73.
26 Wiliam Scrope, *Days and Nights of Salmon Fishing in the Tweed; with a short account of the natural history of the salmon, instructions to sportsmen, anecdotes, etc.* (London: John Murray, 1843), p. 106.
27 Pierre Nora, 'Between Memory and History: Les Lieux de Mémoire', *Représentations* 26 (1989), pp. 7–24.
28 Gerald Finley, *Landscapes of Memory: Turner as Illustrator to Scott* (Berkeley and Los Angeles: University of California Press, 1980), pp. 132–3, pls 57, 58, 136.
29 Finley, *Landscapes of Memory*, p. 182.
30 Walter Scott, *The Fortunes of Nigel* (Edinburgh: Archibald Constable; London: Hurst, Robinson, 1822), vol. 1, p. 107.
31 *Fortunes of Nigel*, by the Author of 'Waverley', p. 6.
32 *The Miscellaneous Prose Works of Sir Walter Scott, Bart.*, vol. 7, *Provincial Antiquities of Scotland* (Edinburgh: Robert Cadell; London: Whittaker, 1834), p. 261.
33 Peveraro, 'Views of the North', pp. 8–9.
34 See n. 1 above.
35 See Kitty Cruft, John Dunbar and Richard Fawcett, *The Buildings of Scotland: The Borders* (New Haven and London: Yale University Press, 2006), pp. 91–8.
36 See Iain Gordon Brown, 'Scott, Literature, and Abbotsford', in Brown (ed.), *Abbotsford and Sir Walter Scott: The Image and the Influence* (Edinburgh: Society of Antiquaries of Scotland, 2003), pp. 18, 20.
37 Talbot referred to Lacock Abbey as his 'house in the country' in letters written in 1839 and 1841 (TCP 3782, 3923 and 4210).
38 Lacock Abbey was also a harbinger of Gothic Revival architecture in England. See John Summerson, *Architecture in Britain 1530 to 1830* (Harmondsworth: Penguin Books, 1963), p. 239, pl. 163b.

39 W. Henry Fox Talbot, 'Some Account of the Art of Photogenic Drawing' (London: R. and J.E. Taylor, 1839), in Beaumont Newhall (ed.), *Photography: Essays and Images* (New York: The Museum of Modern Art, 1980), p. 28.
40 It is depicted clearly in a watercolour of 1832 showing the entrance to Abbotsford guarded by two of Maida's successors. Reproduced in Jeanne Cannizzo, '"He was a gentleman even to his dogs": Portraits of Scott and his Canine Companions', in Brown (ed.), *Abbotsford and Sir Walter Scott*, p. 133.
41 John Gibson Lockhart, *Memoirs of the Life of Sir Walter Scott, Bart.*, vol. 5 (Edinburgh: Robert Cadell, 1837), p. 867.
42 Brown, 'Scott, Literature, and Abbotsford', pp. 22–5.
43 Brown, 'Scott, Literature, and Abbotsford', p. 4.
44 Nora, 'Between Memory and History', p. 7.
45 Walter Scott, *The Lay of the Last Minstrel: A Poem* (London: Longman, Hurst, Rees, and Orme, and A. Constable; Edinburgh: James Ballantyne, 1805), p. 23. On Melrose Abbey, see Kitty Cruft et al., *The Buildings of Scotland*, pp. 533–46.
46 Harriet Beecher Stowe, *Sunny Memories of Foreign Lands*, vol. 1, Letter VIII.
47 Rose Macaulay, *Pleasure of Ruins* (New York: Walker, 1966), pp. xv–xvi.
48 Samuel Johnson, *A Journey to the Western Islands of Scotland* (Glasgow: Stanhope Press, 1817), p. 30.
49 Johnson, *A Journey*, p. 230.
50 See James Buzard, *Disorienting Fiction: The Autoethnographic Work of Nineteenth-Century British Novels* (Princeton: Princeton University Press, 2005), pp. 69–70.
51 Quoted from Elizabeth A. Bohles and Ian Duncan (eds), *Travel Writing 1700–1830: An Anthology* (Oxford: Oxford University Press, 2005), pp. 179–80.
52 Access number NG 2557.
53 Orville Dewey, *The Old World and the New; or a journal of reflections and observations made on a tour in Europe* (London: Simms and M'Intyre, 1844), p. 20.
54 Maria Edgeworth, *The Life and Letters of Maria Edgeworth*, vol. 2, ed. Augustus J.C. Hare (London: Edward Arnold, 1894), 20 June 1823.
55 Gillen D'Arcy Wood, *The Shock of the Real: Romanticism and Visual Culture 1760–1860* (Palgrave: New York 2001), pp. 187, pp. 171–218.
56 Jan Piggott, *Turner's Vignettes* (London: Tate Publications, 1993), pp. 53–6, Appendix B, pp. 76–87, 109–10. In May 1838 Cadell was planning an edition of *The Lady of the Lake* which was to have contained 20 compositions by Turner. See Finley, *Landscapes of Memory*, pp. 184; 258, n. 55.
57 Wood, *The Shock of the Real*, pp. 191–2.
58 Walter Scott, *The Lady of the Lake; A Poem* (Edinburgh: John Ballantyne, Longman, Hurst, Rees and Orme, and William Miller; London; James Ballantyne, 1810), l.14.
59 Cruft, *Buildings of Scotland*, pp. 213–23.
60 The verb 'to Byronise' was already current in the 1840s. See *Blackwood's Edinburgh Magazine* 61(378) (1847), p. 38.
61 Henry James, 'A Passionate Pilgrim', *The Atlantic Monthly* 27 (1871), pp. 352–71, and *The Atlantic Monthly* 27 (1871), pp. 478–99.
62 See Talbot's commentary on plate XVII in *The Pencil of Nature*.

'ART SCIENCE': *THE NORTH AMERICAN INDIAN* (1907–1930) AS PHOTOBOOK

Shamoon Zamir

Published between 1907 and 1930, *The North American Indian* comprises 20 volumes of ethnographic text and photographic images, each volume accompanied by a loose-leaf portfolio of additional photogravures (Figure 1). It is the work of Edward S. Curtis and a shifting team of ethnographers, Native American assistants and informants, and editors and technicians working under his directorial instruction, and it is not only the most photographically accomplished and influential record ever produced of Native cultures in the United States, but also 'the largest, the longest, the most ambitious and the most expensive project ever attempted in photography'.[1] Curtis took some 40,000 photographs, around 2,250 of which were included in the final publication which was intended 'to form a comprehensive and permanent record of all the important tribes of the United States and Alaska that still retain to a considerable degree their primitive customs and traditions', before the opportunity to study them 'shall have passed with the Indians themselves'.[2] If there is nothing quite like it in the history of photography, *The North American Indian* also has no precursor or successor in the history of anthropology.

The singularity of *The North American Indian* does not lie only in its remarkable scale or its sumptuous production values, nor in its pioneering combination of documentary social science and photography, though all of these make the work worthy of continued attention; it resides equally in the consistency with which the book requires us to attend to the claims of aesthetic experience upon our understanding, in a project ostensibly driven by the ends of instrumentalist knowledge. What makes *The North American Indian* distinctive is the *kind* of photography it incorporates and the role it assigns to the image in the communication of meaning. Curtis's choice of pictorialism as his mode of composition and of hand-pulled copperplate photogravure as his print medium align his work squarely with the art photography of its time.

From the perspective of the new scientism emergent within anthropology, this reliance on a deeply expressive and sensual mode of visual communication appears at best a superfluity. And from the point of view of modernist art photography, Curtis's marrying of pictures to ethnographic record seems to be a betrayal of hard-won aesthetic independence. As critics have noted, this same opposition between objective fact and subjective expression has been deployed historically to define the ontology of the photographic image when in fact the true nature of the photograph has always inhered in a perpetual mobility across the spectrum marked by these polarities.[3] What is remarkable about *The North American Indian* is its refusal to work within these boundaries, and its pursuit of a more integrative mode which, following Curtis's own characterization, I call 'art science'.[4]

Curtis's photographs do not merely confirm or decorate textual meanings by visual repetition or supplement, as conventional illustrations, or simply transmit evidence, but assert for themselves an active and independent role in the making of argument. Rather than engender an epistemology divided against itself, the combinatory form of *The North American Indian* produces a mode of understanding doubled and augmented into a dialectic of knowing and affect, record and imagination.

The 12 by 10 inches volumes are bound in Moroccan leather and printed on hand-made Van Gelder paper or Japanese vellum, chosen for their ability to accommodate the rich tones demanded by pictorial photography. High-grade Japanese tissue was used for the larger portfolio sheets, 18 by 22 inches, reserved for images which Curtis considered to be of exceptional quality. Each portfolio consists of around 36 plates, the remainder of the images being distributed across the volumes. Up to the end of the nineteenth century 'one photogravure plate cost as much as the printing of a whole edition of the same picture by one of the other reproductive processes'[5] and this is why each volume of *The North American Indian* was originally priced at either $150 or $192, and the whole set at either $3,000 or $3,850, the higher prices being for the printing on Japanese vellum. As the project progressed, these prices rose considerably.[6] Curtis had planned a limited edition of 500 copies but due to a failure to secure enough subscribers fewer than 300 were produced in the end.[7]

Within the volumes the ratio of text to image varies, but, generally, images are placed at intervals of two to four pages of text, occupying a whole unnumbered page protected by a thin sheet of tissue paper. The most immediate effect achieved by Curtis's photogravures and by the architecture of their placement is to slow down dramatically the pace of attention and to bring to it an intensity of absorption. Curtis's consummate command

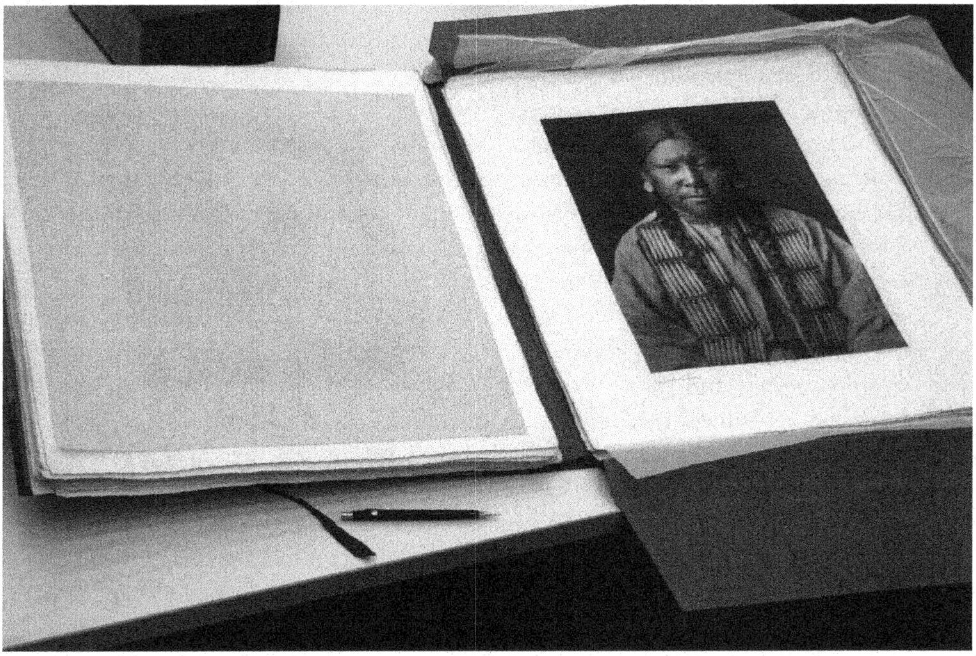

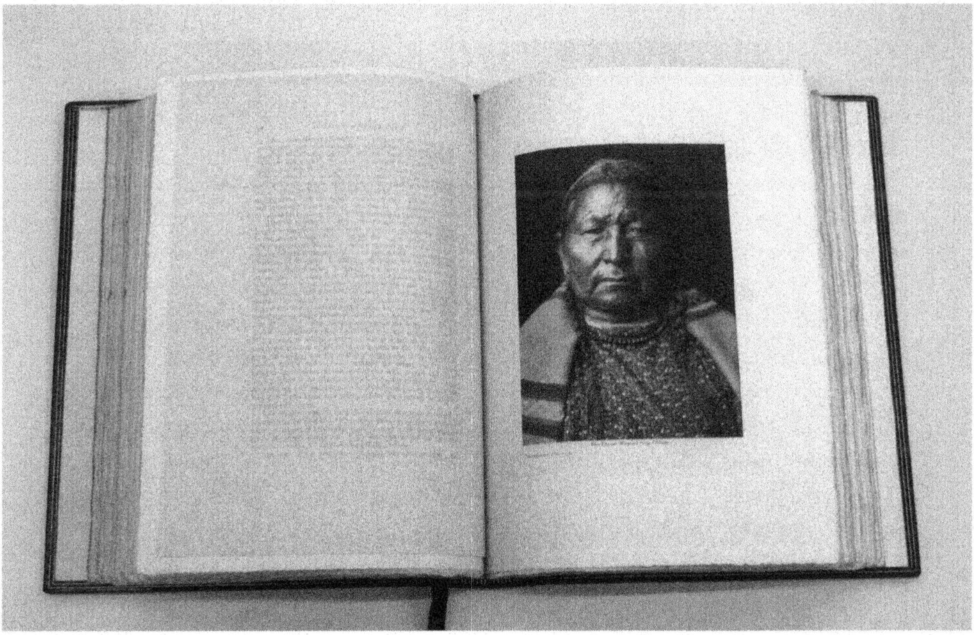

1. Edward E. Curtis, *The North American Indian* (Cambridge, MA and Norwood, MA, 1907–30), loose leaf portfolio and volume with text.

of composition and chiaroscuro contributes greatly to the modulations in the speed of perception and understanding, but the material nature of the photographic reproductions is perhaps a more vital factor. The ink adheres to the surface of the photogravures like a fine dust. Because the prints are available to the touch, their delicacy is also experienced as a more tangible fragility which brings with it the attitude and pace of care. The vigour and clarity of the prose in *The North American Indian* in both its descriptive and narrative modes keeps us moving along at a lively pace while the images stop us in our tracks. Our eyes and thoughts are brought to a stilled reflection. As we turn from text to image we very often go from the abstractions of kinship systems and clan organizations, or the minutiae of ritual practices and religious beliefs, to a more embodied and sensual perception.

Whatever connections we make between image and text in *The North American Indian*, we must make them by bridging the space between their discrete self-enclosures. As we become habituated to the counter-rhythms of the image-text alternation, it becomes difficult to say if it is the images which accompany the text or the other way around. The relative independence of the images in the portfolios could seem to pose a challenge to this characterization of the relation of text and image; but in focusing our attention exclusively on the images and foregrounding their difference from conventional illustrations, the portfolios in effect serve to underline the images' claim to equality with the text. Volume and portfolio unfold their meanings by relying on the reader's memory of one part while engaged with the other, integrating the two as an associative ensemble.

The texts of *The North American Indian* almost never address or discuss the images which accompany them. It is true that sometimes the connection seems to require little or no comment: this is so, for instance, when an account of a particular ceremony is accompanied by a visual record of its enactment, or when the description of a sacred object is coupled with an image of that object. But more often than not the connection between image and text operates at the level of a greater generality in which a sense of relation across a parallel independence is more openly maintained. We turn in the midst of an account of an initiation rite, an agricultural practice, or a myth, to an image of a small band of warriors in traditional costume looking across to the horizon from a hilltop, or of a young woman kneeling by the edge of a stream, or of the interior of a tipi lodge, or, just about half the time, of an individual face. In Curtis's own words, each is 'an illustration of an Indian character or of some vital phase in his existence', grounding the ethnography in visual depictions of the 'environment that made the Indian much of what he is' (*NAI* 1:xiii). As we look at that group of warriors on the hilltop, or riders crossing the floor of a canyon, Curtis's care in composition evokes a feeling of theatricality. When we come upon the faces, however, the effect can be very different. Instead of an experience of distance and detachment, we are plunged into a powerful and unsettling intimacy produced by the proximity of view. The boundary between typology and portraiture becomes unstable, pushed into the background by the particularity of the individual face, a quiddity which is of culture and history but also outside them.

The failure to attend with exactness to the work of form in *The North American Indian* has narrowed our understanding of the book's ethical and epistemological dimensions and obscured what remains most creative and engaging in the work. Despite the substantial body of existing commentary on Curtis's project we still have no sustained close reading of an image, or of an image group or sequence, or of the interactions of image and text – no account, in fact, of the work as precisely what it is, a photobook. What is available instead are accounts of the image archive as a general iconography and its relation to ideology. By contrast, the present study tries to focus on what Martha Nussbaum refers to as the 'noncommensurability' of 'valuable things' in both ethics and aesthetics, a focus on 'the priority of the particular' against what Edward Said referred to as 'the gross political verity'.[8] I look in some detail at one image and its most immediate textual contexts to open up the meanings of *The North American Indian* in their full complexity, but constraints of space prevent me from addressing them all here – considerations of the relationship of portraiture to time and history, and of the role of Native Americans in the making of the project, two preoccupations central to my thinking about Curtis's work, are notably absent.

Numerous evaluations of *The North American Indian* broadly concur that it is best understood as the product of a romantic imagination inextricably, even if inadvertently, bound in service to the project of empire. There can be no question that the work of Curtis and his team is indeed everywhere entangled in the practices and discursive forms of American colonialism and nationalist consolidation. I do not go over these entanglements again as they have been thoroughly documented already, and not because I wish to redeem the book from its many compromises and failures.[9] But as Gillian Rose warns in her critique of postmodernism's quest for 'uncontaminated ethics', if in 'the rush to espouse ... formerly degraded "others"', we renounce representation and knowledge as power, 'we have disqualified any possible investigation into the dynamics of the configuration and reconfiguration of power – which is our endless predicament'.[10] *The North American Indian* is best read not as a sepulchral monument to hegemony but as a living document of 'our endless predicament'. To argue that Curtis aestheticizes history and transforms the promise of veridical record into the mystifications of myth is potentially to immobilize both the work of representation within *The North American Indian* and the active contribution towards the book's creation of the very Native subjects on whose behalf criticism in effect speaks. It is in the portrait, the most prevalent visual genre in *The North American Indian*, that we can still read the traces of the face-to-face meeting between Curtis and the Native Americans in all its fallibility and creativity.

'A Medicine Pipe' (Figure 2), an image from the sixth portfolio, is an example of the achievement of portraiture in *The North American Indian* and of the integration of documentary illustration with the ethnographic text. It is this very duality, this potential for divided aims, which becomes the enabling condition for an enhanced portraiture. Curtis's image and text explicitly raise the problem of naming and anonymity, of individuation and typology, at the level of the object, the pipe. Through the caption in the portfolio and the text in the corresponding volume, the pipe becomes embedded in a collective life history of the class of objects it represents, a history which is cumulatively shaped from accounts of individual pipes. By contrast, nothing is said about the man in the picture; in this silence, we must pass through the object to see the meanings of the face. The dramaturgy of Curtis's image (the kneeling, the slightly turned head, the extended arms) proposes a particular kind of relationship between the man and the object he holds. As we attend to the ethnography, we come to realize that outside its scientific purposes, the anthropological account of the mythological and ceremonial dimensions of the medicine pipe leads us also towards a more intimate understanding of the gestures and of the diffidence of the face, by offering a fuller comprehension of the religious and cultural weight of the object held up to our view. If the text enables us to come this far, in this moment of seeing we also realize that the image confirms the text as much as it is confirmed by it, and that the image also exceeds the text.

The caption to 'A Medicine Pipe' offers a summary account of the ethnographic interest of this object:

> Medicine-pipes, of which the Piegan have many, are simply long pipe-stems, variously decorated with beads, paint, feathers, and fur. Each one is believed to have been obtained long ago in some supernatural manner, as recounted in myth. The medicine-pipe is ordinarily concealed in a bundle of wrappings, which are removed only when the

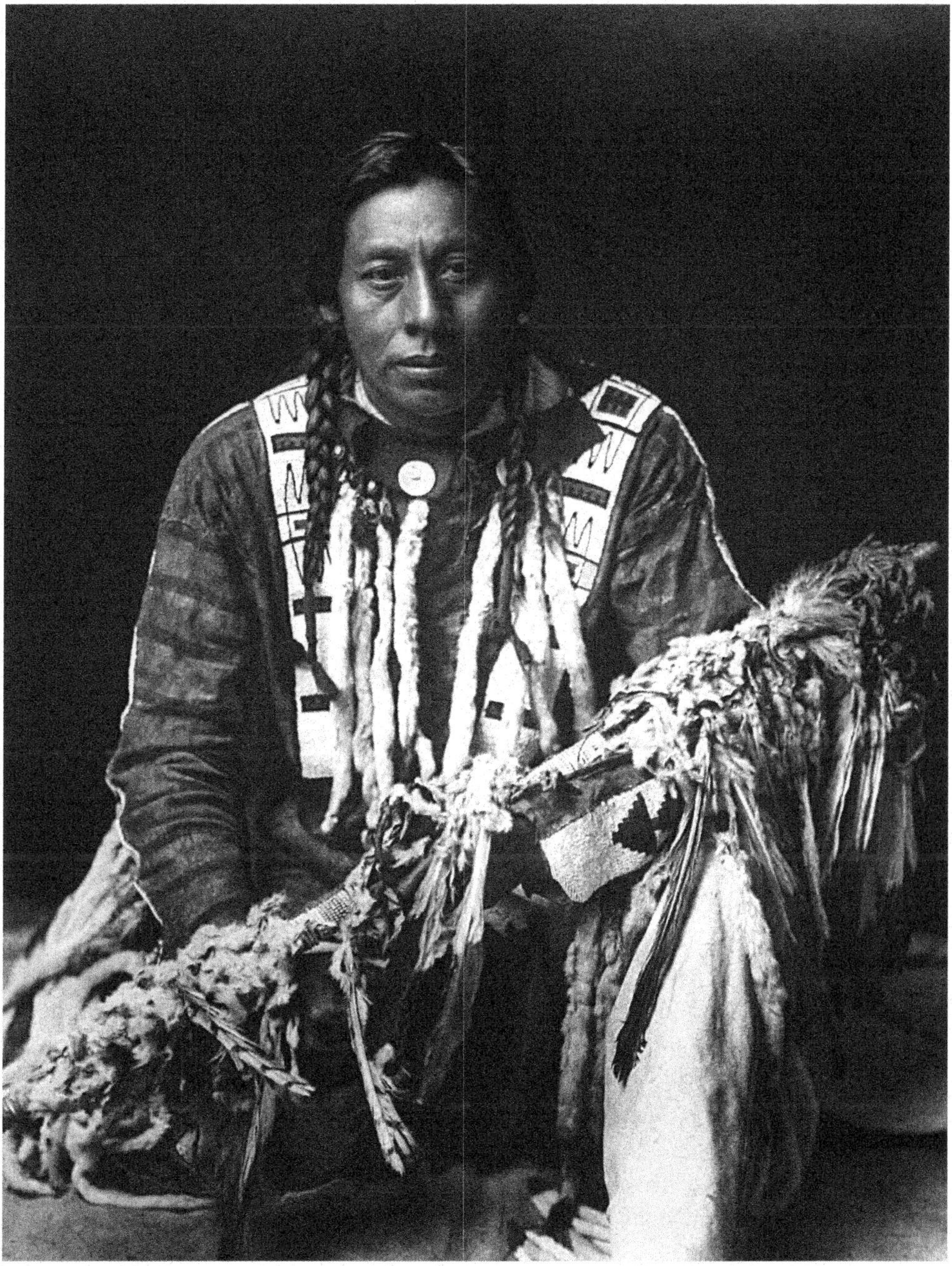

2. Edward E. Curtis, 'A Medicine Pipe', *The North American Indian* (Cambridge, MA and Norwood, MA, 1907–30).

> sacred object is to be employed in healing sickness, or when it is to be transferred from one custodian to another in exchange for property. Such exchanges, occurring at intervals of a few years in the history of each pipe, are attended by much ceremony.

This is a reminder of a more detailed discussion of the role of medicine pipes in Piegan culture that occurs in Volume 6:

> The greatest of all medicine-bundles is that containing the Long-time Pipe. This has been in possession of the tribe as long as the memory of man can tell. The tribe possesses many other medicine-pipes, but this is *the* pipe. Its origin is accounted for in the following myth.
>
> ... A great storm threatened, causing all the people to be filled with fear. A beautiful girl, an only child of a chief, went out and said, 'Thunder, take away the storm and I will marry you!' The thunder ceased, the tumultuous clouds grew quiet and passed away, and the sky cleared. Not long thereafter the girl happened to be alone a short distance from the camp. A man appeared before her, and said, 'I am the man you promised to marry.' The girl, remembering her promise, went with him into the sky. She lived there with him for a time, then began to long for her father, and Thunder allowed her to return, giving her a pipestem for a present to her father. This was the Long-time Pipe. (*NAI* 6:67)

There then follows an explanation of the customary use of such medicine pipes:

> When the first thunder is heard in the spring, the old men who have owned the Long-time Pipe, or at the present time any other medicine-pipe, hurry to the lodge of the custodian. The one who first reaches the place takes down the bundle, burns incense, praying to the Above People, Earth People, and Thunder, removes the wrappings, and exposes the pipe. By this time the other medicine-pipe owners have come in, and they begin to sing the songs, at the close of which the pipe is rewrapped and hung on its tripod.
>
> On rare occasions a person very ill and despairing of recovery asks that the medicine-pipe be opened for him. It is then exposed and rubbed over his body. This is a serious rite and requires the giving of very expensive presents to the custodian. (*NAI* 6:68)

These excerpts from the lengthy commentary on medicine pipes should give a sense of the way in which the text provides for the object a cultural complexity that draws upon mythology and an ethnography of ritual use and social status forming a kind of aura of contextual richness around the object.

But if this textual commentary makes available the data necessary for a culturally and historically informed understanding of the object pictured and the class of object it stands for, the anthropological discourse also constitutes a kind of biography of the object, albeit one which applies simultaneously to a particular example and to the genus exemplified. Comparable narratives and contextual frameworks provided as accompaniments to a human portrait, named or unnamed, would be received as just such an individuation through biography, a greater fleshing out by textual means of the face in the photographic image. Curtis invites the viewer to apprehend the medicine pipe within the terms of such an individuation or naming, to see his image not as an ethnographic illustration but as the portrait of a thing. After all, as the account in Volume 6 tells us, each medicine pipe is named and carries a unique identity and history, a fact illustrated by the narrative of the Long-Time Pipe, the most revered of all pipes and the only one named in Curtis's text. The pipe in the folio image may not be named but, given the narrative of the Long-Time Pipe, we come to see it not simply as an object outside the domain of naming but as more properly anonymous; not as an object unnamed but as an object whose name has been held back. As Paul Claudel has observed, '[o]rdinary objects which have long been used by one master take on a sort of personality, their own face, I could almost say soul, and the folklore of all nations is full of these beings more human than humans, because they owe their existence to people and, awakened by their contact, take on their own life and autonomous activities, a sort of latent and fantastic wilfulness'.[11] It is because the pipe also has a kind of face, a potential personality the possibility of which is revealed indirectly through the textual account, that the image finds its proper home in the portfolio. Seen as a mere illustration, the logical place for the image would be in Volume 6, with the texts dealing with medicine pipes. Here, however, there are no illustrations at all of pipes, though there *are* images of other objects discussed within the ethnography, such as the medicine bags in which the pipes are stored. In each case the objects are pictured alone, without a human presence. In the portfolio accompanying Volume 6 on the other hand, the pipe is the *only* object pictured in its own right. All the remaining folio images are portraits, images of ceremonial activities or scenic views. The caption to 'A Medicine Pipe' of course refers us back to the ethnographic text, but the isolation of the image from the text, its inclusion among the images of exceptional quality reserved for the folio, invite an independent contemplation. Curtis in effect lifts the image of the medicine pipe out of the archive of other objects and folds it into the company of the human portraits which dominate the folio.

The inclusion of the man in the image could be said to underline this fact. At another level, this very inclusion may appear to confirm the failure of portraiture. Since he is referred to neither in the caption nor the anthropological text, is the man not erased even beyond the generality of typology which at least grounds the pipe in a possibility of individuation? Is he not objectified beyond the object itself as a mere prop to facilitate the display of the pipe? It is only possible to argue this if we read only the *textual* erasure of the man and not the visual achievement of the image itself, and also if we approach the relation of the man's image to the text of Volume 6 too literally. If the ethnographic account gives a 'face' to the pipe, it also makes this identification the vehicle for a more profound and more impersonal (more profound *because* more impersonal) human portraiture.

As A.D. Coleman notes, Curtis's portraits 'have a classic purity, simplicity, and strength that seems timeless'. His account of the portraits offers a perceptive understanding of how they were achieved and their aesthetic effects:

> [Curtis's] use of natural light indoors, or inside a tent ... was a determining factor in the look of those images; in combination with the slow speed of the films of his day, it mandated long exposures at wide apertures, with a shallow depth of field and a certain amount of blurring unavoidable. This required of him a technical virtuosity, and a patient self-control that his sitters had to share. One benefit of such a procedure was that it isolated each sitting within its own bubble of slow time; another was that it granted Curtis the fullest possible control over light as a sculptural tool. This allowed him to model each face he contemplated in such a way as to emphasize the bearer's identity and character, as well as to create an unusual sense of depth within a two-dimensional image.[12]

The experience of each image as 'a slow bubble of time' should not be confused with the time of salvage ethnography. The uniformity of style of most of Curtis's photographs, stretching over more than 30 years of work, has confirmed critics in their sense that *The North American Indian* is best understood as a museum display of human and cultural relics. But Coleman puts his finger on a very different experience of the work; his sense of the momentary slowing down of time points us to the artful enabling of a human encounter between the person pictured and the viewer by the very isolation of this encounter from the flow of time. If we rush Curtis's images and our experience of them, then a sense of repetition is inevitable; but if we are attentive to the demands of the pacing that characterizes Curtis's photographs, then each image paradoxically stands out from the flow of images and insists upon the irreducible particularity of the encounter it makes available. It is the very classic timelessness of the portraits that disrupts the spatial and temporal distancing of salvage and makes us confront the possibilities of coevalness across cultures and history.

Coleman is equally perceptive in suggesting that the pace of reflection created by Curtis's portraits erases the distraction of artifacts. Curtis 'resisted the temptation to let artifacts distract him from the faces themselves; by and large, no matter how remarkable it may be in its own right, no artifact steals the scene from a human subject. Instead, such objects are generally de-emphasized by the device of selective focus'.[13] Certainly the medicine pipe cannot be said to steal the scene from the face of the anonymous sitter. But in 'A Medicine Pipe' the classical quality of the composition does insist on a kind of visual balance between pipe and face; it appears, in other words, to propose a relationship.

Throughout the volumes and portfolios of *The North American Indian* there are numerous examples of Curtis photographing objects of cultural importance or aesthetic appeal on their own, without a human presence as a backdrop or a prop. So why does Curtis not do the same with the medicine pipe, an object that could easily stand visually alone with the support of the texts that accompany it? What is the function of the man who holds up the pipe to our view? We can only answer this question if we attend to the nature of the object. The medicine pipe is what the sociologist Violette Morin has referred to as a 'biographical object'. Quoting Morin's argument within an anthropological study of things and the narratives they can tell, Janet Hoskins summarizes how 'the biographical object "imposes itself as the witness of the functional unity of its user, his or her everyday experience made into a thing"'; it is 'formative of its owner's or user's identity, which is both singular and universal at the same time'. Unlike a commodity, which is 'eternally youthful and not used up but replaced', a biographical object 'grows old, and may become worn and tattered along the life span of its owner', anchoring him or her 'to a particular time and place'.[14]

Unlike the objects which concern Morin and Hoskins, a Piegan medicine pipe is not defined by attachment to a single person. Though a pipe may be kept under the custodianship of a particular individual, it transcends private possession; it becomes worn in because its cultural life extends well beyond a single human life span – in the case of the Long-Time Pipe, to the very beginnings of tribal life. The pipe is a biographical object in the sense of a biographical mode in which it is damaging to distinguish sharply between collective and private lives. In his consummate enactment of his privileged custodianship, the man in Curtis's photogravure refuses just such a separation, and it is this refusal which brings into clear view the limits imposed on our understanding of portraiture by too narrow a distinction between typology and individuation.

The man has in fact been identified as Philip Flat Tail, a highly respected member of the Piegan community, who inherited the pipe bundle when he was just a boy following the death of his father, old Flat Tail. The pipe was later transferred to Yellow Kidney, then to the Aims Back and Day Rider families, before being sold to the Provincial Museum of Alberta.[15]

The extensive textual commentary on the medicine pipes comes to bear with great force on Philip Flat Tail's gesture and pose in the folio image. Most important is the holding up to view of the object. The willingness to reveal such a sacred object signals an immense generosity. Noting that the Piegan 'possess a most unusual number of medicine-bundles', all endowed with supernatural powers, Curtis himself acknowledges that 'they are less secretive than other tribes, and will freely discuss them and occasionally even part with them' (*NAI* 6:66). In the picture, however, the holding on to the pipe, the refusal to have it photographed on its own, suggests a certain withdrawal – not a resistance to its exposure but an underlining of its inalienability from the person who holds it and from the culture for which he stands in. If this insistent human presence thwarted the photographer's tendency to photograph objects in isolation, then what is remarkable is the manner in which Curtis turns the hindrance into an opportunity for exceptional aesthetic achievement. The medicine pipe is an object which comes to life by setting in motion communal participation. The willingness to reveal and hold forth a sacred object of ritual importance is a gift offered to both Curtis and the viewer. It is not, of course, the object itself that is offered; it is the openness with which it is shared that is the gift, and Curtis's image is a testimony to the manner in which he receives this gift.

I do not want to appear excessively sanguine here. The manner in which Curtis obtained some of the ritual and religious information published in *The North American Indian*, and the means by which he secured at least some of his views of sacred objects were, judged by the standards of today, unethical to say the least. During a visit to the White Mountain Apache in 1905, for example, Curtis had tried to buy a sacred buckskin chart depicting their creation myth. The owner refused, arguing that he would be killed by the other medicine men if he were to sell the chart and reveal its meanings. By the time Curtis returned to Apache country in 1906, the owner of the chart had died and a rivalry had developed between two medicine men. Curtis exploited the situation, persuading the widow of the owner to sell him the chart and then working the rivalry to obtain an account of the creation story from one of the medicine men.[16] But in the case of the Piegan, as he himself points out, Curtis appears not to have met with such reluctance. The sheer number of Piegan objects and interiors photographed supports Curtis's claim. But perhaps the best verification is the face of the man who holds the pipe. Its poise and composure appear to confirm better than the textual claim about Piegan openness Curtis's sense of the generosity of that culture.

Emmanuel Levinas argues that 'objects are not objects when they offer themselves to the hand that uses them, to the mouth and the nose, the eyes and the ears that enjoy them'. The 'objectivity' of an object resides then not in a material residue, not in 'what remains of an implement or a food when separated from the world in which their being comes into play'; rather '[i]t is *posited* in a discourse, in a *conversation* ... which *proposes* the world'. For Levinas, objects and tools become in the hands of the Other vehicles for an address, a kind of speech by indirection. The Other 'can, to be sure, speak of himself – but then he would announce himself as signified and consequently as a sign in his turn'; he would become, as it were, reified, a passive content available for our knowing, rather than a being that always exceeds the limits of what we can know of it. This is why the Other 'manifests himself in speech by speaking of the world and not of himself; he manifests himself by proposing the world, by *thematizing* it'.[17] Levinas's phenomenology of the face-to-face encounter with the Other allows us to catch the spirit in which Flat Tail holds up the medicine pipe, both in display and invitation; but it also suggests that the directness of the gesture of extension can be read as an indirection that leads our eyes back to the human face that appears otherwise to shy away from our direct regard.

Curtis takes great care in bringing to light the lineaments and expression of the face. The head, melting into the darkness behind, seems almost to float above the body, its isolation and the chiaroscuro effect of the lighting upon the face imparting to it a sense of weightlessness by comparison with the more directly lit mass and detail of the pipe below. The face is turned ever so slightly away to the right, and the eyes do not look directly at the pipe, nor do they meet the viewer's gaze. This is certainly not a reflection of awkwardness in the presence of Curtis or a sign of shame at having violated the object through inappropriate exposure; the self-possession and confidence of the face (as much as the text) speak against such a reading. The slight turn of the head and the averting of the eyes seem better understood as a gesture of deference towards the sacred object (almost a reflex against the light that appears to emanate from it), just as the half kneeling pose enacts a willing subjugation of the self to the authority and aura of the pipe. Curtis avoids sharp contrasts; the soft and even tonalities enhance the roundness of the face and seem to propose a gentle diffidence within the poised composure. The eyes of the man are not highlighted and do not stand out from the darkness that surrounds the figure, as they do in other portraits in the portfolio. Light does not shine out from them but is drawn in by them. They appear, therefore, to signal self-absorption and a contemplative interiority. But the gesture of holding the pipe up to view moves outward. If we read it as a gesture of both sharing and a holding on, we see that the face enacts this same double movement in its willingness to reveal and in maintaining its diffidence. The image moves, then, between inwardness and a reaching out, between a certain withdrawal into the self and a will to communicate. It is through this double movement that the image shifts out of its self-enclosure to address the viewer and to question his or her detachment. If the achievement of portraiture in 'A Medicine Pipe' goes beyond the requirements of ethnographic knowledge or illustration, the coming into view of the face does not so much undermine this project of knowing as completes it by making the embodied human dimension of the face the condition of its proper apprehension. At the same time, if the face transforms scientific understanding, so too the ethnography paradoxically helps ground the face's resistance to a culturalist delimiting of its own meanings. The ethnography of traditional beliefs, ritual uses and social structures help place the face, and threaten to reduce the man figured to an object of knowledge among other objects which is the work of typology; but these accounts can also be read as enabling an understanding of the difference which must be passed through and held on to in order for identification to be achieved. The care with which Curtis as photographer responds to the face of the man in 'A Medicine Pipe' speaks of a recognition that beyond ethnographic understanding and beyond the conventions of portraiture also there 'lies something that defeats understanding'. And it is exactly here, as Max Kozloff argues, that 'critical interpretation begins – in bewilderment'.[18]

I have read the holding out of the medicine pipe towards the viewer and the demeanour of Philip Flat Tail's face in Curtis's picture as a visual dynamics that opens up a structure of reciprocity or gift. In his attempt to understand the workings of reciprocity and responsibility in art through the anthropology of gift exchange, Lewis Hyde writes of the gratitude felt by the recipient of a gift as a kind of labour that can effect the transformation of both the recipient and of the gift alike:

> Between the time a gift comes to us and the time we pass it along, we suffer gratitude. Moreover, with gifts that are agents of change, it is only when the gift has worked in us, only when we have come up to its level, as it were, that we can give it away again. Passing the gift along is the act of gratitude that finishes the labor. The transformation is not accomplished until we have the power to give the gift on our own terms.[19]

Curtis's portraits, more than any of his other images, bear witness to the fact that he comes up to the level of the gift that is passed to him by the Native peoples with whom he worked. These photographs testify that the labour of Curtis's gratitude survives the many failures of reciprocity that can be easily documented in *The North American Indian*. And this labour needs to be understood precisely as a labour of transformation that is in keeping with the spirit of the gift, a passing on of the gift by Curtis in his own terms.

The compositional richness of 'A Medicine Pipe' honours Flat Tail's address to the viewer through the objects of his world. But Curtis's transformation of the gift passed to him cannot be properly approached at the level of vision alone; it must be grasped through the material dimension of his image work. The visual and haptic experiences of Curtis's gravure together construct a single and more complete experience. The medicine pipe is held out not only for our eyes to see but also, if only symbolically, for our hands to take hold of it, a passing of an instrument of reciprocity and community from Flat Tail as representative of Piegan culture to Curtis's white viewers who are his contemporaries or to us across a whole century. '*Ceci n'est pas [aussi] une pipe.*' However, unlike Magritte's well-known painting, what seems most important here is not that the object has been replaced by its representation but that one material object, the pipe, rich in its promise of tactile experience, metamorphoses as we hold it in our hands and before our very eyes into another, the gravure, itself delicate to the touch. 'A Medicine Pipe', it must be remembered, is one of the loose-leaf photogravures that make up the portfolios of *The North American Indian*. As we lift it towards us, we also take up the pipe. The fineness and seeming fragility of Curtis's gravures (qualities further accentuated today by the increased rarity and value of these objects) induces in the viewer what I referred to earlier as an attitude of care. Our carefulness in handling the loose-leaf image mirrors the care with which Flat Tail handles the medicine pipe, our fingers and hands in a sense re-enacting what we see in the image. This structure of mirroring underlines the fact that Curtis's gravure generates a form of equivalence or translation between the Piegan object and itself.

Those who look at Curtis's photographs with care receive a doubly burdened gift. They receive the gift passed by the Native Americans to Curtis but also Curtis's transformation of this gift. If we accept that there is much in *The North American Indian* which comes to us in the spirit of the gift and does not violate it, then in receiving it we are under an obligation to respond in the same spirit, an obligation to continue the transformations of the gift in its circulation. This chapter is part of an attempt to articulate such a response and sense of responsibility.[20]

Notes

1 Martin Parr and Gerry Badger, *The Photobook: A History*, 2 vols (London: Phaidon, 2004, 2006), vol. 1, p. 73.

2 Edward S. Curtis, *The North American Indian*, 20 vols and 20 loose-leaf portfolios (Cambridge, MA: The University Press [vols 1–5] and Norwood, MA: The Plimpton Press [vols 6–20], 1907–30), vol. 1, pp. xiii, xvii. Hereafter *NAI* followed by volume and page number.

3 See, for example, Allan Sekula, 'On the Invention of Photographic Meaning' (1975), in Victor Burgin (ed.), *Thinking Photography* (London: Macmillan, 1982), pp. 84–109.

4 Curtis in Christopher M. Lyman, *The Vanishing Race and Other Illusions: Photographs of Indians by Edward S. Curtis* (Washington DC: Smithsonian Institution Press, 1982), p. 17.

5 Helmut and Allison Gernsheim, *The History of Photography* (New York: McGraw-Hill, 1969), p. 409.

6 Mick Gidley, *Edward S. Curtis and the North American Indian, Incorporated* (Cambridge: Cambridge University Press, 1998), pp. 109–10. This is by far the most thorough and balanced account of the cultural contexts of Curtis's work.

7 For a printing history of the project, see the website of Flury & Company, pioneer dealers in Curtis's materials: http:fluryco.com/Curtis/naip.htm (last accessed 28 October 2011).

8 Martha Nussbaum, *Love's Knowledge: Philosophy and Literature* (New York: Oxford University Press, 1990), pp. 36–7; Edward S. Said, *Orientalism* (London: Routledge & Keegan Paul, 1978), p. 15.

9 Gidley, *Edward S. Curtis*. See also Lyman, *The Vanishing Race*; Alan Trachtenberg, *Shades of Hiawatha: Staging Indians, Making Americans, 1880–1930* (New York: Hill and Wang, 2004); James C. Faris, *Navajo and Photography: A Critical History of the Representation of an American People* (Albuquerque: University of New Mexico Press, 1996); and Martha A. Sandweiss, *Print the Legend: Photography and the American West* (New Haven: Yale University Press, 2002).

10 Gillian Rose, *Mourning Becomes the Law: Philosophy and Representation* (Cambridge: Cambridge University Press, 1996), p. 21.

11 Paul Claudel, 'Meditation on a Pair of Shoes', Prose Works (Bibliothèque de la Pléiade, 1965), in Janet Hoskins, *Biographical Objects: How Things Tell the Stories of People's Lives* (New York: Routledge, 1998), p. 1.

12 A.D. Coleman, 'Edward S. Curtis: The Photographer as Ethnologist', *Depth of Field: Essays on Photography, Mass Media, and Lens Culture* (Albuquerque: University of New Mexico Press, 1998), p. 137.
13 Coleman, 'Edward S. Curtis,' p. 137.
14 Janet Hoskins, *Biographical Objects: How Things Tell the Stories of People's Lives* (New York: Routledge, 1998), p. 8. See also A. Henare, M. Holbraad and S. Wastell (eds), *Thinking Through Things: Theorising Artefacts Ethnographically* (London: Routledge, 2006), and the special issue of *Critical Inquiry* 28(1) (2001) on 'Things', ed. Bill Brown.
15 Adolf Hungry-Wolf, *Pikunni Ceremonial Life, The Blackfoot Papers*, vol. 2 (Skoomumchuck, BC: Good Medicine Foundation, 2006), p. 459.
16 Makepeace, *Edward S. Curtis*, pp. 94–5; and Mick Gidley (ed), *Edward S. Curtis and the North American Indian Project in the Field* (Lincoln: University of Nebraska Press, 2003), pp. 37–47.
17 Emmanuel Levinas, *Totality and Infinity: An Essay on Exteriority*, trans. Alphonso Lingis (Pittsburgh: Duquesne University Press, 1969), pp. 95–6.
18 Max Kozloff, *Lone Visions, Crowded Frames: Essays on Photography* (Albuquerque: University of New Mexico Press, 1994), pp. 4–5.
19 Lewis Hyde, *The Gift: Imagination and the Erotic Life of Property* (New York: Vintage, 1983), p. 47.
20 The present discussion is drawn from a book-length study of Edward Curtis.

EMIL OTTO HOPPÉ, AUTOBIOGRAPHY, AND CULTURAL MOMENTS

Mick Gidley

Emil Otto Hoppé, who is only now emerging from a long period of relative neglect, was during his heyday perhaps *the* most famous photographer in the world. Born in 1878, he was the child of a Bavarian family of Huguenot extraction. In 1900 he was sent to England to be instructed in his father's profession, banking. Instead, he learnt photography and rapidly established himself as the leading studio portraitist in Edwardian London. In this essay I explore the nature of the connection between Hoppé's photographic output, in particular his photobooks, and the larger culture within which he functioned, to show how they partake of their cultural moment and play their part in its construction.

Hoppé exhibited at the Royal Photographic Society, was an editor of *Colour*, and helped found The Plough Club, an avant-garde venture of visual artists, dramatists and musicians keen to promote new work. He turned his studio into a salon: new music was heard, short experimental plays were performed, batik and other 'new' art forms were exhibited, and young artists such as the poet Ezra Pound rubbed shoulders with establishment dignitaries and great beauties of the day, such as Lady Lavery. Hoppé himself became, in effect, a celebrity. He made much-reproduced likenesses of members of the Royal Family, parliamentarians, performers and painters, socialites and socialists, explorers and sports figures. His portraits of a range of writers – from established and emerging 'artists' to popular denizens of 'Modern Grub Street' – are particularly notable; he contributed the photographic portraits to two book-length sketches of the British literary scene, and later did the same for a similar book on American writers. One of his claims was that he had created, in a 1912 portrait, what he called 'the recognized face' of Henry James.[1]

In this initial phase of his fame, Hoppé was probably best known for taking athletic and atmospheric studies of the dancers from Diaghilev's *Ballets*

Russes when they burst upon the world. In fact his very first major publication in 1913 – more a portfolio than a photobook, in that picture titles constitute its only verbal element – was devoted to the Russian ballet. But, at the same time, at a more populist level, he also cut a dash as a photographer of 'fair women'. He was so successful that in 1919 he was able to open a second studio, which he operated himself, in New York City. For the next few years, during the annual four months he spent there, he photographed 'everybody who was anybody', as the cliché has it, including presidential candidates, Albert Einstein during his first American visit in 1921, film stars, newspapermen, serious writers and countless theatre people. During his New York sojourns, apparently prompted by the extraordinary ethnic diversity of the city, Hoppé also began to photograph what he termed 'human documents' – 'types of the lower strata of society whose faces tell their life story' – and was responsible for two photobooks of types. While Hoppé claimed that such faces tell their life story', of course they do not: accompanying words, whether just a caption or pages of text in a book, tell more, and over the years he released some of them with a variety of titles, sometimes just 'human document' but at others granting the same referent *different* ethnic identities. When in 1922 he exhibited a selection of the human documents gathered in the United States, he called them his 'American types', and contrasted them to a range of British 'types', the latter heavily class-based.[2]

From the mid-1920s onwards – including a period during which Hoppé ran yet another successful studio in Berlin – he concentrated more on topographical work, especially for the Orbis Terrarum volumes *Picturesque Great Britain* (1926) and *Romantic America* (1927), and for the studies of German technology collected in *Deutsche Arbeit* (1930). The urban and industrial views in these books are definitely modernist in conception and execution – for example, a depiction of the elevated railroad on New York's 2nd Avenue anticipates in structure some of Walker Evans's views from under Brooklyn Bridge – and some critics have seen in them, especially in such *Deutsche Arbeit* images as the construction of the Zeppelin airship, the influence of the German New Objectivity.[3] By contrast, I think of his work as protean, and not characterized by any marked individual style. I will come back to this point.

The industrial photographs contrast with the images Hoppé made for his succession of photobooks on London, the first entitled just *London* (and published in 1932), which mainly offer striking Pictorialist views of landmarks, such as St Paul's Cathedral framed by a thick ship's cable, and small-scale, almost intimate studies of 'curiosities'.[4] The industrial views also contrast with the kind of pictures that he produced during the 1930s, especially the later 1930s, of the landscapes and peoples of Australia, India, Bali and African colonial territories – places often then considered 'exotic' by residents of the industrialized world. He published these world views in a series of lavish books and illustrated articles and wrote about his itinerant experiences in such works as *Round the World with a Camera* (1934). He also sold even more 'middlebrow' journalism, on an endless variety of topics, than had characterized his earlier years and – a feature that has largely been ignored in what little critical work there is on him – he did much commercial work. He himself celebrated the fact that, for an important advertising campaign, in 1921 he photographed the first 'Nippy' (waitress) employed at one of the sparkling new Lyons Cornerhouses in London. As he repeatedly claimed in later years, he never failed to take commercial opportunities.

The Second World War meant an enforced rest from travel, and in 1945 Hoppé produced a much-read memoir, *Hundred Thousand Exposures*, which was introduced by Cecil Beaton.[5] In the late 1940s he set about turning his own massive negative archive into a picture agency, thus vastly increasing the circulation of his work. (Many people have seen Hoppé images, now mostly circulated under licence by the Corbis agency, without realizing their connection to him.) After his 'retirement', while producing a variety of further publications, Hoppé lived in relative obscurity until his death in 1972.

Autobiographical Elusiveness

For the most part, I have recounted Hoppé's career as if it – and our knowledge of it – were straightforward. But this is not the case, and if we look at his autobiographical writings, especially *Hundred Thousand Exposures*, itself a photobook, we can register some of the ways in which it is not. The photo-historian Bill Jay interviewed Hoppé in his old age and noted that he was very unsure of dates, but there are discrepancies in *Hundred Thousand Exposures* that indicate something more than just memory loss. In a nutshell, when we examine the verbal and visual aspects of this text quite closely we cannot help but be aware that he used it to *construct* his own reputation and to *fashion* his own persona.

Witness how Hoppé recounted, in notably precise detail, his good fortune to be on hand at just the right moment to catch a pivotal instant at the Franco-British Exhibition mounted at London's White City in 1909:

> I had just exposed my fifth plate ..., when a tremendous detonation shook the ground. A balloon close by, which was to have lifted people

> up for a bird's-eye view of the Exhibition ..., had exploded and was in flames. Fortunately, my big camera was still screwed on its tripod. All I had to do was to swing it round, adjust the focus, reverse the slide and expose the last plate left ... This was a real piece of luck since there was no other camera in sight.

This opportunistic moment led to a front page 'exclusive' in the *Daily Mirror*, and a big fee. 'Although I may modestly claim to be somewhat of a pioneer in illustrated journalism,' Hoppé continued, 'the balloon story was the only occasion on which I have worked as a press photographer proper'.[6]

In fact, Hoppé did *not* work as a press photographer on this occasion either. In 1955 Heinrich Hoffman, who had been one of Hoppé's operatives in 1909 and who went on to earn the dubious distinction of becoming Hitler's favourite photographer, had his autobiography translated into English, and in this *he* claimed the explosion picture: 'Hoppé's picture – my pictures, really – were printed in all the leading newspapers in England and abroad, and the *Daily Mirror* put one on the front page. My employer netted a tidy sum in fees, and my own share was by no means to be despised'. Photo-historian Helmut Gernsheim, on realizing the discrepancy between the two accounts, wrote to Hoppé for clarification. Hoppé responded in a laconic, matter-of-fact manner: 'I have not read Hoffmann's [*sic*] Book [*sic*]; it is quite true that he came to me as a pupil & did take the Balloon Explosion picture together with another of my pupils'.[7] It has been far from rare in the history of photography for studio owners to claim rights in and credit for their operatives' work, but Hoppé's appropriation in this instance was not just a common business practice. It had a dimension peculiar to him.

It was in fact congruent with several other seemingly quirky episodes. Despite all the previous evidence (including data he had himself provided) that he had been born in the German city of Munich, in the last months of his life Hoppé told Jay that he was an Austrian, and that he had been born in Vienna! More curiously, during his last years Hoppé claimed to have made portraits not only of Mussolini, which he did, but also of Hitler (who, apparently, 'sipped milk'). On one occasion he even asserted that Hitler, not realizing Hoppé understood German, had insulted him personally, saying to an underling 'these decadent English – decadent to the top of his head'.[8] There are no negatives or records of any Hitler sitting, or any other evidence that could support the story.

These happenings affirm Hoppé's presence, but it is a removed, shadowy presence. He is a shifting, spectral figure lacking in precise, individualistic features. In certain places in the autobiographical writings Hoppé seems to have gone a step further, and to have positively hidden himself. An instance in *Round the World with a Camera* occurs when he described photographing, in Austria, 'an old farmhouse that an English family [had] adapted and made into a beautiful home'. He even named it ('Edhof') and detailed clashes between the English family and local villagers – all without stating that he and his wife were the new owners of the actual Edhof farmhouse and that the events described had happened to him and to his own family![9] These episodes transmit mixed messages: of attention-seeking egotism and elusiveness, self-importance and a kind of reserve, openness and near deceit.

Moreover, as the three words of the autobiography's title (*Hundred Thousand Exposures*) together indicate, it renders a life – or, at least, a career – *in* images, a veritable hundred thousand of them. Memoirs by photographers are, of course, likely to have this dimension. Edward Steichen, for example, entitled his autobiography *A Life in Photography* (1963), indicating that the life itself might be registered *through* images, a fusion exaggerated in Cecil Beaton's choice of title for his *Photobiography* (1951). In the case of *Hundred Thousand Exposures*, the book's constant oscillation between event, photographic depiction of the event, and the photographic techniques by which it was achieved, permits it to do double service as a technical ('how to') manual: its very chapter titles all begin with 'How' ('How an amateur turns professional', 'How to break into new fields with the camera') – and such a device means that, in a very exact sense, the photographs reproduced in it become exemplary. Indeed, even the extended captions for each reproduced image offer both technical data ('I used my old Leica with the Elmar lens, stopped down to *f*6.3 and gave one second exposure on Kodak Panatomic film for this portrait') as well as the historical circumstances of their making ('Taken at the poetess's London flat near Marble Arch').[10] The photographs and their supplementary captions constitute testimony to a life – in fact, they carry and *are* the autobiography.

As we have seen, Hoppé made portraits of many writers, and these would often appear as frontispieces in their own works. Perhaps most notably, in 1925 Hoppé's photographs of George Bernard Shaw, by then established as an indisputably major modernist figure, and of Shaw's biographer Archibald Henderson, were used in the famous *Table-Talk by G.B.S.* and they open the book in scene-setting manner, as if to depict *visually* the characters featured in the conversations to follow. Shaw himself had a serious interest in photography, both aesthetically and as a modern system of communication, and he apparently discussed such matters with Hoppé. In 1933 Hoppé made a particularly interesting portrait of Shaw (Figure 1): pen in hand, the writer looks up quizzically at someone who appears to have just entered the room.

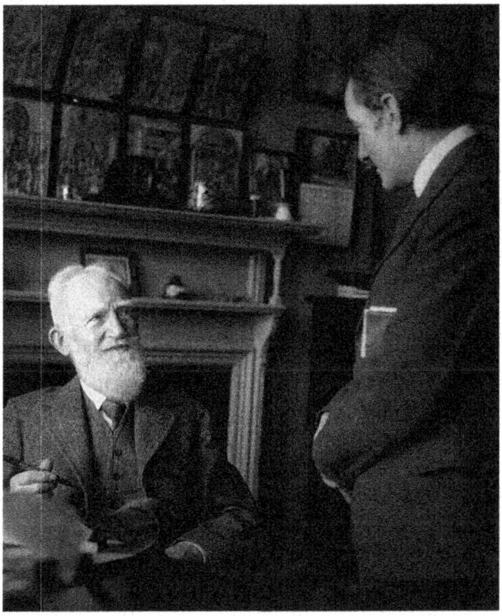

1. Emil Otto Hoppé, portrait of George Bernard Shaw, 1933.

This figure, in profile, with folded hands in front of him, inclines his head a little, as if questioningly. The image, it seems, has captured a moment of shared intimacy. In fact, as Hoppé recorded in *Hundred Thousand Exposures*, the inquiring interlocutor was himself:

> I think this is the most amusing of my pictures. It was made at his flat in Whitehall with the delayed action device incorporated in the Contax camera. This is the caption which Shaw wrote himself: 'This is my celebrated performance as a genial and charming old man: blessings on his kindly voice and on his silver hair – and Hoppé pretending to be taken in.'

If, as Shaw intuited, *both* men were performing, Shaw playing himself, Hoppé, with a book or notepad visible under his elbow, presented himself as a fellow writer or intellectual.[11] In this image, Hoppé *is* 'taken in', but not in the sense intimated by Shaw; in a gesture suggestive of reciprocity, he is taken into the circle of creative production, one that encompasses both photography and writing. And, of course, obscured though Hoppé's role as photographer is, he also presses the button to take the picture: it represents, as might be said today, his take on the scene. In other words, the image hints at Hoppé's then prevalent *self-conception* as a participant in the making of high modernism.

The other image in *Hundred Thousand Exposures* in which Hoppé himself appears is very different. Entitled 'One Fisherman', and apparently made in Australia early in 1931, it depicts a lone figure against the immensity of a literally – or, rather, a graphically – high sea. The figure would not be recognizable without the caption:

> May I confess that I am ... a keen fisherman and that my rod accompanies me on all my journeys ... Surf-fishing off the Sydney Heads is famous all over the world, and in this photograph I may be seen, precariously balanced, making a cast after having previously set the shutter of the *Leica* to 1/500th second and stopped down to *f* 0.8; a friend pressed the button.[12]

Here Hoppé projects himself as competent traveller, outdoorsman, adventurer – and, by implication, as a well-rounded person able to cope not just with the conundrums of art, but also with the pleasures and pressures of life. Note, too, that from both of these images, as in the case of the autobiographical writing, we get less than a clear view: in the Shaw photograph Hoppé is turned away from the camera, in hidden profile, and as a fisherman he is so far off, as it were, that his specific features cannot be recognized.

This presence when ostensibly absent is actually the situation with regard to *all* of the images reproduced in *Hundred Thousand Exposures*. We might think from the use of 'exposures' in the title of Hoppé's autobiography that we will have revelations, even tabloid ones. What this photobook actually offers is a series of half truths as it constructs – both verbally and visually – a *composite* persona. The autobiography creates 'E.O. Hoppé' as an entity somewhere between a fictional character and a trademark. The task of the autobiographical photobook as a sub-genre is to provide a narrative, necessarily visual as much as verbal, that connects the 'character' of the photographer to the trademark. 'Emil Otto Hoppé' should be seen, as it were, in quotation marks – as just the name on the title page, or a signature, to stand for certain trends in the photography of the middle decades of the twentieth century.

The Cultural Moment of the Orbis Terrarum Series

No matter how extraordinary Hoppé himself was, as a person or as a phenomenon, he should be seen as only one factor in the making of his photobooks. They may best be viewed as sites of contestation between artistic aspirations, commercial imperatives, cultural assumptions current at the time(s) of their creation, and the constraints of tropes inherited from both written and photographic genres. I will restrict my comments to *Romantic America* and, to a slightly lesser extent, *Picturesque Great Britain.*[13]

Both these texts are coffee-table books, collections of over 300 toned, large-size photogravures made from photographs by Hoppé. They appeared in the Orbis Terrarum series, a very popular line of picture books on various countries and regions which originated in Germany in the early 1920s and was published on both sides of the Atlantic, principally in Berlin and New York, during the remainder of the 1920s and early 1930s. Many of the volumes were produced by a single photographer-writer, most notably Kurt Hielscher, but varied forms of collaboration also took place. For example, Hoppé was just one of a number of photographers to contribute to the Orbis Terrarum volume on South America, *SudAmerika*, edited in 1931 by Karl Schumacher. Orbis Terrarum items were not always published or distributed by the same companies in each country in which they appeared, so to some degree the series itself enjoyed an identity which transcended those of the specific publishers who brought it out, a reputation enhanced by the fact that in some countries, most notably Germany, it was possible to take out a subscription at a reduced rate to the whole series ('the countries of the world in pictures', as a frequent Orbis Terrarum advertisement translates). Each volume contained a lengthy introduction, essentially a history and description of the locale concerned, and the plates were preceded by more or less detailed topographical notes on each image; both of these features were usually printed in the language of the country of publication, and Hoppé himself contributed them to *Romantic America.* To save on manufacturing costs, the images themselves were produced in long print runs with their captions or titles in four languages – English, German, French and Spanish – so that they could be bound into any edition. The format was so successful that a number of non-Orbis Terrarum books – including Hoppé's own study of picturesque old German towns, *Romantik der Kleinstadt* (1929), published by F. Bruckmann of Munich – used it as a template.[14]

The interwar years, especially the 1920s, might justly be labelled an 'Age of Travel'. By 'travel' I mean travel itself, of course, but also the *discourse* of travel: travel writing, travel journalism and travel *photojournalism.* As admirably demonstrated by Paul Fussell in *Abroad* (1980), his study of travel literature of the period, there was a tremendous sense of release, both actual and metaphorical, after the restrictions of the First World War. And the automobile came of age as a supreme mode of transport to cater for the desire to get about felt by the publics of the technologically advanced world, but especially in the United States. It is not an accident that in 1924 Hoppé himself was sponsored by the Sunbeam Motor Car Company to travel to Italy to produce *To Rome on a Sunbeam*, a travelogue that, naturally, featured both pictures of tourist landmarks along the way, usually with the elegant Sunbeam in view, and anecdotes detailing the travellers' antics and the car's exemplary performance.[15] When, in 1926, he came to undertake the long trip around the United States necessary for *Romantic America*, an automobile was the obvious preferred mode. But this was also the period of lavishly designed ocean liners, air-streamed transcontinental trains, and, with the most visually evident modernist associations, aeroplanes – each photographed by Hoppé, sometimes on commercial commission. By the late 1920s the publication of a veritable deluge of travel writing addressed to middle-class travellers, both actual and armchair, was in full spate. The cover picture of Hoppé's own book on Australia, *The Fifth Continent* (1931), summons all the relevant associations: a pith-helmeted figure with a camera (actually Hoppé himself) straddles a large globe which, in turn, is marked by the routes taken by planes, trains and ships.

Publishing houses competed with one another in issuing their own series of travel books, and the tropes of travel writing were rapidly codified. One such trope, renewed but old, involved, of course, the appeal of the exotic 'other' as encountered by the inquisitive and intrepid traveller. A typical instance was Hoppé's journey, with Native American guides, to Rainbow Bridge, a huge natural arch of stone in southern Utah's Navajo country (Figure 2a). In successive books Hoppé claimed that he was 'the first white man', then 'the first European', then 'the first Englishman' to see this wonder, presumably changing the specifics of his claim as he discovered that the arch had in fact been known abroad for somewhat longer than he at first wished to believe.[16]

Interestingly, none of the urban 'types' I mentioned earlier were included in *Romantic America*, and the types that were tend towards the stereotypical: a grandly befeathered Indian, for example, or a Hispanic performer with a guitar, or an elderly African-American man belittlingly captioned as 'Uncle Remus'. To a degree, this was due to the demands of Orbis Terrarum as a series, in that it exerted a specific rubric to concentrate on landscape and architecture. Several factors lay behind this rubric, including a genuine interest in landscape and architecture, and it was 'natural' for Hoppé to capture both already famous sites, such as Niagara Falls and the Woolworth Building, and such lesser-known spectacles as Bryce Canyon and an innovative early Chicago skyscraper by Burnham and Root. But the sacrifice of people as subject matter (other than as stereotypes) also enabled this transnational series to transcend – or, perhaps, simply evade – nationalist imperatives. Also, more negatively, as Roland Barthes and others have noted, in travel and tourist

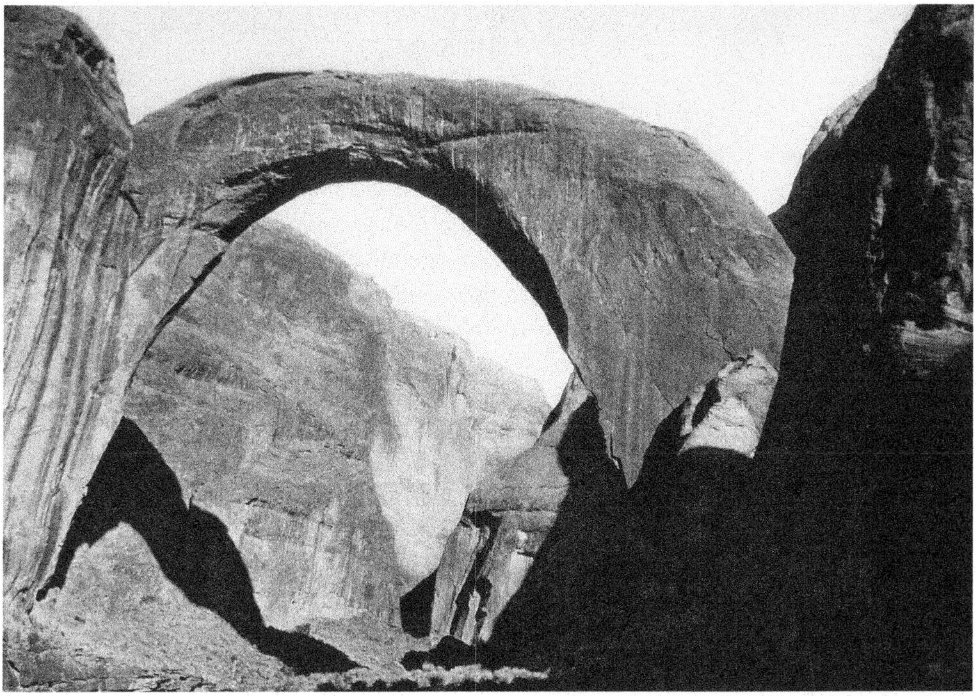

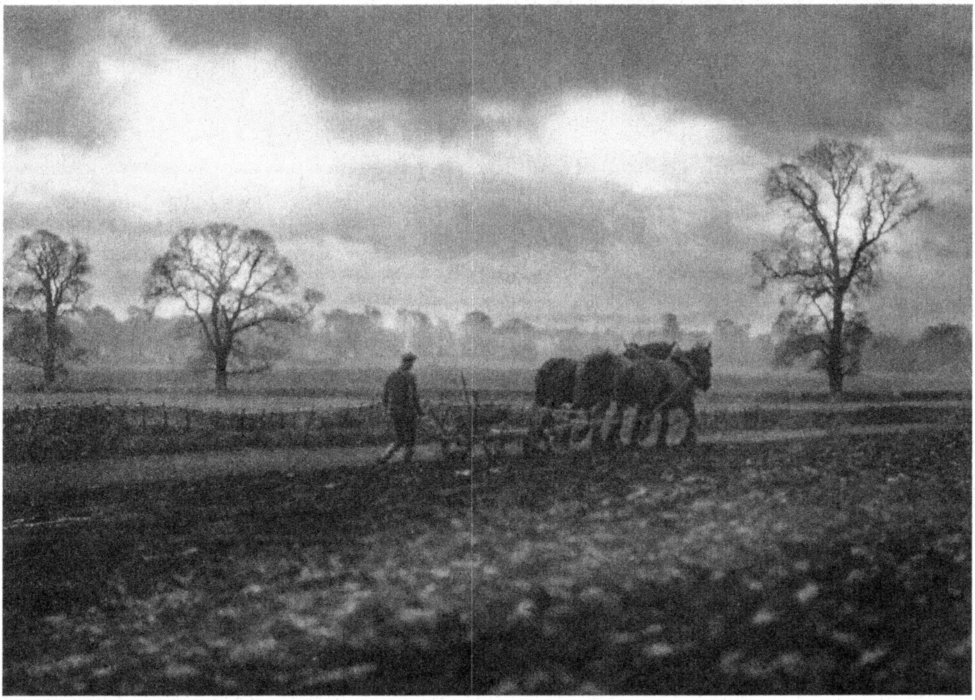

2a. Emil Otto Hoppé, 'Rainbow Bridge, Utah', *Romantic America* (New York, 1927).

2b. Emil Otto Hoppé, 'Hampshire', *Picturesque Great Britain* (Berlin, 1926).

discourse generally 'the human life of a country disappears to the exclusive benefit of its monuments', with peoples reduced to mere types.[17]

Another determinant in the formation of *Romantic America* was the sheer power of existing visual tropes in representations of American natural landscapes and cityscapes, perhaps best gauged by comparison with the British volume. The Introduction to *Picturesque Great Britain* was written by Sir Charles F.G. Masterman, the Liberal cabinet minister who had steered the first National Insurance Act through parliament: a quintessential Edwardian liberal. When he composed the Introduction to *Picturesque Great Britain*, he had written two enormously popular diagnostic books about Britain, *The Condition of England* (1909) and *England after War* (1923). In both of these he had been concerned by class divisions and by lack of investment in future manufacturing developments, as well as by the ugliness of industrial waste, but the dominant tone of his Introduction to *Picturesque Great Britain* was somewhat different. He pointed out that urbanization was making sharp inroads into all aspects of the British scene, but then added: 'Mr Hoppé has seized the period *before* the change which is coming. He has not been compelled to go to specially reserved beauty spots, or to special buildings embedded in the hectic and feverish disease of twentieth century development'. Rather, Masterman claimed, Hoppé had 'wandered through these islands; selecting indeed many historic places familiar through the world, but also landscapes and seascapes and old houses and churches of which he could have found many similar examples. Here is the England ... our ancestors have seen and rejoiced in for so many passing generations'.[18]

So to be picturesque here is to be familiar, old, commonplace, traditional (Figures 2b, 3a and 3c) – and this even applies to the industrial scenes which are often depicted as if they were already the deserted archaeological sites they were to become later in the twentieth century. Two views of Manchester on opposite pages, for example, present not the Manchester factories that Masterman reminds his readers that Engels knew, with all their inequities *and* energy, but deserted stacks left marooned by unmoving canal waters (Figure 3b). This is not the 'black' Britain Masterman knew existed – as opposed to what he called the 'green' one. In the main, even when teetering on the edge of lifelessness, as in some of *Picturesque Great Britain*'s northern cityscapes, it is a *comfortable* vision. Usually the urban sites that merit coverage are cathedral cities (Durham rather than Newcastle), but more often than not they are small towns or villages, with timber-framed schools, covered butter markets, colonnaded shops and pack-horse bridges. The dwellings are manor houses and mills beside streams and rivers, thatched cottages that jostle stone-built village inns on cobbled streets, or landmark castles, often moated. And most

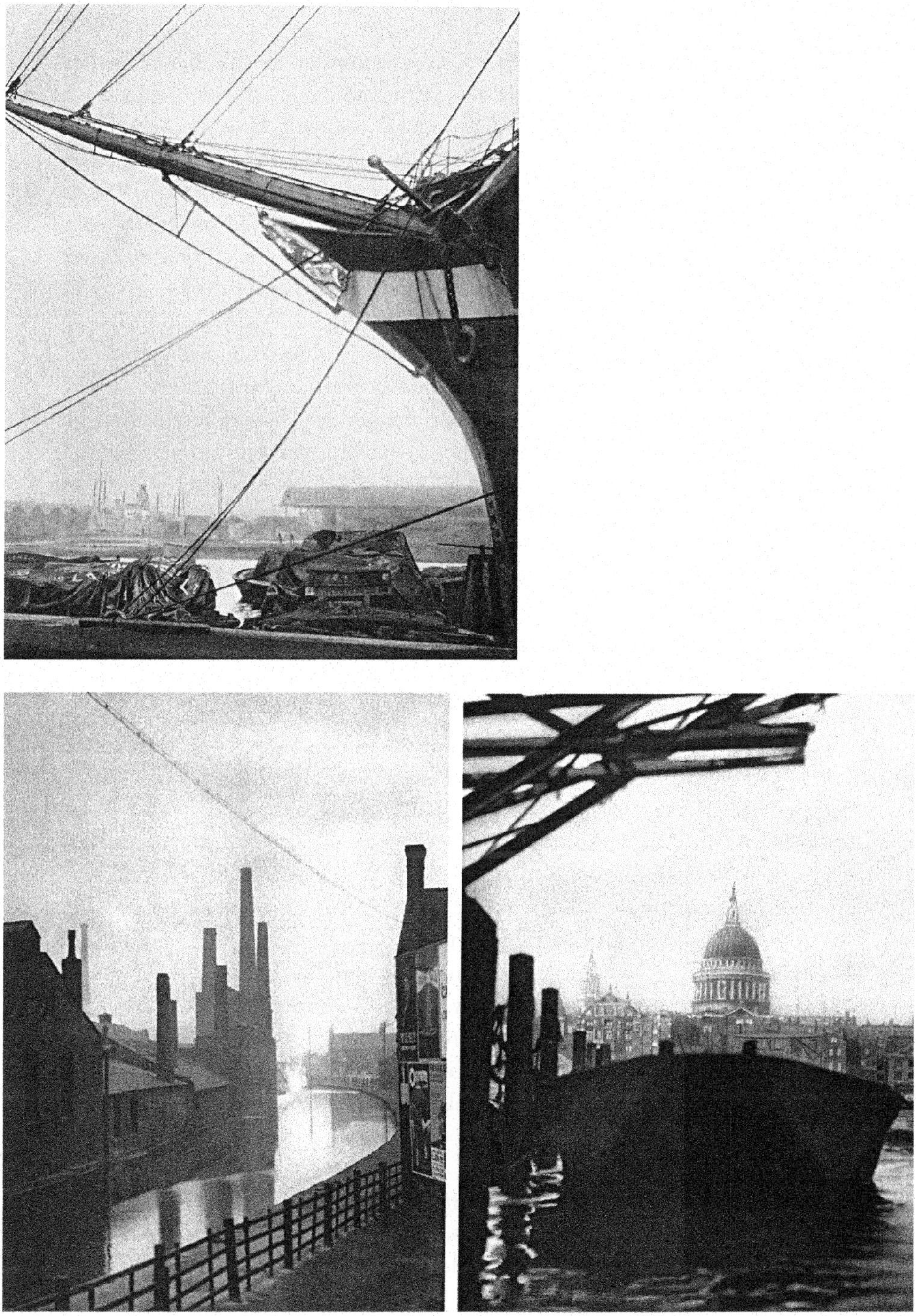

3a, b, c. Emil Otto Hoppé, from *Picturesque Great Britain* (Berlin, 1926).

of the scenes are rural – rolling pastures surmounted by the distant spires of country churches – which give the impression not only that they have not changed for a long time, but that they are unchangeable. In 'Selworthy, Somerset' a thatched cottage with logs and branches leaning against it appears as rooted as the surrounding trees and, as the vantage point is from above, it seems to crouch into the hillside behind it. 'Ploughing, Hampshire' shows a man behind a plough pulled by three horses, the distance he still has to travel accentuated by the successive horizontal lines of the fence, the hedges, and the trees behind him under a high mottled sky (Figure 2b). All told, it is as if Keats's 'season of mists' and, usually, 'mellow fruitfulness' had been stretched from the autumn through the winter and on down the years.

When Hoppé came to produce the images for *Romantic America* he sometimes seems to have tried the same sort of representation of the United States. In the case of the image of the 'Superior City Smelting Works' in Arizona, for example, the scale and aggression of the industrial is naturalized by framing it within foregrounded leafy trees (Figure 4a). But, generally speaking, this strategy did not produce images that were wholly convincing; in this case there is an unsettling disjuncture between the smelting works and the trees, as if the latter were stage props. To put Hoppé's dilemma into bald terms, when faced with America's natural landscapes – not just the obvious sites, such as the Grand Canyon and the Half-dome of Yosemite, but also, for instance, the vertiginous cliff faces of Zion in Utah – Hoppé was more often than not wrestling with the *sublime*, as classically described by Edmund Burke and Immanuel Kant, rather than the picturesque. And, when dealing with urban landscapes, the sheer scale of so many American buildings, bridges, dams and other structures meant that he was confronted by what David Nye has described as 'the double of nature', the 'technological sublime', a term first widely circulated by Leo Marx. Indeed, while it must also be admitted that this distinction between the picturesque and the sublime was not one which was recognized with consistency in Orbis Terrarum publications, one primary meaning of the slippery term 'romantic' in Hoppé's title must be – in fact and in effect – 'sublime'.[19] We see it in the span of the Brooklyn Bridge, in the huge and then brand new Ford plant at River Rouge, Michigan (Figure 4b), and in an oilfield, awesome in its extent, its derricks seemingly infinite in number (Figure 4c).

Hoppé said that in *Romantic America* he pursued 'the spirit of a new romance'. The newness – in the images, if not in the written text – consisted of the fact that it was a romance of a land without history: abstract, almost wholly modern, almost without human beings altogether – and when humans are there they are mostly presented *en masse*, as design elements in a complex,

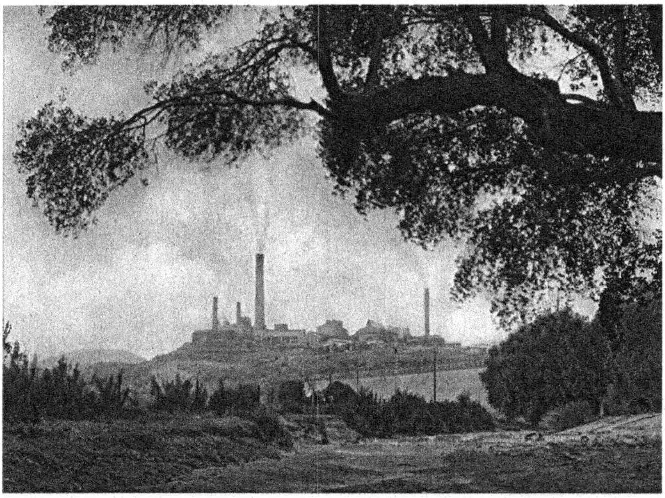

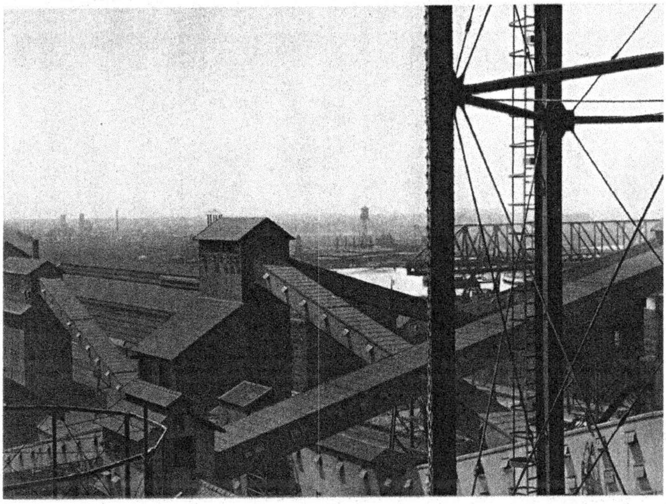

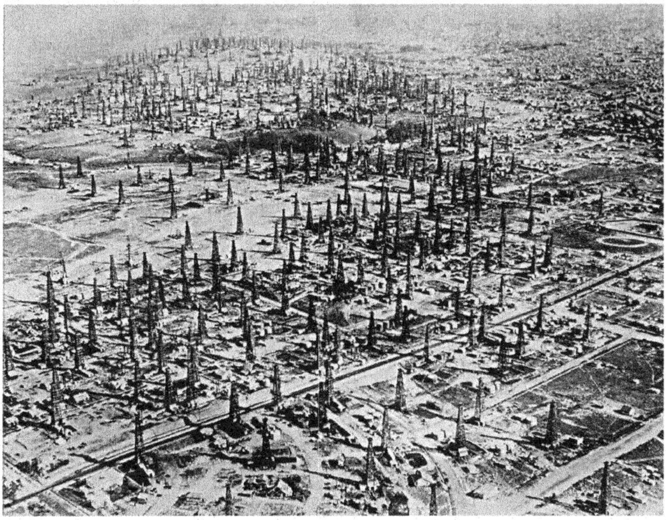

4a, b, c. Emil Otto Hoppé, from *Romantic America* (New York, 1927).

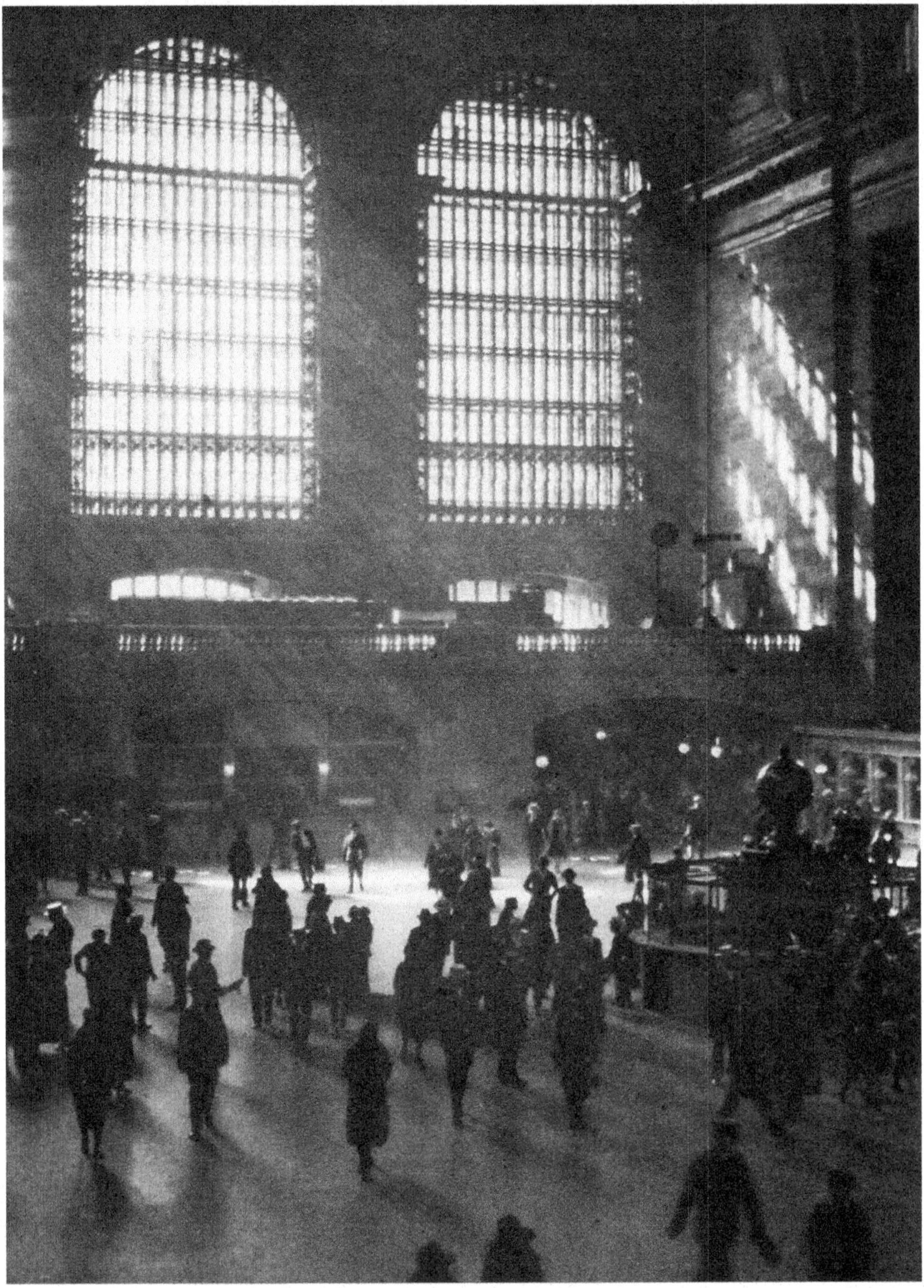

5. Emil Otto Hoppé, 'Grand Central Station', *Romantic America* (New York, 1927).

aestheticized pattern (Figure 5). By excluding people in this way Hoppé in effect represented America as a land without the ethnic, regional and other inter-communal tensions we know existed. His work in this respect is at one with – if not explicitly so – the advice of many contemporary guide books that advised tourists to avoid any interaction with ethnic minority people. In all these travel books, in Barthes's words, 'the real spectacle of conditions, classes, and professions' is missing.[20]

Despite the fact that they were not cheap, both *Picturesque Great Britain* and *Romantic America* sold more than 15,000 copies within their first year of publication, and *Romantic America* went on to become the most popular volume in the series. Its representation clearly proved highly palatable to the middle classes of Europe in the late 1920s and early 1930s, many of whom were trying very hard not to see their own inter-communal divisions. It is noticeable in this respect, for example, that the reworking of the Orbis Terrarum genre performed by Martin Hürlimann in the 1931 compilation on Germany to which Hoppé contributed – unlike its 1924 Kurt Hielscher predecessor – now contained such images as a modernistic store in Chemnitz, the Siemens steel works, and some Bauhaus-style homes in Frankfurt, but when it depicted people they remained types wearing varieties of folk costume, and the overwhelming visual impression is one of a settled, storied past. It does not remotely hint at the eruptions of Nazism then readily apparent. Closer to Hoppé's home, while Masterman's long introduction mentioned that in Ireland 'the English conqueror's attention' was not given to 'construction' but to 'plunder and burning', he did not reveal that Hoppé's grounds for the limited coverage of the Irish scene was that he was prevented from travelling far and wide by the violence of the country's civil strife. Masterman could evoke the storied plunder of centuries but not the inter-communal miseries of the present. That is, the coverage of these illustrated travel books is analogous to the construction of 'heritage', as David Lowenthal and others have distinguished it from 'history' – and perhaps in this there is a clue to the nature of their cultural work as representations. When setting out on his American journey in 1926, Hoppé secured a letter of introduction from the British Embassy in Washington that stated his travel was 'for the purpose of obtaining material for a book upon social, industrial and economic questions'.[21] But, of course, just as *Picturesque Great Britain* avoids the *politics* of Ireland, *Romantic America* in actuality hardly touches upon either 'social' or 'economic' issues in North America. The 'industrial' is there, in a sense – but sublimated, as we have seen, into the technological sublime.

On both sides of the Atlantic, heritage, while seeming to commemorate the past or preserve the beauties of the present, actually monumentalizes an aspect of the past or cordons off a privileged space of the present. Interestingly, in a blurb written for Hoppé's contemporaneous illustrated book on German small towns, *Romantik der Kleinstadt*, Thomas Mann wrote as follows: 'Hoppé, whose extraordinary skills I have known for a long time, testifies in these motifs of the German Idyll, to his complete sensitivity and his mastery of photographic heritage'. The plates in that collection are idyllic and radically *unlike* Hoppé's views of industrial sites in *Deutsche Arbeit*. The towns, each seemingly sheltered by an ancient cathedral or castle, have a sleepy air, and their people, when present, wear folk costumes and seem tied to the land.[22] It is not surprising that Hoppé translated its title as 'Cities Time has Passed By'. The individual images in each of these books – *Picturesque Great Britain*, *Romantik der Kleinstadt*, and *Romantic America* – tend, if in different ways, however seemingly anchored by their captions, to float free as 'compositions', and the books themselves, as unified entities, in lacking a coherent narrative, are removed from, precisely, history.

Obviously, much more could be said about the way nations are represented in these photobooks. The key point is that almost none of it begins with Hoppé himself; it is inherited and paradigmatic rather than original. The same must be said of the *form* of these texts. Paradoxically, they live most fully as silent tableaux. They are not enactments – or even re-enactments – but projections. They are not yet kinetic in the manner of Werner Gräff's *Es kommt der neue Fotograf!* (*Here Comes the New Photographer!*) (1929) – or, even, in the manner of the opening of Hoppé's own *The London of George VI* (1937). But in much of their photography they do exhibit similarities with other modernist work pervasive in the Orbis Terrarum cultural moment, such as that of Albert Renger-Patzsch in Germany and Alfred Stieglitz in the United States – both figures Hoppé knew.[23] The point about such links is *not* that they indicate artistic influence – though this may also be true – but that, like pollen in the air, they signify a *season*. I'm suggesting a tension between the auto/biographical and the paradigmatic. Each of the works I have discussed is indeed Hoppé's, but it is also, however partial, a codification of a shared cultural moment via the medium of the photobook.

Notes

1 Hoppé's work has been returned to the public realm largely through the efforts of the E.O. Hoppé Trust, Curatorial Assistance, Pasadena, California (hereafter CA), including the publication of Phillip Prodger, *Hoppé's Amerika* (New York: W.W. Norton, 2007), Graham Howe (with Erika Esau), *E.O. Hoppé's Australia* (New York: W.W. Norton, 2007), and Phillip Prodger and Terence Pepper, *Hoppé's Portraits:*

Society, Studio and Street (London: National Portrait Gallery, 2011). Any unreferenced data are taken from Hoppé's own writings. See also Mick Gidley, 'E. O. Hoppé Photographs the Recognized Face of Rabindranath Tagore', *Moving Worlds* 4/1 (2004), pp. 47–59.

2 For examples of Hoppé's pictures of female beauty, see his *The Book of Fair Women*, introduction by Richard King [pseudonym for Richard King Huskinson] (London: Cape, 1922). On Hoppé's types see Mick Gidley, 'Hoppé's Impure Portraits: Contextualising the "American Types"', in Graham Clarke (ed.), *The Portrait in Photography* (London: Reaktion, 1992), pp. 132–54, 215–18; also, Brian Stokoe, 'Class Tourism and Photography: The Typological Portraits of E.O. Hoppé and J.D. Beresford', *History of Photography*, 31/2 (2007), pp. 180–200.

3 See David Mellor, 'Patterns of Naturalism: Hoppé to Hardy', in *The Real Thing: An Anthology of British Photographs 1840–1950* (London: Arts Council of Great Britain, 1975), pp. 25–35, 27. Hoppé's modernist German work is *Deutsche Arbeit: Bilder vom Wiederaufstieg Deutschlands*, introduction by Bruno H. Bürgel (Berlin: Ullstein, 1930).

4 See also Brian Stokoe, 'The Image of London: The Metropolitan Photography of E.O. Hoppé', *The London Journal* 30 (2005), pp. 40–65; and Mark Haworth-Booth, *Hoppé's London* (London: Michael Hoppen Gallery, 2006).

5 Hoppé, *Hundred Thousand Exposures* (London: Focal Press, 1945); Beaton's preface is pp. 5–6.

6 *Hundred Thousand Exposures*, p. 154.

7 Hoffman, *Hitler was my Friend*, trans. Lt.-Col. R.H. Stevens (London: Burke, 1955), pp. 26–27; and Hoppé, postcard, n.d., to Helmut Gernsheim, Gernsheim Collection, Harry Ransom Center, Austin, TX.

8 Interview with Bill Jay, 1 May 1972, Center for Creative Photography, University of Arizona, Tucson (hereafter CCP). Other sources of Hitler stories include the transcript of Hoppé's BBC broadcast on 6 May 1968, CA.

9 Hoppé, *Round the World with a Camera* (London: Hutchinson, 1934), p. 40. The evidence that Edhof was Hoppé's own house is 'The Edhof, Molln', an article published in an unidentified magazine, photocopy in CA.

10 Steichen, *A Life in Photography* (Garden City, NY: Doubleday, 1963) and Beaton, *Photobiography* (London: Odhams Press, 1951). The caption quotations are taken from those for Queen Mary (p. 65) and Alice Meynell (p. 47). See also Linda Haverty Rugg, *Picturing Ourselves: Photography and Autobiography* (Chicago and London: University of Chicago Press, 1997) and Jay Prosser, *Light in the Dark Room: Photography and Loss* (Minneapolis and London: University of Minnesota Press, 2005).

11 The frontispiece photographs, based on *actual* sequences of negatives, appear in Archibald Henderson, *Table-Talk of G. B. S.: Conversations on Things in General by George Bernard Shaw and his biographer Archibald Henderson* (London: Chapman and Hall, 1925). Typescript memoirs of Shaw at CA and especially at CCP: folder marked 'Reminiscences [iv]', AG: 1/6. The 1933 portrait of GBS appears, with this caption, in *Hundred Thousand Exposures*, p. 65. See also Bill Jay and Margaret Moore (eds), *Bernard Shaw on Photography: Essays and Photographs* (London: Equation, 1989).

12 *Hundred Thousand Exposures*, p. 199.

13 See also Mick Gidley, 'Silence, Grandeur: Emil Otto Hoppé's Popular American Landscapes', in Mick Gidley and Robert Lawson-Peebles (eds), *Modern American Landscapes* (Amsterdam: VU University Press, 1995), pp. 151–71.

14 I used Hoppé, *Picturesque Great Britain* (Berlin: Ernst Wasmuth, 1926) and *Romantic America* (New York: B. Westermann, 1927); Karl Schumacher (ed.), *SudAmerika* (Berlin and Zurich: Atlantis, 1931). Hoppé, *Romantik der Kleinstadt* (Munich: F. Bruckmann, 1929). Other data from Orbis Terrarum leaflets.

15 Fussell, *Abroad: British Literary Traveling Between the Wars* (New York and Oxford: Oxford University Press, 1980). Hoppé, *To Rome on a Sunbeam* (Wolverhampton: Sunbeam Motor Car Company, 1924); Richard Hoppé, Hoppé's grandson, kindly showed me a copy of this rare publication.

16 Hoppé, *Romantic America*, p. xxxvi; *Round the World with a Camera*, p. 229; and *Hundred Thousand Exposures*, p. 189. While the Bridge had been known by non-Indians for some time, and was first photographed in 1909, as Ian Walker rightly pointed out to me it *was* indeed rarely visited when Hoppé ventured to it.

17 Barthes, *Mythologies*, ed. and trans. Annette Lavers (London: Paladin, 1973), p. 82.

18 Masterman, 'Introduction' to E.O. Hoppé, *Picturesque Great Britain*, p. vi.

19 Nye, *American Technological Sublime* (Cambridge, MA: MIT, 1994); see also Leo Marx, *The Machine in the Garden: Technology and the Pastoral Idea in America* (New York: Oxford University Press, 1964). For contrarieties of 'romantic', see Jacques Barzun's *Classic, Romantic and Modern* (Garden City, NY: Anchor, 1961), pp. 155–68.

20 A typical example is Fremont Rider, Frederic Taber Cooper, et al., *Rider's New York City: A Guide Book for Travelers* (New York: Henry Holt, 1923). I am grateful to Richard Haw for drawing such guides to my attention. Barthes, *Mythologies*, p. 82.

21 These Orbis Terrarum volumes, both entitled *Deutschland: Landschaft und Baukunst*, are Hürlimann, Introduction by Ricarda Huch (Berlin: Atlantis Verlag, 1931) and Hielscher (Berlin: Ernst Wasmuth, 1924). For Masterman on Ireland, see *Picturesque Great Britain*, pp. xxvi–xxvii; evidence on Hoppé's Irish travails taken from an autobiographical note in CA. Lowenthal, *The Past is a Foreign Country* (Cambridge: Cambridge University Press, 1985). The British Embassy letter, dated 18 June 1926, was examined at CA.

22 Mann's words, kindly translated for me by David Stirrup, appeared on the dust jacket of *Romantik der Kleinstadt.*

23 Werner Gräff, *Es kommt der neue Fotograf!* (Berlin: Herman Reckendof, 1929). Evidence of Hoppé's relationships with Renger-Patzsch and Stieglitz is taken from unpublished letters to be reproduced in Mick Gidley, *Emil Otto Hoppé at Large: Photographing the Modern World* (forthcoming).

RECALCITRANT INTERVENTION: WALKER EVANS'S PAGES

David Campany

What more is there to say about Walker Evans? Along with the work of Eugène Atget and August Sander, Evans's photography is perhaps the most discussed and debated in the history of the medium. Built on formal restraint and the rhetorical ambivalence of the classical document, the work of all three has been subject to the vicissitudes of history and the shifting fortunes of readability. Each produced a body of work that *could* yield a great deal so long as the necessary skills or disposition were in place. Sander's inter-war portrait survey *could* be a training manual (as Walter Benjamin had suggested); Atget's agile documents *could* be redemptive history or proto-modernism; Evans's 'documentary style' *could* be a complex dialectical engagement with the behaviour of the document. Yet Sander's work could be reduced so easily to an authoritative imprint of the face of Weimar Germany, Atget's to a wistful record of a disappearing Paris and Evans's to an evocation of fading Americana for a metropolitan elite. Such images forever risk becoming the reality that they were in the first instance bold attempts to understand, articulate and comment upon. It is one of the deepest ironies of the medium that such approaches to photographic representation could lend themselves to the most astute, aesthetically rewarding and semantically rich of readings but also to the most reductive. (This was of course an ambiguity well exploited by the provocatively 'dumb' documents of Conceptualism and Pop later in the century, scrambling the distinction between the intelligence and the lumpenness of the photographic record.) It is this very gap between such extremes of interpretation, a gap that is inescapably political, which remains at the heart of the continuing claims made for such work.

Thirty-five years after his death, the understanding of Evans's work has become markedly split between seeing it as essentially belonging either to the gallery wall and the modern museum, or to the very different orbits of the page and the library. Evans the 'museum artist' is of course the legacy of a long-standing if fitful relationship with New York's Museum of Modern Art that began in the 1930s and culminated with a retrospective in 1971, the terms of which still define the mainstream approach to his work. His relationship to the page was arguably less fitful and also began in the 1930s with photographic contributions to various journals including *Architectural Record, Creative Art, Hound & Horn, Architectural Forum*, culminating with a 20-year tenure at *Fortune*. Plus there were a number of books. Some of these contained folios by Evans accompanying writing by others: Hart Crane's *The Bridge* (1930); Carleton Beals's *The Crime of Cuba* (1933); *Let Us Now Praise Famous Men: Three Tenant Families,* co-authored with James Agee (1941); and Carl Bickel's *The Mangrove Coast* (1942). Here Evans's photographs stood apart from the text, resisting the slick and usually unreflective integration of word and image that dominated magazine photo-essays and photobooks from the 1930s onward. In addition Evans published three monographic books: *American Photographs* (1938), *Many Are Called* and *Message from the Interior* (both 1966).

In his 40-year career Evans produced more than enough striking 'pictures' to warrant a place in any history of art or art photography, but he showed relatively little desire to present them that way. Instead his approach was shaped by a background in literature, by early ambitions to be a high modern writer and, soon after he found the camera, a realization that one of the central characteristics of photographic modernism was the intelligent assembly of images for the printed page. *American Photographs* and *Let Us Now Praise Famous Men* have come to be seen as significant works of Modernist documentary (a form of highly reflexive record-making that Evans all but invented with the sequential arrangement of *American Photographs*, perhaps the first 'difficult' photobook to emerge in the US context). But recognition came with a significant delay. Having been remaindered when they were first published, *American Photographs* and *Let Us Now Praise Famous Men* were reviewed widely and received positively when reissued at the beginning of the 1960s. These were books whose time had come precisely insofar as their moment had gone. Their latent critical success derived less from their being urgent contributions to the understanding of their own historical moments than from their coming to be seen as perplexing responses to an increasingly distant past. For Evans the timing was significant. Most of the images were at least a quarter of a century old, and from a period before the war, but still within living memory. As Martha Rosler put it subsequently:

> in the game of waiting out the moment of critique of some cultural work it is the capitalist system itself ... that is the victor, for in cultural

> matters the pickings of the historical garbage heap are worth far more than the critical moves of the present, and by being chosen and commodified ... even the most directly critical works in turn affirm the system they formerly indicted, which in its most liberal epochs parades them through the streets as proof of its open-mindedness. In this case of course [the publication of *Let Us now Praise Famous Men*], the work did not even see publication until its moment had ended.[1]

Rosler describes a kind of canonization that seals off the work from the historical and political complexity of its moment and turns modernist documentary reflexivity into a formal game. But a more profound ambiguity remained. Certainly, for some the historical remove made the photographs easier to read as art but for others their indexical force secured them status as historical records in the popular imaginary. Indeed they still looked 'documentary' enough to appeal to a constituency looking for models of campaigning realist practice from the past (it was in the 1960s that the myth was born of a 1930s possessed of a widespread cultural politics of dissent when the reality was a matter of important pockets of progressive activity in a predominantly conservative era). All this has allowed Evans's books to be aligned with his reputation as a modern photographic artist, distant from the cut and thrust of documentary and the compromises of the 'applied image'.

The work Evans produced for magazines is another matter entirely. The photobook form always has at least half an eye on posterity but the illustrated magazine has a very different temporality and cultural significance. It is not made to last but lives and dies, succeeds or fails in the space of its short shelf life. This presents profound problems for understanding the history of photography, particularly documentary and photojournalism. As the 'genres of record' these practices evolved and presented themselves in contexts that were essentially ephemeral. The representation of documentary and photojournalistic images in monographs and museums does little to capture the contingent complexity of their initial page presentation. And only in the last decade has the difficult work of assembling a history of the illustrated magazine begun to come into focus, if somewhat less clearly than the emerging history of the photobook.

In the revival of interest in Evans's work that gathered momentum through the 1960s he was heralded as several contradictory things at once: a detached observer of 1930s America; a committed documentarian; a pioneer of Modern art in photographic form; and a proto-Pop artist of the American vernacular. But he was not heralded as an editor, or a writer or a designer and certainly not a 'working photographer', all of which he had been in his engagement with the magazine page. Art's assessment of Evans, like its assessment of so many photographers working for magazines, preferred to overlook the actual conditions in which the imagery was made, to see it as simply the catalyst for the artistic production of photographs. The 1971 retrospective, curated by John Szarkowski, confirmed the growing resurgence of interest and secured Evans a significant reputation, introducing his photographs to a new generation of practitioners, writers and critics. But the terms were too narrow to reflect fully Evans's concerns and achievements. The show and the accompanying book (entitled simply *Walker Evans*) skirted his particular grasp of the page as a working site and the centrality of editing, sequencing and writing to his practice.[2] Szarkowski's approach, soon emulated by other museums, privileged the significant single, exhibitable photograph over the internally organized body of work. The only sequence Szarkowski adopted was a uniform chronology (although nearly half of the 200 images selected for the show dated from 1935 to 1936, the 'FSA' period). He had nothing particular to say about the specificity of any of Evans's books or magazine work. *American Photographs*, which had been published by MoMA, was for him a collection of exceptional images; an anthology, not an articulated statement and certainly not a 'work'. Its ambitious and demanding two-part structure, modelled on modern photography's two key modes of assembly – the associative sequence and the archival album – meant little to Szarkowski. He also dismissed Evans's 20 years at *Fortune* as a long autumn of comfortable compromise following a creative 'hot streak' in the 1930s born of youthful energy and artistic exploration. He assumed Evans was softened by regular employment into producing very few images of the 'fierce conviction that identifies his best work' since the 'continual vigilance' required of working for a magazine 'frustrates free expression'.[3] This missed the point. At *Fortune* Evans's work was not *only* about the making of photographs. It was about synthesizing the whole craft complex associated with the production and presentation of photographic work for a magazine while seeing what an independent mind could do with it. Images of 'fierce conviction' (singular, rhetorically charged, formally unified, museum friendly) are often resistant to such synthesis and it should be conceded that Evans produced comparatively few of these for *Fortune*. But the boundaries Evans was testing there were less to do with composition and picture-making than those of the mainstream magazine itself. Three examples from *Fortune* should illustrate the point well enough here.

Evans's disdain for the working practices of American magazines is well documented.[4] It is part of his posthumous artistic identity that although the American vernacular was his lifelong subject he saw its magazine culture as generally vulgar and regressive, too in thrall to advertising, commerce, kitsch and the management of popular opinion. *Fortune* was founded in 1930 by Henry R. Luce who had established *Time* magazine in 1923 and went on to launch *Life* in 1936. In the immediate aftermath of the Wall Street Crash and the onset of the Depression it was an unlikely venture: a luxurious and extravagant magazine specializing in the coverage of business, science and industry. Luce expected it to run at a loss, as a worthwhile indulgence subsidized by his other enterprises. The editorial statement in the first issue (February 1930) announced the aim of presenting 'clear and readable text, profusely illustrated with pictures, in a form ample and agreeable to the eye' and 'planned upon an economic scale which permits it to go toward that end beyond the technical limitations of most magazines'.[5] Many of *Fortune's* pages were printed in high-quality gravure rather than the halftone typical of most non-art publications. It also used colour reproduction in great quantity. At eleven by fourteen inches it was larger than most magazines and it had more pages, printed on heavy stock. It set out to commission the best photographers, writers, artists and illustrators, which meant looking beyond the scope of those working within journalism. Noting its blend of free marketeering and advanced artistic values, Douglas Eklund has described *Fortune* as 'an experiment in the aesthetics of capital'.[6] But as the effects of the Depression continued to take their toll well into the 1930s (there were five million unemployed in 1931), *Fortune* could not cleave easily to its brief of celebrating the bounties of capital. As Evans himself remarked, it 'didn't really know what role it should play during the depression. They didn't know what they were doing since they were founded to describe in a stimulating way American business and industry, and that was falling apart'.[7] And with the coming of the Second World War its position was if not contradictory then at least sensitive to the breadth and uncertainty of social and cultural attitudes of that fraught period.

As a freelance photographer, Evans contributed to *Fortune* as early as 1934 (seven photographs for a piece on the Communist Party in the September issue). In 1943, after around 13 years working without a permanent job, he joined Luce's Time Incorporated as a writer (primarily an art, film and book reviewer for *Time*). He continued to take photographic commissions, including some from *Fortune*. Two years later he was offered a post at *Fortune* as a photographer and writer; and in September 1948 he was named Special Photographic Editor, a title and position he had carved out for himself.[8] It was his artistic credentials, his avowed interest in American culture and his ability as a writer of copy that secured him a unique role. While *Fortune* was sheltered from the sharp demands of commercial viability, it in turn sheltered

Evans, giving him more than usual freedom. Once established on the staff he cultivated a high degree of autonomy. He shot competent portraits of businessmen as a trade-off for picking and choosing his photographic assignments, as well as compiling features from archival images. He answered not to the art department but directly to the managing editor, securing near total control of the pages he bargained for. An editorial from May 1948 informed the readership about him:

> Walker Evans ... is a writer of delicacy and evocative power. He is more widely recognized, however, in many discerning circles as one of the most distinguished photographers in the U.S. Aesthetic officialdom has leaned strongly towards that judgment: Evans had the first one-man show of photography ever given by New York's Museum of Modern Art, had held a Guggenheim Fellowship, and has only recently exhibited at the Chicago Art Institute. The power of Evans's photography has always proceeded from an eye that is as lively, direct, responsive and acidly probing as the eye of the great Civil War photographer Matthew Brady. Evans is not in the least interested in photographic attitudinizing, in camera schmaltz or grandiosity; he wishes through the instrumentality of photography, to make you see, with maximum directness, the great accuracy of tone and detail, the sights that have arrested him in his straight staring around the amazing crust of the visible world. [9]

Despite the high regard, Evans's work received no special billing or auteurist presentation in the magazine. This entirely suited its nature, as we shall see. Evans never used *Fortune* simply to showcase his talents as an image-maker. It was not a forum for 'art'. Rather he worked with and against the received conventions of the magazine page, producing features that both did and did not fit within *Fortune*'s editorial remit. With increasing frequency he wrote the texts to accompany his features.[10] He also determined the look of his pages, including the cropping of images, layout, graphics and titles. He understood that photographic meaning did not begin and end with the individual photograph. It was, vitally, a matter of editing, designing and writing. While he had pursued all these skills before, *Fortune* gave him the opportunity to do so with a steadier schedule, sufficient freedom and a regular income. It was an enviable position that few photographers have ever achieved, particularly on American magazines.

'Main Street Looking North From Courthouse Square' (May 1948), his first feature as Special Photographic Editor, included none of his own photography but drew instead on his archive of vintage American postcards (Figure 1).[11] He saw that the regional postcards that were typical of the early twentieth century provided an unlikely but telling measure of that era. They were predominantly colour-tinted views of provincial streets, bridges, transportation and factories – not the glorifications of leisure and tourist spots that soon came to dominate the form. The imagery is clear, unpretentious, restrained and quite anti-promotional, similar in many ways to Evans's own photographic aesthetic. Even so, he knew very well they could be misread as nostalgia (an acute awareness of the possibilities of misreading is the common thread that unites all of his work for magazines). So Evans crafted a succinct page-long introduction that made deft connections between period and image, making the case that the passing of particular moments in modern history always involve the passing of their distinctive mode of self-representation:

> In the 1900's, sending and saving picture postcards was a prevalent and often a deadly boring fad in a million middle-class family homes. Yet the plethora of cards printed in that period now forms a solid bank from which to draw some of the most charming and, on occasion, the

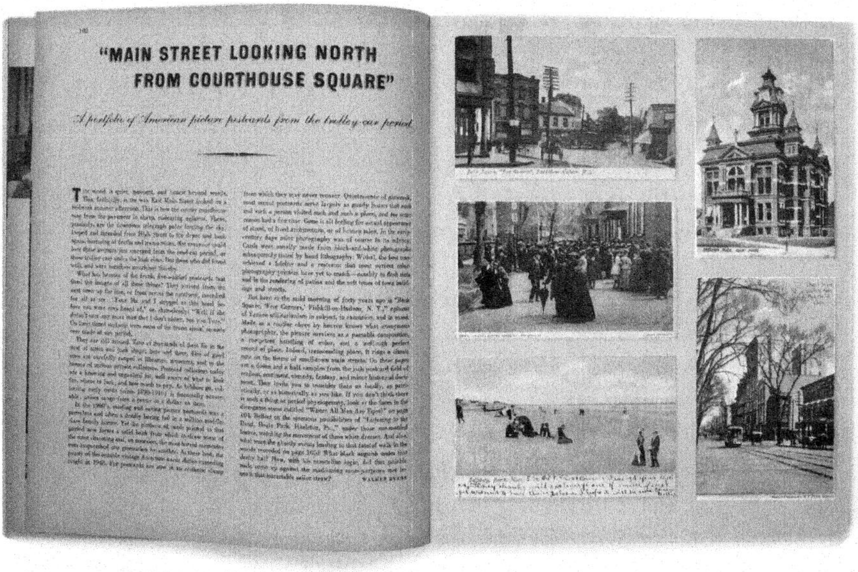

1. Walker Evans, 'Main Street Looking North from Courthouse Square', *Fortune* (1948).

> most horrid mementos ever bequeathed one generation by another. At their best, the purity of the humble vintage American cards shines exceeding bright [*sic*] in 1948. For postcards are now at an aesthetic slump from which they may never recover. Quintessence of gimcrack, most recent postcards serve largely as gaudy boasts that such and such a person visited such and such a place, and for some reason had a fine time. Gone is all feeling for actual street, of lived architecture, or of human mien. In the early-century days color photography was of course in its infancy.

What might at first look like a mildly sentimental feature is in fact a concise and accessible reflection on photography, history, material culture and memory, presented in a magazine with an even shorter active life than a postcard.

The majority of Evans's *Fortune* features had a historical consciousness that was out of step with the magazine's commitment to the modern and the new. Many focused upon vestiges of the past and the imminent obsolescence of everyday things. 'Vintage Office Furniture' (August 1953) showcased nineteenth-century office fittings and equipment still to be found in businesses of long standing in the Boston area. 'Before they Disappear' (March 1957) was a suite of colour images of vanishing railroad company insignia, standardized but still hand-painted on the sides of freight cars. Even the titles of his features are indicative: 'The Small Shop', 'One Newspaper Town', 'Is the Market Right?', 'The Wreckers', 'These Dark Satanic Mills', 'Downtown: A Last Look Backward', 'The Last of Railroad Steam', 'The Auto-Junkyard'. However, it would be hasty to dismiss this work and its presence in *Fortune* as nostalgic, as a kind of sentimental looking back in the knowledge that the juggernaut of American progress could not be stopped. Certainly many business-oriented magazines were (and still are) prone to bouts of that kind of wistful hand wringing but Evans was adamant that it was not so simple and he became increasingly explicit on the matter. In 'Collectors Items' (*Mademoiselle*, May 1963) he railed: 'Pray keep me forever separated from an atmosphere of moist elderly eyes just about to spill over at the sight of grandmother's tea set'.[12] And in interview he insisted: 'To be interested in what you see that is passing out of history, even if it's a trolley car you've found, that's not an act of nostalgia. You could read Proust as "nostalgia" but that's not what Proust had in mind at all'.[13] Evans's interest in the lingering evidence of the past was complex. The nearly, or recently forgotten could, if approached correctly, serve an allegorical meditation on the present and the nature of modernity. More to the point, in *Fortune* Evans's tempered and reflective take on modernity extended beyond the subject matter to the nature of images themselves, to the very structure of photographic representation and its capacity to transport the present into history and summon the past into the present. Looking across his output one can see clearly how Evans grasped that in modernity a period and the pictorial means by which it comes to know itself are as short-lived as each other. (In another context this was a phenomenon central to the thought of Walter Benjamin: 'Just as the entire mode of existence of human collectives changes over long historical periods so too does their mode of perception'.[14]) Modernity implies not just a succession of epochs but also a succession of ways those epochs understand and picture themselves. Looking at the overlooked and the throw(n)away Evans sensed that the act of representation *could* produce a mode of attention that would allow photography's relation to the past to be grasped dialectically. Paradoxically then, *Fortune*'s focus on the new and the future was both Evans's foil and the best context for his concerns.

In the early months of 1946 the editorial board was preparing a special issue on housing. There was an acute shortage of dwellings in America, the result of a suspended building programme exacerbated by the return of military personnel from overseas. There was great popular interest both in the innovative construction methods that had been developed in wartime and in new ways of living. Solving the housing problem was vital to America, prerequisite to any other kind of 'advance'. *Architectural Forum*, the sister publication of *Fortune*, was also planning a housing issue and both appeared in April 1946. Most of the articles were descriptive and informational, covering topics such as the economics of building, innovations in construction, new modes of interior design and home appliances. The cover design featured Buckminster Fuller's hi-tech Wichita House, a development of his modular Dymaxion House of 1944, which was receiving much publicity.

Evans's contribution 'Homes of Americans' took a starkly different approach.[15] It covered five double spreads, comprising an introductory text, 33 photographs and captions reserved for the concluding page. The presentation was almost austere amid the magazine's colour reproductions and graphic flamboyance. The typesetting was pared-down, the layout neutral and grid-like and the images black and white. None were shot especially for the feature and only seven were by Evans himself, taken much earlier in the 1930s. The picture credits were tucked away on the issue's general credits page and they were from three federal sources. But this was not an archival research exercise since most of the prints were actually from Evans's own collection, as the brief editorial on page 2 points out.[16] Where the rest of the magazine put photographic illustrations to use in enthusiastic and

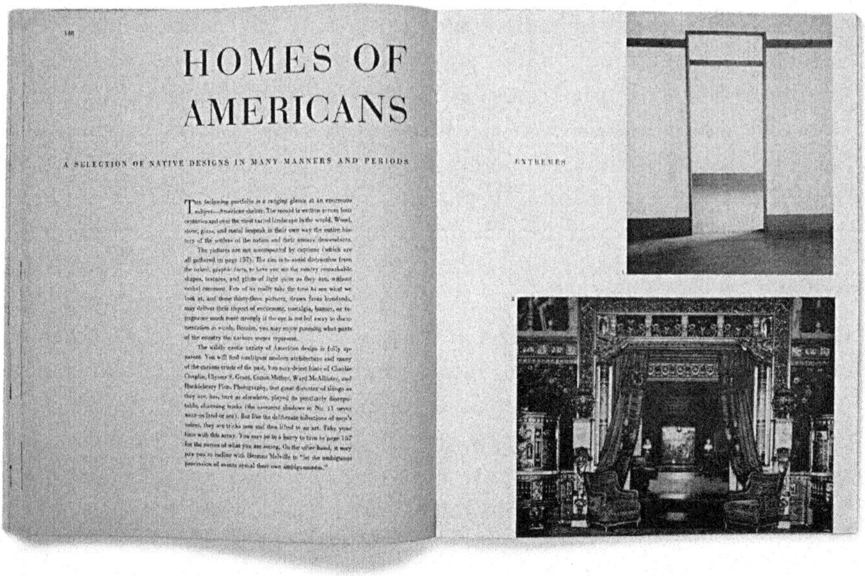
HOMES OF AMERICANS

A SELECTION OF NATIVE DESIGNS IN MANY MANNERS AND PERIODS

2. Walker Evans, 'Homes of Americans', *Fortune* (1946).

explanatory articles, 'Homes of Americans' was much more ambiguous, even deliberately awkward (Figures 2, 3 and 4).

Evans was well aware of the open meaning of these documents, and here he strategically turned the risks of misreading into the very subject of the piece. This is the introductory text:

> The following portfolio is a ranging glance at an enormous subject – American shelter. The record is written across four centuries and over the most varied landscape in the world. Wood, stone, glass and metal bespeak in their own way the entire history of the settlers of the nation and their uneasy descendants.
>
> The pictures are not accompanied by captions (which are all gathered on page 157). The aim is to avoid distraction from the naked, graphic facts, to have you see the sundry remarkable shapes, textures and glints of light quite as they are, without verbal comment. Few of us really take the time to see what we look at, and these thirty-three pictures, drawn from hundreds, may deliver their impact of excitement, nostalgia, humor or repugnance much more strongly if the eye is not

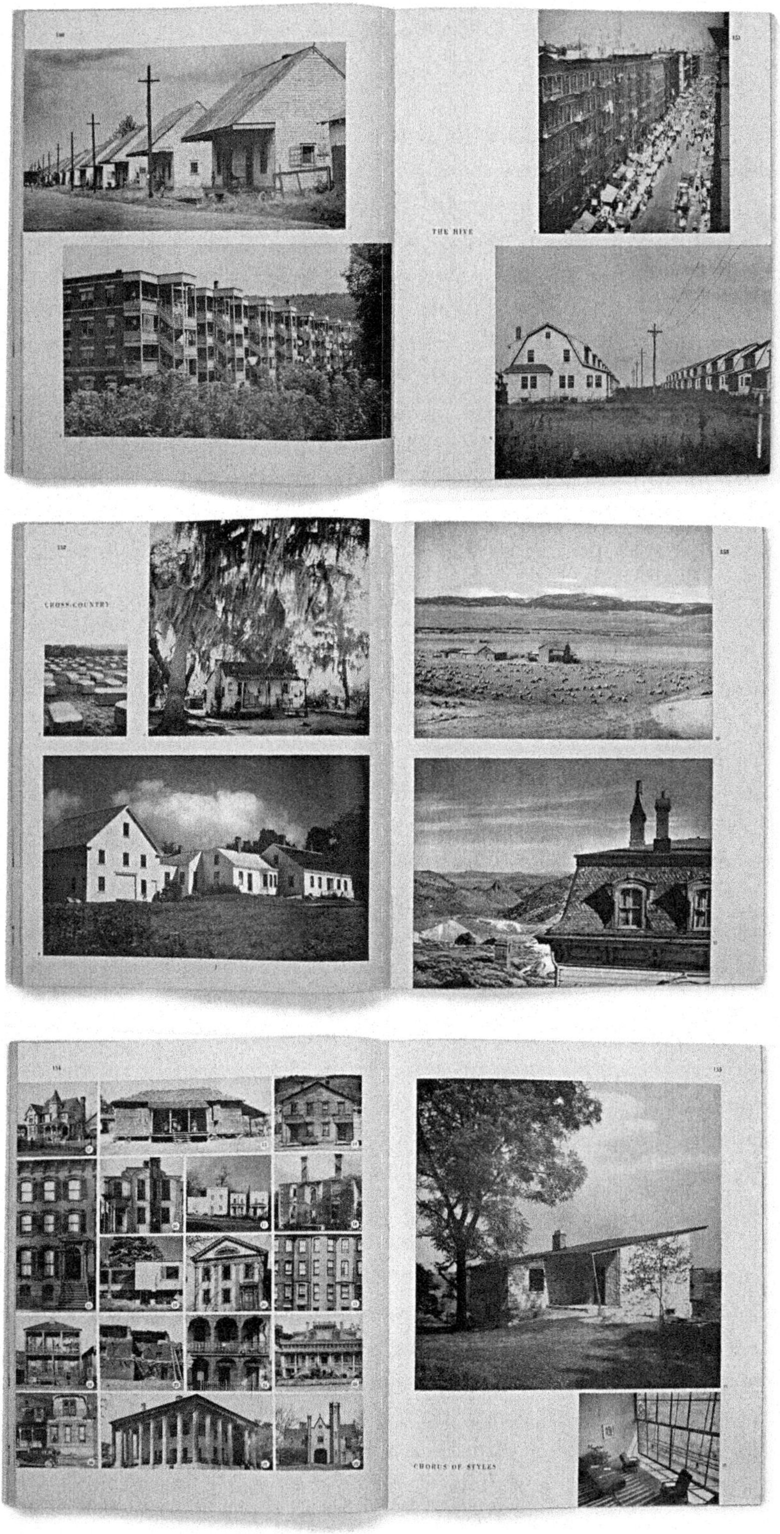

3. Walker Evans, 'Homes of Americans', *Fortune* (1946).

> led away to documentation in words. Besides you may enjoy guessing what parts of the country the various scenes represent.
>
> The wildly exotic variety of American design is fully apparent. You will find intelligent modern architecture and many of the curious crusts of the past. You may detect hints of Charlie Chaplin, Ulysses S. Grant, Cotton Mather, Ward McAllister, and Huckleberry Finn. Photography, that great distorter of things as they are, has, here as elsewhere, played its particularly disreputable, charming trick ... But like the deliberate inflections of men's voices, they are tricks now and then lifted to an art. Take your time with this array. You may be in a hurry to turn to page 157 for the names of what you are seeing. On the other hand it may pay you to incline with Herman Melville to 'let the ambiguous procession of events reveal their own ambiguousness'.

The tone continues at the rear in the caption for the first two images:

> These are a Shaker doorway in New Lebanon, New York, built in 1819 and Mrs. Cornelius Vanderbilt's New York drawing room as of 1883. That Shaker reticence should meet cupids, ormulu and brocade in the same nation, while no great surprise, is certainly a telling matter for pictorial juxtaposition. There could scarcely be a more vivid parable concerning the extreme diversity of American manners or character.

Neither could there be a more vivid parable of the vicissitudes of the photographic document. 'Homes of Americans' inverts *Fortune*'s embrace of the new and the rational not just by lingering on images of old things, but by wrong-footing easy reading and making interpretation pointedly difficult. The Modernist-looking interior was actually 133 years old, predating the Baroque-looking drawing room by 64 years. This opening pair also alerts the reader to the fact that photography has always been attracted with equal appetite to the typical and the untypical, the banal and the exotic, but with a sharp reminder that photographs cannot guarantee their status in this regard. The reader is deprived of a documentary standard by which to make shorthand sense, but is unable to suspend the documentary claim in the name of art or something else. Further on we see a field of Airstream caravans that is a temporary home for defence workers, but the caption talks of the trailer's emancipatory mobility and its long-standing popularity as a mainstay of American culture. An image of a Long Island housing development of the 1930s is captioned 'A Life-time Opportunity. Steam Heat, with Gas, Electricity and Water. On Easy Terms...', mocking the rhetoric of the

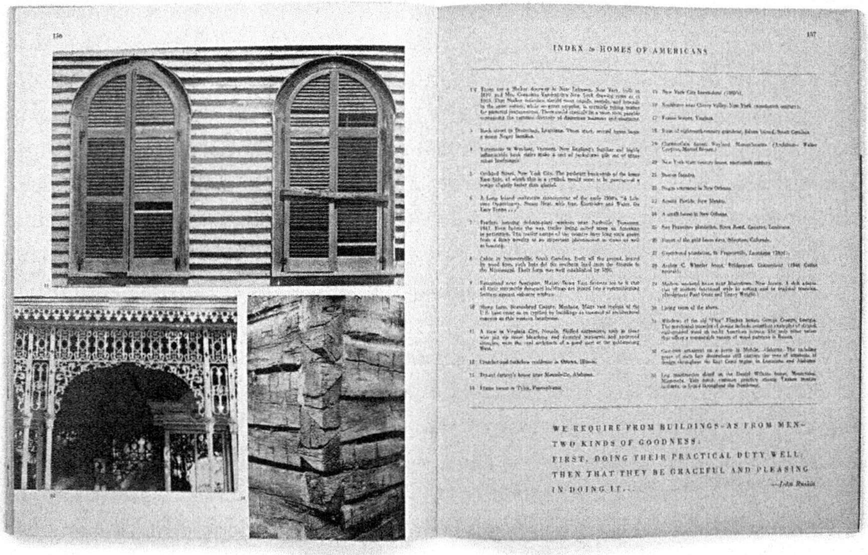

4. Walker Evans, 'Homes of Americans', *Fortune* (1946).

real estate sales pitch to be found elsewhere in the magazine. The sleek functionalism of the latest High Modern home by Walter Gropius and Marcel Breuer is squashed into a grid with vernacular flatroofed, wood-frame houses from the nineteenth century. Captions suggest repeatedly that the beauty of built form is rooted in pragmatism, tradition, experience, prudence and anonymous craft, not in high architecture and its star pioneers. Many of the images are left deliberately undated to suggest – in this future-oriented issue of *Fortune* – that if these dwellings still exist and are occupied, they are as contemporary as anything new and have a valid future.

Conventionally, captions serve to 'anchor' the polysemy of the image while helping to imply that photographic meaning is straightforward and natural.[17] 'Homes of Americans' foregrounds the function of the caption by actively withholding or delaying its delivery, and setting it at odds with the photograph. Word and image are deployed against convention to slow down audiences rather than hasten them into the tempo necessary to consume a photo-essay as information or entertainment. As in so much of Evans's work for the printed page 'Homes of Americans' sets out to establish a reflective pace at which it is possible to think not just about the purported subject matter, but about the conditions and limits of photography and writing.

The feature was presented anonymously, with no name on its opening page, leaving it to be attributed to the magazine in the abstract. This was uncommon in the pages of *Fortune* (although Evans often reduced his credit to a minimal 'W.E.'). But given the interventionism involved here it seems entirely plausible this was done to allow it the fullest potential quietly to disrupt and subvert. The presence of a name, any name, may well have contained the deliberate awkwardness, personifying and bracketing it off as something distinct from the body of the magazine (much the way art magazines declare their 'artists' pages' in which the graphic rules and values of the host are lifted to indulge the art/artist).

Most of Evans's features for *Fortune* were billed on the contents pages as 'Portfolios', but this had less to do with artistic aspiration or a need to separate his pages from the rest of the magazine than a desire to put clear water between his concerns and those of photo-essay formulae being honed in the popular press, spearheaded by *Life* with its pacy design, narrative flow, over-emotional tone and often trite 'messages'. Henry Luce had set out to ensure *Life* was 'the best magazine for look-through purposes', while its first editor Daniel Longwell had proclaimed excitedly 'the quick nervousness of pictures is a new language'.[18] Evans's portfolios have no beginnings, middles or ends and they resist speed at every turn. Each is a deliberating and monotone meditation on a small cluster of related themes. It is suggestive, inconclusive, open and at odds with its setting. This recalcitrance was a resistance to what John Tagg has described as 'those dreams of transparency, efficiency, and accelerated exchange that marked the instrumentalization of photographic meaning, in social administration as in commercialized communications, in the documentary archive as in the photojournalistic picture file'.[19] In another context such refusals of clear meaning might have looked indulgent or prankish but for Evans part of making effective work for *Fortune* entailed knowing the context well enough to be able to operate a kind of micro-intervention, confounding assumptions and diverting expectations.

With his name confined to the credits page and only seven of the images being his, it is not surprising 'Homes of Americans' slips below the radar of those looking for Evans's more obviously formal or pictorial hallmarks. Moreover, while the selection of the photographs was his, the text was the outcome of conversations with his good friend and member of *Fortune*'s editorial board, Wilder Hobson, who had been first assigned a piece on American housing. So we must proceed with care before we declare Evans the absent auteur here. Nevertheless, the whole disposition of the feature chimes with Evans's outlook, while the writing is very close in attitude and rhetorical flourish to his other pieces for *Fortune*. The tactic of using straight photos made complex by sequence and text was in keeping with his suspicion of anything easy while the stronger remarks bear his characteristic distrust of magazine manipulation. There is the warning that 'Photography, that great distorter of things as they are, has ... played its particularly disreputable, charming trick'. There is the injunction to 'Take your time with this array' and the hint that 'it may pay you to incline with Herman Melville to "let the ambiguous procession of events reveal their own ambiguousness"'. Similar sentiments can be found throughout Evans's pronouncements on his own photography and the medium in general.[20]

Clearly none of the meaning of 'Homes of Americans' would survive if the images were disaggregated and re-presented. It is an entirely 'site-specific' assembly. Indeed most of the images had been used before in one context or another and Evans could pluck and reuse them precisely because they functioned loosely as archival stand-ins for (almost) unknown subjects or objects. They were not obviously 'arty' pictures. This is a photographic tradition in which Evans is an exemplary figure, not just in his adherence to the 'straight' photo and his preference for vernacular subjects, but in his understanding that the more neutral the document appears the more dependent its meaning upon the way it is deployed. And insofar as its meaning is made through placement, sequence and language, it is archival to its core. There could be no *definitive* place for such images. Photographs would be what you did with them (and even the museum would have to concede that it could never provide the definitive meaning or last word).

An even starker example of this kind of contingency is 'Labor Anonymous', published seven months after 'Homes of Americans' (November 1946). It is a double-spread of 11 images and text which at first glance looks like a serial typology of anonymous workers, perhaps taken surreptitiously as they leave their place of work. That is how these portraits by Evans are regularly recycled and presented in exhibitions and monographs. But in the spread itself there are many details that complicate and even contradict such a reading. The short but crucial text makes no reference to the end of a working shift, while only three of the subjects are wearing clothes associated exclusively with labour (Figure 5).

The feature is in fact subtitled 'On a Saturday Afternoon in Downtown Detroit', suggesting this may not be a day of work at all, even if this is one of America's foremost industrial cities. These may well be workers but they are not working here. The text occupies a space the size of one of the portraits, as if word and image were of a piece and interchangeable, but once read it is clear the purpose is to uproot that assumption. Evans reminds the reader

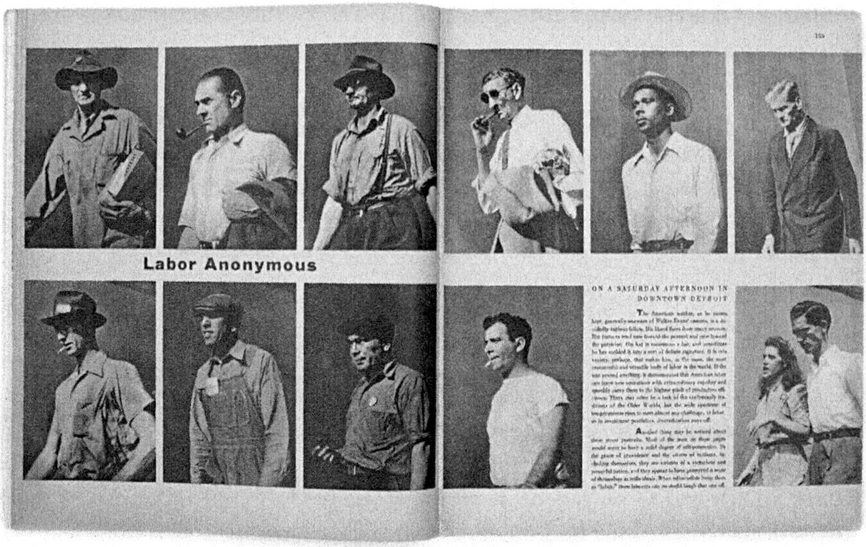

5. Walker Evans, 'Labor Anonymous', *Fortune* (1946).

that there is no classifiable physiognomy on show here. Labourers cannot be stereotyped, neither in appearance, nor disposition, nor dress: 'His features tend now toward the peasant and now the patrician. His hat is sometimes a hat, and sometimes he has molded it into a sort of defiant signature.' In other words these photographs offer no sure measure and the reader will still have all their interpretive work ahead of them. He concludes: 'When editorialists lump them as "labor" these laborers can no doubt laugh that one off.' It is an obvious point but easily forgotten: a person cannot be anonymous in and of themselves but only to, or for, another. 'Labor Anonymous' is revealed to be an ironic title, critical of the assumptions of mainstream editorialists and readers, including those of *Fortune* itself (the feature appeared in an issue dedicated to 'Labor in U.S. Industry'). Looking again at the photos we see they are not entirely serial, even though this was about as serial as Evans's work ever became (more so than his New York subway portraits). In the first frame a man in overalls seems to look directly at the photographer. The brim of his hat overshadows his eyes, giving the impression he notes the presence of the camera while keeping something of himself hidden. It stalls the ethnographic fantasy of invisibility, of observing and classifying unsuspecting specimens. Placed top left in the grid, the image helps to suggest the subsequent shots should not be taken too readily 'at face value'. The final photo shows a man and a woman together as a couple in the same frame, complicating any simple distinction between labour relations and sexual relations. All this is in the space of a single spread. It is a rare example of a photographer adopting the conventions of the visual typology, only to undermine the instrumental authority they usually invoke. Suffice it to say, when removed from their layout and presented simply as a suite of formally innovative street portraits, their meaning is doomed not just to 'revert to type', but to turn the original intention on its head.

It would be another two decades at least before this kind of attention to the discursive limits and ideological underpinnings of documentary and photojournalism was to come into focus in the USA, and only then in the context of conceptualism and its art-educational spin-offs. In 1946 'Labor Anonymous' parried the growing trend for voyeuristic portraits, while 'Homes of Americans' offered housing to its readership 'in two inadequate descriptive systems', to paraphrase the title of the much-celebrated conceptual documentary work by Martha Rosler from 1974 to 1975.[21] And when Dan Graham produced the still endlessly celebrated photo-text 'Homes for America' in 1966 (in ignorance of Evans's precedent), its appearance as a piece of subversive print journalism was scuppered first by the artist's failure to get it published in the mainstream press and then by *Arts* magazine's replacement of his intended images with one by ... Evans.[22] But Graham's magazine work survives where Evans's has not precisely because Graham saw himself as an artist making 'Works' for magazines, which permitted him to recycle and recuperate them in the post-conceptual art museum, whereas Evans was working for a magazine with no eye on the future but a very sure eye on intelligent intervention in the moment and context of publication. Unaware of his magazine work, the conceptual art generation of the 1960s and 1970s inherited and largely rejected Evans as a modernist/formalist museum artist, when in fact he had been a significant precursor.

Evans's use of the page gives us a far better understanding of what he may have meant by his notoriously elusive description of his work as 'documentary style'.[23] The museum tends to take this to mean an Evans image looks like a documentary photograph but is 'really' art, either because it is formally more ambitious than documentary demands, or more riskily because once exhibited the museum suspends the documentary claim. But if we take documentary to mean not a type of image but a type of image *use* (also involving modes of editing, writing and design), then Evans's work for the magazine page was indeed 'documentary style' rather than 'documentary'.

When John Szarkowski presented Evans as a modern museum artist, he had the photographer's opportunistic blessing and in some senses this was inevitable. In working at *Fortune* Evans addressed himself to a specificity and timeliness of the page that the art history of photography cannot adequately accommodate. It would have been not just inappropriate but pretty much impossible for posterity to rest upon such work. Exhibiting or reprinting those features would have had 'merely' anecdotal interest. The recent interest in the photographic book, of which the present volume is an instance, marks a tentative step towards the barely charted and possibly unchartable chaos that is the history of the photographic page. Indeed the photobook represents something of a bridging point between the auteurism and permanence demanded by the culture of the museum and the near-anonymous ephemerality of the magazine which was photography's most significant site for the four decades in which Evans was active (1930–70). So what does it mean to return to the specificity of magazine work and to reproduce it here? For Denis Hollier,

> The significance of the reprint is not the same for a book as it is for a periodical. A novel is republished because it has had some success or because the time has come to rediscover it. *Habent sua fata libelli.* With a journal, the transposition from the aorist to the imperfect alters the textual status of the object, its punctuality. Like an event condemned to linger on.[24]

I cannot tell if Evans himself thought this way but given the manner in which he worked at *Fortune* it should not surprise us if he did. His eyes were not on the future but on *that* audience, for *that* feature in *that* magazine, *that* month. Plus of course posterity cannot deploy the same criteria of judgement as the present. Evans barely spoke about his magazine work, but when he did it was clear he thought highly of it. It was for him among his most significant achievements. When asked about his favourite *Fortune* features, he even opted for ones that did not involve his own photography but allowed him to operate as an editor.[25] And when asked about the essentials of photography he downplayed the significance of single images in favour of the intelligence of their arrangement:

> The essence is done very quickly with a flash of the mind, and with a machine. I think too that photography is editing, editing after the taking. After knowing what to take you have to do the editing.[26]

Individual images are not without merit, not least many of Evans's, but however singular they may seem, sooner or later they must be put together. In 1969, in what turned out to be his last significant work for the page, Evans was invited by Louis Kronenberger to select the section on photography for the anthology *Quality: Its Image in the Arts*. He chose what he felt were exemplary photographs from across the history of the medium. He insisted on a simple layout, typically stark in this messy publication, with a single image on the right and an invariably terse paragraph opposite. But even here Evans considered very carefully the sequencing of these apparently unrelated photos, and he let the reader know as much: 'No individual evaluation is implied in the order and manner of presentation of the photographs that follow. The picture placement has been arranged solely with regard to the visual effect of the plates in relation to one another, and to their impact collectively'. Nearing the end of a long career, he was still working out the complex dialectic between the one, the many and the word that had interested him at the outset, wanting his audience to feel their way into it but without too strident a guide.

Notes

1 Martha Rosler, 'In, Around, and Afterthoughts (on Documentary Photography)' (1981), in Richard Bolton (ed.), *The Contest of Meaning: Critical Histories of Photography* (Cambridge, MA and London: MIT, 1989), footnote n.18, p. 338.
2 John Szarkowski, *Walker Evans* (New York: Museum of Modern Art, 1971).
3 Szarkowski, *Walker Evans*, pp. 9–20.
4 See Lawrence Bergreen, *James Agee: A Life* (New York: Dutton, 1984), p. 161.
5 See Chris Mullen and Philip Beard, *Fortune's America. The Visual Achievements of* Fortune *Magazine 1930–1965* (Norwich: University of East Anglia Library, 1985).
6 Douglas Eklund, '"The Harassed Haven of Detachment": Walker Evans and the *Fortune* Portfolio', in Maria Mouris Hambourg, Jeff L. Rosenheim, Douglas Eklund et al. (eds), *Walker Evans* (New York: Metropolitan Museum of Art and Princeton: Princeton University Press, 2000), p. 121.
7 Evans in James R. Mellow, *Walker Evans* (New York, Perseus Press, 1999), p. 308.
8 See Lesley K. Baier, *Walker Evans at* Fortune *1945–1965* (Wellesley, MA: Wellesley College, 1977).
9 'Freewheeling Cameraman', *Fortune* (May 1948), p. 32.
10 See also Baier, *Walker Evans at Fortune*, p. 12.
11 This was the first of three portfolios Evans published on the subject: 'When "Downtown" was a Beautiful Mess', *Fortune* (January 1962), pp. 100–6; and 'Come on Down', *Architectural Review* (July 1962), pp. 96–100. See also Jeff Rosenheim et al., *Walker Evans and the Picture Postcard* (New York: Steidl/The Metropolitan Museum of Art, 2009).

12 Walker Evans and Malcolm Bradbury, 'Collector's Items', *Mademoiselle* 57 (May 1963) p. 182.
13 Leslie Katz, 'Interview with Walker Evans', *Art in America* (March–April 1971), pp. 82–89.
14 Walter Benjamin, 'The Work of Art in the Age of Its Technological Reproducibility', second version (1935–6), *The Work of Art in the Age of Its Technological Reproducibility and Other Writings on Media*, ed. Michael Jennings et al. (Cambridge, MA and London: The Belknap Press of Harvard University, 2008), p. 23. The parallels between Evans and Benjamin run deep and can be best grasped by a comparative reading of Evans's 'The Reappearance of Photography' and Benjamin's 'A Little History of Photography', both published in 1931.
15 'Homes of Americans', *Fortune* 33 (April 1946), pp. 148–57.
16 See David Campany, 'Almost the Same Thing: Some Thoughts on the Collector-photographer', in Emma Dexter and Thomas Weski (eds), *Cruel and Tender: the Real in the Twentieth Century Photograph* (London: Tate Publishing, 2003), pp. 32–35.
17 Roland Barthes coined the term 'anchorage' in 'The Rhetoric of the Image' (1964), in Stephen Heath (ed. and trans.), *Image-Music-Text* (London: Fontana, 1977).
18 Luce and Longwell in Loudon Wainwright's *The Great American Magazine* (New York: Alfred A. Knopf, 1986), pp. 21 and 29.
19 John Tagg, 'Melancholy Realism: Walker Evans's Resistance to Meaning' (2003), *The Disciplinary Frame: Photographic Truths and the Capture of Meaning* (Minneapolis and London: University of Minnesota Press, 2009), p. 96.
20 See, for example, Leslie Katz, 'Interview with Walker Evans', *Art in America* 59 (1971), pp. 82–89.
21 I am referring to Martha Rosler's *The Bowery in Two Inadequate Descriptive Systems* (1974–5), a sequence of straight shots of shop fronts in New York's Bowery distinct accompanied by endless euphemisms for drunkenness.
22 See David Campany, 'Conceptual Art History, or, a Home for *Homes For America*', in John Bird and Michael Newman (eds), *Rewriting Conceptual Art* (London: Reaktion Books, 1999).
23 'The term should be *documentary style* ... You see, a document has use, whereas art is really useless. Therefore art is never a document, though it certainly can adopt that style.' Katz, 'Interview with Walker Evans', p. 87.
24 Denis Hollier, 'The Use-Value of the Impossible', *October* 60 (1992), p. 23.
25 See the interviews with Walker Evans conducted by Paul Cummings in October and December 1971, in The Smithsonian Archives of American Art.
26 Katz, 'Interview with Walker Evans', pp. 82–89.

SCULPTURE, PHOTOGRAPH, BOOK: *THE SCULPTURES OF PICASSO* (1949)

Patrizia Di Bello

The Sculptures of Picasso, with an essay by Daniel Henry Kahnweiler and 'Photographs By Brassaï', was published in London and Paris in 1949.[1] Commissioned in 1943, the book had been ready for its French publisher Editions du Chêne since 1945 or 1946, but publication had been delayed by postwar paper shortages.[2] In the end it came out first in London, published by Rodney Phillips.[3] Like many art books of its kind, the issue of authorship is somewhat ambiguous. Library catalogues consider Kahnweiler the author of the book, yet its fame and current circulation on the market rest far more on its photographs by Brassaï,[4] while Kahnweiler's bibliographer defines his essay as the introduction to a book by Picasso.[5] Kahnweiler, who had been Picasso's dealer on and off throughout his career, was one of the champions of modern sculpture and had written important essays on art such as *The Rise of Cubism* (1916), which was translated for Documents of Modern Art, the series edited by Robert Motherwell, in 1949,[6] and 'The Essence of Sculpture' first published in 1919.[7]

As Brassaï recollects, it was the publisher who asked Picasso to do 'an album of his complete sculpture', and Picasso agreed only on condition that the photos be done by Brassaï.[8] Brassaï's biographer, however, thinks that only Picasso could have 'accomplished the amazing feat' of convincing a publisher to produce such a book in the middle of a war.[9] In this chapter, however, I am going to focus on the book itself, rather than its authors, to see what it tells us about the role of sculpture photobooks in the development of sculptural aesthetics circa 1949. The actual object I have looked at and reproduced here is from the 1949 English edition. It was given to me as a present by a friend, a surprise I decided to interpret in the spirit of the Surrealist 'found object', as a kind of 'involuntary' sculpture case-study. In other words I do not come to this as a scholar of Picasso, Brassaï or Kahnweiler, but as someone interested in sculpture photobooks as a particular type of photographic object.

The cover of the book (Figure 1a) emphasizes Picasso as the author of what we are about to see: sculptures, rather than photographs in a book. The title is split in two and pushed to the edges of the cover. *The Sculptures Of* at the top and *Picasso* in a larger typeface at the bottom are separated by a photograph of the cast of Picasso's hand, raised as if in greeting. It reminds us of the tangibility of sculpture and underscores the importance of the touch of the artist in what we are about to experience; it invites us to touch, grab hold of the book, and turn its pages. As we do so, our hands meet that of the artist. The photograph was taken by Brassaï in 1943 as part of his commission, as was the first one inside the book (Figure 1b), where Picasso's hand is now grasping the neck of one of his figures. The photograph highlights how different Picasso's sculpture was from the aesthetics of direct carving, which at the time dominated in Britain, favouring artists who worked 'directly on the stone' such as Henry Moore and Barbara Hepworth.[10] This was a highly serious sculptural aesthetic of demanding physical work and emotional earnestness, based on 'truth to material' and 'truth to nature', as elaborated by the influential Herbert Read in the 1949 edition of *Henry Moore: Sculptures and Drawings*.[11] In this lavishly illustrated volume, Moore is portrayed in a rather formal photograph by Alfred Carlebach, a head-and-shoulder portrait in which the sculptor is gazing into the distance.[12] Brassaï's photograph of Picasso, instead, vividly recasts the cliché image of the sculptor chiselling away at his masterpiece[13] into one of the artist simply holding or strangulating his creation – a Pygmalion who brings sculpture to life not by hard work from the original block, nor by loving caresses, but by shaking or squeezing it. The involvement of Picasso's hands is emphasized here not as work, but as a kind of rough magic, appropriate to his mythical fame as an artist whose touch could metamorphose any surface, support or bit of scrap into something more valuable than gold – in this sculpture, chicken-wire and corrugated cardboard or metal are clearly visible. This 'truth to materials', however, is very different from the one Reed describes. Rather over-literal, it emphasizes the ingenious economy with which Picasso could prompt the viewer's imagination into transforming one material into another – lacy fabric, crumpled trousers or a pleated skirt.

For art books of this time, educating a new and widening public for modern art after two world wars, it was important that sculpture should be presented as autonomous art, issuing forth from the artist's creativity and use of materials, rather than in response to architectural, civic or religious commissions, as sculpture had traditionally been. Sculpture was 'no longer something to be seen only in public places ... a thing for the public building or the market square, or ... the Church'; it had 'become domestic as well as

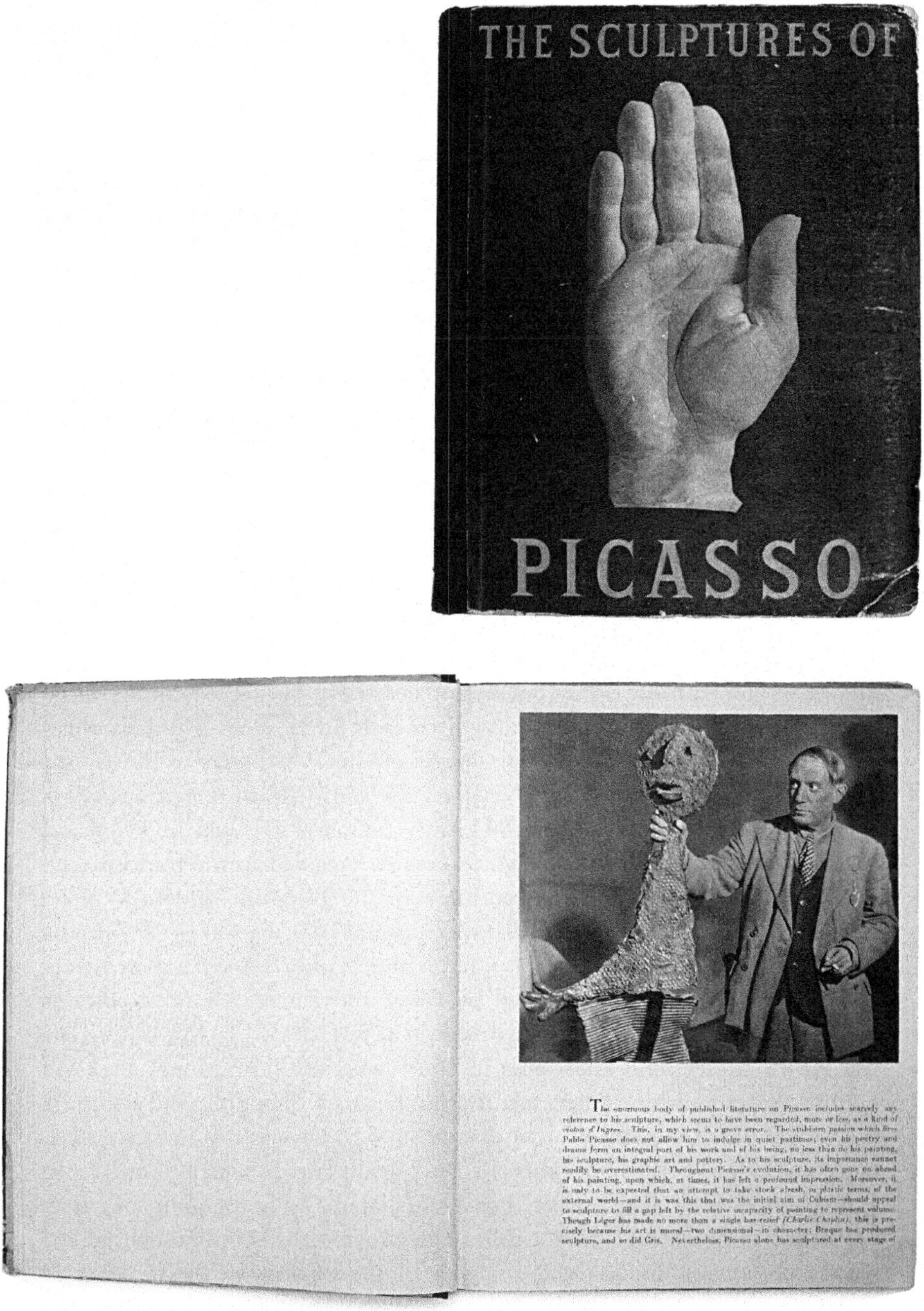

1a, b. *The Sculptures of Picasso, with Photographs by Brassaï* (London, 1949).

public or religious', as Arthur Broadbent wrote in 1944 in a small photobook of sorts on *Sculpture Today* (12.5 by 18.5 centimetres, two pages of text, 40 photographs). Yet the difference between sculptures and decorative objects, or fetishized commodities, should also be clear. There was no place in modernist aesthetics for the Parian statuettes so popular in the nineteenth century, as 'the average man is beginning to distinguish between the cheap reproduction and the exclusive work of the sculptor'. The sculpture-collecting urges of the modern middle classes should be satisfied not by mass-produced miniatures, but by a few well-chosen original objects, 'a little something on the mantelpiece, or in the entrance hall',[14] be as they may sculptures or well-chosen pebbles and driftwood,[15] augmented by photographs of sculptures. As Valerie Holman argues, in the twentieth century it was photography, film and eventually television, which made sculpture available to more viewers than ever before, and made artists more self-conscious about exploiting the mass media to create artistic identity.[16] This process had been halted by the Second World War but reinvigorated by the cultural ideals and idealism of postwar publishing. In a culture that seemed to seek in art a form of redemption or an antidote for the horrors of war, books on art were published in spite of paper shortages. Penguin books, for example, made art affordable to the masses not as cheap reproductions, but as intellectual packages wrapping visual pleasure and aesthetic understanding into each other. Even if usually small in format and brief in content, art books of the 1940s were well designed and carefully illustrated.[17] Eric Newton's *European Painting and Sculpture*, for example, first published in 1941 and 1942, was reissued in 1944 as a Penguin book 'for the use of H.M. forces' (as specified in the frontispiece), illustrated with 32 plates, and reprinted in the Penguin Modern Painters series in 1950. Clive Bell's 1914 *Art* was reissued after the war in 1947 and a new edition published in 1949 by Chatto and Windus. And Herbert Read's *The Meaning of Art* was published by Faber and Faber in various editions and reprints before the Second World War (1931, 1936, 1943), during the war (1945, 1946), and afterwards in 1949 'with 46 illustrations'. By 1949 books were 'establishing a new relationship between the public and sculpture independent of function or architectural support. It was not just critical ... texts that helped bring about this change, but the way in which photographs of sculpture were taken, selected and circulated'.[18] Photography not only brought sculpture to a wider public, but also took this public behind the scenes, 'to anchor the aesthetic integrity of the artwork to the presence of the maker in that unique site of creation: the sculptor's studio'.[19] It was only thanks to photography that the artist's studio could emerge as the ideal setting to see modern sculpture.

It is fitting, then, that the third photograph in the book is one of Picasso's studio, the only one accompanied by a caption (Figure 2a). This opening sequence highlights that the book does not just give us access to pictures of sculptures, but to Picasso's own artistic agency (the hand), identity (his looming presence by the sculpture), and working space (the studio). It constructs the experience of leafing through the book as a visit to meet him and his work in the studio, regardless of the various anonymous locations in which the photographs were actually taken.

As Alex Potts highlights in his discussion of the twentieth-century sculptural imagination, the idea of modern sculpture as a significant aspect of a modernist aesthetic 'gathered momentum relatively late, in the 1930s, coming to a head with the spate of publications in the 1950s ... specifically dedicated to the subject', yet remained a sideline 'to the master narratives of modern painting'.[20] This places *The Sculptures of Picasso* at the beginning of the postwar flowering of a process Brassaï had been very much part of, with his involvement with the Surrealist French magazine *Minotaure*. He had first met Picasso in 1932 when working on a series of 'sixty previously unpublished reproductions' of 'recent sculptures by Picasso' and photographs of his studios in Paris and Boisgeloup, appearing with an André Breton article in the first issue of *Minotaure* in February 1933.[21] He went on to photograph for the magazine the studios of, amongst others, Giacometti, Brancusi and the Cubist sculptor Laurens.[22]

Kahnweiler's essay argues against the marginalization of sculpture, and for its central role in Picasso's development. For Kahnweiler, Cubism allowed Picasso to solve the problems of modern sculpture. Rather than being a derivative from, or secondary to his painting,[23] sculpture had actually been the driving force in the development of Picasso's aesthetics. According to Kahnweiler, many of his paintings were actually of sculptures Picasso did not have the money or the commissions to execute, so he had to paint them instead.[24] After his essay, which refers directly to only a few of the sculptures that follow, we have a list of plates, arranged more or less in chronological order, specifying materials, dates and sizes, but no titles.

Sculpture had had a problematic role in modernist aesthetics since the nineteenth century, and continued to do so for much of the twentieth. For Baudelaire, modern sculpture was 'boring'.[25] For Leonardo da Vinci, as Read pointed out, sculpture was 'less "intellectual" than painting'.[26] In the twentieth century sculpture became what you bump into when you back up to see a painting, a much quoted quip variously attributed to Barnett Newman in the 1950s[27] or to Ad Reinhardt in the 1960s.[28] For writers on art from Baudelaire to Pater, Rilke to Simmel, modern sculpture was problematic

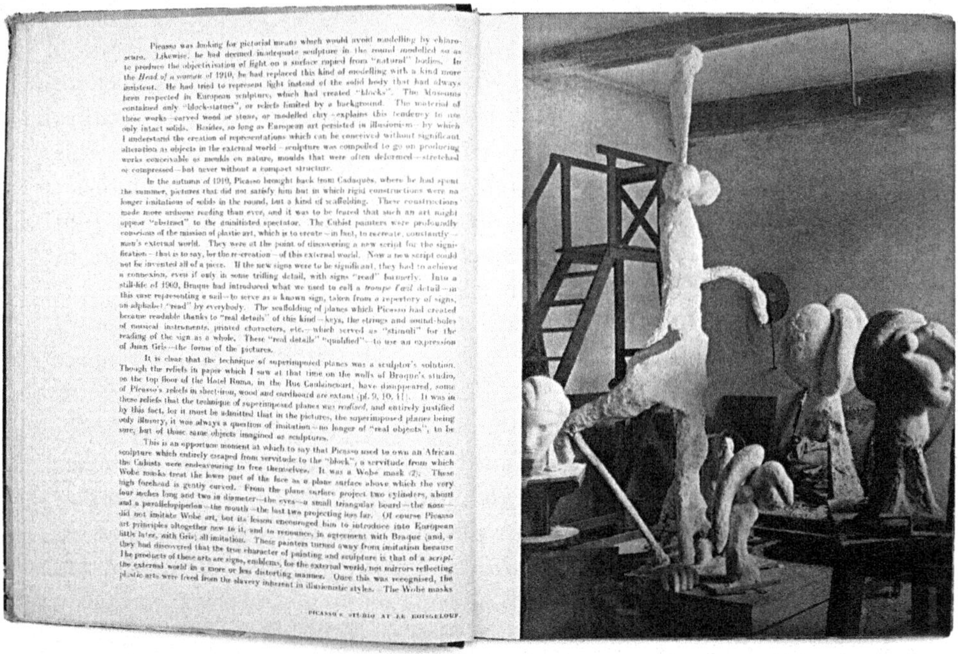

Picasso was looking for pictorial means which would avoid modelling by chiaroscuro. Likewise, he had deemed inadequate sculpture in the round modelled so as to produce the objectivisation of light on a surface copied from "natural" bodies. In the *Head of a woman* of 1910, he had replaced this kind of modelling with a kind more insistent. He had tried to represent light instead of the solid body that had always been respected in European sculpture, which had created "blocks". The Museums contained only "block-statues", or reliefs limited by a background. The material of these works—carved wood or stone, or modelled clay—explains this tendency to use only intact solids. Besides, so long as European art persisted in illusionism—by which I understand the creation of representations which can be conceived without significant alteration as objects in the external world—sculpture was compelled to go on producing works conceivable as moulds on nature, moulds that were often deformed—stretched or compressed—but never without a compact structure.

In the autumn of 1910, Picasso brought back from Cadaquès, where he had spent the summer, pictures that did not satisfy him but in which rigid constructions were no longer imitations of solids in the round, but a kind of scaffolding. These constructions made more arduous reading than ever, and it was to be feared that such an art might appear "abstract" to the uninitiated spectator. The Cubist painters were profoundly conscious of the mission of plastic art, which is to create—in fact, to recreate, constantly—man's external world. They were at the point of discovering a new script for the signification—that is to say, for the re-creation—of this external world. Now a new script could not be invented all of a piece. If the new signs were to be significant, they had to achieve a connexion, even if only in some trifling detail, with signs "read" formerly. Into a still-life of 1909, Braque had introduced what we used to call a *trompe l'œil* detail—in this case representing a nail—to serve as a known sign, taken from a repertory of signs, an alphabet "read" by everybody. The scaffolding of planes which Picasso had created became readable thanks to "real details" of this kind—keys, the strings and sound-holes of musical instruments, printed characters, etc.—which served as "stimuli" for the reading of the sign as a whole. These "real details" "qualified"—to use an expression of Juan Gris—the forms of the pictures.

It is clear that the technique of superimposed planes was a sculptor's solution. Though the reliefs in paper which I saw at that time on the walls of Braque's studio, on the top floor of the Hotel Roma, in the Rue Caulaincourt, have disappeared, some of Picasso's reliefs in sheet-iron, wood and cardboard are extant (pl. 9, 10, 11). It was in these reliefs that the technique of superimposed planes was *realised*, and entirely justified by this fact, for it must be admitted that in the pictures, the superimposed planes being only illusory, it was always a question of imitation—no longer of "real objects", to be sure, but of those same objects imagined as sculptures.

This is an opportune moment at which to say that Picasso used to own an African sculpture which entirely escaped from servitude to the "block", a servitude from which the Cubists were endeavouring to free themselves. It was a Wobe mask (2). These Wobe masks treat the lower part of the face as a plane surface above which the very high forehead is gently curved. From the plane surface project two cylinders, about four inches long and two in diameter—the eyes—a small triangular board—the nose—and a parallelopipedon—the mouth—the last two projecting less far. Of course Picasso did not imitate Wobe art, but its lesson encouraged him to introduce into European art principles altogether new to it, and to renounce, in agreement with Braque (and, a little later, with Gris) all imitation. These painters turned away from imitation because they had discovered that the true character of painting and sculpture is that of a *script*. The products of these arts are signs, emblems, for the external world, not mirrors reflecting the external world in a more or less distorting manner. Once this was recognised, the plastic arts were freed from the slavery inherent in illusionistic styles. The Wobe masks

PICASSO'S STUDIO AT LE BOISGELOUP.

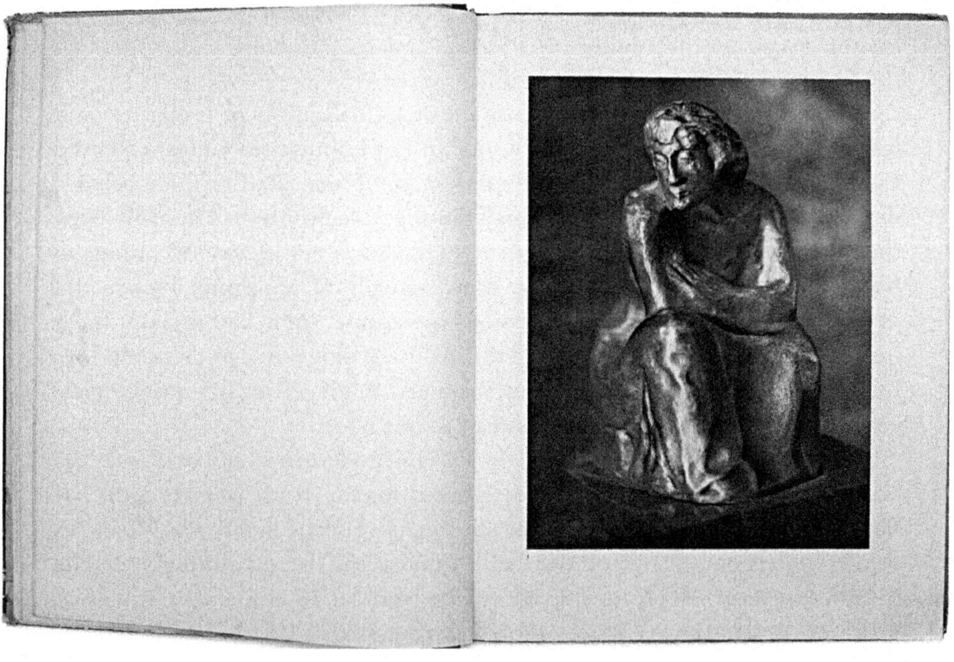

2a, b. *The Sculptures of Picasso, with Photographs by Brassaï* (London, 1949).

because of the fundamental disparity between its solidity and permanence as a thing of durable material and the fluid modern sense of self, permanently in a state of flux, immersed in the restless dynamics of a society where 'all that is solid melts into air'.[29] For Walter Pater, writing in England in the nineteenth century, more dematerialized media such as painting, music and poetry were better suited to a modern sensibility.[30]

My argument here is that photography and the photobook in particular did more than just make modern sculpture and the artist's studio available to the masses, they actually played an important role in attending to the problems posed by the solidity of sculpture, offering a way to place it and to learn to see it in a modernist aesthetic.

Plate 1 is of a 14-centimetre bronze from 1899 (Figure 2b). We would not remember this, however, as the information is somewhere in the pages behind. The photograph disrupts our sense of scale, and we cannot really tell how big it is. This is the most traditional-looking piece in the whole book, in the sketchy style of Rodin, the hero of modernist sculpture at the turn of the century. It is also the smoothest, most touch-inviting object in the whole book. Looking at a photograph, we do not have the pleasure of holding a statuette, or of moving around a full-sized version. But then, in modernist aesthetics and viewing protocols, you are not actually supposed to touch sculptures; any tactile pleasures or sensations are supposed to remain imaginary. The photograph, however, is not in itself disembodied. The tactility of the sculpture is replaced by that of the photograph. This tactility is at one level conceptual: the photograph is a sensitive surface touched by the light that touched the subject,[31] generating a two-dimensional copy or version that has not been mediated or contaminated by the photographer's hands.[32] But it is also actual: we can handle and get close to prints, we can turn and caress the pages of a book, or casually finger a corner while looking. Mechanical reproductions allow the beholder to disavow the work involved in their making, and to imagine the connection between original and reproduction as indexical – directly from the touch of the artist to the hands of the owner of the book. Touching mechanical reproductions enables an imaginative intimacy with their originals, even as they are dislocated by differences in size or materials, or between two and three dimensions. Like photography itself, touch can bridge 'space and time' and become a way of asserting 'domination' over objects and people.[33]

Looking at this photograph of a sculpture, our touch is dislocated. If we were in a gallery, we would be looking and imagining the feel of the sculptural material. Since we are in a book, we are also feeling the paper, and, in my old edition, the dusty texture of the ink. In the gallery, we might barely glance at this piece (it is the size of a child's hand). Looking at it in a book, we feel at once big over the image, yet small enough to imagine entering into it, and moving around what Rilke conceptualized as the space, movements and atmosphere generated by the sculpture itself, the 'vibrating air' of which a sculpture is 'only the firm, fruitful kernel'.[34] For Rilke, sculpture is, like a fruit, not just a solid core of hard material, but a soft, mutable and mobile, airy flesh around it.[35] We are here, holding a book, and there, in the space of the photograph, the flesh of the sculpture. At an imaginative level, our body hovers and shifts between the two – the peculiar physicality of the experience of being *in* a book we become aware of when we are suddenly called away from it.

It might seem a waste to use Brassaï, famous for his capacity to capture in his images fleeting and hidden moments in the flow of urban life, to photograph a still object. But what is being captured and stilled here is not the sculpture, but rather our movements around and towards it, the play of light on the metal, our desire to pick up and hold the piece. The photograph thus solves one of the problems Baudelaire had identified in explaining 'Why Sculpture is Boring'. For him, sculpture was too literally, 'a palpable thing that even the most untutored can seize upon and marvel at', possessing none of painting's 'mystery that cannot be touched by fingers'.[36] While not imaginative enough, the experience of sculpture for Baudelaire was also too undetermined, too unruly, too unguided by the intentions of the artist:

> Sculpture ... exhibits too many surfaces at once. ... the spectator, who moves around the figure, can choose a hundred different points of view, except for the right one, and it often happens that a chance trick of the light, an effect of the lamp, may discover a beauty which is not at all the one the artist had in mind – and this is a humiliating thing for him. A picture, however, is only what it means to be; there is no other way of looking at it than its own terms. Painting has but one point of view; it is exclusive and absolute, and therefore the painter's expression is much more forceful.[37]

But here, the photograph endows the sculpture with its own light and point of view, without having to make Picasso paint it. It removes it from our fingers, reinstating some of its mystery, our frustrated wonder at what it would be like to hold it. The photograph finishes the sculpture – not by removing its rough edges, but by taking to some logical conclusion the process that the object made by the artist had only started. Yet the photograph allows this conclusion to be provisional, temporary and conceptualized as fugitive while also dependably visible. If the photograph freezes our experience of sculpture into one moment of perfect viewpoint and lighting, the book format reinstates movement, not around a statue or through the studio, but as we move from one picture to the next, guided by the sequence of pages as if on a tour, stopping at a series of ideal viewpoints (Figure 3).[38] Unlike a guided tour, however, we determine the temporal dimension of our visit, and of course we can subvert its order by looking at the pages out of sequence.

Plates 29 and 30 take us around one object, from 1931, then close to a different but related piece in Plate 31 (Figure 3a). This different layout is required because Picasso's sculptural practice has changed. These are the pieces Kahnweiler refers to as crucial in the evolution of Picasso's sculpture, because instead of reproducing volume by enclosing its skin, its outer mass, volume is suggested by the interplay of protruding and concave, hollow and convex geometrical shapes that require the viewer's imagination to fill in the blanks, in a play where ambiguity and variety, as we move around an object, are exploited rather than a problem.

The erasure by the photographs of the material differences between the sculptures – one in bronze, the other in plaster – emphasizes their skinlessness. In the first photograph, we tend to read the round shape made by the two colanders as a skull (as Rosalind Krauss does),[39] and the dish as the face. In the second photograph, however, 'face' is now signified by a combination of the curve of the dish and the wire outlining a portion of grey background. The lips, instead of puckering out, are smirking to the side. The two cones now visible suggest breasts, and in this different anatomical configuration the colanders read as belly, or perhaps open out to 'say' buttocks. What before seemed a sign for long hair, now could be a skirt. According to Kahnweiler, Picasso is no longer reproducing volumes, or drawing in space, but inventing signs whose meanings are determined by context and viewpoint. The viewer's own movements and imagination no longer confuse or humiliate the artist's work but are a crucial part of it.

Plates 50 to 52 are all photographs of small sculptures from 1931, one in bronze and two in plaster, respectively 48, 29 and 39 centimetres high (Figure 3b). Both materials are imaged as pliable, emphasizing the roughness of their surfaces, the way they bear the marks of having been manipulated. The sequencing suggests a stop-motion effect, as if the same lump of malleable matter were reshaped and morphed from one figure to the next, in a state of flux only temporarily halted. The photographs here are teaching us to see bronze not as the material of everlasting monuments, those fixed lumps of matter so antithetical to a modernist sensibility, but as fluid material, sensitively indexing the traces left by the touch of the artist, with a status no

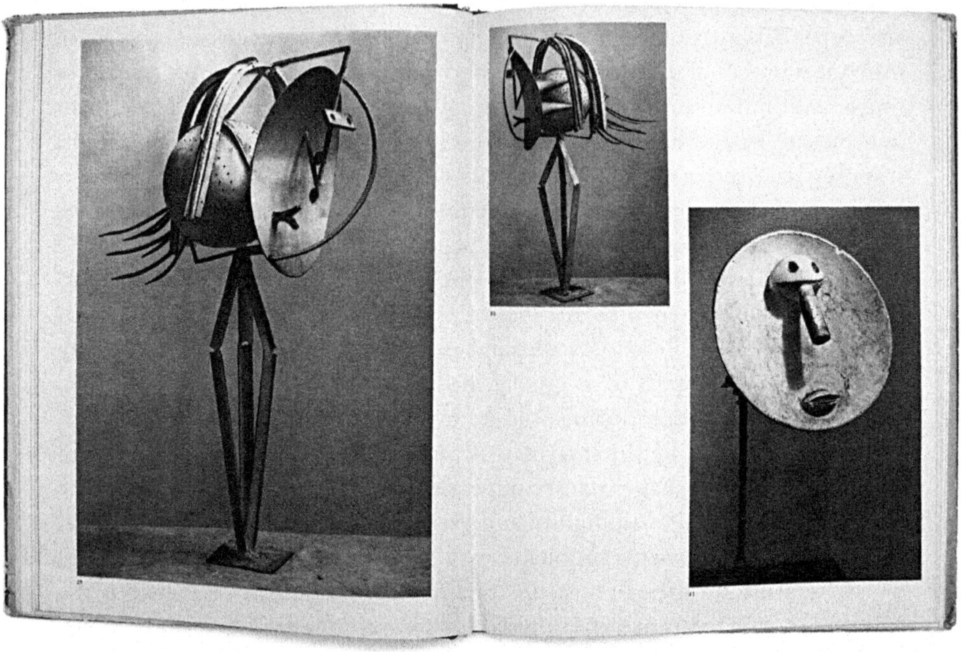

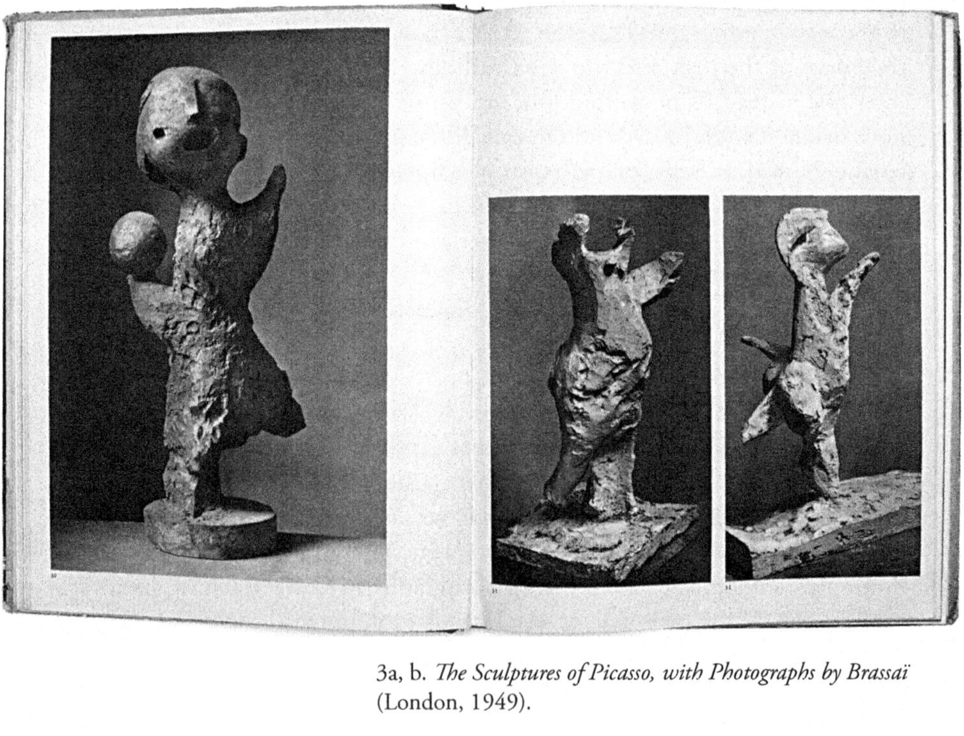

3a, b. *The Sculptures of Picasso, with Photographs by Brassaï* (London, 1949).

different from plaster, usually reserved for models and maquettes. The book is here taking further a sculptural aesthetic, first elaborated in relation to Rodin's work, of sculptures as unfinished, experimental, provisional fragments from a work never quite completed.

While small, unfinished and informal, however, these objects also remain clearly sculptures, existing in an autonomous space removed from everyday life, even that of the artist. Photography, again as in previous plates, is answering the problem of small works: how to retain their intimacy and informality, yet also the distinction between them and 'other things, ordinary things, which anyone may lay hold of'.[40] To retain its identity as an autonomous work of art, sculpture for Rilke must somehow be made 'untouchable, sacrosanct ... solitary and strange',[41] 'an image we carry within ourselves [rather than] a thing permanently planted in the landscape of our everyday life'.[42] This is why he conceptualized the artist's studio as the ideal site of encounter with sculpture.[43]

The artist's studio, however, could not accommodate the demands of a growing public, or in doing so, it would have to be turned into a museum. At the same time, a photograph of a sculpture, displayed onto the wall at home, would become part of the landscape of everyday life, blending in with domestic clutter. The book format stops that, isolating the image from everyday life. Between its covers, the book brackets the objects and spaces contained within into an experience intimate and informal yet still marked as special and different from everyday life by the act of taking the book off the shelf or the table, holding it for a second to consider the cover, and then turning the pages.

About half-way through the book, the issue of materials, of the status of the piece (finished or unfinished; fixed or in a state of flux) becomes even more interesting. Materials for the object in Plate 78 are given as: 'matches, drawing pins, blades, leaves and a butterfly' (Figure 4a); whoever prepared the list gave up, and pieces 79 to 84 are listed simply as 'relief treated with sand', while 85 is in more traditional bronze again (Figure 4b). As Mark Godfrey has noted, photography in this book works in two slightly different registers, one of 'reproducing' the sculpture, the other of replacing traditional sculptural process by photography.[44] This is particularly evident where the original is no more than a three-dimensional torn-paper shape (Figure 5b). Here, the photograph bypasses all the sculptural processes Picasso would have used to turn these little scraps into sculptures – the moulding and casting he used earlier to turn cardboard and chicken wire into bronze – to go directly from maquette or idea, to photomechanical reproduction, bypassing the making of an object we could classify as a sculpture. And anyway casting would have

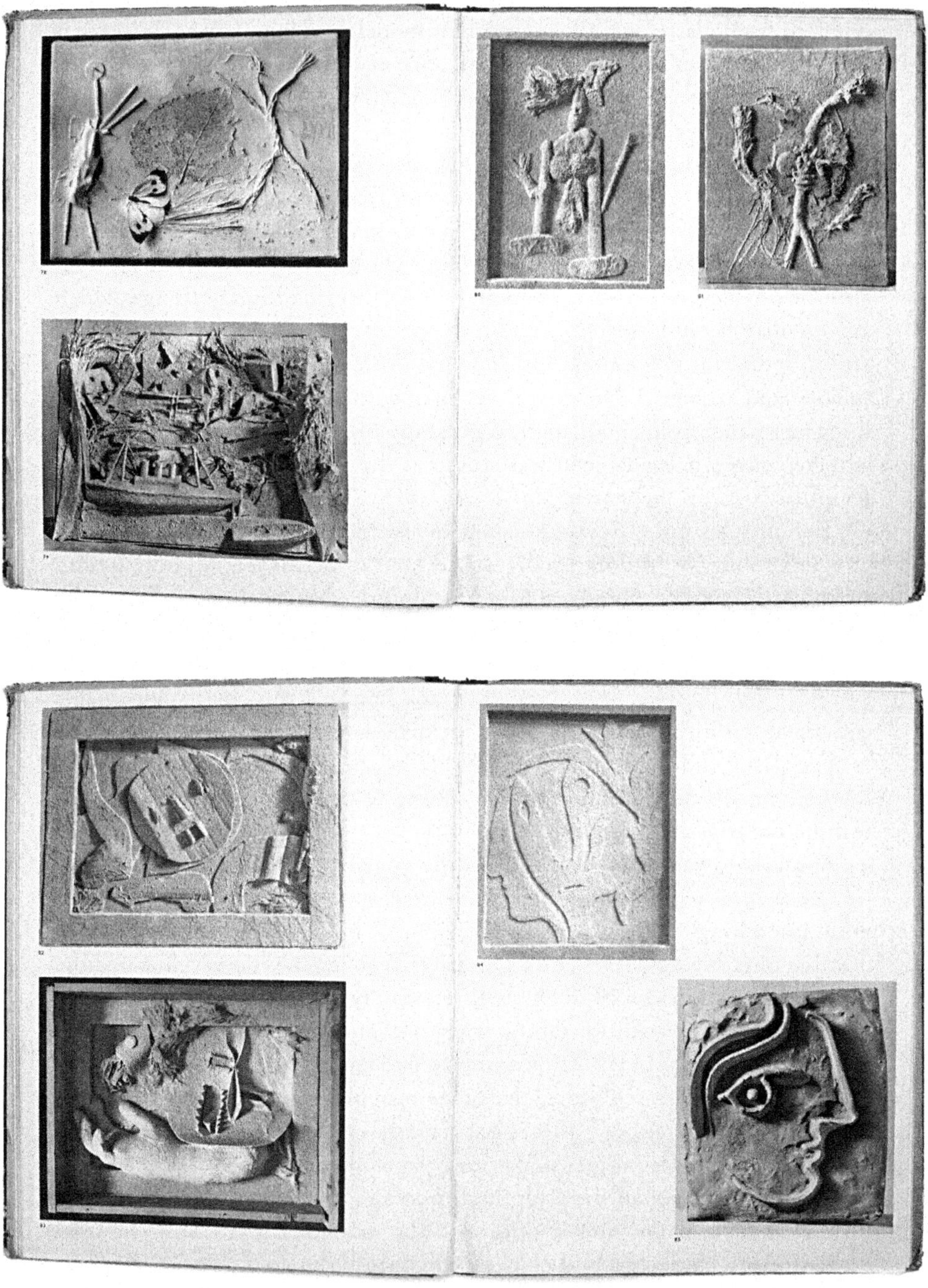

4a, b. *The Sculptures of Picasso, with Photographs by Brassaï* (London, 1949).

destroyed the point of having a real butterfly stuck on the surface of the relief in Plate 78 (Figure 4a). As Potts highlights, even for those interested in Cubist sculpture, 'informal studio works' and 'small-scale experiments in non-traditional materials' are often more interesting than when transformed into more 'mainstream sculptural' objects, losing the informality that was the main strength of the experiments.[45] Photography retains this informality and spares the viewer from having to bump into lumpy Cubist sculptures while backing to see the more famous Cubist paintings.

The material listed for Plate 117 (Figure 5a) are: 'Piece of wood on a match box', 1941. For 118: 'Piece of bread and paper flower', 1941; and for 119: 'scooter and feather', 1942. This is a collaboration almost on a par with the one published in issue 3/4 of *Minotaure*, where Dalí and Brassaï had anonymously collaborated on a pseudo-scientific article on 'Involuntary Sculpture', for which Brassaï had contributed moody photographs of smeared toothpaste, rolled up tickets, bits of paper and a bread roll. Much has been written about these photographs and how they relate to the Surrealist's interest in the found object as 'an emissary from the external world [that] carries a message informing the recipient of his own desire'.[46] In *The Sculptures of Picasso*, the chance encounter between a matchbox and a piece of wood reveals the semantic potential of even the most fragmented, least mimetic object as sculptural sign: the piece of wood would not look so much like a cigar if it was found on a beach or in the garden (Figure 5a).

This highlights the problem of exhibiting 'found objects'. How can an object be both found and staged to be viewed, without the viewer losing the experience of a chance encounter? One Surrealist solution was articulated by Michel Leiris in *Documents* in 1929, in an essay about Giacometti's work: by visiting the artist's studio, where 'beautiful objects', as he prefers to call them rather than sculptures, would lack 'the formality and aesthetic pretensions of conventional sculpture' and be 'intimate enough' to fulfil the Surrealist fantasy of an encounter precipitating a 'genuine crisis where what is outside us seems ... to respond to the summons that we give to it from within ourselves'.[47] My argument is that, more than the artist's studio, photography was the ideal medium to construct and disseminate this experience, capable as it is of staging a 'chance encounter' (with a found object, with people in the street ...) and make it available to be viewed.

We are reminded of the importance of this 'chance encounter' in Plate 188 (Figure 6a). Here, elements of the artist's studio have been incorporated in the description of the sculptural object, as the materials in the list of plates read: 'wooden head placed on a radiator, 1943' – was the head made or placed on the radiator in 1943? The casual placement of the head and of the

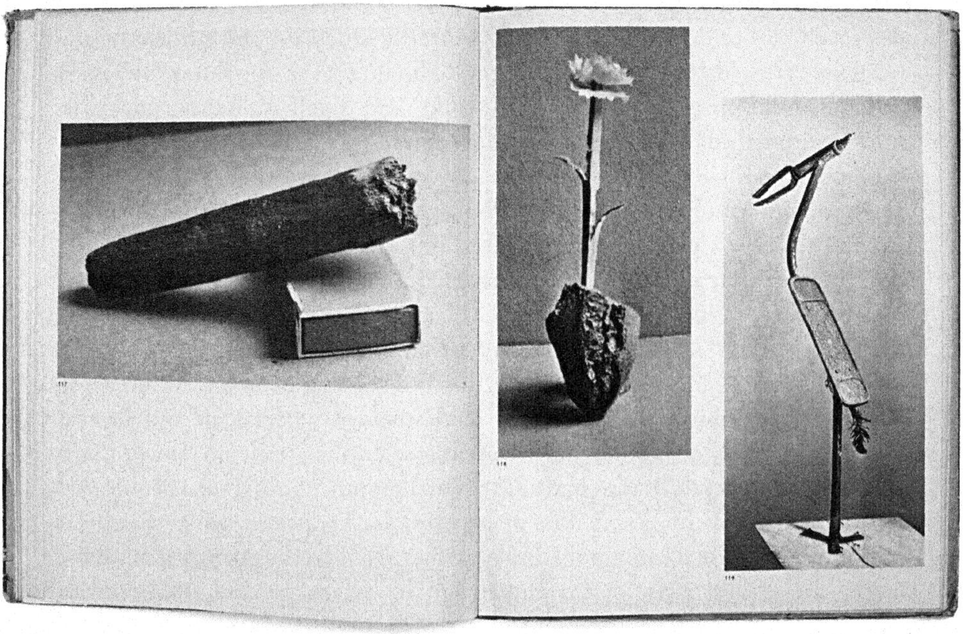

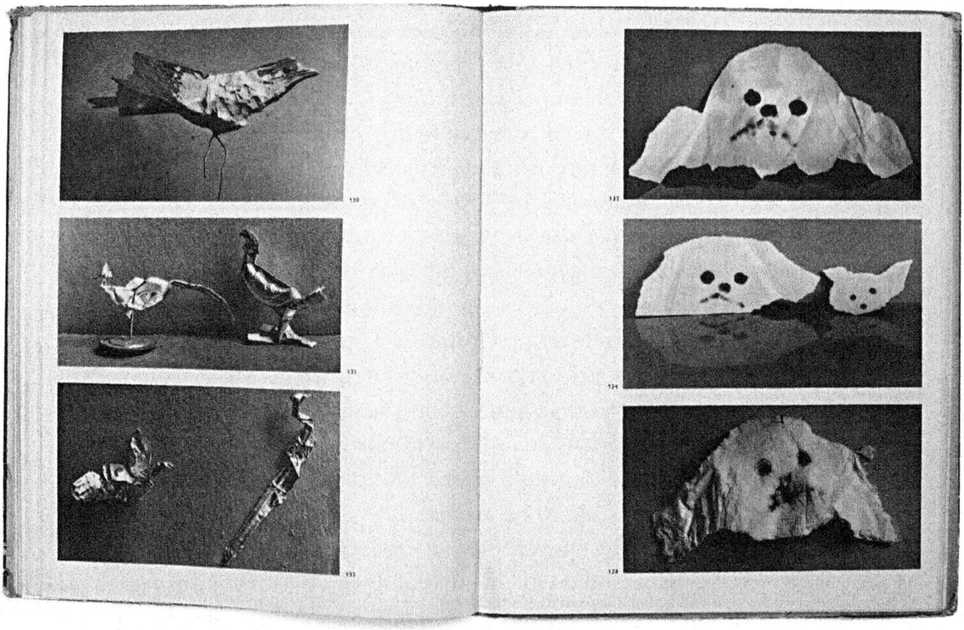

5a, b. *The Sculptures of Picasso, with Photographs by Brassaï* (London, 1949).

composition of the photograph itself, not bothering with careful lighting or isolating the head from the background, appears to be the result of chance rather than contrived arrangement. There is no sense that we are forced to 'read' the radiator as the vertical element supporting the head – as column or body. The photograph seems to have been included only because a better one was not available. The fiction created is not simply of a sculpture casually propped up on a radiator, as if Brassaï or Picasso were following the advice given in *Vogue* in 1934 of displaying modernist sculptures at home, not on the mantel but 'above a chromium radiator', but rather of an arrangement we – including artist and photographer – have chanced upon. If found objects are being turned into sculptures, here the reverse is also happening: a sculpture is being turned into a found object.

At the very end of the book, a bronze of a closed fist seems to suggest that the book is itself a magic hand, which is first opened and then closed, only when we touch it (Figure 6b); that photography books are evocative objects not only through their contents, visual or textual, but through their being objects – things – where 'the contagious magic of touch' can meet 'the sympathetic magic of visual representation',[48] and design meets use.

The *Sculptures of Picasso* makes possible a privileged meeting with the artist, an intimate and evocative encounter with his sculpture, or a Surrealist chance encounter with a found object available to many. It dematerializes sculpture's 'thingness' into an image we can take home, not to be displayed amid the clutter of 'ordinary things' and 'objects of daily use', but enclosed in its own space, bracketed from the hubbub of modern life to facilitate instead 'the imaginative projections' of the 'close encounters' Rilke envisaged as the ideal experience of modern sculpture.[49] The book's open and close dynamics, its somewhat fragile nature, allows it to resolve but not erase the gap between 'the permanence of sculpture and the restless dynamics of a modern society'.[50] Photography 'petrifies' our experience of sculpture – I am here paraphrasing Lindsay Smith[51] – as one of the many fluid and contingent modern experiences 'caught' by photography, petrifying an instant so that, at the click of a button, all that is melting into air appears momentarily solid; not trapped into old-fashioned monumental permanence, but rather launched in the ambiguous temporality of photography, where duration is better ensured by constant reproduction than by the durablity of its materials. So the photobook not only preserves sculpture 'as an image we carry within ourselves', it also has a reassuring dimension as something we can store without, safely on the bookshelf, containing within its covers the possibility of opening our domestic space into the imaginative space of the sculpture and the artist's studio.

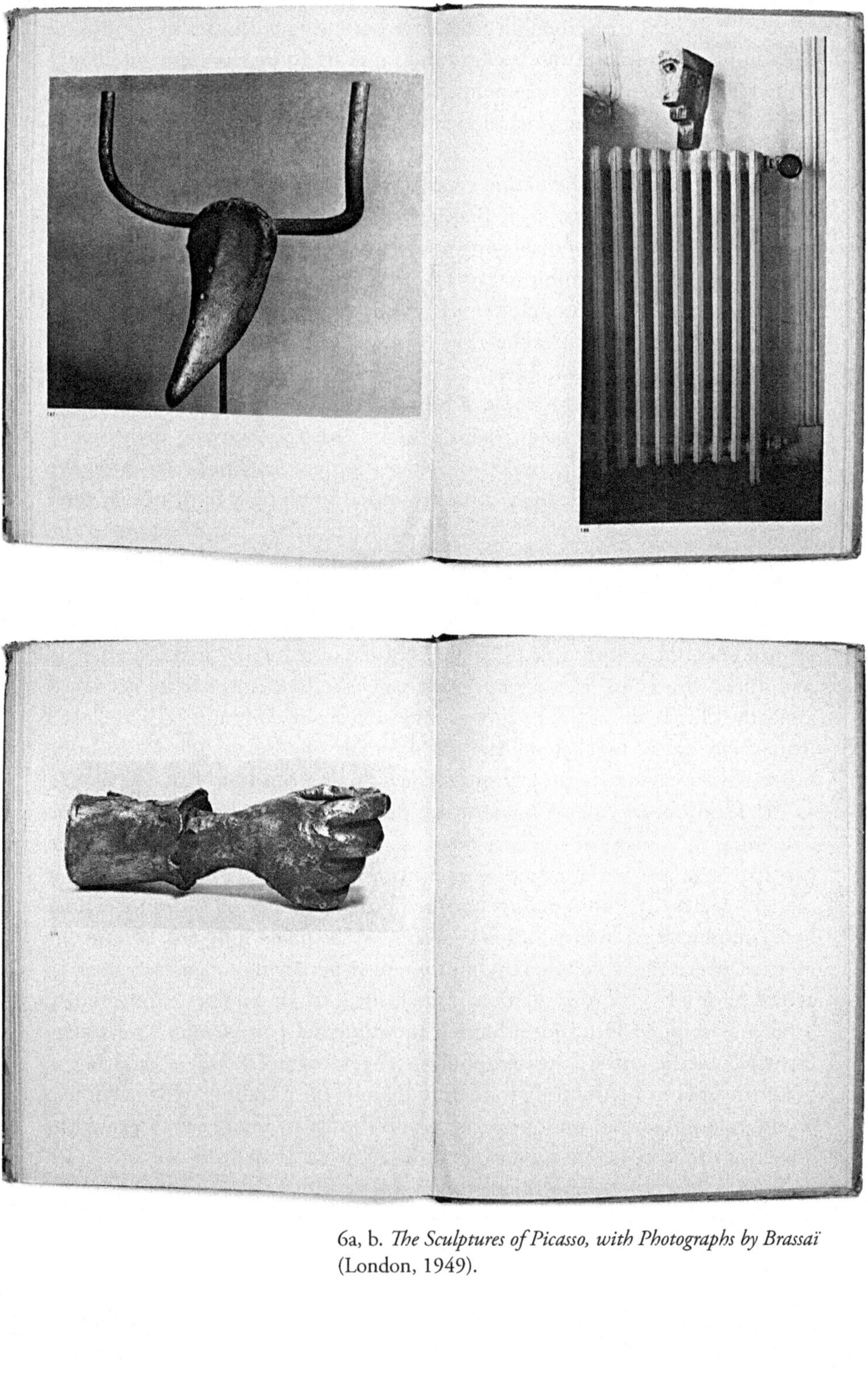

6a, b. *The Sculptures of Picasso, with Photographs by Brassaï* (London, 1949).

If the tension between reification and dematerialization was, as Potts argues, a key aspect of a modernist sculptural aesthetic, the photobook negotiates it by creating a dialectic between highlighting and resolving this tension, dematerializing sculpture and rematerializing it into its humble, semi-permanent, tactile materiality.

Notes

1 (London: Rodney Phillips & Co, 1949), title page.
2 Brassaï, *The Artists of My Life*, trans. Richard Miller (London: Thames and Hudson, 1982), p. 172. Brassaï gives the publication date as 1947, which is incorrect.
3 Diane Elizabeth Poirier, *Brassaï: An Illustrated Biography*, trans. Jennifer Kaku (Paris: Flammarion, 2005), p. 158. Poirier gives the publisher as Thames and Hudson, which is incorrect.
4 The book is listed under 'works published by Brassaï' by Poirier, p. 204. It is still in print, reprinted by Assouline.
5 Bernard Karpel, 'Bibliography: The Writings of Daniel-Henry Kahnweiler', in Daniel-Henry Kahnweiler, with Francis Crémieux, *My Galleries and Painters* (1961), trans. Helen Weaver (London: Thames and Hudson, 1971), pp. 140–55 (p. 143).
6 Daniel Henry Kahnweiler, *The Rise of Cubism*, trans. Henry Aronson (New York: Wittenborn, 1949). See also Karpel, pp. 140–1 (p. 145), and Charles Harrison and Paul Wood (eds), *Art in Theory: 1900–1999* (Oxford, UK and Cambridge, MA: Blackwell, 1992), p. 203.
7 Karpel, pp. 141, 145.
8 Brassaï, *Artists of My Life*, p. 172.
9 Poirier, *Brassaï*, p. 130.
10 Sue Malvern, 'The Identity of the Sculptor, 1925–1950', in Penelope Curtis, Denise Raine, Matthew Withey et al. (eds), *Sculpture in Twentieth-Century Britain* (Leeds: Henry Moore Institute, 2003), pp. 77–87 (p. 77). Carvings dominated, for example, the exhibition *40,000 Years of Modern Art: A Comparison of Primitive and Modern* (London: ICA, December 1948–January 1949), where Henry Moore was the best-represented modern sculptor and Picasso the star of modern painting.
11 Herbert Read, 'Introduction', *Henry Moore: Sculptures and Drawings* (London: Lund Humphries, 1949), pp. xi–xxx (p. xv).
12 Opposite p. xxx.
13 Several are reproduced in Jon Wood, *Close Encounters: The Sculptor's Studio in the Age of the Camera* (Leeds: Henry Moore Institute, 2001). The image predates the age of the camera and can be traced as far back as the myth of Pygmalion in Ovid's *Metamorphoses*, which Picasso illustrated in 1931 for Albert Skira's first foray into publishing deluxe artists' books.
14 This and preceding quotes from Arthur Broadbent, *Sculpture Today in Great Britain 1940–1943* (London: Tiranti, 1944), unpaginated. On the Arts Council's ultimately unsuccessful efforts to sell small sculpture to the general public, see Robert Burstow, '*Sculpture in the Home*: Selling Modernism to Post-war British Homemakers', *Sculpture Journal* 17:2 (2008), pp. 37–50.

15 Both Picasso and Brassaï collected pebbles. Displays of pebbles and driftwood seem to have been common in modernist interiors at the time, as can be seen in the architect Ernö Goldfinger's house at 2 Willow Road, London, and in Kettle's Yard, the house of the curator and collector Jim Ede in Cambridge. Le Corbusier collected pebbles, driftwood and other 'found objects' which he described as 'objet[s] à réaction poétique'; see Thomas Mical, *Surrealism and Architecture* (London: Routledge, 2005), p. 4.

16 Valerie Holman, 'Reception: The Context of Reproduction and Dissemination, 1925–50', *Sculpture in Twentieth-Century Britain*, pp. 125–35 (p. 128).

17 Valerie Holman, *Printing for Victory: Book Publishing in England 1939–1945* (London: British Library, 2008), p. 112.

18 Holman, 'Reception', p. 133.

19 Holman, 'Reception', p. 122; Wood, *Close Encounters*.

20 Alex Potts, *The Sculptural Imagination: Figurative, Modernist, Minimalist* (New Haven and London: Yale University Press, 2000), p. 103.

21 André Breton, 'Picasso dans son élément' [Picasso in His Element], *Minotaure* 1 (1933) pp. 8–29, quote from the unnumbered contents page (my translation).

22 'Les ateliers de Brancusi, Despiau, Giacometti, Laurens, Lipchitz, Maillol, photographiés par Brassaï', *Minotaure* 3–4 (1933) pp. 39–53. See also Wood, *Close Encounters*, pp. 15–23, and his translation of Raynal's article, pp. 92–3.

23 Alfred Barr, for example, considered 'Cubist sculpture ... secondary to Cubist painting', in *Cubsim and Abstract Art* (1936) (London: Secker and Warburg, 1975), p. 103.

24 Kahnweiler, *Sculptures of Picasso*, unpaginated.

25 Charles Baudelaire, 'XVI. Pourquoi la sculpture est ennuyeuse', in 'Le Salon de 1846', *Oeuvres Complètes*, ed. Y.G. Le Dantec, rev. Claude Pichois (Bibliothèque de la Pléiade, Paris: Gallimard, 1961), pp. 874–952 (p. 874) ; trans. into English as 'The Salon of 1846', *Art in Paris 1845–1862*, by Jonathan Mayne (Oxford: Phaidon, 1965), pp. 41–120. Here and in the next quote from Baudelaire I follow, instead, Potts's more colloquial translation in *Sculptural Imagination*, p. 62.

26 *Henry Moore*, p. xi.

27 By Rosalind Krauss in *The Originality of the Avant-Garde and Other Modernist Myths* (Cambridge, MA and London: MIT, 1985, 1988), p. 281.

28 By Lucy Lippard in 'As Painting is to Sculpture: A Changing Ratio', *American Sculpture of the Sixties*, ed. Maurice Tuchman (Los Angeles: County Museum of Art, 1967).

29 This sentence, originally from Karl Marx's *Communist Manifesto* (1848), has become such a widely used characterization of modernity – see, for example, Marshall Berman, *All that Is Solid Melts into Air: The Experience of Modernity* (1982) (London: Verso, 1999) – that Potts uses it as an unreferenced quotation in *Sculptural Imagination*, p. 80.

30 Walter Pater, *The Renaissance: Studies in Art and Poetry* (1873, 1893), ed. Adam Phillips, using the last version revised by Pater in 1893 (Oxford: Oxford University Press, 1986), esp. pp. 134–9.

31 This was first noted by David Brewster in 'Photogenic Drawing, or Drawing by the Agency of Light', *Edinburgh Review* 76 (1843), pp. 309–44 (pp. 330–1).

32 Steve Edwards, *The Making of English Photography: Allegories* (University Park, PA Pennsylvania State University Press, 2006).

33 Constance Classen, 'Touch in the Museum', in *The Book of Touch* (Oxford and New York: Berg, 2005), pp. 278–9.

34 Rainer Maria Rilke, 'The Rodin-Book: First Part (1903) Second Part (1907)', in *Rodin and Other Prose Pieces*, trans. G. Craig Houston (London, Melbourne and New York: Quartet Books, 1986), pp. 1–70 (p. 42).
35 Naomi Segal, 'Words, Bodies and Stone', *Journal of Romance Studies* 6 (2006), pp. 1–18.
36 Baudelaire, 'Salon de 1846', in Potts, *Sculptural Imagination*, p. 62.
37 Baudelaire, 'Salon of 1846', in *Art in Paris*, p. 111.
38 This is how Helmut Gernsheim conceptualized his photographs of sculptures in *Focus on Architecture and Sculpture: An Original Approach to the Photography of Architecture and Sculpture* (London: Fountain Press, 1949).
39 Rosalind Krauss, *Passages in Modern Sculpture* ([1977] Cambridge, MA and London: MIT, 1993), pp. 135–7.
40 Rilke, 'Rodin-Book', p. 8.
41 Rilke, 'Rodin-Book', p. 8.
42 Rilke cited and translated in Potts, *The Sculptural Imagination*, p. 84.
43 Potts, *Sculptural Imagination*, p. 80.
44 Mark Godfrey, 'Image Structures: Mark Godfrey on Photography and Sculpture', *Artforum International* (February 2005), online at: thefreelibrary.com (accessed 26 September 2008). Thanks to David Campany for bringing this text to my attention.
45 Potts, *Sculptural Imagination*, p. 103.
46 Rosalind Krauss, *The Originality of the Avant-Garde and Other Modernist Myths* (Cambridge, MA and London: MIT, 1985, 1988), p. 112.
47 Leiris in Potts, *Sculptural Imagination*, p. 118.
48 Susan Stewart, 'Prologue: From the Museum of Touch', in M. Kwint, C. Breward and J. Aynsley (eds), *Material Memories: Design and Evocation* (Oxford and New York: Berg, 1999) pp. 17–36 (p. 30).
49 Rilke in Potts, *Sculptural Imagination*, p. 88.
50 Potts, *Sculptural Imagination*, p. 80.
51 In 'The Wont of Photography, or the Pleasures of Mimesis', in Luisa Calé and Patrizia Di Bello (eds), *Illustrations, Optics and Objects in Nineteenth-Century Literary and Visual Cultures* (Basingstoke and New York: Palgrave, 2010), pp. 65–86.

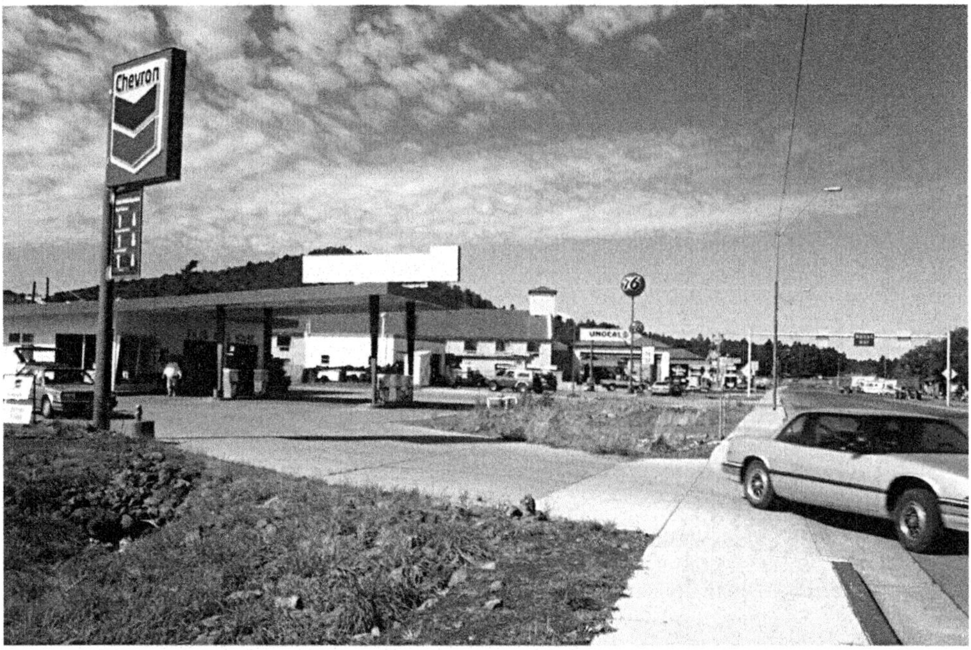

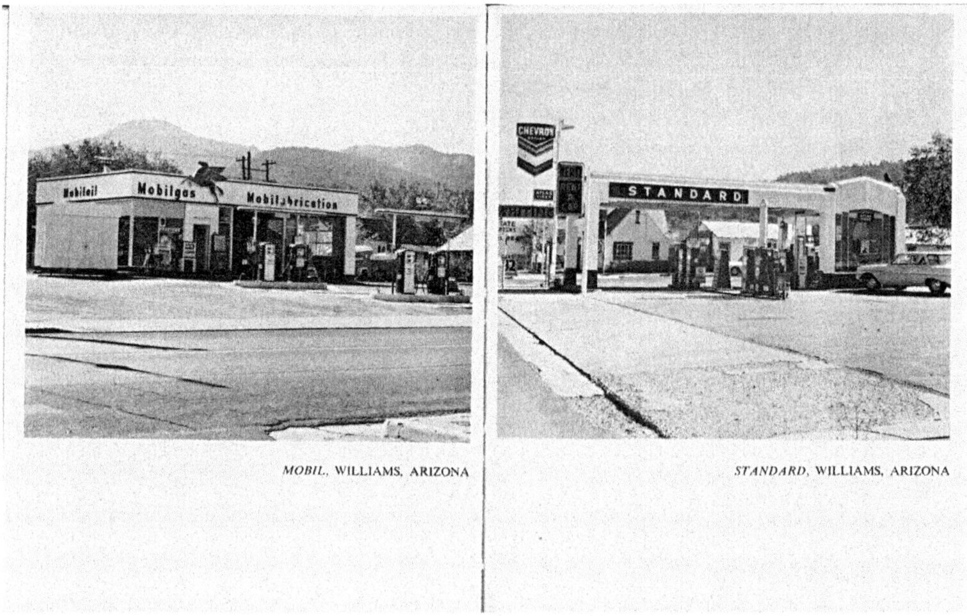

1a. Williams, Arizona, 1992. Photograph by Ian Walker.

1b. Ed Ruscha, '*Mobil*, Williams, Arizona' and '*Standard*, Williams, Arizona', *Twentysix Gasoline Stations* (Alhambra, California, 1962).

'A KIND OF A "HUH?"': THE SITING OF *TWENTYSIX GASOLINE STATIONS* (1962)

Ian Walker

We never intended to go to Williams, Arizona, but, if we had not, I am not sure I would have written this essay. That afternoon, we had driven across from Monument Valley to the Grand Canyon, arriving much later than expected. After staring open-mouthed at the view for a while, we went over to the Visitors' Center to book a room for the night, but there was nothing available. Williams, about 60 miles south of the Grand Canyon, was apparently the nearest place to find a motel, so we rang one at random, reserved a room and drove for an hour through a darkness lit only by the car headlights.

In the hard white light of the following morning, I went for a walk down the main street of Williams – a wide drag lined with motels, restaurants and supermarkets. All along it, signs indicated that this was a remaining section of the 'Historic Route 66'. In the 1960s and 1970s the old road had been gradually replaced by Interstate Highway 40. Indeed, I discovered later that Williams was the last town to be bypassed in 1984.

Despite – or perhaps because of – its demise, Route 66 is probably still the most famous road in America. This was the road that the Joad family travelled from Oklahoma to California in John Steinbeck's 1939 novel *The Grapes of Wrath* and it was Steinbeck who called Route 66 the 'Mother Road'.[1] Bobby Troup's popular song 'Get Your Kicks on Route 66' was recorded by, among others, Nat King Cole and the Rolling Stones; in the early 1960s there was also a police show on US television called *Route 66.* [2] It is a mythic road and now the subject of much nostalgia, though this is to forget that, as Larry McMurtry has remarked, 'it was always a dangerous road, with much more traffic to carry than it could carry safely. Dead bodies in the bar ditch and smushed cars on wreckers were always common sights along old 66'.[3] (One of those roadside accidents was photographed by Robert Frank in 1955 – a small group of bystanders huddled in a snowstorm next to a body covered in a rough blanket.[4])

I remembered, however, that there was something else to see in Williams. I walked down to the end of the strip and there I discovered what I was looking for: a gas station (Figure 1a). In fact there were two gas stations facing each other on either side of the road – a Chevron station and a Mobil station. And I photographed them because they reminded me of two other gas stations in Williams – also Chevron and Mobil – which I had seen before in the book *Twentysix Gasoline Stations*, made by Ed Ruscha in 1962 (Figure 1b).[5]

As the book's title indicates, it contains images of twenty-six gas stations, photographed along Route 66 between Los Angeles and Oklahoma (though it is also important to emphasize that the road itself is never actually depicted or indeed referred to in the book). The two stations at Williams sit opposite each other in the seventh and eighth photographs in the book. I did not know if the gas stations I was now looking at were standing in the same place as the ones Ruscha had photographed in 1962 (nothing changes as fast as the everyday), but still my reaction was far from innocent. Just as my view of Monument Valley was filtered through the films of John Ford and my view of the Grand Canyon through the paintings of Thomas Moran, so I saw the gas stations of Williams, Arizona, through the photographs of Ed Ruscha.

The *Twentysix Gasoline Stations* that we would look at today is of course not the same as the book that Ruscha made in 1962. Not only does it show us a landscape that has long disappeared, but how we think about the book has also changed, and this is because of the contextualizations and recontextualizations that have formed around it. Some of these are personal, like my story of going to Williams. Some of them are cultural – to do with America, the West, the automobile – and a full account would have to take them all into consideration.

Rather, what I want to do here is to examine the ways in which this modest little book has been repositioned over the last 40 years within the evolving history of art and photography. My emphasis will be on the later and less well-known part of the story, from the mid-1970s on, when Ruscha's work found a place within the developing understanding of photography. The earlier part of the story, where *Twentysix Gasoline Stations* moved during the 1960s to a central position within the advanced art of the period, has been more thoroughly discussed, but it will need to be briefly sketched before moving on. But first of all, it is useful to outline where the book came from and what influences may have affected its formation.

In 1962 Edward Ruscha was 25 years old. He had moved in 1956 from his home town Oklahoma City to study at the Chouinard Art Institute in Los Angeles, where he has been based ever since. His work centred on the iconic presence of ordinary everyday objects and a desire to push back the boundaries of art. One of the artists who influenced him in this was Marcel Duchamp, with his concept of the 'Readymade', but Duchamp was also an important influence for a whole generation. In 1962, the year that Ruscha made the book, Andy Warhol exhibited at the Ferus Gallery in Los Angeles his series of paintings of Campbell's soup cans – each one the same, each one different. There are obvious parallels here with *Twentysix Gasoline Stations* in the concentration on an everyday subject matter presented in an uninflected, repetitive manner, but, of course, there is also a big difference. *Twentysix Gasoline Stations* is not a set of paintings, it is a book of photographs (Figure 2a). And we know from later interviews that Ruscha was also aware of what were then (and arguably still are) the two most important books of American photographs.

His interest in Walker Evans's work went back to his youth growing up in Oklahoma, where he probably came across it as a social document of the American South. He would surely then have seen Evans's classic book *American Photographs* when it was republished in 1962 and responded to his 'documentary style' presentation of the everyday.[6] Then in the late 1950s Ruscha saw Robert Frank's *The Americans* and took to it immediately; much later, when he had some money, Ruscha was to buy a print of Frank's picture of a gas station in Santa Fe.[7] But it was not the style that would have interested him, rougher and darker than Evans's. Rather, it was the poetic idea of travelling the land, driving down endless highways. *Twentysix Gasoline Stations* is also in its own way a sort of travel book, a 'road movie'.

Ruscha certainly related to Evans and Frank as he did to Duchamp and Warhol, but at the time this photographic context remained unacknowledged. Interviewed in 1965 by John Coplans, Ruscha said, 'I think photography is dead as a fine art; its only place is in the commercial world, for technical or information purposes'.[8] It is the kind of ironic, negative stance that many young artists were adopting at the time, but perhaps Ruscha really did not think of the work of Evans or Frank as 'fine art'. Certainly, their work was set apart from the avant-garde context in which Ruscha's work was sited.

All this is retrospective. At the start, it seems that most viewers were genuinely puzzled by *Twentysix Gasoline Stations*. The first review of the book came in the Los Angeles-based magazine *Artforum* in September 1963, when Philip Leider remarked: 'It is perhaps unfair to write a review of a book which, by now, is probably completely unavailable. But the book is so curious, and so doomed to oblivion, that there is an obligation, of sorts, to document its existence, record its having been there'.[9] Yet astonishingly *Twentysix Gasoline Stations* did not simply disappear; as we will see, its reputation steadily grew and grew.

If, in 1963, anyone had wanted to define *Twentysix Gasoline Stations*, it would have been as a piece of Pop Art. (In his review, Leider is definite on this point: '*Twentysix Gasoline Stations* is a Pop Art book'.) Pop, after all, was then the latest movement in American art, connecting California with New York. In the fall of 1963 Andy Warhol made a return trip to Los Angeles, driving across country with Gerard Malanga, Wynn Chamberlain and Taylor Mead. Later, in his book *POPism*, he recalled the trip: 'The further West we drove, the more Pop everything became ... Once you "got" Pop, you could never see a sign the same way again. And once you thought Pop, you could never see America the same way again'.[10]

Ruscha himself emphasized this Pop reading in 1963 when he based one of the most iconic and precisionist of his early paintings on the photograph of a Standard gas station at Amarillo (Figure 2b). In this new guise, it becomes a sort of heroic, ideal gas station – a 'standard' station in the other sense of the word (Figure 3a).[11] When, in 1966, the painting 'Standard Station, Amarillo, Texas' was illustrated in Lucy Lippard's anthology *Pop Art*, it was accompanied by a caption referring to the painting's source in *Twentysix Gasoline Stations*.[12]

Seven years later, in 1973, Lippard published another book, *Six Years: Dematerialization of the Art Object from 1966 to 1972*, which charted some of the dramatic changes that had taken place within the avant-garde since Pop.[13] On the very first page Lippard cited Ruscha's books as important precursors and, throughout the anthology, she referenced his subsequent books which played variations on the format established in *Twentysix Gasoline Stations*. Their titles suggest something of this: *Various Small Fires* (1964), *Some Los Angeles Apartments* (1965), *Every Building on the Sunset Strip* (1966), *Thirtyfour Parking Lots* (1967), *Nine Swimming Pools* (1968), *Real Estate Opportunities* (1970). Whereas *Twentysix Gasoline Stations* had been made on the obscure periphery of advanced art, these later books were seen to be central to the shifting zeitgeist.

At around the same time that Ruscha was taking delivery of his first edition of 400 identical copies, another Californian artist, John Baldessari, made a sequence of photographs: 'The backs of all the trucks passed while driving from Los Angeles to Santa Barbara, California, Sunday 20 January, 1963'.[14] It would be another few years before this sort of art would be named. In 1967 Sol LeWitt wrote a short text, 'Paragraphs on Conceptual Art', which he defined thus: 'In conceptual art the idea or concept is the most important aspect of the work. When an artist uses a conceptual form of art, it means that all the planning and decisions are made beforehand and the execution is a perfunctory affair. The idea becomes the machine that makes the art'.[15] According to Ruscha, that is almost literally what had happened with *Twentysix Gasoline Stations*: 'The title came before I even thought about the pictures'.[16]

Ruscha's books were very influential for younger artists such as Robert Smithson or Dan Graham, but what they found in them was complex. Certainly, there is the concentration on an everyday, somewhat degraded environment – where Ruscha in California was interested in gas stations and parking lots, Graham and Smithson were interested in the housing estates and industrial wasteland of New Jersey.[17] But they were also struck by the inartistic form of the books and Ruscha's espousal of what came to be called 'anti-photography': seemingly casual, anonymous and functional (but in fact quite strategic).

By the late 1960s, then, Ruscha's books had come to occupy a central if quixotic position within Conceptual Art, though some more theoretically minded artists were sceptical of Ruscha's attitude. Victor Burgin later told John Roberts: 'in that period I remember thinking that he wasn't anybody one should take seriously. Because basically he seemed to be some sort of Californian stand-up comedian'. [18] But humour and irony were embedded elsewhere in Conceptualism and its use of photography, albeit that it was necessarily of a deadpan variety.

In 1972, for example, Eleanor Antin began producing a series of photographs distributed as postcards, showing 100 boots embarking on an odyssey across America from California to an exhibition at the Museum of Modern Art in New York.[19] The following year Antin published an essay which can in fact be seen as another variety of art work. Entitled 'Reading Ruscha', the essay looked closely at the construction of *Twentysix Gasoline Stations* and the order of the pictures within it. She seemed to take the book literally, describing it as

> a sort of travel narrative. Most of the shots were taken by day except for three night shots, one in Daggett, California, and two in New Mexico and Texas. That marks it as an actual trip lasting three days and two nights ... Ruscha was born in Oklahoma City and now lives in Los Angeles. The book proves he went home at least once, which makes it an autobiographical narrative ... In order to cover 1400 miles in three days he probably drove about 500 miles daily. That's a civilized driving pace for an American.[20]

Of course, as Antin well knew, the book was not the straightforward documentation of a real trip and her reading of it as such was wilfully naïve.

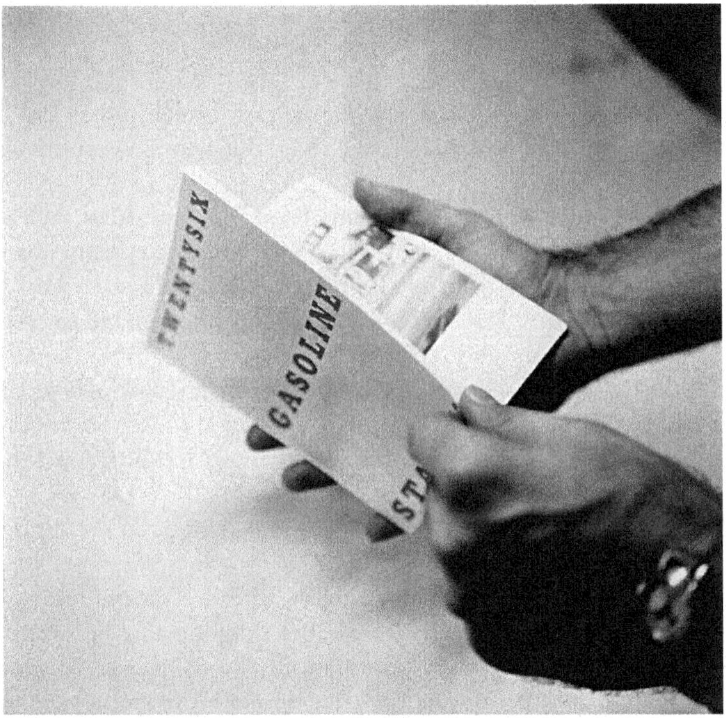

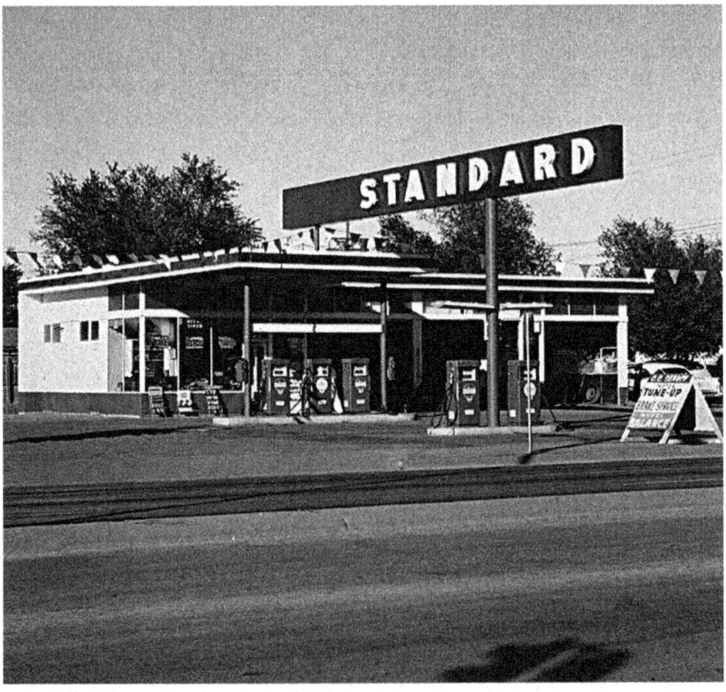

Figure 2a. Ed Ruscha, 'Hands Flipping Pages', 1963.
Figure 2b. Ed Ruscha, '*Standard*, Amarillo, Texas', from *Twentysix Gasoline Stations*, 1962.

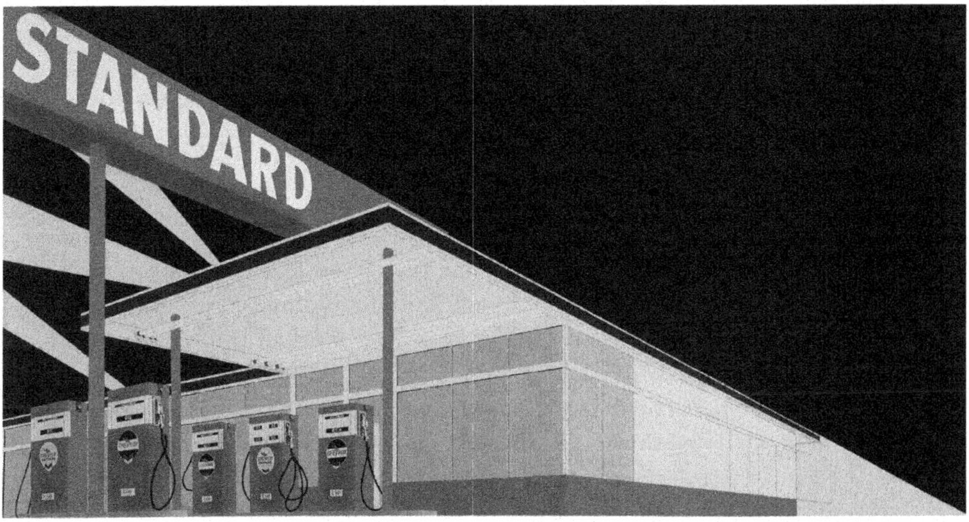

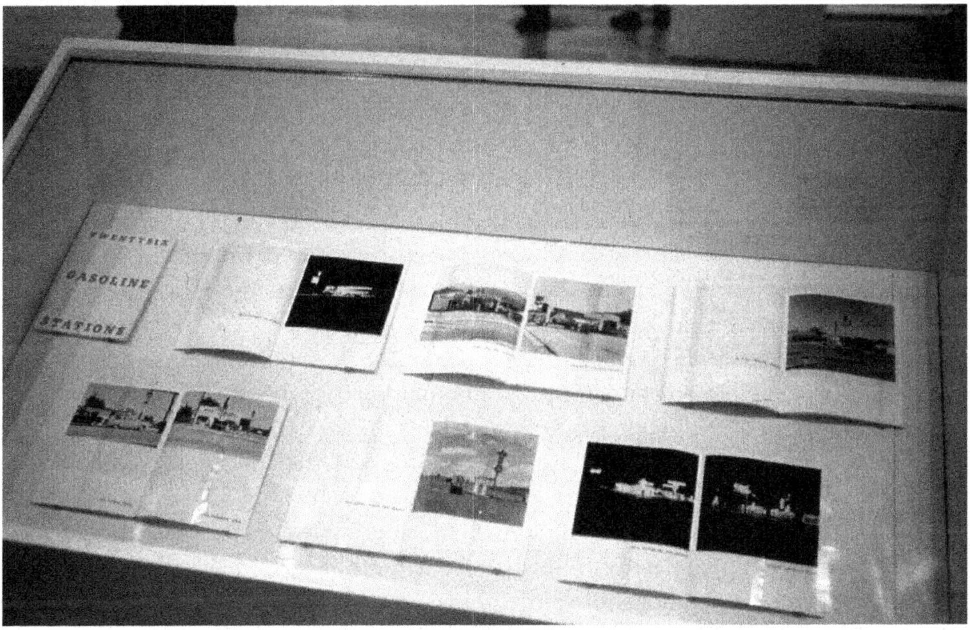

3a. Ed Ruscha, *Standard Station, Amarillo, Texas*, 1963.

3b. Seven copies of *Twentysix Gasoline Stations* in the exhibition *In Visible Light*, Museum of Modern Art, Oxford, 1997. Photograph by Ian Walker.

With its emphasis upon the realities of an actual journey along an actual road (Route 66) and the way that this intersects with the autobiography of Ruscha himself, Antin's essay rubs against the very lack of these references in *Twentysix Gasoline Stations*. Yet once we know these facts about the journey, the road and the artist, we cannot forget them again and they give the book an additional weight. Antin brought out the subtle mix of factuality and artifice, flatness and depth, dumbness and intelligence, that underpins *Twentysix Gasoline Stations* and made it both a key work of its own time and a touchstone for succeeding generations of artists.

From then on, any art-historical placement of Ruscha's early books would put them in that loose category we might call 'photographic conceptualism'.[21] Yet as Kevin Hatch has observed, any definitive attempt at categorization is inherently unstable: 'Not quite Pop paintings in book form, not exactly eccentric documentary projects, and not merely a pit stop on the road to Conceptualism, Ruscha's curious books ... become increasingly difficult to categorize the more one considers them'.[22] This task becomes no more straightforward as one moves on to consider the role that the *Twentysix Gasoline Stations* came to play in the discourses of photography itself.

Just as, in the mid-1970s, the art world suddenly woke up to photography, so, from the photographic direction, there was a breaking-down of barriers and it is clear that Conceptualism helped photographers themselves to think more critically about the particularities and paradoxes of their medium. In 1975 Ruscha's photographs were directly referenced in the catalogue of a small exhibition which had enormous influence: *New Topographics*, mounted at the George Eastman House in Rochester, New York. [23] The show signalled a decisive shift away from the heavy Romanticism that had pervaded American landscape photography post-Ansel Adams and Minor White. The work of Robert Adams, for example, made around Denver, Colorado, offered a dispassionate look at the suburbanization of the landscape. Adams was angry about what was happening but his pictures do not display that. Rather he aimed for a calmness that he felt would ultimately be more effective. Elsewhere he wrote: 'Pictures that embody this calm are not synonymous, of course, with what we might see casually out a car window. (They may however be more effective if we can be tricked into thinking so.)'[24]

Adams's analogy of the view from the car window can be interestingly connected with Ruscha's apparently casual photographs, though it is less convincing when it is applied to his own rather classically controlled work. However, other New Topographicists responded quite directly to Ruscha's work, among them Stephen Shore. In the 1960s he had worked in Warhol's studio and thus had perhaps more sympathy for avant-garde art. He had first come across Ruscha's books in 1967 or 1968 and, by his own account, 'for me and my friends they were a delight'.[25]

A number of the New Topographics photographers were working in Ruscha territory and, indeed, one of them, John Schott, travelled along Route 66, photographing not gas stations but motels. In his text for the *New Topographics* catalogue, the exhibition's curator William Jenkins begins by stating: 'It would seem logical to regard these pictures as the current manifestations of a picture-making attitude that began in the early 1960s with Edward Ruscha'. He lists a number of points of comparison: rigorous purity, deadpan humour, a stripping away of artistic frills. But, he says, there is an important difference and he quotes Schott: 'They [Ruscha's pictures] are not statements about the world through art, they are statements about art through the world'.[26] It is a comment that suggests that Ruscha's work was still primarily seen within the framework of Conceptualism, a placement that, while evidently valid, undervalued the role of *Twentysix Gasoline Stations* as a commentary on contemporary culture (a role that would become increasingly evident with greater retrospection). But one can understand that for the New Topographicists, Ruscha's deliberate casualness was finally too overt and in conflict with the clear and precise presentation of the exterior world which they espoused.

There was one pair of artists in the *New Topographics* exhibition who stood somewhat apart from the rest. They were not American, they did not photograph the West and they worked in a far more systematic way than any of the others. They were Bernd and Hilla Becher and oddly they had travelled a similar route to Ruscha, having been fêted by the New York avant-garde in the late 1960s before being accepted as photographers by the photographic establishment.[27] The comparison between the Bechers and Ruscha was to arise again and again over the next 30 years, but ultimately the ethos of the Bechers, derived from German *Neue Sachlichkeit*, was quite different from that of Ruscha. All three made undemonstrative, neutral photographs of a vernacular architecture. But where Ruscha deliberately eschewed photographic skill, the Bechers operated like artisans of the medium. Where Ruscha's work could be read as a parody of photography's archival ambition, the Bechers evidently still believed very seriously in that ambition.

Through the 1980s there was a growing interest within photographic practice in the tactics of 'typologization' – the focused analysis of particular sets of artefacts or sites, usually photographed in a direct, frontal, disengaged manner. One key exhibition that summarized this approach was curated in 1991 by Marc Friedus for the Newport Harbor Art Museum in California.[28]

The list of artists in the show is revealing. On the one hand, there were four representatives from Germany – the Bechers as well as their former students, Candida Höfer, Thomas Ruff and Thomas Struth. It was the emergence in the 1980s of this younger generation of German photographers developing the concerns of the Bechers in different directions that focused attention on this way of working. The North American contingent was more disparate – Lynne Cohen, Roger Mertin and Judy Fiskin as well as Ed Ruscha – but it was clear that Ruscha was seen as the progenitor of this approach in the USA as the Bechers had been in Germany.

Ruscha was represented in the show by *Twentysix Gasoline Stations*, but the actual presentation of the work was significant. The exhibition did include three copies of the book itself, but alongside that was placed a set of ten individual photographic prints. These had been first produced by Ruscha in portfolio form in 1989 – a significant indication that he himself accepted that the photographs could have a role outside of the book. But whether this should be regarded as a contradiction of his original intentions or more positively as a re-evaluation and opening out of the work is an open question.

The interest in typologization as a key photographic strategy continued to develop through the 1990s and, in Britain, this was marked by the exhibition *In Visible Light* at the Museum of Modern Art, Oxford in 1997.[29] Curated by Russell Roberts, this was a wide-ranging analysis of 'Photography and Classification in Art, Science and the Everyday'. The show presented photographs made for actual archives, alongside the work of modernist photographers whose ambition was archival, from Atget and Sander through to the Bechers. Finally, there were contemporary artists such as Joachim Schmid, Christian Boltanski and Joan Fontcuberta who critiqued these notions of order.

It was in this final category that *Twentysix Gasoline Stations* found its place, as a cryptic comment on the problematic aspirations of classification that predated most of the work in this mode by 30 years (Figure 3b). One feels that the Bechers would, if they could, have recorded every minehead or water tower in existence, but failing that, sought to picture a representative sample. Ruscha, on the other hand, set himself parameters that verged on the absurd – either at once both too specific and random (*Twentysix Gasoline Stations*, *Nine Swimming Pools*) or simply too vague to be helpful (*Some Los Angeles Apartments*, *Various Small Fires*). This seeming off-handedness disturbed the very logic of the class or category as a careful and rationally considered structure of thinking.

So, if an account of late twentieth-century art would most likely place *Twentysix Gasoline Stations* at the beginnings of Conceptualism, then any account of recent photography would site it as one of the founding works and (simultaneously) earliest critiques of 'typologization'. But the book has also appeared in some other, very different sites. In 1985 Warhol's former lieutenant Gerard Malanga edited a curious anthology entitled *Scopophilia*. The book was a strange mix of soft porn and psychoanalytic theory, but it contained work by some important artists and had insightful things to say about the intractable problems of voyeurism within photography. Then, suddenly, in the middle of all the naked bodies, there was a spread of some of Ruscha's gas station photos, with his own comments. Of the man getting out of a car next to the Phillips 66 station at Flagstaff Ruscha remarks, 'He was a passing customer and wanted to know what was up. It was hard to explain to him how insignificant he was to the picture, but he finally understood'.[30] Strange as the context is, it does give us yet another perspective on these pictures. Andy Warhol had apparently once told Ruscha he really liked the pictures because they were empty.[31] In fact, it seems they are not so empty after all.

In 1981 the discourse around *Twentysix Gasoline Stations* had taken another turn, when Douglas Crimp published his essay 'The Museum's Old / The Library's New Subject'.[32] Crimp was one of a number of radical critics buzzing around a new concept, Postmodernism, and intending to discredit thoroughly Modernist distinctions between High and Low. Photography – with its multiple forms and indeterminate status – was an important weapon in this campaign.

In the essay, Crimp told the story of how he had once been doing some picture research in the New York Public Library and he found a copy of *Twentysix Gasoline Stations* filed not under 'art' but under 'transportation'.[33] At the time, he says, he found this merely funny. 'But now, because of the considerations of postmodernism, I've changed my mind; I now know that Ed Ruscha's books make no sense in relation to the categories according to which art books are catalogued in the library and that is part of their achievement. The fact that there is nowhere within the present system of classification a place for *Twentysix Gasoline Stations* is an index of its radicalism with respect to established modes of thought'.[34] In one sense, this might be considered a recategorization of *Twentysix Gasoline Stations* as 'postmodern', or at least 'proto-postmodern', but it does also point to something less categorizable, something fluid and unstable in the book, which continually seems to evade any attempt at definition.

Ed Ruscha is now a much respected artist and, with time, an inevitable process of retrospection has occurred. *Catalogues raisonnés* of both his prints and paintings have been published and his writings and interviews were collected in 2002 in the October book *Leave Any Information at the Signal* (from which many of the quotations in this essay have been garnered).[35] In turn, the archivization of his photographs was marked in 2004, when the donation of his photographic work to the Whitney Museum of American Art, New York, was followed by a major exhibition and book.[36] In 2006 a second major show of Ruscha's photographs was seen in Paris, Zurich and Cologne, accompanied by a new publication with an essay by Margit Rowell.[37]

It may be difficult here not to feel a certain regret at the disappearance of the self-contained purity of Ruscha's books, though, as we have seen, this has been a gradual and incremental process. In recompense, however, the early photographs made public with the Whitney donation also make it clear what a radical gesture *Twentysix Gasoline Stations* was in 1962, not only in the broader context of the artist's book but also within Ruscha's own practice. The year before, Ruscha had travelled round Europe with a 2¼ square format Yashica. It was a serious professional camera and these early photographs show that Ruscha was well versed in composition and framing. Yet it seems as if, with *Twentysix Gasoline Stations*, he deliberately threw that competence out of the window. Making himself work like an amateur, his contact sheets show that he rarely made more than one image of any one gas station (Figure 4a). He really did just get out of the car, walk across the road, make the picture and drive on. So after all the layers of meaning that have subsequently been wrapped round the book, this return to the moment of its making can refresh our understanding of it. And, ironically, the publication of Ruscha's photographs actually emphasizes the importance of the book as container for those photographs. The meaning of *Twentysix Gasoline Stations* still lies as much in its layout and typography, its presence as an object, as it does in the twenty-six photographs it contains.

The influence of Ruscha's books has been thoroughly pervasive and almost incalculable. But, as a final coda, one must note not only that general influence but also some very specific acts of *hommage*. In 1992 the Californian photographer Jeff Brouws produced a small volume, *Twentysix Abandoned Gasoline Stations*, deliberately following both the design and style of the original.[38] In 2008 the French photographer Eric Tabuchi in turn paid homage to this homage with his own collection of *Twentysix Abandoned Gasoline Stations*, a portfolio of formal colour images made across France.[39] Also in 2008 Frank Eye in England produced his book *Twenty-Four Former Filling Stations*,[40] while Peter Calvin, based in Dallas, Texas, has photographed a series of *26 Repurposed Gasoline Stations*, each transformed into another sort of establishment.[41] In 2009 the German artist Michalis Pichler published

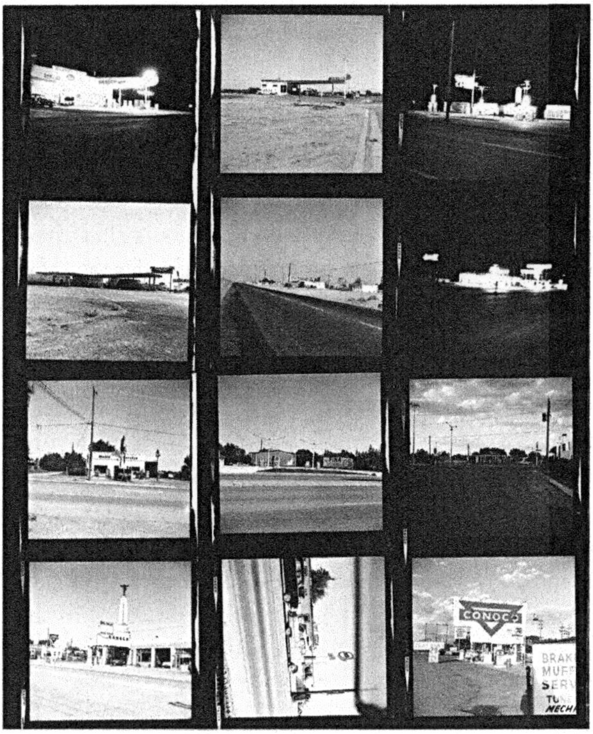

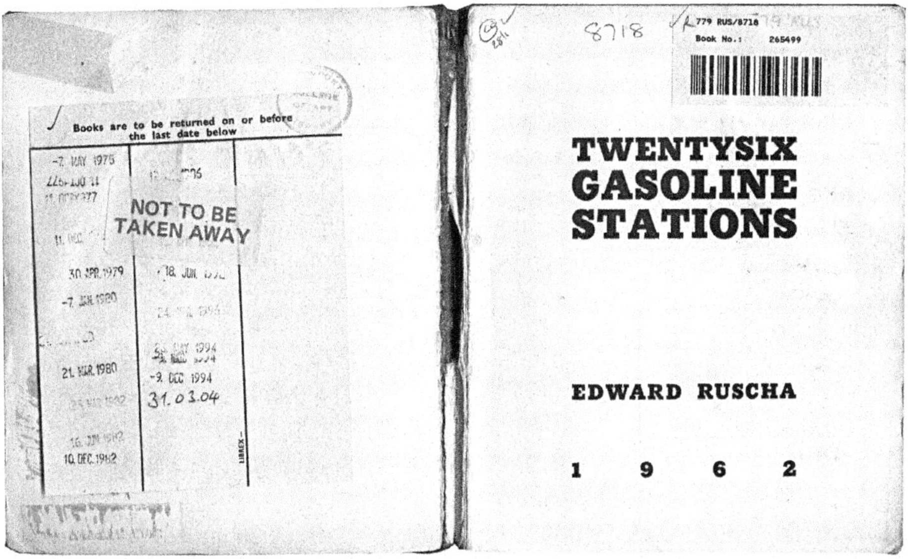

4a. Ed Ruscha, contact sheet for *Twentysix Gasoline Stations*, 1962.

4b. Title page of the copy of *Twentysix Gasoline Stations* in the collection of the Library of the University of Wales, Newport. Photograph by Ian Walker.

his own *Twentysix Gasoline Stations*, photographed across Germany and presented in an identical format to Ruscha's original; it concludes with a photo of a piece of paper on which is written: 'The eccentric stations were the first ones I threw out'.[42]

What is striking in most of these later projects is that their motivation derives primarily from an interest in environmental and social questions. The abandonment of the gasoline stations may seem insignificant in itself, but it can act as a marker of larger changes. As Emily King has remarked of *Twentysix Gasoline Stations*: 'Looking at it now, it describes an era when local businesses were making a plucky stand against the incursions of global capitalism. Beehive Gas in Holbrook, Arizona is pitted against numerous Mobil stations scattered across several states; with hindsight the playing field seems hopelessly uneven'.[43] It is a useful reminder that part of the richness of the book lies in the two orders of change which weave through its history. In this essay, I have examined the recontextualizations related to the changing discourses of art and photography, but, beyond that, the world has also been changing, and these two forms of change cannot and should not be disconnected.

Almost five decades now separate us from the moment when *Twentysix Gasoline Stations* was first published. In one sense, the book is absolutely of that moment, yet it is not merely an archaeological curiosity. As we have seen, its meaning has also shifted throughout that time and it has, at the same time, remained in the present. Thus, one feels a curious mix of connection with and distance from it. That was what I sensed that morning in Williams and it is what I sense now when I pick up the book and leaf through it.

In doing that, I am also suddenly made aware of a tendency in this discussion to talk about 'the book', as if it were a unitary, single object. But of course, *Twentysix Gasoline Stations* was always a multiple work and one can appreciate Ruscha's description of 'the thrill of 400 exactly identical books stacked in front of you'.[44] In fact, *Twentysix Gasoline Stations* is actually comprised of 3,900 individual *books*: 400 from the first edition in 1962, 500 from the second in 1967 and 3,000 from the third in 1969. Each book may have started off the same but, since publication, each has gone its own way and undergone a different history.

In 1972 Ed Ruscha talked in an interview about an imaginary person he had invented whom he called 'The Information Man'. He is 'someone who comes up to you and begins telling you facts about a particular subject in your life. He came up to me and said, "Of all the books of yours that are out in public, only 171 are placed face up with nothing covering them;

2026 are in vertical positions in libraries, and 2715 are under books in stacks ... 58 have been lost; fourteen have been destroyed by water or fire; 216 could be considered badly worn. 18 of the books have been deliberately thrown away or destroyed. 53 have never been opened."'[45] And so on.

It seems appropriate then to end this account by telling the story of just two specific copies of *Twentysix Gasoline Stations*; they are sitting side by side on the table in front of me as I write. One of them is mine. It is from the third edition; I bought it in 1976 and it cost £1.85 from Nigel Greenwood's gallery in London. Ever since, I have kept it in an envelope in a box in a filing cabinet and it still has its cellophane wrapping around it. Which is just as well, since at the time of writing one can find clean copies from that edition priced on the Internet from £750 upwards. Ruscha originally said that he wanted to 'get the price down, so everyone can afford one. I want to be the Henry Ford of book making'.[46] Now, however, copies are as valuable as any *livre d'artiste*.

Next to it is another copy of the book, bought at the same time as mine, and originally exactly identical. But this one has spent its life in the library of the University of Wales, Newport. Until 1994 it could be taken out by students, and thus was subject to all the rigours and accidents of bedsit life. Then it was withdrawn from the shelves and put on reserve – but too late, I am afraid. The spine has been cracked open, the pages are creased, its cover has a brown stain (coffee?) spreading from the right, while various library stickers and stamps have left a plethora of smudgy marks across its title page (Figure 4b).

These two copies of the book can be seen as a kind of physical analogue of the ways that its meaning has shifted and turned over the past 40 years. It is almost a sort of 'Picture of Dorian Grey' story in reverse, with the raddled, besmirched copy out in public and the pure, clean copy hidden away. Though, of course, it cannot after all this time be quite as pure and clean as the day it rolled off the presses. Behind it, as intimated earlier, there is the *idea* of the book – untarnished by time or experience; a sort of 'platonic' *Twentysix Gasoline Stations*.

It is ironic perhaps that a book so perfectly dumb and passive should have excited so much commentary, so much exegesis. But perhaps that is the reason – because almost anything *can* be read into that dumbness. What is extraordinary, however, is that all these interpretations have not destroyed the ultimate inscrutability of the book. In 1973 Ruscha tried to evoke 'an inexplicable thing' he was looking for and felt he had found in his books. He called it 'a kind of a "Huh?"' – the reaction which someone might have when they encounter the book for the first time.[47] With that apparently simple but ultimately gnomic formulation, Ruscha himself alluded to the resistance to categorization in *Twentysix Gasoline Stations*, a resistance to which both Kevin Hatch and Douglas Crimp referred and which paradoxically has enabled the book to carry, at the same time, so many different meanings. And *Twentysix Gasoline Stations* can still have that disconcerting effect. Even now, I might find myself picking it up and looking through it and the only reaction that really seems appropriate is just that: Huh?

Notes

1 This is part of an extended evocation of Route 66 at the start of Chapter 12 of John Steinbeck, *Grapes of Wrath* (London: Penguin, 2000), p. 123.
2 See Michael Wallis, *Route 66: The Mother Road* (New York: St Martin's Press, 1990). Bobby Troup wrote the song 'Get Your Kicks on Route 66' in 1946 while en route to live in California; his own account of its genesis is on pp. 9–15.
3 Larry McMurtry, *Roads* (London: Phoenix, 2001), p. 14.
4 The caption to the photograph indicates that it was taken in Arizona between Winslow and Flagstaff (Robert Frank, *The Americans*, 1st US edn: New York: Grove Press, 1959. Subsequent editions have varying pagination, but in Manchester: Cornerhouse, 1993, this picture is on p. 79).
5 Edward Ruscha, *Twentysix Gasoline Stations* (Alhambra, CA: The Cunningham Press, 1962). The date of the book is variously given as 1962 or 1963. Even in the book itself, the title page gives 1962 and the colophon 1963. It seems that, while the book was made in 1962, it was not actually published until early 1963.
6 Walker Evans, *American Photographs* (New York: Museum of Modern Art, 1938). The 1962 edition was also published by the museum. 'Documentary style' is Evans's famous description of his work in an interview with Leslie Katz, *Art in America* 59 (1971), pp. 82–9 (p. 87). He used it to distinguish his photography from 'real' documentary such as 'police photography of a scene', which has use, whereas, says Evans, 'art is really useless'. See also David Campany's chapter in this volume.
7 Frank, *The Americans*, p. 93.
8 John Coplans, 'Concerning *Various Small Fires*: Ed Ruscha Discusses His Perplexing Publications', *Artforum* (February 1965), pp. 24–5; repr. in Ed Ruscha, *Leave Any Information at the Signal* (Cambridge, MA: MIT, 2002), pp. 23–7 (p. 23).
9 Philip Leider, 'Books', *Artforum* (September 1963), p. 57.
10 Andy Warhol and Pat Hackett, *POPism* (London: Pimlico, 1996), pp. 39–40.
11 'Standard Station, Amarillo, Texas', 1963, is now in the Hood Museum of Art, Dartmouth College, Hanover, New Hampshire.
12 Lucy Lippard (ed.), *Pop Art* (London: Thames and Hudson, 1966), p. 151.
13 Lucy Lippard, *Six Years: Dematerialization of the Art Object from 1966 to 1972* (New York: Praeger, 1973).
14 See Coosje van Bruggen, *John Baldessari* (New York: Rizzoli, 1990), pp. 14–15.
15 Sol Le Witt, 'Paragraphs on Conceptual Art', *Artforum* (Summer 1967), p. 79.

16 Coplans, 'Concerning *Various Small Fires*', in Ruscha, *Leave Any Information at the Signal*, p. 23.
17 See Dan Graham, 'Homes for America', *Arts Magazine* (December 1966), pp. 21–2, and Robert Smithson, 'The Monuments of Passaic', *Artforum* (December 1967), pp. 48–51.
18 John Roberts, 'Interview with Victor Burgin', in *The Impossible Document: Photography and Conceptual Art in Britain 1966–1976* (London: Camerawork, 1997), p. 93.
19 The images were collected with supporting essays in Eleanor Antin, *100 Boots* (Philadelphia: Running Press, 1999).
20 Eleanor Antin, 'Reading Ruscha', *Art in America* (November–December 1973), pp. 64–71 (p. 66).
21 Two important later texts in this respect are Benjamin Buchloh, 'Conceptual Art 1962–1969', *October* 55 (Winter 1990), pp. 105–43, and Melanie Mariño, 'Almost Not Photography', in Michael Corris (ed.), *Conceptual Art* (Cambridge: Cambridge University Press, 2004), pp. 63–74.
22 Kevin Hatch, '"Something Else": Ed Ruscha's Photographic Books', *October* 111 (Winter 2005), pp. 107–26 (p. 108).
23 William Jenkins (ed.), *New Topographics* (Rochester, NY: George Eastman House, 1975). The exhibition included work by Robert Adams, Lewis Baltz, Bernd and Hilla Becher, Joe Deal, Frank Gohlke, Nicholas Nixon, John Schott, Stephen Shore and Henry Wessel Jr. The *New Topographics* exhibition has now been examined in great detail in Britt Salvesen and Alison Nordström, *New Topographics* (Tucson, Ariz.: Center for Creative Photography, Rochester, NY: George Eastman House, and Göttingen: Steidl, 2010); Salvesen discusses the exhibition's relationship to Ruscha's work on pp. 26–8. This publication presents a much fuller collection of photographs than the original catalogue and makes clearer the technical and aesthetic differences between, for example, the work made by Ruscha and Schott along Route 66.
24 Robert Adams, introduction to *Denver* (Boulder: Colorado Associated University Press, 1977), unpaginated.
25 Susanne Lange, 'A Conversation with Stephen Shore', *Bernd and Hilla Becher: Festschrift, Erasmuspreis, 2002* (Munich: Schirmer/Mosel, 2002), p. 48.
26 Quotations in this paragraph are from Jenkins, 'Introduction', *New Topographics*, pp. 5–7.
27 See Susanne Lange, *Bernd and Hilla Becher: Life and Work* (Cambridge, MA: MIT, 2007).
28 Marc Friedus, *Typologies* (Newport Harbor, CA: Newport Harbor Art Museum and New York: Rizzoli Press, 1991).
29 Chrissie Iles and Russell Roberts (eds), *In Visible Light: Photography and Classification in Art, Science and the Everyday* (Oxford: Museum of Modern Art, 1997).
30 Gerard Malanga, *Scopophilia* (New York: Van der Marck, 1988) p. 92.
31 See Willoughby Sharp, '"... A Kind of Huh": An Interview with Edward Ruscha', *Avalanche* 7 (1973), pp. 30–9; repr. in Ruscha, *Leave Any Information at the Signal*, pp. 64–72.
32 Douglas Crimp, 'The Museum's Old / The Library's New Subject', *Parachute* 22 (Spring 1981); repr. in Crimp, *On the Museum's Ruins* (Cambridge, MA: MIT, 1993), pp. 66–81, and Richard Bolton (ed.), *The Contest of Meaning: Critical Histories of Photography* (Cambridge, MA: MIT, 1989), pp. 3–13.

33 Oddly, if one goes now to the online catalogue of the New York Public Library, it seems that they do not actually possess a copy of *Twentysix Gasoline Stations*.
34 Crimp, *On the Museum's Ruins*, p. 78. Crimp's essay is accompanied by a pair of photographs by Louise Lawler which show pages from the book in mid-turn, a subtle play on the very element of undecidability emphasized by Crimp.
35 See Edward Ruscha, *Catalogue Raisonné: Editions 1959–1999* (Minneapolis: Walker Art Gallery, 1999) and *Catalogue Raisonné of the Paintings* (Göttingen: Steidl), *Volume One: 1958–1970* (2004), *Volume Two: 1971–1982* (2005), *Volume Three: 1983–1987* (2007) and *Volume Four: 1987–1992* (2009).
36 Sylvia Wolf, *Ed Ruscha and Photography* (New York: Whitney Museum of American Art and Göttingen: Steidl, 2004).
37 Margit Rowell, *Ed Ruscha, Photographer* (New York: Whitney Museum of American Art and Göttingen: Steidl, 2006); the exhibition was shown at the Jeu de Paume, Paris, the Kunsthaus, Zurich and the Museum Ludwig, Cologne.
38 Jeffrey Brouws, *Twentysix Abandoned Gasoline Stations* (Santa Barbara, CA: Handjob Press/National Gas-n-Go Publications, 1992).
39 Eric Tabuchi, *Twentysix Abandoned Gasoline Stations* (Paris: Florence Loewy, 2008).
40 Frank Eye, *Twenty-Four Former Filling Stations* (n.p., self-published, 2008).
41 See online at: www.petercalvin.com/26repurposedgaso.html (accessed 9 September 2009).
42 Michalis Pichler, *Twentysix Gasoline Stations* (New York: Printed Matter Inc., 2009). In addition to these specific reworkings of *Twentysix Gasoline Stations*, there have been other projects which expand on the original. In 2010 Joachim Schmid produced the book *Twentysix Gasoline Stations, Every Building on the Sunset Strip, Thirtyfour Parking Lots, Nine Swimming Pools, A Few Palm Trees, No Small Fires*; it consisted entirely of photographs of these objects seen from above and produced by satellite technology (see online at: www.blurb.com/bookstore/detail/1096054 [accessed 30 September 2010]). Other artists have referenced Ruscha's books more widely; see, for example, the work of Tom Sowden online at: www.tomsowden.com [accessed 30 September 2010]. A good discussion of this area is Yann Sérandour, 'Serial Readers: Fortunes et infortunes des livres d'Edward Ruscha', *Nouvelle Revue d'esthétique* 2 (2008), pp. 51–6.
43 Emily King, 'Look, No Words!' in Maria Fusco and Ian Hunt, *Put About: A Critical Anthology of Independent Publishing* (London: Book Works, 2004), p. 36.
44 Coplans, 'Concerning *Various Small Fires*', in Ruscha, *Leave Any Information at the Signal*, p. 27.
45 A.D. Coleman, 'My Books End Up in the Trash', *New York Times* (27 August 1972), D12; repr. in Ruscha, *Leave Any Information at the Signal*, pp. 46–50 (p. 47).
46 Douglas M. Davis, 'From Common Scenes, Mr. Ruscha Evokes Art', *National Observer* (28 July 1969), 1; repr. in Ruscha, *Leave Any Information at the Signal*, p. 28.
47 Sharp, '"… A Kind of a Huh"', in Ruscha, *Leave Any Information at the Signal*, p. 65.

BEYOND THE EXHIBITION – FROM CATALOGUE TO PHOTOBOOK

Liz Wells

The Land: Twentieth Century Landscape Photographs, selected by Bill Brandt, was published in 1975 by Gordon Fraser Gallery to coincide with an exhibition of the same title.[1] In the acknowledgement section, the publication is described by Mark Haworth-Booth as 'the principal illustrated record of the exhibition of the same title held at the Victoria and Albert Museum (V&A), London ... and thereafter at Edinburgh ... Belfast ... and Cardiff' (p. 8). The book is slim, with 48 duotone pages of photographs, one by each of 46 named photographers, and 32 pages including three essays and five poems. The written contributions are printed on brown paper in what might now be seen as a proto-environmentalist gesture. My copy has a stated price of £2.75, although I actually paid £28 many years later. Copies are rare, although nowadays it can be found online (priced lower than my copy). Had my copy been signed by Brandt it would have been considerably more expensive!

Twenty-two years later, in 1997, Princeton University Press published the book, *Photography: An Independent Art*, by Haworth-Booth, to coincide with the opening of the permanent photography gallery at the V&A.[2] It is large-format, 195 pages long (not counting forematter, notes and index) and includes 75 illustrations printed in full colour as well as 25 duotones. This is before the days of digital photo-printing; full colour was expensive and would have posed design challenges in terms of the organization of the book. In business terms this was clearly a 'long tail' initiative, a publication intended to have an active sales life beyond its immediate relationship to the exhibition of the same title with which the gallery was launched. It is not a 'record' or catalogue of an exhibition, nor is it a complete inventory of the photography collection at the V&A – as is pointed out in the introduction, 100 images have been selected from a total of over 300,000. Rather, it is a free-standing book, the first to draw exclusively on this particular collection. But it was no doubt produced with expectations of enhanced sales during the exhibition.

This paper investigates the development from exhibition catalogue to photobook. For the sake of establishing some parameters, the focus will be on publications related to British exhibitions (including many examples relating to land and landscape since this is central to my personal interests as a researcher and curator). My primary objectives are, first, to identify patterns of change and associated motivators, and second, to evaluate consequences for the content and styling of publications and, related to this, implications for emergent histories of exhibitions. As Mary Kelly has observed, catalogues are significant as they outlast specific exhibitions, transforming from exhibition-related publications to historical records of events that once took place.[3] If there is no leaflet, catalogue or book, an exhibition 'disappears'. My interest, then, is not in photographs as objects catalogued, but in catalogues or books as objects in themselves. Third, I shall indicate interwoven sets of factors, from immanent ones such as printing technologies to broader social shifts, whereby we might begin to account for such changes. Following Jacques Rancière, I take it that art, whilst distinctive in terms of being or materiality and also in formal and semiotic terms, is integrally interrelated to social experience.[4] Whilst my focus is not on the political (although some examples discussed below suggest political critique), Rancière's emphasis on ways in which the aesthetic is simultaneously an autonomous sphere of developments *and* grounded in, as well as informing, the social offers a useful point of departure. If we conceptualize photography (and the photobook) as testing its own modes and potential whilst *simultaneously* having some influence on ways of being, doing and seeing, then we have a useful critical model through which to think about photographic modes of communication.

For the purposes of this research, 'catalogue' is defined as 'a list, register or complete enumeration; now *spec.* one systematically or methodically arranged, often with brief particulars or descriptions aiding identification etc.'[5] allowing that a '*brief* description' might well be an image reproduction or, as Haworth-Booth phrased it in *The Land*, 'principal illustrated record'.[6] A catalogue refers to something else, to a collection or exhibition external to itself. Catalogues as exhibition guides later become key records of events. Differing styles of catalogue imply different purposes beyond their function as a guidebook; for example, they may be designed as souvenir items, or intended as works for scholarly study.[7]

Catalogues differ from photobooks, defined by Badger as 'a book – with or without text – where the work's primary message is carried by photographs. ... It has a specific character, distinct from the photographic print, be it the simply functional "work" print, or the fine-art "exhibition' print"'.[8] He emphasizes the primacy of the photographic and distinctive character (achieved through design concept, layout, sequencing, and, where applicable, inter-relation of image and text). The 'book' is an autonomous art form with inherent cohesion and is usually produced as a free-standing and marketable object. A booklet (small book) may likewise be published to coincide with an exhibition, but differs from a catalogue as it would not include an exhibition inventory, and differs from a book in that it would not achieve distribution via established book distribution channels (although it may remain subsequently available from the photographer or the gallery that hosted the exhibition).

I am interested in the historical emergence of books occasioned by photography exhibitions, so it is not the limited-edition art book, comparable to other artworks, that is central to my attentions – although there may be instances where exhibition-related products have themselves been limited-edition, bespoke, craft objects. In considering books, my focus is on those produced in conjunction with an exhibition but with a view to broader circulation (although in practice, the market, and consequent print-runs, may be relatively limited). For the purposes of research I distinguished loosely between 'catalogue', 'monograph' (produced in conjunction with an exhibition of work by a single photographer), and 'critical compilation', photobooks accompanying themed exhibitions involving work by several photographers (territory with which I am familiar having curated several such exhibitions).

The origins of the catalogue lie, literally, in the listing of objects included in an exhibition (or a collection). Later, lists started to be illustrated, precisely because of the possibilities allowed by photography and lithography that developed towards the end of the nineteenth century, supplanting the need for hand-printing and tipping-in of each photographic illustration within an edition.[9]

The Royal Photographic Society (RPS) Collection includes several examples of catalogues and photographic periodical reviews (journals) towards the latter decades of the nineteenth century, by which time photographic illustration was common. Periodicals often acted as vehicles for exhibition inventories.[10] For example, *The Photographic Journal* included 'transactions of the Photographic Society of Great Britain'; thus the issue of Saturday, 28 September 1889 is devoted to 1889 annual exhibition information, and includes a catalogue in the form of a full list that consists of title (*process*) and name of photographer, followed by a full list of exhibitors in alphabetical order. Other issues for the year (vol. XIV, 1889–90) include papers given at meetings, information on processes and abstracts of publications, plus news and events.

Sixteen years later, in 1906, *The Photographic Journal* (vol. XLV1 – now monthly) similarly includes an annual exhibition catalogue in the form of a list by title and photographer, although now there is also a price, and, in some instances, a brief description. For example, 'A Study of Wych Elms', 15/- (shillings) *Alfred W. Dennis* is described as:

> A series of seven photographs showing the same pair of trees leafless, and in leaf, together with the trunks, the blossom, the fruit, the leaf, and winter buds. The special interest lies in the completeness of the study. All the detail photographs are from specimens obtained from the trees shown in the general views.[11]

As can be seen, the description is followed by an appreciation based on a particular notion of 'study' or thorough documentation of natural phenomena. Some other examples give context, for instance:

> 'Sand-Waves left by a dried-up stream', *Vaughan Cornish, D.Sc., F.R.G.S.* The stream by the side of a cliff-path at Bournemouth was caused by a thunderstorm. The water having been absorbed by the porous ground, the sandwaves are uncovered.

Since this particular image is not reproduced, we can suppose that this was contextual material for reference when enjoying the exhibition, as well as a 'take-away' for subsequent reference.[12]

To return to the notion of 'catalogue': two examples of publications associated with the RPS are worth particular comment. First, Malcolm Arbuthnot's 'A Series of Impressions Rendered by Photography' which is termed 'catalogue' and is about 5 x 4 inches, with a grey light card outer cover and 10 cream colour pages listing 43 images by number, title and price. There are no images. The exhibition was at the 'Little Gallery' of the Amateur Photography and Photographic News, 52 Long Acre, March/April 1909, and the catalogue notes that the edition of each photograph will be limited to 12 copies, after which the plate will be destroyed (prefacing the art market manoeuvres by Brett Weston and others by some 70-odd years). It is not that there could not be illustrations – as I have pointed out, these are by then common in magazines; rather, the catalogue is intended specifically for reference at the exhibition and the objective is that the photographs as limited editions should command a good market price.

A second and earlier example is 'Photographs of the Year', subtitled 'descriptive notes and critical review of the Photographic Society's exhibition, 1891, by H. P. Robinson'. This is strictly speaking a portfolio rather than a catalogue; it includes 12 photographs, listed on the front cover and reproduced in Woodbury-Gravure, which is advertised on the inner back cover of the publication as a new process. The portfolio price was half a guinea, which was expensive at the time. The accompanying introductory essay by Robinson is on a sheet of A2, folded and printed as four sides. The introduction indicates something of criteria and concerns (as well as local 'politics') that for him emerge in considering this exhibition. He remarks:

> As usual, there is a good deal of work which reaches the high average of technical excellence that has obtained since the introduction of gelatine plates; a few pictures that stand out prominently either for their real art qualities or their eccentricity; and a good deal that had no claim to be accepted on artistic grounds … . Exhibiting has a distinct educational value to the photographer. By contrast he gauges the value of his work; by emulation he progresses; but common sense, without much technical knowledge, ought to be some guide to the photographer in judging the suitability of his productions for exhibition.[13]

He comments on the number of prints on extra rough paper 'the charity which covers many photographic sins' as it 'puts atmosphere into photographs which were devoid of that landscape beauty, helps to hide defects, and in some cases is undeniably effective; but in the hands of many … it is a stumbling-block in the way to that better art which comes from knowledge'.[14] One has the sense of a telling-off and there is an interesting 'teacherly' tone! The essay is quite discursive. It is not clear whether the portfolio was sold at the exhibition, or subsequently as a souvenir, but it is stated that selected pictures are discussed 'in their order on the walls' which suggests either that the catalogue essay was written and printed after the hanging or that exhibition spaces were allocated to named photographers in advance with no consideration to the overall hang or impact. There is no list of pictures exhibited – maybe there was a separate list – but the highest number referenced by Robinson is a series, '596 etc.', which suggests that the exhibition was extensive. The tone of the essay is one of critical appreciation mixed with advice to those who, for various reasons, have not come up to Robinson's standards in some respect – for example, he dismisses Mr Cassel's use of a French title for a 'thoroughly English picture' and suggests an alternative title. Detailed analysis would reveal several of Robinson's preoccupations, but this is not my primary concern. What is of interest is the explicit critical address to selected photographs; the 'could do better' tone that might suit an exhibition *review* would be totally out of place in any equivalent catalogue or souvenir publication now. Catalogue essays in exhibition-related publications now function to introduce, overview, situate and evaluate the import of a body of work in a supportive manner; the expectation is different from that of an independent (critical) review.

Photography exhibitions, and their significance, in the early twentieth century in Britain, are difficult to track and analyse. Camera club shows persisted, and the RPS continued to host annual exhibitions and other group shows. There are also accounts of photographers hiring galleries to exhibit their work, but photography did not normally feature in major art institution events; as is well known, the first major photography exhibition at the Royal Academy was not until 1989 (the 150th anniversary exhibition). In terms of innovation in the first half of the twentieth century, it is the printed page, rather than exhibition, that begs historical analysis. The history is well charted, and articulates multiple strands of practice. In Britain these particularly included enhanced use of photography within social surveys, political campaigning, journalism and documentary whilst the burgeoning of society magazines and developments in advertising kept studio photographers busy. Image-text experimentation became common within art movements and manifestos – albeit more evident elsewhere in Europe than in Britain. For example: Dada, then Surrealism, in Switzerland, France and Belgium; New Objectivity within the Germanic tradition; Constructivism in Soviet photography. This was an exciting era for experimental photography publication, and for developments in the mass circulation press, that was not necessarily reflected in exhibition catalogues. In other words, whilst one could use local and national archives to track exhibition inventories for camera club shows, this would offer an extremely partial view of debates and developments in the medium and its uses in the modern era.

The notion of the 'academic text' has some bearing on the development from catalogue to photobook, as arts education became an influence within the museum and gallery sector in the second half of the twentieth century. In relation to this, David Chandler, erstwhile senior curator at The Photographers Gallery in London, later Director of Photoworks, Brighton, noted the late 1970s to late 1980s as a 'cathartic decade'.[15] Susan Butler, editor of *Creative Camera* in the mid-1980s, commented on the influence of the educational concerns of the Arts Council on photography publishing in that era.[16] Analysis of various exhibition-related publications of the time indicates a multiplicity of interests. First, there was concern to situate specific contemporary projects socially, and in terms of visual literacy. As is evident from magazines such as *Ten/8* or *Camerawork* from the period, this was grasped socio-politically as well as in academic terms. Second, a developing map of the history of photography is reflected in essays in archive-derived exhibitions. Examples of publications from the 1970s and 1980s point to the influence on photography education of the Arts Council itself, as well as to initiatives by specific early publicly financed photography galleries. Third, photographers whose work was exhibited within a contemporary art context, such as Arnolfini Gallery, Bristol, had publications along the lines of those common in the art sector of the period. For instance, *Remnants and Prenotations, The Photographs of Thomas Joshua Cooper and Paul Hill* is a booklet, not a catalogue, as there is no full list of photographs.[17] However, it is in the style of a catalogue in that the pictures included act as a partial inventory. The brief commentaries, two paragraphs and three paragraphs respectively, operate to situate the work in some respect; as such this can be seen as a precursor of the longer essay now typical of catalogues or books for solo or two-person events. But the comments are traditional; *how* the work was contextualized was not innovatory. Post-modern challenges within art theory leave no trace here.

Concern with photography history becomes particularly manifest in catalogues and booklets from the 1970s and 1980s, a period when the work of several historically acclaimed photographers was organized for exhibitions (often tours). The Arts Council itself ran a themed series on photographers, typically accompanied by a booklet or fold-out offering biographical and historical contextualization, albeit with reference to the socio-political somewhat muted. For example, *Peter Henry Emerson 1856–1936: A Victorian Photographer of Life and Landscape in East Anglia* is introduced by Norbert Lynton, Director of Exhibitions at the Arts Council of Great Britain (ACGB), who tells us that this is the 'second touring exhibition in a series devoted to the work of major individual figures in the history of photography in England' (the first one was on Bill Brandt).[18] The leaflet is a fold-out of six pages, landscape format, that would be relatively cheap to produce and easily carried when viewing the show as well as for subsequent reference. The precise date of the exhibition is not noted, although an essay on Emerson, by Peter Turner, is dated 1973. Turner emphasizes Emerson's theoretical interests in 'Naturalistic Photography', his subject matter, and his disagreement with his contemporary Robinson. There is a separate section on 'Emerson's Techniques' (page 5 of the fold-out) and the final page includes a list of books, in three sections; discussion of Emerson (by figures such as Gernsheim, Newhall, or Time-Life Books), original books by Emerson and modern reprints, and pictorial books on the work of Emerson. The educational purpose is clearly manifest; we are encouraged not only to view and respect the work, but to go off and read more about it and related histories. In 1974 the Arts Council published a folio of eight facsimile Benjamin Stone prints, with explanatory notes based on his original publication of 1905. The introduction is by Barry Lane, the first photography officer at the Arts Council (appointed in 1973). The Arts Council also promoted exhibitions about photographers from elsewhere. For example, in 1976 they published the booklet, *Walker Evans Photographs*, to support a show of 80 pictures selected by John Szarkowsky at MoMA New York, which came over to MOMA Oxford.[19] The booklet, which consists of 16 A5 sides plus light card cover, includes an essay by Valerie Lloyd (circa 2,000 words) that is structured biographically, introduces Evans's work and identifies visual style in terms of literalness, faith in intuition and lack of interest in Art. (There are no further reading references in this instance.)

Parallel to Arts Council initiatives were a number of museum exhibitions; for example, *The Hill/Adamson Albums: A Selection of Victorian Prints* (London: Times Newspapers Limited, 1973), includes a seven-page (circa 2,500 words) essay by Colin Ford, then Keeper of Film and Photography, National Portrait Gallery, on 'The Beginnings of Photographic Art'.[20] He situates their work in terms of the early history proceeding from Daguerre and Niepce, via Talbot, to Hill and Adamson, remarking that after Hill and Adamson no one other than Nadar, or Julia Margaret Cameron, approached their skill, and, without offering any clear criteria for his assessment, acclaims them as the 'finest' of Victorian portraitists. Meanwhile, to return to my starting point, the V&A had identified photography for specific historical focus, and started to mount shows in the temporary exhibition galleries, including Bill Brandt's 1975 selection, *The Land*, which was simultaneously a themed landscape exhibition and an opportunity to introduce work by 46 increasingly acclaimed photographers from the United States or elsewhere in Europe to a London audience. One of the things that is interesting about this is that a range of different types of writing, including poetry, sits alongside the – maybe more predictable – introductory essay on landscape photography.

Independent galleries perhaps had more leeway than the Arts Council or national organizations. There were certainly several initiatives in the later 1970s by galleries such as Impressions, then based in York (with Val Williams as Director) or the Scottish Photography Group based at Stills Gallery, Edinburgh. For example, *Paul Strand, The Hebridean Photographs*, 1978, published in conjunction with a tour (Stills, Aberdeen Art Gallery and Museum, MOMA Oxford and Kelvingrove Art Gallery and Museum, Glasgow) is a *catalogue* in terms of the definitions that I have suggested, as it includes an inventory of 45 pictures on the penultimate page, with title (place) and print size.[21] There are 24 pages in total, but only six images, including the front cover, are actually reproduced, so it is clearly primarily for reference when viewing. But what makes it unusual is that, like *The Land*, it includes three diverse types of writing: a Gaelic folksong and an essay on the history and culture of the Hebrides precede the images, and an (unaccredited) essay on Strand (circa 1,500 words) follows. The emphasis is as much on the context in which these images were made as on the photographer himself. Likewise, a 1977 Impressions publication, delightfully titled *Mondays Children*, the work of 'Paul Tanqueray and four of his contemporaries', benefits from a long (circa 4,500 words) essay by Terence Pepper who conceived, researched and curated the exhibition. He offers a substantial historical mapping of portrait studios, as set up in London in the 1920s and 1930s, with some social contextualization and also biographical information about the five photographers (the others are Hugh Cecil, Marcus Adams, Bertram Park and Dorothy Wilding). Pepper makes the argument that photography was taken seriously in this era, with terms such as 'Camera Portrait', 'Portrait Study', 'Camera Study' used (instead of the more banal term 'photograph'), and photographers referred to as 'Camera Artists'. The booklet appears more as an illustrated essay than an exhibition catalogue – there is no inventory as such, and it is not even clear whether the 23 pictures reproduced were all included in the show. By the mid-1980s, Arts Council-supported galleries such as Camerawork and The Photographers' Gallery were also producing touring exhibitions. The eight-page booklet for *Striking Women: Communities and Coal*, toured by The Photographers' Gallery, reminds us that it was not only more radical organizations such as Camerawork and the Cockpit that were engaging with the politically critical strands of work typical of the decade.[22]

The Arts Council itself no longer specifically promotes photography exhibitions, although, of course, photography may feature in its South Bank touring programme. Museums and galleries continue to situate and contextualize work, particularly from their own collections or that of artists for whom they act as agents, but this now takes the form of producing or commissioning books that have an *intended* 'long-tail' shelf-life beyond any specific exhibition and a broad reach beyond any particular gallery or museum context. Two recent examples serve to illustrate this. First, *Coming to Light* (Birmingham City Libraries, 1998) was 178 pages long with 80 plates, and cost £13.50.[23] It was designed to introduce the history and contents of the City Collection, and to contextualize it in terms of British photo histories more generally, as well as acting as 'take-away' from the winter exhibition of the same name, which opened in September 1998. But there was also a 24-page catalogue which, in accordance with strict definitions of 'catalogue', included an inventory of the exhibition as well as an alphabetical list of photographers with summary biographical notes. This was free and easy to reference when viewing the show, whereas the book involves reading the essay, cross-referencing to the various illustrations and was clearly intended for later perusal. In addition it acts as a historical account for the future, one focused primarily on developments in the Midlands and framed by 1990s concerns and perceptions. The book has a long life and potential for subsequent editions as the Collection enlarges through acquisitions and also becomes more fully catalogued. Second, *A Record of England*, on Sir Benjamin Stone and the National Photographic Record Association (NPRA), 1897–1910,[24] was motivated by a transfer in 2000 of photographs from the British Museum to the V&A that included the archive of the NPRA. The book was published by Dewi Lewis in 2006, and includes essays by Martin Barnes, Elizabeth Edwards and Peter James. Biographies of the writers include the note that Edwards is currently completing an ethnography of the 'Photographic Record and Survey Movement' in England, which I assume includes NPRA, and that James, who is Head of Photography at Birmingham Central Library and has been researching the work of Stone for many years, is working on a major exhibition about Stone and his photographic collection. The exhibition took place in the open air in Centenary Square in 2008, and was accompanied by a small booklet offering some historical contextualization and, perhaps most crucially, giving the website address for further information about Stone. The catalogue as inventory has migrated online. The 2006 book served as an adjunct publication – an opportunity that the publisher no doubt took into account from the onset.

So, towards the end of the twentieth century, catalogues gave way to books. These took at least two forms: first, monographs of particular projects or of a particular photographer's work often, although not always, published to coincide with a specific exhibition (new work, or retrospective). Second, thematically conceptualized texts produced to accompany exhibitions, although not entirely anchored to their companion show.

Parr and Badger date photobooks from Anna Atkins (1843–53), but the date depends rather on the definition of the photography *book* that is in play (see discussion above). The Hasselblad Exhibition, *Open the Book* (2004), took John Thomson's *Street Life in London* (1878) as a starting point. Arguably this is not strictly a *photography* book, as Thomson worked with journalist Adolphe Smith, in effect as illustrator of a report in 12 parts, each with three stories, relating lives of the London poor; the selection of 36 photographs was determined by the story to be illustrated. In other words, although they worked in tandem, the editorial process was text-led.

We can define the monograph as a bound publication by a single photographer including one or more bodies of work that might also include critical essays subservient to the photography and generated in response to it. Contemporary monographs commonly have specific themes, or, if featuring work from more than one series or project, cohesion in terms of aesthetic style, subject matter and socio-political perspective. The distinction between 'monograph' and 'artist's book' is imprecise but it has something to do with sources and starting points, the monograph being a 'treatise' on something, whereas the artist's book is more concept-driven and self-expressive.

As Ute Eskildsen has commented, improvements in printing techniques and a burgeoning of newspaper and magazine publishing boosted the photography book after the First World War.[25] The interrelation of aesthetics and technologies is obviously central. The introduction of colour film and print techniques was another key development in terms of book quality. But colour reproduction remains expensive and finance 'packages' have to be put together.[26] There is now a common mode of monograph whereby a photographer seeks a publisher for a particular project, and seeks exhibition possibilities to help tempt the publisher. Exhibition prints may be large-scale, selected from a full series and presented in a style that takes gallery space and audience into account. Commonly, at least one writer will be commissioned for the book with a particular brief related to the work and the overarching thematic concerns of the project. From a writer's point of view this is a specific type of commission with expectations or objectives agreed with the photographer and the publisher.

There is a sliding scale between two types of monograph. First, those designed primarily to foreground the work of a specific photographer or project. Second, those whose motivation is very evidently social or political, although, by dint of being single authored, they also foreground a particular body of work. *Inscape*, by John Blakemore, is an example of the former.[27] It was published in 1991, with an accompanying exhibition at Zelda Cheatle Gallery which then represented him. It includes a couple of poems, by Goethe and by Gerald Manley Hopkins, and an appreciation by Val Williams. The title of a later booklet, *John Blakemore – Photographs*, published on the occasion of a British Council tour, is even more explicit.[28] This includes a preface by Brett Rogers, then Head of Exhibitions at the British Council, and a reprint of Val Williams's essay from *Inscape*. The booklet functions as a catalogue, with some works illustrated. By contrast, the relationship between *Inscape* and the exhibition was the other way round; the exhibition acted as a launch for the book, rather than the book acting as a catalogue for the show. I labour this point in order to emphasize that the relationship between exhibition and book may take a number of forms. In this instance, the gallery was also Blakemore's dealer and publisher, so the business interrelations were not complex. More commonly a triangular relationship between photographer, gallery or museum, and publisher emerges within which the photographer, unless he or she has a curator, agent or agency acting on his or her behalf, becomes a broker within a complex set of financial and time-line negotiations.

Ian Walker's 1989 publication, *Civitas*, is interesting in this respect.[29] The commission was to photograph Southampton Civic Centre in the lead-up to an exhibition marking its 50th anniversary. On closer inspection, *Civitas* turns out to be *about* Southampton Civic Centre and 'other similar buildings'; the author has included other civic buildings dating from the same period, the 1930s. Not all the images are as reverent as might perhaps have been expected by the civic leaders as magazine tear sheets on office walls, deteriorating billboards, and some rather wry titling suggests, for instance, 'order' for a couple of computers delightfully situated below a cable box with wire protruding in disorganized fashion next to a pinned-up image with 'welcome to organized chaos' emblazoned horizontally across it. Apparently the opening of the exhibition was cancelled as the electricity went out; as Walker suggests, 'sort of CIVIC CENTRE BITES BACK'![30] But my interest in this small book, which definitely is not simply an exhibition catalogue, stems from the fact the photographer and writer are the same. This allows for image-text strategies involved in the captioning to extend to the interrelation of the 10 colour photographs and the written texts, a series of eight discontinuous brief commentaries. He tells us that in the exhibition the pictures were grouped in themes: 'DEMOCRACY, ORDER, ART, WORKSPACE and so on'. This is not echoed in the publication that, instead, takes the opportunity to reflect the civic in terms of classical allusion, façades of order and the rhetoric of power. In other words, although described as a catalogue, this turns out to be a complexly layered bookwork in its own right. Whilst no doubt the exhibition was pictorially striking, especially as this was in what were still the early days of colour documentary, the book builds to a critical sting that I am sure the photographer as exhibition curator avoided, if only out of courtesy to his commissioners – although, of course, as already noted, the building clearly caught the drift.

Image-text montage is a classic strategy, one that was effectively employed by John Kippin in his earlier work, but that he no longer deploys, because he is particularly aware that tactics become commonplace if over-used. He seeks new conceptual points of departure through questioning social phenomena as well as experimenting with photographic methods and aesthetics. His 2001 book, *Cold War Pastoral*, was based on a commission to photograph the legacy of the American nuclear missile base formerly stationed at Greenham Common.[31] Kippin draws attention to the aftermath of occupancy, reminding us of the then perceived threat of war and annihilation, through documenting traces of military presence such as remains of wire fences and bunkers as well as more incidental legacies. The series was first exhibited at the Imperial War Museum in London – a context which specifically inflected interpretation of the imagery in terms of war, conflict and military histories. It was then shown near Greenham, where the context re-inflected it more in terms of environmental legacy and local community. It will be many generations before memories of the impact of a high-security military base, a peace camp, several high-profile peace demonstrations, traffic re-routing, and the general impact upon the natural habitat of the region in terms of flora, fauna and wildlife, are forgotten.

The project was also published as a book which, of course, is more long-lasting than an exhibition. By contrast with exhibitions, books offer a certain intimacy, and the possibility of repeat consideration. Kippin's book includes 31 photographs. Individual images are not captioned; symbolic allusion is allowed to transcend specificity of place. The publication includes four essays, each variously contextualizing the work: in terms of the history of Greenham Common as open land (written by a local environment officer), in relation to the history of the peace camp (by one of the activists), through reference to debates about English landscape imagery (myself), and in relation to Kippin's previous bodies of work (an elegant essay by Mark Durden). Two of the essays directly reference the photographic approach that Kippin adopted; the other two offer broader historical and political contexts. This multiplicity acknowledges varying ways and contexts in which Greenham resonates. The photography itself works through accretion; whilst any single image may seem silently to aestheticize particular traces, the accumulative effect is narrative; we come to perceive this as an uneasy environment. The four essays variously intersect with this, revisiting histories and politics through written rhetoric; the essays are more or less prosaic in idiom, but they articulate stories that add resonance, thereby enhancing the import of the imagery. Obviously, choice of writers, and ways in which we were briefed by Kippin, were absolutely crucial to determining the final tenor of the book which was intended for broad circulation.

The examples mentioned are detailed, but they serve as a basis for a few summary comments on catalogues and exhibition-related books. Marketing is now a driving force within publishing. Publishers are unlikely to be interested in catalogues simply as exhibition (or collection) inventories as there is no broad sales potential. Museum collections have to fund-raise, publish and distribute inventories themselves. Publishers are interested in book proposals if they have long-tail sales potential, preferably international. Curators explore themes and exhibitions are often interrogative, so there is a discussion to be sustained not only through exhibition installation – a particular form of theatre – but also through associated writings and related debates to which the publication may contribute over a period of time. Likewise, photographers producing monographs are concerned that their work should communicate to as wide an audience as possible. As I have emphasized, it is through book publication, rather than exhibition or the catalogue as inventory, that a broader audience can be sought.

Notes

1 Bill Brandt, *The Land: Twentieth Century Landscape Photographs* (London: Gordon Fraser Gallery Ltd, 1975).
2 Mark Haworth-Booth, *Photography: An Independent Art* (Princeton: Princeton University Press, 1997).
3 Mary Kelly, 'Reviewing Modernist Criticism', *Screen*, 22:3 (1981).
4 Jacques Rancière, *The Politics of Aesthetics* (London, 2004). Originally published in French (Paris: La Fabrique-Editions, 2000).
5 Lesley Brown (ed.), *New Shorter Oxford English Dictionary* (Oxford: Clarendon Press, 1993).
6 Mark Haworth-Booth, acknowledgements, in Bill Brandt, *The Land: Twentieth Century Landscape Photographs* (1975).
7 Clare Barclay, *The Exhibition of Japanese Artefacts in Britain Historically and Now: Exhibition Catalogues and their Functions* (Unpublished Masters dissertation, University of Plymouth, 2007), p. 23.
8 Gerry Badger, in Martin Parr and Gerry Badger, *The Photobook: A History*, 2 vols (London: Phaidon Press, 2004, 2006), vol. 1, p. 6.
9 Fox Talbot's *Sun Pictures in Scotland*, based on a journey made in October 1844, although strictly a portfolio (without text other than picture captions) may be seen as a progenitor of the photographically illustrated book or catalogue. As an edition of 1,000, all pre-subscribed, it involved printing 23,000 handmade salted paper prints from calotype negatives, each pasted in by hand! The labour-intensive nature of such illustrated books obviously rendered them relatively unusual. Source, John Hannavy (ed.), *Encyclopedia of Nineteenth-Century Photography* (Abingdon: Routledge, 2008) (Also see the essay by Graham Smith elsewhere in this volume.)
10 I should acknowledge the keepers at The Royal Photographic Society Collection, National Media Museum, Bradford. On making contact with the curators in September 2008 an immediate question arose as to whether I wanted to look at 'catalogues' or 'reviews'.
11 *The Photographic Journal* 46 (1906).
12 This issue of the journal consists of 62 pages of editorial, plus 38 pages of advertisements, and cost one shilling. It also includes 24 pages (12 printed double-sided) of photographs from the exhibition; the selected illustrations are marked by asterisks in the listings so this was clearly pre-planned (as opposed to inserted subsequent to the exhibition

hanging). There is no indication of criteria for selection of photographs; it is not clear whether photographers paid for their inclusion.

13 H.P. Robinson, *Photographs of the Year* (London: Photographic Society, 1891), p. 1.
14 H.P. Robinson, p. 1.
15 Interview with author, 24 February 2009.
16 Photobook workshop, Birkbeck College, University of London, 31 January 2009.
17 Thomas Joshua Cooper and Paul Hill, *Remnants and Prenotations, The Photographs of Thomas Joshua Cooper and Paul Hill* (Bristol: Arnolfini Gallery, 1975).
18 Arts Council, *Peter Henry Emerson 1856–1936, A Victorian Photographer of Life and Landscape in East Anglia* (London: The Arts Council, n.d.).
19 *Walker Evans Photographs* (London: The Arts Council, 1976).
20 Colin Ford, *The Hill/Adamson Albums: A Selection of Victorian Prints* (London: Times Newspapers Limited, 1973).
21 Scottish Photography Group, *Paul Strand: The Hebridean Photographs* (Edinburgh: Stills Gallery, 1978).
22 The Photographers' Gallery, *Striking Women: Communities and Coal* (London: The Photographers' Gallery, n.d.). Work by Izabela Jedrzejczyk, Raissa Page, Brenda Prince and Imogen Young.
23 Birmingham Museum and Art Gallery, *Coming to Light*, exhibition catalogue (Birmingham: Birmingham Museum and Art Gallery, 1998) and *Coming to Light: Birmingham's Photographic Collections* (Birmingham: Birmingham Libraries and Birmingham Museum and Art Gallery, 1998).
24 Elizabeth Edwards, Peter James and Martin Barnes, *A Record of England* (Stockport: Dewi Lewis Publishing and London: V&A Publications, 2006).
25 Ute Eskildsen, 'Photographs in Books', in Andrew Roth (ed.), *The Open Book*, (Göteborg: Hasselblad Center, 2004), p. 11.
26 Visual standards of digital colour print have improved massively in the last five years which, along with possibilities for print-on-demand, means that unit costs for book production may be reduced.
27 John Blakemore, *Inscape* (London: Zelda Cheatle Press, 1991).
28 John Blakemore, *Photographs* (London: The British Council, 1995).
29 Ian Walker, *Civitas: Photographs of Southampton Civic Centre* (Southampton: Southampton City Art Gallery, 1989).
30 Letter to myself from the photographer, included with my copy of the book (n.d.).
31 John Kippin, *Cold War Pastoral, Greenham Common* (London: Black Dog Publishing, 2001). Greenham Common, a public area of heathland in Southern England, was the site of a continuous women's peace camp, 1981–2000.

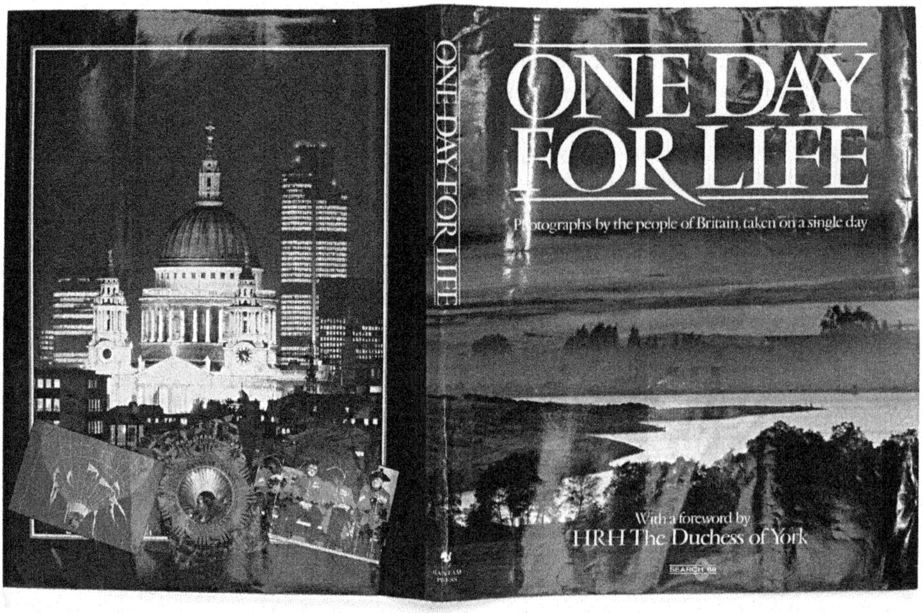

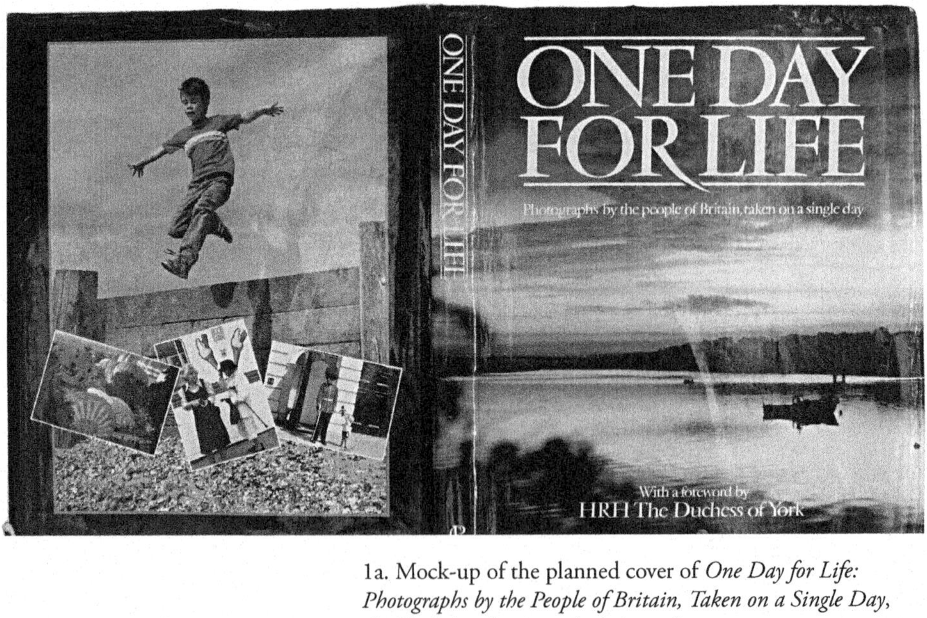

1a. Mock-up of the planned cover of *One Day for Life: Photographs by the People of Britain, Taken on a Single Day*, ahead of the photographs being taken.

1b. Cover of *One Day for Life: Photographs by the People of Britain, Taken on a Single Day* (London, 1987).

'THE BOOK THE NATION IS WAITING FOR!': *ONE DAY FOR LIFE* (1987)

Annebella Pollen

Existing photobook models have so far failed to provide convincing theorization for popular and populist publications as they have tended to consider what Gerry Badger and Martin Parr describe as 'the "literary novel" amongst photographic books'[1]: that which is produced for an elite audience and 'a niche market' with 'most ... published in editions of around 2,500'.[2] The 1987 book *One Day for Life: Photographs by the People of Britain, Taken on a Single Day* exceeds this print run a hundred times and, featuring image templates recognizable from greetings cards and illustrated calendars, is less literary novel than mass-market bestseller.

The aim of this chapter is to explore the circumstances by which a group of apparently ordinary photographs of everyday life by unknown photographers came to top the British book charts and feature in the national news. At a time when so-called vernacular photographic practice generates ever more exhibition space and academic scrutiny, this essay argues that *One Day for Life* presents a unique, multilayered and large-scale opportunity to examine the complex expectations applied to mass-participation photography, and a prism through which to assess the compromises necessitated by its commercial publication. While the democratic aims and documentary effects of *One Day for Life* as a convincing portrait of national life in the Thatcher era are curtailed by the conditions of its production, this essay posits that the process by which photographs were elicited, judged, organized, published and promoted can tell us much about the ways that 'coffee table' photobooks may be marketed and consumed as humanist products. As a charitable project that featured and was endorsed by television personalities and members of the royal family, the relationship between charity and celebrity in *One Day for Life* can also serve to illuminate fundraising practice in the post-Live Aid period.[3] Ultimately, as a demonstration of the way that photographic meaning and intention can be reconstructed through publication, *One Day for Life* provides potent evidence of the pliable malleability of photographs and their ability to support a myriad number of stories according to the various desires of their editors, publishers and promoters and the discursive locations in which they are presented.

One Day for Life was the culmination of an ambitious fundraising endeavour. Via 30 million entry forms, participants were asked to send in a photograph of everyday life in Britain on 14 August 1987, accompanied by a pound per photograph, to raise money for the Search 88 Cancer Trust and to compete for a place in a commemorative book.[4] The project aimed to be 'the biggest charity fundraising event since Live Aid'[5] and 'the largest national fund-raising campaign against cancer of its kind'.[6] It was claimed that *One Day for Life* would be 'the largest photographic event the world has ever seen'[7] and the resulting publication was intended to be 'the biggest-selling hardback photographic book ever'.[8] The desire for monumentality in *One Day for Life* was made material in the form of what the publishers described as a 'magnificent, large format, colour, hardback' book,[9] and through the 220,000 copies sold. Structured around a 24-hour format, the book aimed to present 'an image of a nation in all its moods'.[10] The 350 winning photographs, chosen 'for the fact that they represent the creation – and character of ordinary people everywhere',[11] show daily experiences of labour, leisure, customs and rituals across Britain, ranging from the whimsical to the poignant.

As a publication, *One Day for Life* was shaped by several different intersecting demands that might be best summarized as aesthetic, commercial and charitable. The aesthetic demands include the competitive angle of the project whereby participants vied for a place in the publication and were judged, first by the 'serious amateurs' of the 18 regional camera clubs who selected a longlist of 4,000 prints from the 55,000 submissions, and then by the professional 'celebrity' photographers – including Don McCullin, Linda McCartney and Terence Donovan – who acted as judges. These requirements overlap with the commercial desire for the book to be a bestseller (the August date had been chosen with Christmas retail schedules in mind), to make good the sponsorship of the numerous high-profile corporate backers, and also to profit the publisher – who trumpeted the publication as 'The book the nation is waiting for!'[12] – as only the royalties from the sale of the book went to charity. Not least, the book was shaped by the project's charitable aims: cancer fundraising was the project's *raison d'être*, with photography principally utilized as an innovative means of encouraging mass participation and donation. Promotion of the project centred on cancer research, and the charitable aspect of *One Day for Life* was the pivotal motivation for participation for many of the contributors.

There were other broad shaping factors that influenced the content and form of the publication, and these can be found both in the rhetoric by which the project was publicized and through evidence in the book and in the larger archive of submissions, housed since 1990 in the Mass Observation Archive at the University of Sussex. These diverse imperatives can be grouped into three themes: historical, national and everyday. *One Day for Life*'s aim was to create a manufactured historical event, marking 14 August 1987 as a day to remember, with the book intended to function as 'a lasting record'.[13] This historical element attracted numerous contributors to participate, and influenced the content of images submitted, whether this was by literally commemorating the date through photographs of calendars and clocks, for example, or by documenting the event itself through pictures of the project's wide media publicity. A significant number of explicitly historical statements are present in both the collection and in the book, evident in photographs that depict the enduring or the topical as subjects, from Stonehenge and stubble burning to the trend for aerobics and the notorious 'Spycatcher' book of the period, as just a few examples.[14]

As a collective endeavour, the project was promoted as a kind of national portrait by its organizers, and this encouraged the submission of imagery relating to British institutions and traditions, from the most literal of photographs that include the Union Jack to depictions of British customs, practices and 'iconic' objects, such as, for example, the enormously popular photographic subjects of red telephone boxes and fish and chips. While the quotidian national intentions of *One Day for Life* might best be described, after Michael Billig, as a form of 'banal nationalism'[15] rather than an explicitly political endeavour, numerous interviews with participants have confirmed that a sense of what Benedict Anderson calls 'imagined community'[16] was a powerful emotional motivator for many contributors.

The third dominant theme among submissions can be understood by the project's focus on the 'ordinary' and the 'everyday'. *One Day for Life* asked for images of everyday life and thus enabled non-professional photographers to contribute a range of photographic material that challenges and expands what Richard Chalfen has called the 'selective prohibitions' of the family album, where he notes there is an emphasis on special occasions and ceremonial events and 'a general neglect of daily life'.[17] While the project claimed to celebrate the amateur, the 'ordinary' that the book promoted was, as evidenced by its hierarchical structure and selection process, an 'other' rather than a synonym for everyone.

Even before the first of the photographs had been submitted, the book's design, from cover to layout, was fixed. Entry forms already showed an image of the projected book's cover (Figure 1a) and a sample spread (Figure 2a). This mock-up enabled participants to visualize the prize that they were competing for and also doubled as a saleable image of the book which could be pre-ordered with the same form. The images on the entry envelope correspond to the publisher's promotional dummy, created to 'sell the book in' to trade catalogues. As a template layout, devised by the book's designers to serve as a grid into which submitted photographs and captions could be dropped, this dummy also reveals the overall aesthetic and format to which submissions were expected to conform. Comprising images sourced from picture agencies in a variety of sizes, and imagining a range of names, ages, genders and countrywide locations for the credits of its projected participants, the dummy photographs of national monuments and landscapes alongside representations of labour and the family established the inclusive demographic and ordinary-to-extraordinary, private-to-public, celebratory aesthetic that the book was to fulfil.

The design team appointed by Bantam Press for *One Day for Life* was Associated Design Consultants, headed by Bob Searles. Searles told me, in interview, that he mocked up the pages of the dummy for the benefit of the publishers long before the event, with no knowledge of the kinds of subjects that might be submitted.[18] The close resemblance between the 10 images of the dummy, which include tweed-clad older men, fairground rides in motion and sleeping babies, and the chosen subjects in the published book is, however, remarkable. Searles's presence at the judging and his steering role in the final selection, ordering and formatting of the final 350 images from the 650 finalists shortlisted by the 'celebrity' photographers should not be overlooked. Arguably, as artistic director, Searles (and the publisher who oversaw him) had more influence on the look of the finished book, particularly in relation to the cover, than any of the organizers, 'big name' photographers or the tens of thousands of participants who took part in the project.

The key organizing characteristic of the *One Day for Life* book is the temporal format of a single day. This conceit of selecting a single 'ordinary' day to act as a metonym for a longer period was clearly not invented by *One Day for Life* – it is at least as old as the Greek tragedies. Circadian narrative devices, as they might be described,[19] have long-standing popularity, and intersect with photography in particular in their common appearance as a motif in interwar illustrated magazines.[20] Nor was *One Day for Life* the first glossy hardback book to take up this temporal structure. The South African businessman, Gareth Pyne-James, who was Project Director of Search 88, had been inspired by *A Day in the Life of South Africa*, which had raised money

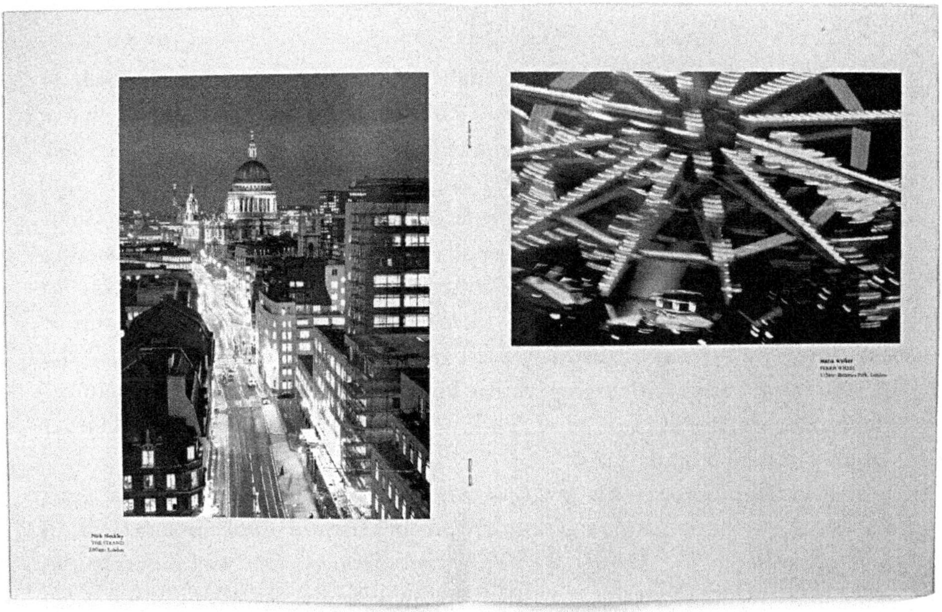

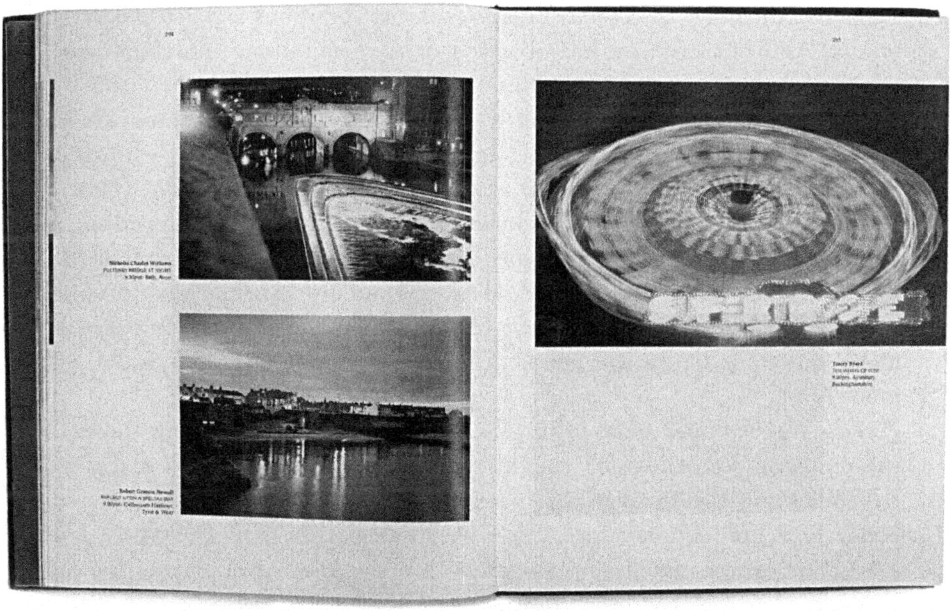

2a. Mock-up of a planned spread in *One Day for Life: Photographs by the People of Britain, Taken on a Single Day*, ahead of the photographs being taken.

2b. Double-page spread from *One Day for Life: Photographs by the People of Britain, Taken on a Single Day* (London, 1987).

for visual impairment charities through the sale of a large-format book of photographs taken on 26 May 1982.[21] This book had, in turn, been explicitly modelled on *A Day in the Life of Australia* which had taken 6 March 1981 as its 'typical day'.[22] As the first of a long-standing series of *Day in the Life* photobooks which, along with their later *24/7* reinvention, can now claim to be the best-selling photobooks of all time,[23] Rick Smolan's blockbusting projects set the template for many copycat versions, including *One Day for Life*. At the same time that *A Day in the Life of America* was at the top of the American bestseller lists in 1987, *One Day for Life* was at the top of the British book charts with a very similar format but a slightly different name – the phrase 'A Day in the Life of' had, by then, been copyrighted by Harper Collins to deter competitors.[24]

All of the photographic projects mentioned so far are indebted, at least in spirit, to the 'sentimental humanism' of Edward Steichen's exhibition and photobook *The Family of Man*.[25] *One Day for Life* was described in contemporary news coverage as 'Britain's own family album',[26] and its seven ages of man-type content of births, marriages and deaths is just one connection that can be drawn between the two projects. Similarly blockbusting and number-crunching, *The Family of Man* had vast ambitions and achieved vast results. As Blake Stimson has observed of the exhibition: 'Numbers were bandied about incessantly from the beginning: 503 photographs taken by 273 photographers from 68 countries seen by 9 million exhibition-goers in 37 countries'.[27] These impressive numbers do not include those who own or have seen the book, which has never gone out of print. Hilton Kramer, writing at the time of the book's release, predicted that 'judging from advance sales, *The Family of Man* will become as much part of the family library as the Bible'.[28] Heroic ambitions, a universal address and monumental sense of scale were equally intrinsic to *One Day for Life*. As Pyne-James put it: 'In order to make something big, you've got to do something big. That's what Search 88 is all about'.[29]

One Day for Life's sense of historical value was articulated both through the temporal format which sought to institute a single day as a day to remember and also through the material qualities of the lavishly illustrated book's high production values. These were indebted to their *Day in the Life* precursors, whose stated aim was a book of the kind of quality to 'be on people's coffee tables 40 years from now'.[30] The term 'coffee table' is usually used as a pejorative reference to a large illustrated book heavy on style and low on substance, but the large-format photography book may also be built to convey gravitas or even inspire awe, in the case of the Exhibit Format books published during the 1960s by the American conservation society, The Sierra Club, featuring landscape images by photographers such as Ansel Adams alongside inscriptions by writers such as Thoreau. While *One Day for Life*'s 29 by 23 centimetre format is slightly smaller than both Sierra Club and *Day in the Life* books, it nevertheless appears indebted to Exhibit Format principles, which Finis Dunaway has noted were designed to simulate the experience of an art exhibition. David Brower, executive director of the Sierra Club, claimed, 'It has long been recognized that the book, for all that television, radio, and periodicals may do, still has a status of its own ... . It lasts. It is kept and referred to. It is quoted. This is particularly true of the exhibit-format books'.[31] The substantial, literally heavy-weight, photography book was seen as something that would endure and make a lasting statement. Exhibit Format books were prestige items, objects of display, and expensive (and *One Day for Life* was not cheap at £16.95 in 1987). The specific materiality of photobooks matters. As Elizabeth Edwards has argued, 'The role of the book ... as a material object, constructed through clearly articulated design values, becomes key in mediating the information presented'.[32]

As a book designed to appeal to a mass market and that aimed to raise the largest possible sums for charity, the content of the book is, as one might expect, a feel-good, picture postcard look at life in Britain in the 1980s. Elements of British national character are depicted fondly through queues and pub lunches; universal stages of life are displayed, from adorable babies and young lovers to grandmothers with ice-creams. Labour is frequently traditional, from thatching to blacksmithing, and sometimes spectacular, as in the case of the many images of street performers. A small number of images comment on the cancer aspect of the project and show gravestones, a funeral or surgery but these are not as confrontational as images rejected for inclusion that show graphic mastectomy wounds, for example. Photographs of the destitute are popular in both the larger archive and the published book, where 'the tramp' appears as an enduring street photographic 'type' as much as a symbol of social critique. Certainly, in the book, the inclusion of numerous images of the homeless or street drinkers appears to be utilized as 'local colour', and is distinct from the significant number of excluded critical images which comment on the daily reality of unemployment, for example. It is worth remembering that the book represents less than 1 per cent of the total photographs submitted to the project.

Notable exclusions from the book, which are very visible in the archive, are those that camera clubs would have rejected in the first edit, from the obscene or banal in subject matter to the blurred and technically inept. Photographs with indistinct focus, framing or fingers-in-the-lens were cast aside. Images that did not conform to the brief in format, location or date were also excluded. One of the most compelling features of the archive as a whole – and something that is barely seen in the book – is the wealth of accompanying documentation, sometimes in the form of comments on the back of photographs, that reveal competitive aspirations or unseen, poignant cancer connections, and which can extend to poetry and personal letters of some length. Textual captions in the book give only the time and a location alongside a five-word title, which was interpreted as a description by some and a competition-style slogan by others.

James Buzard has described literary works 'which offer to contain all life within the single day' as characterized by a dialectic that 'oscillate[s] between the operations of mythologizing the ordinary and "normalising" the mythic'.[33] Indeed, there is a fluctuation of commitment between the ordinary and the special in *One Day for Life*, which aimed to be both typical, as a cross-section sample, and 'a day unlike any other'.[34] While *One Day for Life* differs from its *Day in the Life* precursors by being non-professional in its photographic focus, the layout of the book, within the single-day format, is organized around time zones, each of which is topped and tailed by a 'celebrity contribution', from singer Aled Jones to author Catherine Cookson. In addition to these photographs – which are the only ones permitted any substantial textual accompaniment – the final pages include submissions by press and professional photographers alongside those by television celebrities, which in total make up 10 per cent of the book. The very first and last images of the book are by members of the monarchy. The newly married Duchess of York was the project's high-profile patron, and *One Day for Life* was her first charitable endorsement. Her image (taken by her husband, Prince Andrew, who was a keen amateur photographer at this time) appeared on each of the entry forms, and both this image and the Duchess's photographic contribution preface the book.

In this context, the use of the term 'the people' in the book's title seems more akin to 'subjects' than convenient shorthand for 'everybody'. The evidence that 'the ordinary' is a category rather than a synonym for 'the population' is reiterated by this segregation of 'ordinary' people's photography from the 'celebrity' and thus 'non-ordinary' contributions. While the book's promotion of 'ordinary people' *could* be read as a radical social agenda; as committed or community photography, or as a democratic means of providing a voice for those likely to suffer the condescension of history, the editorial process of *One Day for Life* with its 'distinguished panel'[35] of professionals suggests that stratification of value was very much embedded in the project. This was certainly the case in *One Day for Life*'s coverage in the contemporary press, where the participation of 'stars' was foregrounded and provided the principal motivation for the story.[36]

The layout of the book, while framed by a midnight-to-midnight structure, does not follow a strict sequential narrative based on the time that the photographs were taken. Within chapters that separate out 'The Early Hours' from 'The Morning' and 'The Middle of the Day', photographs move forwards and backwards in time at the convenience of the designers. Of the photographs that comprise the main body of the book, the first image is of illuminated London. Taken at 1.15 a.m. by E. Aldred, and originally entitled 'Lambeth Bridge – Nightlife' on the photographer's entry form, the photograph's title is changed in the book to 'Good Morning Britain', marking from the outset the prioritization of the book's editorial narrative over the photographers' intentions. The following photograph, of a sunrise over Windsor, jumps forward in time to 5.20 a.m. Two photographs later the clock returns to 2.30 a.m. This peculiar chronology – from night to morning and back again – demonstrates that photographs were ordered for harmonious comparisons or arresting contrasts between images rather than for temporal correctness.

The reason for the grouping of certain pages is obvious: for example, a woman delivering the post in rural Somerset faces a woman delivering milk in a Devon village, suggesting universal equivalence in daily activities across the land (Figure 4a). Elsewhere photographs are brought together as opposites – a smartly dressed man outside the draped flags and polished railings of the Royal Academy, for example, is scaled to the same size as 'Ray' the park sweeper on the opposing page, suggesting the co-existence, within one nation and one day, of extremes of experience (Figure 3a). Prints submitted to *One Day for Life* were required to conform to a standard enprint format, to fit into the entry envelope. Any full-page bleeds and double-page enlargements in the book thus represent the aesthetic choices of the editorial team, informed by the conventions of mass-market publications and the necessity for variety, rhythm and contrast to relieve the monotonous pace and texture of repetitive sizing. It is formal rhythms in the shape of the photographs – emphasized by cropping or resizing – that position, for example, the elongated heads of children seen in a distorting mirror against the narrow shape of a punt on the River Cam (Figure 5a). Elsewhere the formal repetitions are internal to the image: the trailing wake of a model of a ship in a Royal Navy exhibition on the upper left of a spread, corresponds with the vapour trail from a skydiver in spiralling descent on the bottom right of the facing page (Figure 5b). Later in the book, in a grid of four photographs spread across pages 296 and 297, the silhouette of a kissing couple before the fiery colours of a sunset is echoed by the shadows and flames of a chef's burning pan in the image below. On the facing page, two photographs, first of hedgehogs on a paving stone and, below, of a tabby kitten on a beige carpet, are clearly linked by their sympathetic colour tones as well as the sentimental appeal of their animal subjects.

Rather than the unfolding of narrative like a filmic sequence, then, the shifting patterning of time and subject matter reiterate the simple, universalizing rhetoric of the publication: simultaneously, across the nation, multiple people took part in an abundant variety of activity. The book's structure brings order to the disparate elements and creates linked sets of relationships through juxtaposition. Alan Trachtenberg has written that layout constitutes the ultimate meaning of a photobook text. 'What the pictures say, they say in and through the texture of relations that unfold – continuities, doublings, reversals, climaxes, and resolutions'.[37] Similarly, Stimson has suggested that '[a]gainst the frozen time of the single image and the pregiven temporality provided by film, the photographic essay in book or exhibition form opens out to an interactive and dynamic relation between viewer and text'. But he goes on to add: 'At least this is its promise'.[38]

For it is important not to overstate the formal complexity of the book's layout. Although *One Day for Life* was described in contemporary news reports as 'a montage of life in the 1980s',[39] it is not a radical aesthetic project. *One Day for Life* may not be read satisfactorily as an avant-garde publication, nor can it be critiqued convincingly for its deficiencies as a serious ethnography of national life when this was not among its intentions. The larger body of photographs was never even intended to become an archive: as the day of the book's launch was on Bonfire Night, 5 November 1987, plans were floated for a spectacular pyre of the rejected prints to mark the event.[40] It was only due to financial difficulties at the close of the project and the hurried necessity of disposing of Search 88's assets that an institutional home was sought for the photographs.[41] The peculiarities of *One Day for Life*'s biography mean that it falls outside the boundaries of the photo-essay methodologies that currently exist for the interpretation of photobooks, based as they are on readings of the careful selection, sequence and structure of image and text. The production of *One Day for Life* took place within incredibly tight deadlines, with only around a month to spare between the submission deadline and the launch date. Within this narrow schedule, the final selection and layout were completed in a weekend, and the shape and content of the book must be read accordingly.

One Day for Life is best described as a product of multiple intentions, which include the particular stories that the various promoters, judges and

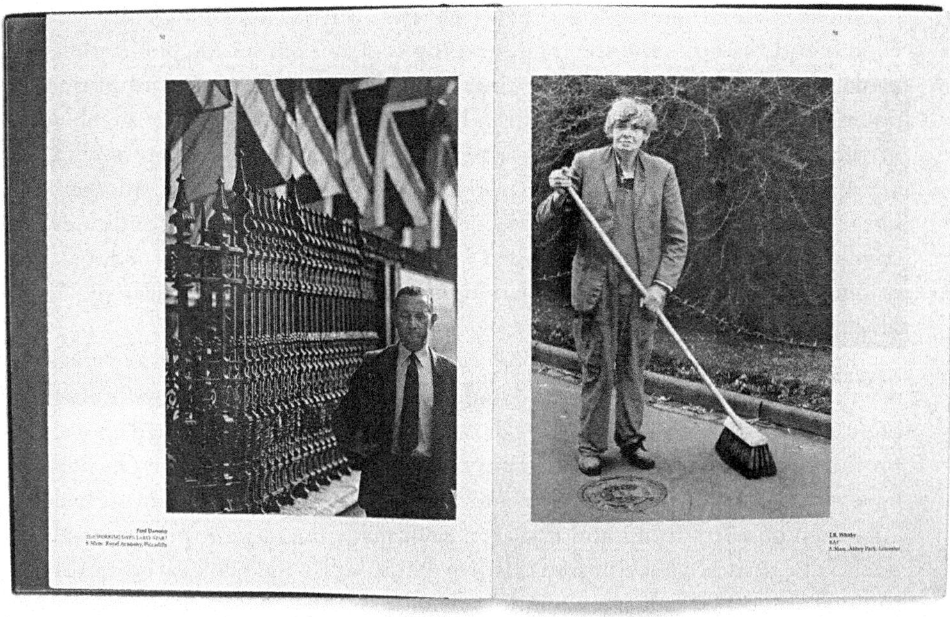

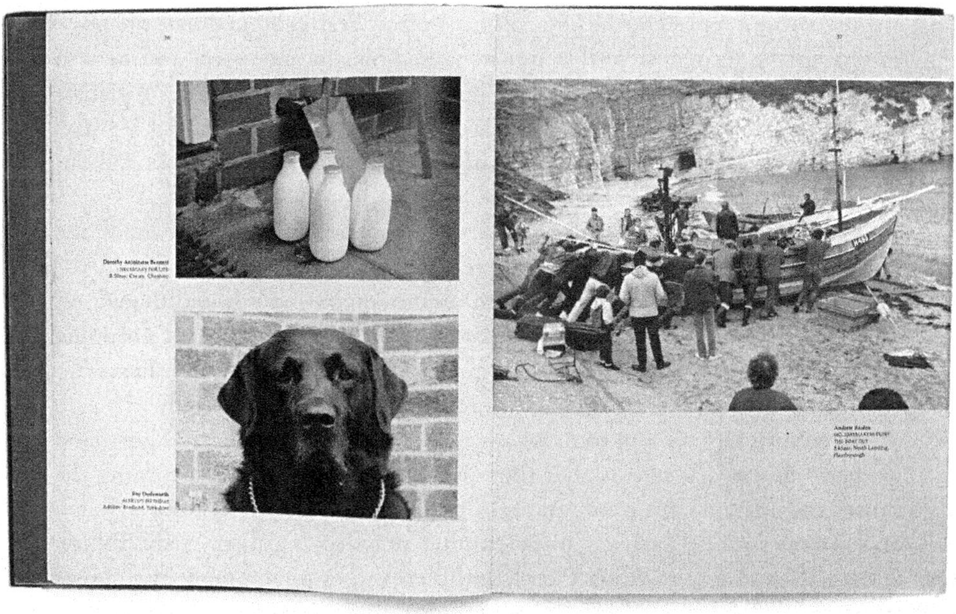

3. *One Day for Life: Photographs by the People of Britain, Taken on a Single Day* (London, 1987).

publishers wanted the photographs to tell: the everyday and the special; the famous and the ordinary; the tragic and the comic. The uses the publication made of submitted images were at times at odds with the motivations of the photographers, not least because this information was not always transferable in the photograph. Many of the 130 *One Day for Life* participants who answered questionnaires for this research attribute a significance to their images that exceeds its visible subject, where, for example, a dog indicates comfort in the face of chemotherapy ('Alfred's birthday', Figure 3b) or a man reading a newspaper in a park functions as a memorial to a dead relative ('A lunchtime break', Figure 4b).

There are some key points when a clear disjuncture between intentions occurs, and this is most clearly demonstrated in the case of the winning photograph – the one chosen for the cover of the book. As mentioned above, for the purposes of publicity, a dummy book cover for *One Day for Life* had been mocked up in advance from a commercial picture library. This image had circulated on entry forms and had even been made into a giant promotional book to be used as a backdrop to celebrity photo calls. The book's art director thus felt compelled to locate a winning cover image that looked similar to the one already in use (Figure 1). In order to do this, he made a selection that went against the wishes of the judges who thought that the cover should be a 'people' shot to represent the aims of the project. Searles argued that the book would not be recognizable if it did not resemble the mock-up, and he also argued that their suggestions 'would not look like a photo book'. A picture of a person on the cover, he argued, would suggest at a glance that it was a book about that person; just as a picture of a dog would suggest a book about dogs, and so on.[42]

In fact, the final cover image used was one that had not even made the final cut by the judges. Searles gathered a list of possible sunsets from the camera club-compiled longlist of 4,000 photographs and selected the closest fit. The sunset chosen had to be substantially doctored through cropping and recolouring to imitate the dummy cover, and to provide the necessary contrast with the book's lettering in order 'to show up on the telly'.[43] As an image appropriate for a photobook, Searles stated that sunsets are 'shorthand for photography'. It is true that there is a certain currency in assuming the sunset and the amateur photograph in particular to be synonymous – Julian Stallabrass's article on mass photographic practice is called 'Sixty Billion Sunsets', for example, while Pierre Bourdieu uses a photograph of a sunset as a focal point by which to examine hierarchies of aesthetic distinction.[44] There are also very many sunsets in both the *One Day for Life* archive and in the book, although this is likely to be as much to do with entries that sought

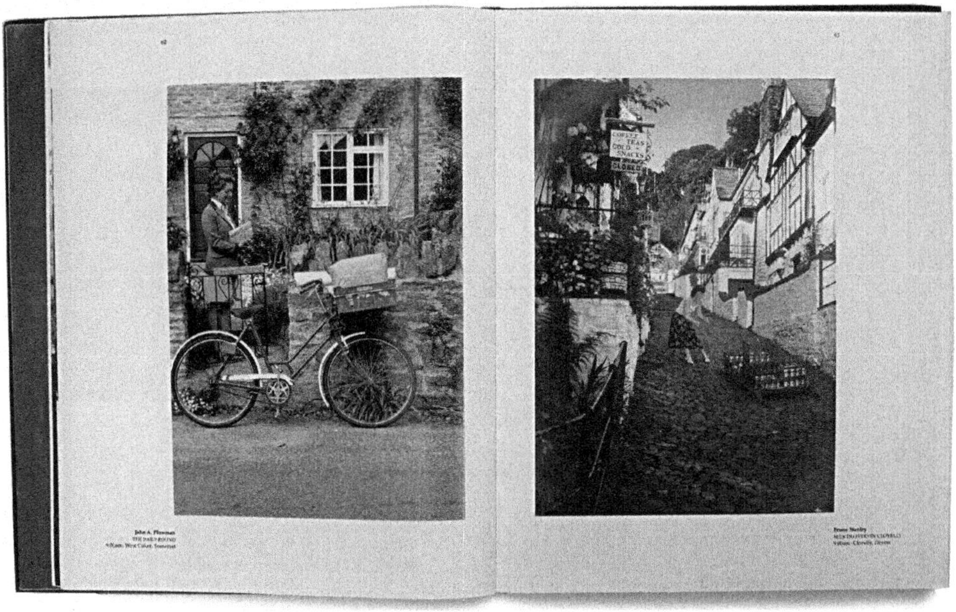

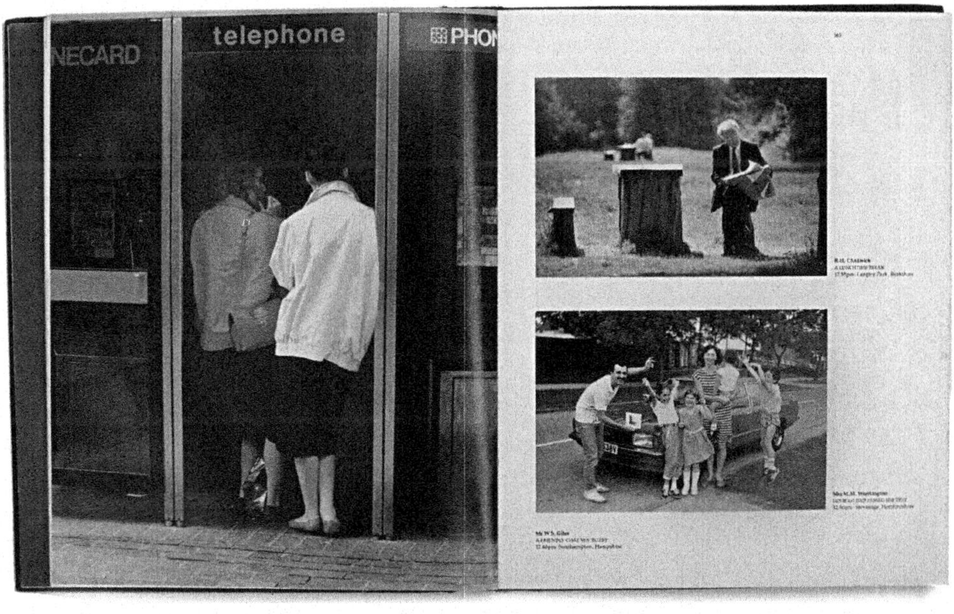

4. *One Day for Life: Photographs by the People of Britain, Taken on a Single Day* (London, 1987).

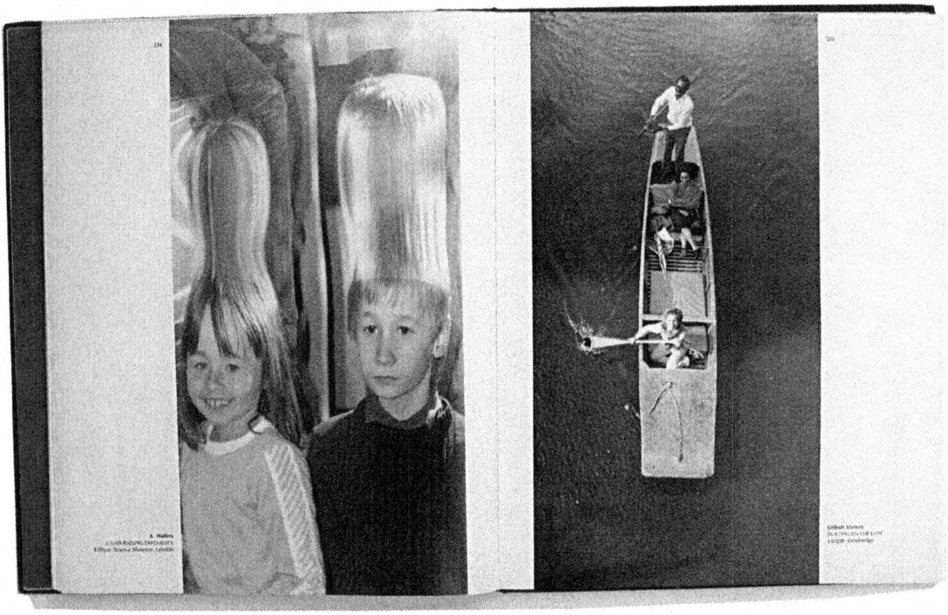

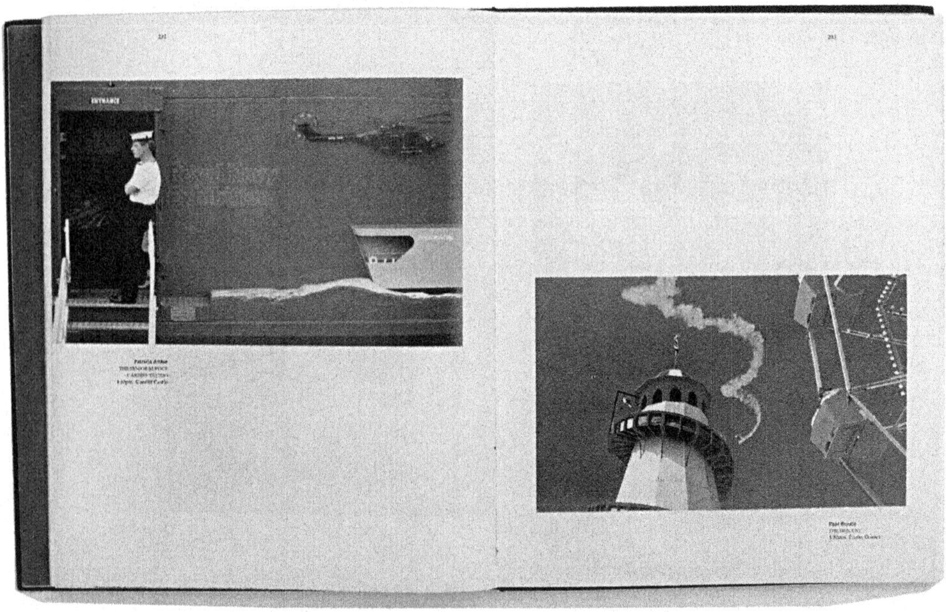

5. *One Day for Life: Photographs by the People of Britain, Taken on a Single Day* (London, 1987).

to mark a visible time of day as it is to do with the sunset as a supremely popular 'photographable' amateur subject.

Searles's conviction that a photograph of a sunset works as photobook shorthand can be seen again in the cover of the 1988 Bantam Press follow up, *One Day for Life in Ireland*, which Searles also art-directed.[45] *Heart of Britain*, a 1996 royalty- and celebrity-endorsed photographic fundraiser modelled on *One Day for Life*, and which again used the same design team, also ended up with a sunset on its cover.[46] Despite the *One Day for Life* judges not liking the image, the organizers thinking it was 'too easy',[47] and Searles himself stating, 'It's a bit of a cliché',[48] the sunset photograph he selected made the cover, and the winner was presented with a prize by the Duchess of York and an invitation to appear on Terry Wogan's television chat show.[49] The photographer, meanwhile, had a whole different set of ideas for his photograph. A Catholic born in Northern Ireland, John F. Bradley told me that his photograph depicted the Derry and Donegal border, the site of the siege of Derry and the origin of the term 'No Surrender'. He wanted to show a different view of Ireland than the one commonly depicted during the Troubles, and he believed his image to be more of an Irish photograph than one about what he called 'Britain in inverted commas'.[50] His sunset-as-political-statement became entangled in the complex and frequently conflicting multiple intentions that characterize *One Day for Life* – variously envisaged as a national family album, a democratic historical record, a celebrity-studded spectacle, a social document of everyday life, a public display of compassion, a monumental photographic competition, a bestselling book and, above all, 'a lovely Christmas present'.[51]

Notes

1 Martin Parr and Gerry Badger, *The Photobook: A History*, 2 vols (London: Phaidon, 2004, 2006), vol. 1, p. 8.
2 Parr and Badger, *The Photobook*, vol. 2, p. 8.
3 Live Aid, 13 July 1985, was a large-scale international rock concert in aid of famine relief in Ethiopia that raised millions of pounds in public donations.
4 The Search 88 Cancer Trust was a co-ordinated fund-raising initiative, founded in 1987, that aimed to raise money for cancer charities through a series of major public events.
5 Alan Hamilton, 'Duchess Heads Photo Fund', *The Times* (10 August 1987), p. 5.
6 Lee Rodwell, 'Charitable Snaps', *The Times* (7 August 1987), p. 8.
7 Search 88, *One Day for Life: Photographs by the People of Britain, Taken on a Single Day* (London: Bantam Press, 1987), flyleaf.
8 Paul Eastham, 'Orders for Charity Book Soar', *The Times* (2 September 1987).

9 *One Day for Life* entry form, 1987.
10 Search 88, flyleaf.
11 Search 88, flyleaf.
12 Stocklist, Transworld Publishers Limited, October/November/December 1987, cover.
13 Richard Hambro, 'Afterword', Search 88, p. 316.
14 Peter Wright's banned book *Spycatcher: The Candid Autobiography of a Senior Intelligence Officer* (New York: Viking Press, 1987) was a topical issue in the summer of 1987 when English newspapers took their appeal against a ban on its reportage to the High Court. Several participants photographed the book, or posed reading it, for their *One Day for Life* submission.
15 Michael Billig suggests that in contrast to an overt and often fiercely expressed political nationalism, banal nationalism is a sense of nationhood embedded in the routines of everyday life. Billig, *Banal Nationalism* (London: Sage, 1995).
16 Benedict Anderson argues that nationalism is best understood as a kind of imagined community in the minds of its members. He states, 'It is imagined because the members of even the smallest nation will never know most of their fellow-members, meet them, or even hear of them, yet in the minds of each lives the image of their communion'. Anderson, *Imagined Communities: Reflections on the Origin and Spread of Nationalism* (London: Verso, 1983), p. 15.
17 Richard Chalfen, *Snapshot Versions of Life* (Ohio: Bowling Green University Press, 1987), pp. 46 and 94.
18 Interview with Bob Searles, 11 July 2008.
19 I have adapted this term from John Mullan's conception of circadian novels. He writes, 'You may not have heard of "circadian novels", but you have probably read one. They are novels that fit all their action into a single day'. John Mullan, 'Ten of the Best: Circadian Novels', *The Guardian*, Section 'Review' (25 October 2008), p. 13.
20 Notable examples include Bill Brandt, 'The Perfect Parlourmaid', *Picture Post* (29 July 1939), pp. 4–6. For further reference see the chapter 'A Day in the Life: The Documentary Photobook in the 1930s', in Parr and Badger, *The Photobook*, vol. 1, pp. 117–45.
21 *A Day in the Life of South Africa* (South Africa: A Day in the Life of South Africa (Pty.), 1982).
22 Andy Park and Rick Smolan, *A Day in the Life of Australia: Photographed by 100 of the World's Leading Photojournalists* (Australia: DILTA Pty. Ltd, 1981), p. 12.
23 Rick Smolan and David Elliot Cohen, *24/7 Media Group*, online at: http://www.247mediagroup.com/projects/index.html (accessed 27 May 2009).
24 Rick Smolan and David Cohen (eds), *A Day in the Life of America* (New York: Collins, 1986).
25 Edward Steichen, *The Family of Man* (New York: Museum of Modern Art, 1955).
26 As described in a news item on the book, BBC *News at Ten* (5 November 1987).
27 Hilton Kramer, 'Exhibiting the *Family of Man*: The World's Most Talked About Photographs', *Commentary* 20 (October 1955), p. 365 cited in Blake Stimson, *The Pivot of the World: Photography and Its Nation* (Cambridge, MA: MIT, 2006), p. 65.
28 Stimson, p. 65.
29 Rodwell, p. 8.
30 Robert Sam Anson, 'A Day in the Life of America Revisited', in Smolan and Cohen (eds), *A Day in the Life of America*, p. 256.

31 David Brower, 'About the special help the Sierra Club needs for its role in saving Grand Canyon' (1964), carton 30, folder 39, David Brower Papers, Sierra Club Members Papers, Bancroft Library, University of California at Berkeley quoted in Finis Dunaway, *Natural Visions: The Power of Images in American Environmental Reform* (Chicago: University of Chicago Press, 2005) p. 119.
32 Elizabeth Edwards, 'Gardens of War: Materiality and the Photographic Narrative', in Illisa Barbash and Lucien Taylor (eds), *The Cinema of Robert Gardiner* (Oxford and New York: Berg, 2007), p. 176.
33 James Buzard, 'Mass-Observation. Modernism and Autoethnography', *Modernism/Modernity* 4 (1997), pp. 93–122, p. 111.
34 Search 88, flyleaf.
35 Search 88, flyleaf.
36 See, for example, 'Stars Click for Charity', *Daily Mail* (14 August 1987), p. 17.
37 Alan Trachtenberg, *Reading American Photographs: Images as History, Matthew Brady to Walker Evans* (New York: Hill and Wang, 1990), p. 259, quoted in Stimson, pp. 33–4.
38 Stimson, p. 98.
39 From news item on *One Day for Life*, BBC *News at Ten* (5 November 1987).
40 Interview with Christopher English, formerly of the Search 88 *One Day for Life* organizing team (26 March 2008).
41 English (26 March 2008).
42 Searles (11 July 2008).
43 Searles (11 July 2008).
44 Julian Stallabrass, 'Sixty Billion Sunsets' in *Gargantua: Manufactured Mass Culture* (London: Verso, 1996); Pierre Bourdieu, *Distinction: A Social Critique of the Judgement of Taste* (Cambridge, MA: Harvard University Press, 1984), pp. 34–47.
45 Irish Cancer Society, *One Day for Life in Ireland: Photographs by the People of Ireland, Taken on a Single Day* (London: Bantam Press, 1988).
46 Royal Brompton Hospital, *Heart of Britain: The People's Photographs Capture the Soul of the Nation* (London: Bookman Publishers, 1996).
47 Interview with Lucinda Mackay, née Pugh, formerly of the Search 88 *One Day for Life* organizing team (1 May 2008).
48 Searles (11 July 2008).
49 Bradley was due to feature on a special edition of the television chat show 'Wogan' on 6 November 1987, but the death of popular entertainer Eamonn Andrews on the previous day resulted in a change in the programme's content. Interview with John F. Bradley (26 April 2008).
50 Bradley (26 April 2008).
51 *One Day for Life* entry form (1987).

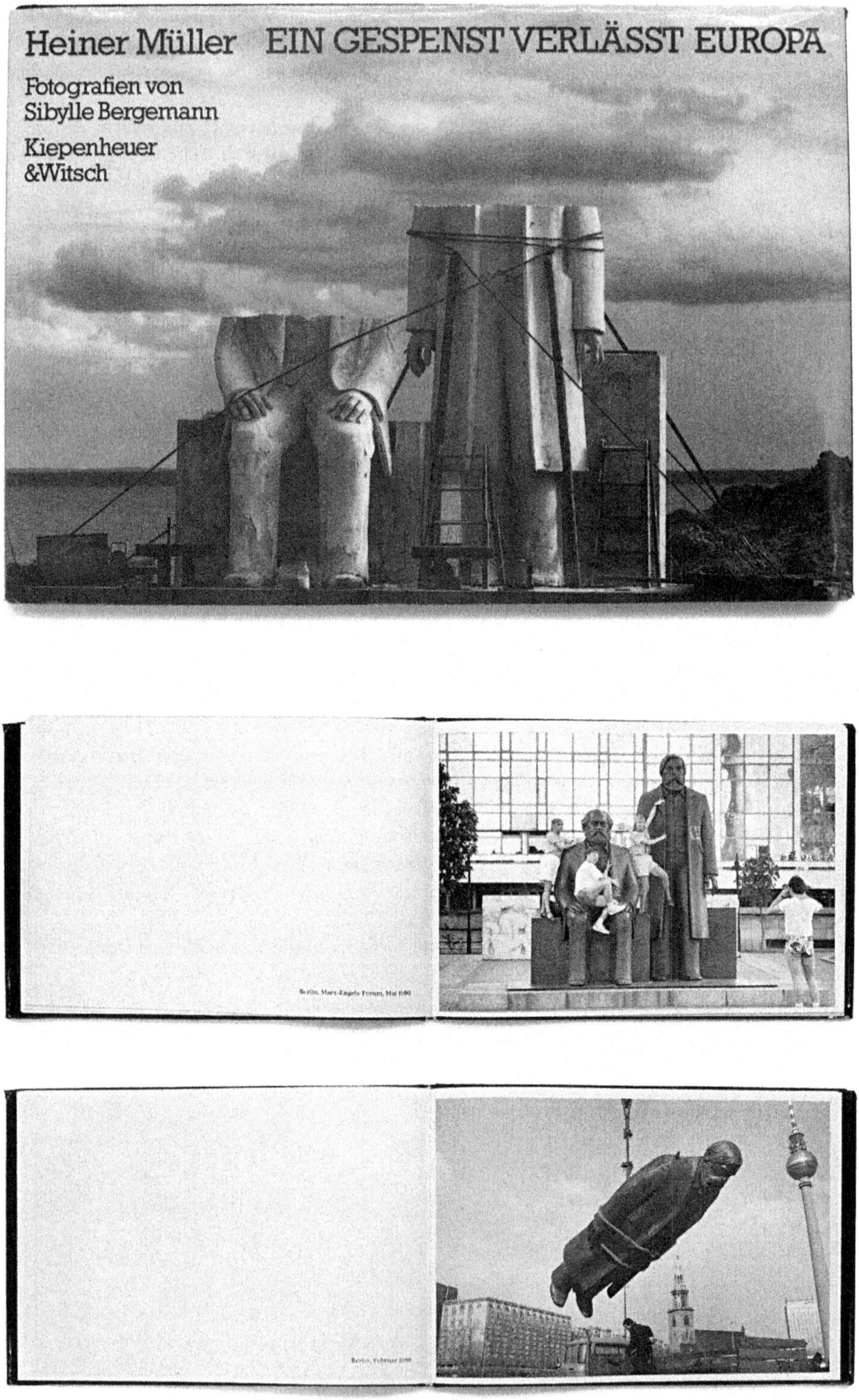

1. Heiner Müller and Sibylle Bergemann, *Ein Gespenst verlässt Europa* (Cologne, 1990).

A SPECTRE IS LEAVING EUROPE (1990): APPROPRIATION IN A POST-COMMUNIST PHOTOBOOK

David Evans

Ein Gespenst verlässt Europa (*A Spectre Is Leaving Europe*) is a book published in Cologne in 1990 by the writer Heiner Müller (1929–95) and the photographer Sibylle Bergemann (1941–2010).[1] The title alludes caustically to the ominous boast of Karl Marx and Friedrich Engels that famously opens *The Communist Manifesto* of 1848: 'A spectre is haunting Europe – The spectre of Communism'.[2] Müller and Bergemann had both lived and worked in the German Democratic Republic (East Germany) and their book is a response to the rapid collapse of a staunchly pro-Soviet regime that began during 40th birthday celebrations in 1989, and concluded with political unification with the Federal Republic of Germany (West Germany) in the following year. *A Spectre Is Leaving Europe* is my main case study in an essay about appropriation, post-Communism and the photobook.

1

The photobook, post-Communism and appropriation are all terms that require preliminary clarification. The noun appropriation means taking possession of something, usually without authority. It has been a constant in all forms of imperialism, from ancient times to date, and in all forms of society in which one group dispossesses another of the products of its labour. In the modern era, it can also be used to describe the processes of de- and re-contextualization that informed the emergence of museums after 1789. The Musée des Monuments Français, for example, was opened in 1795 to provide a safe refuge for artefacts associated with the discredited *Ancien Régime* and Church, now stripped of their regal and divine attributes and represented as mere objects of art or historical documents. Similar developments took place across Europe and amounted to art's 'conceptual redefinition'.[3]

Appropriation can also be used in relation to a number of art activities across the last 100 years or so that involved taking over real objects, including other works of art. Indicative examples include (photo)collage, (photo) montage, the found object and the readymade, all neologisms associated with the avant-garde groups that were particularly active in the early decades of the twentieth century; assemblage, *décollage* and *détournement* from the mid-twentieth century; and more recently, postproduction, re-mixing or sampling. The contexts continuously change, with earlier initiatives marked by the emergence of cinema and the illustrated press in the early twentieth century, and the pervasive digital culture of the last two or three decades having a comparable impact on contemporary artwork. Yet there is continuity, too, as succeeding generations of artists develop their own version of what Louis Aragon called in 1930 'the personality of choice'.[4]

An expansive notion of appropriation art could take on board the various examples sketched above from the late eighteenth century to date. Yet its widespread use as a term by artists and critics is far more recent, primarily in connection with a small number of artists who came to prominence in New York in the late 1970s and 1980s and who were regularly referenced in ambitious debates around the postmodern. The debates remain unresolved, but a radical – even revolutionary – *frisson* was initially generated by the frequent use of the word appropriation. The implication was that activities like Richard Prince's re-photographing of Marlboro advertisements involved appropriating the appropriators, and was a sophisticated, cultural equivalent to colonial resistance, the occupation of land by peasants, or the takeover of factories by workers.[5]

Appropriation art is close to, but distinct from, the copy, the replica or the forgery.[6] Copying was an essential element of academic art training from the seventeenth century onwards, informed by the assumption that emulation of the masters of antiquity was the best way of gaining competence. During the same period, replication involved artists or supervised apprentices creating versions of a studio's popular work to satisfy the demand of more than one patron. In theory, at least, the copy and the replica can both be clearly differentiated from the fake or forgery, understood as an unauthorized work that aims to be recognized as an 'original'. In the twentieth century, famous forgers included Han van Meegeren, a Vermeer specialist, and Elmyr de Hory who copied numerous famous artists and provided the inspiration for the Orson Welles film *F for Fake* (1974). Copying, replicating or forging might seem apt terms to describe the re-photographing of reproductions of the 1930s work of Walker Evans by Sherrie Levine. Unlike van Meegeren or de Hory, however, Levine draws attention to her actions and intentions with a title like *Untitled (After Walker Evans)* (1981) and the addition of her own name. Note also Eric Doeringer, whose series *Bootlegs* includes an inkjet print of an Evans photograph used by Levine with the title *Sherrie Levine (Walker Evans)* (2007), mischievously implying that Levine's questioning of Walker's authority has been a way of establishing her own.[7] Many of the wilder claims relating to the activities of the New York appropriationists have now been abandoned or seriously modified. In addition, the term appropriation art is no longer centred on one American city around 1980, and regularly crops up in the writings on very diverse topics, including feminism, post-colonialism and post-Communism.[8]

post-Communism is another term that can give rise to confusion. Usually, it refers to those states that emerged after the implosion of the Soviet Union and its Central and Eastern European satellites, as well as Yugoslavia, between 1989 and the early 1990s. It is also used to describe dissident currents within Communist states whose activities predated formal collapse at the political level. Thus the artists' collective *Neue Slowenische Kunst* (NSK), probably best known for its musical wing called *Laibach*, can be generally characterized as post-Communist.[9] However, the NSK existed for around a decade before Slovenia broke away from Yugoslavia to become an early, internationally recognized, post-Communist state in 1990. Comparable distinctions are made within a Soviet context, so art theorist Boris Groys champions what he calls Moscow Conceptualism (for him, a major instance of cultural post-Communism that had been operating since the 1970s), yet the Soviet Union was only dissolved in December 1991.[10] In both of my examples, then post-Communism can simultaneously refer to a dissident cultural phenomenon within a Communist state, and the political form that emerges after the disappearance of a Communist state.

And the third term that requires some initial commentary is the photobook. Not all books of photographs are photobooks. The latter, it is widely assumed, refer to one or more printed volumes which foreground the work of a photographer who frequently takes an active part in the overall design. Such a description can be applied to most of the items in *The Book of 101 Books: Seminal Photographic Books of the Twentieth Century*, the recent guide by Andrew Roth and others that helped launch the current enthusiasm for the photobook as an object to be analysed and collected.[11] Yet it is worth noting that this book also contains a number of publications in which a writer is also clearly credited. *La Banlieue de Paris* (Paris, 1949), for instance, is primarily photographs by Robert Doisneau with an introduction and captions by writer Blaise Cendrars, whose better-known name dominates the cover. In contrast, writer James Agee and photographer Walker Evans are given the same prominence on the cover of *Let Us Now Praise Famous Men* (Boston, 1941), as are Paul Eluard and Man Ray on the cover of *Facile* (Paris, 1935), a book combining poetry and photography.[12]

The name of Heiner Müller is more conspicuous than that of Sibylle Bergemann on the dust-jacket of *A Spectre Is Leaving Europe* (Figure 1). Yet the book is more than poems supplemented by photographs. Rather, it is a photobook in which images and poems are given equal status, and in this respect is comparable to the otherwise very different *Facile*. It is a *Post-communist* photobook in both senses of the term. That is, the critiques by Müller and Bergemann of 'Actually Existing Socialism'[13] pre-date the collapse of the German Democratic Republic, but this particular book also deals with that collapse as recent history. And finally, it is a post-Communist photobook as *appropriation* most obviously in the sense that Bergemann de- and re-contextualizes photographs that were originally made for the Party.

2

A Spectre Is Leaving Europe includes 10 poems by Heiner Müller plus a suite of photographs by Sibylle Bergemann that officially record the creation and installation of what proved to be one of the last Communist monuments in Europe. In 1974 East German sculptor Ludwig Engelhardt received a commission to create a memorial spot for Marx and Engels in East Berlin that would have a sculpture of the two founders of Communism as its central focus, and in 1986 the Marx-Engels Forum was officially opened by the President and Communist Party Leader, Erich Honecker. (The statue is still standing, though the parliamentary building originally behind it, Erich Honecker and the German Democratic Republic are all long gone.)[14]

Sibylle Bergemann trained in the mid-1960s with the established photographer Arno Fischer, whom she married in 1985. For several decades Bergemann worked as a photojournalist and fashion photographer in the GDR, as well being hired for different types of Party work that included research trips abroad with her husband. In certain respects, then, she was a cultural worker above suspicion, specializing in a medium that was widely believed to be a minor, yet useful, art form. In general, the Party assumed that photography's 'immediacy and its unique ability to appear factual' made it the perfect 'didactic tool for imaging the utopian collective'.[15] In addition, Party leaders 'manipulated the medium's special relationship with "reality" in order to imprison individualism' and they 'surreptitiously used – and abused – the various definitions of photographic "truth" to build up their personal power'.[16] In short, Communist regimes like the GDR valued photography's reputation as hard evidence, making it the medium of preference for adding visual credibility to their various projects.

The Party's underestimation of the critical potential of photography also provided opportunities and recent commentators have been keen to identify Bergemann as a discreet dissident. Such a perspective informed her recent retrospective at the German Academy of the Arts, Berlin. The catalogue essay of Matthias Flügge, for example, associates her with the 'subjective "author" photography' that emerged in the GDR in the 1970s, and the photographs 'demonstrate her ability to penetrate far below the polished surfaces of an apparently controlled, pseudo-egalitarian society'.[17] For Flügge, her 'magnum opus' is the documentation of the Marx-Engels Forum: 'images which showed what the end would be, right at the beginning'; 'icons of futility'.[18] Appropriately, one of these 'icons' is used as the frontispiece for the catalogue – the photograph from 1984 of the half-built Marx-Engels monument, ambiguously tied down with ropes. The same image is also on the cover of the catalogue for the major exhibition *Art of Two Germanys: Cold War Cultures* (Los Angeles, 2009). The reason for this prominent position appears in a catalogue note by Jodi Kovach:

> Sibylle Bergemann's photographs reveal another insidious side of the GDR, through her use of the uncanny. In one picture of the installation of the Marx-Engels monument in Berlin, Engels appears to hang facedown from a noose. In another shot showing a construction sight in Gummlin, the figures look like human bodies cut cleanly in half. Without knowledge of the dates these photographs were taken, one could readily presume that they are documents of Communist monuments being dismantled. But more importantly, the division of identity that they suggest still resonates today.[19]

Flügge and Kovach both suggest that the Party was getting more than it bargained for when it hired Bergemann. What it wanted was neutral documentation, and what it got was a photographic record permeated with unofficial ideas and sentiments that would now be termed post-Communist.

Bergemann did production shots for Heiner Müller, another critic from within, who was tolerated by the East German authorities because of his international reputation as a poet and playwright who had supposedly inherited the mantle of one of the GDR's cultural heroes, Bertolt Brecht.[20]

Bergemann gave Müller a set of her photographs of the Marx-Engels project as a present, and one can assume that he would have instantly appreciated their sly dissidence. He had them lying around in his apartment for a few years and started to think about using them when Communist monuments throughout Central and Eastern Europe were being wrecked rather than erected.[21]

As Kovach notes, examining the photographs now, the viewer is drawn into a mental montage with post-1989 history as the activating element that unveils the pretensions of pre-1989 Communist ideology. Bergemann's new edit emphasizes this contrast. In general, the sequence proceeds chronologically from 1975 to 1986, but an obvious absence is a concluding image showing Honecker and associates officially unveiling the monument that had been a decade in the making. Instead, the only photograph showing the completed monument (Figure 2a) was taken in May 1990, between the opening of the Wall (November 1989) and formal reunification (October 1990). (The choice of month is obviously an ironic reference to May Day that was an important date in the calendar of the former regime.) Significantly, this photograph opens the new sequence and depicts casually dressed tourists clambering over Marx and Engels for a souvenir snap. That is, the once feared founders of Communism have been reduced to tourist *kitsch*. Her new choice of concluding image is equally significant – an installation shot from 1986 that Kovach refers to above, in which Engels appears to be noosed (Figure 2b).

The dust-jacket of the collaboration between Müller and Bergemann shows her now widely distributed photograph of the roped, half-built monument plus the title *A Spectre Is Leaving Europe* (Figure 1). Together, image and text convey a straightforward, ironic message, but the dust-jacket is not a premonition of what is to follow. On the contrary, Müller's poems and Bergemann's simply captioned photographs occupy their own space, an extreme instance of what Brecht would have called a 'separation of elements'.[22] What, then, are Müller's poems about? And how do they relate to the photographs? *An Explosion of a Memory* is the title of an earlier piece of writing that seems appropriate to describe poetry triggered by the events of 1989.[23] Take the opening poem:

> Light rain is on the light dust
> The willows of the inn-yard
> Will be growing greener and greener,
> But you, Sir, had better take wine ere your departure,
> For you will have no friends about you

When you come to the gates of Go.
(Rihaku/Ezra Pound)[24]

Müller translates into German a poem by Ezra Pound that Pound in turn had translated into English from the Chinese of the eighth-century court poet Rihaku, also known as Li Po or Li Bai. Müller clearly sees parallels between Pound's support for Italian Fascism and his own support for East German Communism, two examples of modern court poets supping with the devil and subsequently experiencing isolation and opprobrium. Müller's isolation is exacerbated by an awareness that disillusionment with Soviet-oriented Communism by no means involved endorsement of the Western alternative enthusiastically embraced by many of his fellow citizens in 1989:

On the tube I see my compatriots
With hands and feet vote against the truth
That forty years ago was my own
What grave will protect me from my youth?[25]

His 'explosion' intertwines the personal, the political and the literary. Most books involving photography and poetry have some kind of dialogue between the two media but this is not the case in *A Spectre Is Leaving Europe*. Here, words and appropriated images offer separate perspectives on the end of an era.

3

Another way of assessing *A Spectre Is Leaving Europe* is to compare it with an earlier photobook by Bertolt Brecht that used a different type of appropriated source material. Brecht's *Kriegsfibel* (War Primer) was originally published in East Berlin in 1955 and represents his most elaborate, practical engagement with photography (Figure 3).[26] The book is mainly a collection of photographs which Brecht clipped from newspapers and magazines during the Second World War and to which he added his own captions in the form of four-line verses. The book's appearance in the mid-1950s is significant. Of course, it deals with the recent war from which the German Democratic Republic drew its legitimacy as the 'better' Germany, anti-Fascist and pro-Soviet. And it is by Brecht, consolidating the reputation of the GDR as the rightful heir of the progressive culture of Weimar Germany. In addition, it confirms that at this point anyway, there was some tolerance of inventive work with photographs.

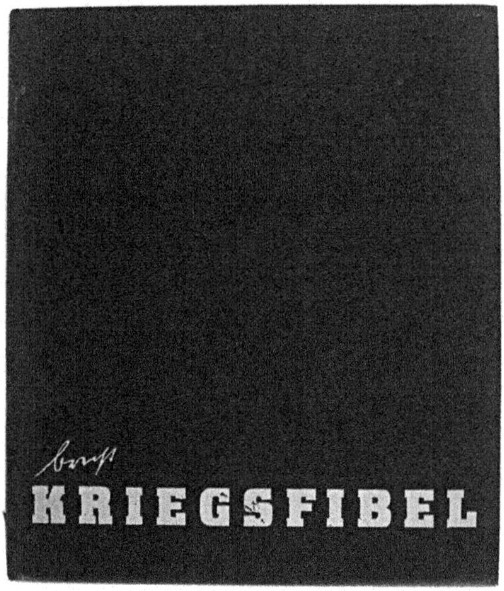

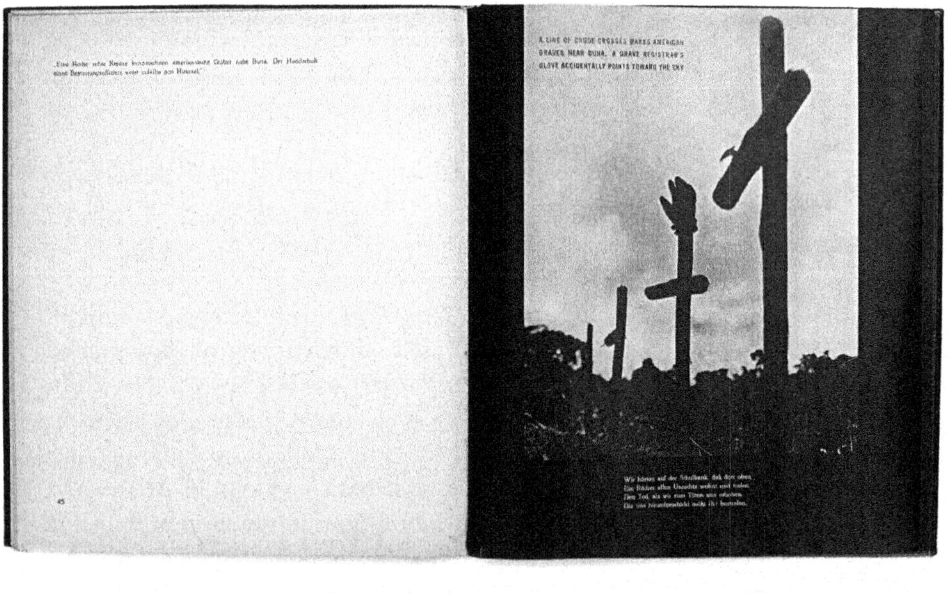

2. Bertolt Brecht, *Kriegsfibel* (Berlin, 1955).

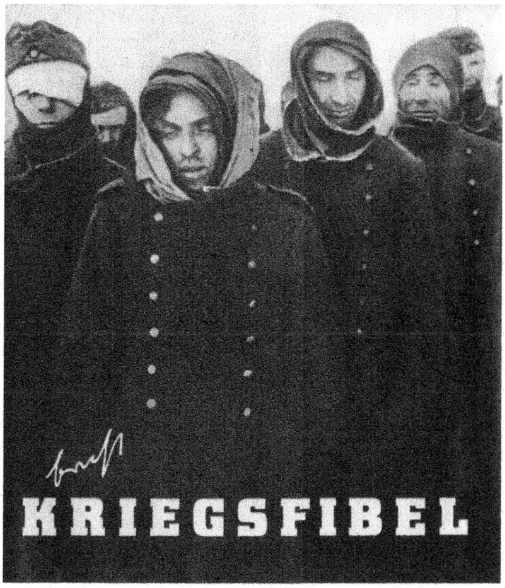

3. Original dust-jacket, Bertolt Brecht, *Kriegsfibel* (Berlin, 1955).

Indeed, Brecht's *War Primer* sits comfortably in any expansive history of appropriation art.

Primers are usually elementary textbooks for teaching children how to read, and *War Primer* is aimed at adults who wish to learn some fundamental lessons about modern warfare from a Marxist perspective. *War Primer* was edited by Ruth Berlau who also provided an introductory note that challenges the idea that the meaning of a press photograph is self-evident:

> The great ignorance concerning social relations, an ignorance nursed carefully and brutally by capitalism, reduces thousands of photos in illustrated journals to hieroglyphs which are undecipherable for the unsuspecting reader.[27]

War Primer was offered, therefore, as a practical manual with Brecht's epigrams demonstrating how to 'read' or 'translate' a press photograph. The implication is that press photographs can be a valuable source of knowledge and an aid to critical remembering, if they are correctly captioned.

War Primer was mainly put together in the Second World War when Brecht was in exile and deprived of a regular theatre audience. It can be plausibly described as the continuation of epic theatre by other means. Take the *gest.*[28] For Brecht, the term encompasses all of the elements – a style of acting, costume, lighting and props, for instance – that cumulatively draw out the social significance of an action, and epic theatre proceeds through an accumulation of *gests*. As a theatre director, Brecht was able to construct his *gests*, but as a 'photo-epigrammist' he had to make do with appropriated press photographs that had *gestic* potential. A good example is a 'photo-epigram' originally made in 1940 involving a photograph of Hitler amiably shaking hands with an elderly woman (Figure 4, right). Where Brecht found this image is unknown but it was widely distributed in Germany in the mid-1930s as a sticker to be collected and inserted in an album devoted to Adolf Hitler.[29] This particular sticker was destined for a chapter in the album called 'Der Führer and das deutsche Volk', written by Dr Otto Dietrich, Press Chief of the Third Reich, with the caption 'Am Tage der Saarrückgliederung' (Day of the return of the Saar) (Figure 4, left). In 1935 a plebiscite took place in the Saarland and a majority voted for the restoration to Germany of a region that

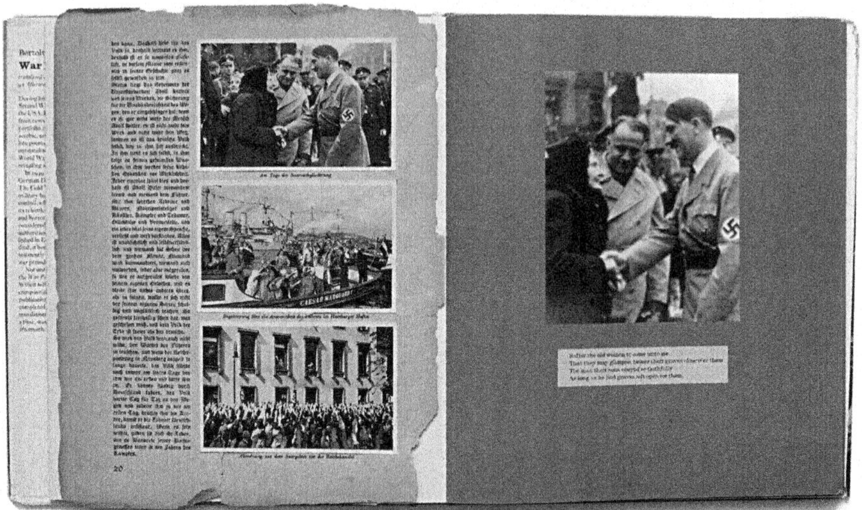

4. (left) 'Am Tage der Saarrückgliederung' (Day of the Return of the Saar), in *Adolf Hitler: Bilder aus dem Leben des Führers* (Altona-Bahrenfeld, 1936)

4. (right) This early 'photo-epigram', dated 15th October 1940, is not in the 1955 edition of *Kriegsfibel*, but appears in the English edition of Bertolt Brecht, *War Primer* (London, 1998)

had been administered by the League of Nations since 1919. For Hitler, the plebiscite was the first victory in an ongoing campaign to reverse the Treaty of Versailles, and in the photograph *Führer* and *Volk* savour the moment. Brecht's epigram reads:

> Suffer the old women to come unto me
> That they may glimpse, before their graves close o'er them
> The man their sons obeyed so faithfully
> As long as he had graves still waiting for them.[30]

Hitler's Messianic pretensions are conveyed in the opening line that rephrases the words of Jesus: 'Suffer the little children to come unto me' (Mark 10:14). Unlike Jesus, Hitler can only greet mothers because their sons are elsewhere, fighting and dying supposedly to liberate Germany. In 1940 Brecht reviews an image of triumph from the mid-1930s and notes premonitions of tragedy: Hitler is now the ersatz saviour whose swastika armband is a perversion of the Christian cross, the older woman's black clothes become mourning shrouds and the touch of the leader's hand is paltry consolation for the loss of a son. In short, the 'photo-epigram' reverses the original message.

The *fable* is another important dimension of epic theatre that informs *War Primer*. [31] Brecht's plays avoid the suspense associated with much conventional drama. Instead, the audience is given the pleasure of assessing a new treatment of familiar material. *War Primer* attempts something comparable. It is taken for granted that the meaning of the recent past, especially the Second World War and its aftermath, is fiercely contested, and it encourages reflection on rival interpretations. One *fable* associated with the Federal Republic of Germany emphasized the war as a victory of democracy over National Socialism. Yet the triumphant revival and extension of the freedoms associated with the Weimar Republic after 1945 were compromised as long as the misnamed German Democratic Republic was under the control of a Soviet regime as authoritarian in its own way as the Third Reich. And another *fable* came from the GDR. This version stressed the role of the Soviet Union in defeating National Socialism. The latter was not an aberration. Rather it was a dictatorial response to capitalism in crisis, and potentially a new Hitler could emerge in the FRG if another economic crisis developed. Such a scenario was only unimaginable in those states that had gone beyond capitalism: the Soviet Union and its allies. *War Primer* is a critique of the first *fable*, without being a straightforward endorsement of the second. Brecht's political sympathies are evident, but there are no glib answers. Rather, there are no winners and many losers in a *fable* that resists easy appropriation by either Germany.[32]

Umfunktionierung (functional transformation) is another key aspect of epic theatre that is found in *War Primer*. Within theatre, Brecht sought to overhaul an invention of the Ancient Greeks to create a relevant forum to 'expose the present'[33] and in *War Primer* he aimed to 're-function' the epigram, also invented by the Ancient Greeks. For them, the epigram was a form of lapidary verse – concise and dignified, and to be inscribed on stone monuments, especially for funerary purposes. Brecht uses his epigrams as alternative captions to photographs that he clipped from the illustrated press, mainly during the Second World War (Figure 4b). He called them 'photo-epigrams', a new hybrid that paradoxically linked a visual form associated with the ephemeral news media of the twentieth century and an ancient verse form intended to last for eternity. Indeed, if the choice of the epigram is meant to suggest ancient inscriptions, then the press photograph can be understood as equivalent to the ancient statue or building for which the epigram was originally intended. From this perspective, *War Primer* can be considered a series of portable monuments, flat memorials to the Second World War that are intended to aid critical remembrance.[34] Needless to say, Brecht's ideas about poor monuments never caught on, and the photographs of Bergemann show that the Party leadership continued to prefer monuments based on solid nineteenth-century precedents.

4

War Primer (1955) and *A Spectre Is Leaving Europe* (1990) frame the emergence and demise of the GDR and can be usefully compared. Consider the respective uses of photography. Brecht selects imagery found in what he would have termed the bourgeois or capitalist press and 're-functions' them to draw out different, revolutionary messages. There are obvious affinities with, say, Heartfield's photomontages of the 1930s that often involved 're-functioning' images from establishment picture agencies. But Brecht's 'photo-epigrams' should also be put in a wider frame that includes Eisenstein's films, Aby Warburg's *Bilderatlas* and the picture editing of Georges Bataille for the journal *Documents*.[35] Within this context, *War Primer* is perhaps the last great achievement of a montage culture focusing on the photograph as historical document that emerged in the 1920s and was especially powerful in Central and Eastern Europe in the interwar years. Bergemann's later appropriations take for granted the thorough institutionalization by the GDR establishment of interwar revolutionary montage, and she attempts something very different. That is, her own photographs are 're-functioned' to emphasize a subtle critique that her Party patrons overlooked. More importantly, their new appearance in 1990 has them stripped of the authority associated with pro-Soviet Communism and makes them analogous to the artefacts of the *Ancien Régime* and Church that became redefined as mere art objects in the early nineteenth century.

The poetry in each book is also very different. *War Primer* is informed by Brecht's model of an epic theatre with a 'collection of people with a desire to improve the world, listening to a report about the world'.[36] Müller rejects this model, especially from the 1970s onwards. Instead, he is drawn to a theatre that permits a flow of memories, fantasies and illusions, without the constraints of officially sanctioned, prescriptive blueprints, and a similar desire to resist interpretation permeates his poems for *A Spectre Is Leaving Europe*. These differences between the two poet-playwrights can be further clarified by examining their respective attitudes towards photography.

Berlau's description of the press photograph as a 'hieroglyph' in need of translation that precedes the first edition of *War Primer* re-echoes earlier remarks by Brecht. In 1930 he endorsed the Communist illustrated journal *A.I.Z.* (Heartfield's main platform in the 1930s) with the following statement:

> The tremendous development of photojournalism has contributed practically nothing to the revelation of the truth about the conditions of this world. On the contrary, photography, in the hands of the bourgeoisie, has become a terrible weapon *against* truth. The vast amount of picture material that is being disgorged daily by the press and that seems to have the character of truth serves in reality only to obscure the facts. The camera is just as capable of lying as is the typewriter. The task of the *A.I.Z.*, which is to restore the truth, is of paramount importance under these circumstances and it seems to me that it fulfills this purpose extremely well.[37]

In the above, he is juxtaposing true and false photographs. But in another well-known quotation from 1930 he suggests that the false image can be made true with appropriate editing:

> The situation has become so complicated because the simple 'reproduction of reality' says less than ever about that reality. A

> photograph of the Krupp works or the AEG reveals almost nothing about these institutions. Reality as such has slipped into the domain of the functional. The reification of human relations, the factory, for example, no longer discloses those relations. So there is indeed 'something to construct', something 'artificial', 'invented'. Hence, there is in fact a need for art. But the old concept of art, derived from experience, is obsolete.[38]

This statement has been interpreted in various ways, for instance, as an endorsement of photomontage, or the staged photograph, or seriality. In Brecht's case, however, the 'photo-epigram' can be considered his practical demonstration of how to make the mute photograph 'speak' the truth.

Müller refers to this quotation in an interview from 1981: 'Here realism doesn't work at all, only stylization works, because East Germany is not photographable – a variation of Brecht's remark that a photograph of the Krupp Works says nothing really about the Krupp Works'.[39]

Here, Müller's advocacy of 'stylization' seems close to Brecht's notion of the 'artificial' or 'invented' that is required to make naturalistic photography a critical medium. On other occasions, however, he simply rules out the possibility of photography being an aid to understanding the past:

> I don't believe photography is an instrument of memory. Language is memory and images are not. Images are too abstract. That's their danger: you blot out memory with these kinds of images. You don't remember the image, you remember your reaction to it. Memory is work, it's not something you can contemplate.[40]

Müller's scepticism about photography was obviously underpinned by his experience in an authoritarian regime that used the medium to record and encourage a bogus collectivist cultural heritage, as well as his awareness of how the complexity of collapse of the GDR became reduced to a small number of emblematic images circulated by news media around the world.

In *A Spectre Is Leaving Europe*, Müller wants to write about that which cannot be photographed, and Bergemann wants to draw out what was in her photographs all along but which her Party patrons failed to notice. Together, they offer complementary instances of what Groys has termed 'privatization of the communist myth'.[41]

Notes

1 Heiner Müller and Sibylle Bergemann, *Ein Gespenst verlässt Europa* (Cologne: Kiepenheuer & Witsch, 1990).
2 *Manifesto of the Communist Party*, in Karl Marx and Friedrich Engels, *Selected Works* (London: Lawrence and Wishart, 1968), p. 35.
3 Sven Lütticken, *Idols of the Market: Modern Iconoclasm and the Fundamentalist Spectacle* (Berlin and New York: Sternberg Press, 2009), p. 40.
4 Louis Aragon, 'The Challenge to Painting' (1930), in David Evans (ed.), *Appropriation* (London and Cambridge, MA: MIT, 2009), p. 28.
5 For a comprehensive assessment of this moment see Douglas Eklund, *The Pictures Generation, 1974–1984* (New York: The Metropolitan Museum of Art and New Haven, NY and London: Yale University Press, 2009).
6 The various terms are analysed in depth in Hillel Schwarz, *The Culture of the Copy: Striking Likenesses, Unreasonable Facsimiles* (New York: Zone Books, 1996).
7 Both works were included in the stimulating exhibition *Seconde Main* (Paris: Le Musée d'Art Moderne de la Ville de Paris, 2010).
8 Evans's *Appropriation* (2009) is deliberately expansive, and includes a section on post-Communism.
9 Alexei Monroe, *Interrogation Machine: Laibach and NSK* (Cambridge, MA: MIT, 2005).
10 Boris Groys, Max Hollein and Manuel Fontán del Junco (eds), *Total Enlightenment: Moscow Conceptual Art 1960–1990* (Ostfildern Ruit: Hatje Cantz, 2008).
11 Andrew Roth et al., *The Book of 101 Books: Seminal Photographic Books of the Twentieth Century* (New York: PPP Editions and Roth Horowitz LLC, 2001).
12 Roth (2001), pp. 86–7, 108–9 and 132–3.
13 The term is particularly associated with the East German dissident Rudolf Bahro. See: Rudolf Bahro, *The Alternative in Eastern Europe: A Contribution to the Critique of Actually Existing Socialism* (London: New Left Books, 1978).
14 Peter Voigt, 'Nachwort', in Müller and Bergemann (1990), n.p.
15 Karl Gernot Kuehn, *Caught: The Art of Photography in the German Democratic Republic* (Berkeley: University of California Press, 1997), p. ix.
16 Kuehn (1997), pp. ix–x.
17 Matthias Flügge, 'Sibylle Bergemann's Photographs', in Sibylle Bergemann, *Photographien* (Heidelberg, Edition Braus, 2006), p. 14–15.
18 Flügge (2006), p. 15.
19 JK (Jodi Kovach), in Stephanie Barron and Sabine Eckmann (eds), *Art of Two Gemanys: Cold War Cultures* (Los Angeles: Los Angeles County Museum of Art and New York: Abrams, 2009), p. 344.
20 See, for example, *New German Critique* 8 (Spring 1976), a special issue devoted to Brecht, Müller and their relations in theatre; and more recently, Jonathan Kalb, *The Theatre of Heiner Müller* (Cambridge: Cambridge University Press, 1998).
21 Conversation between Sibylle Bergemann and the author, Berlin, 1992.
22 In a note to accompany his opera *Aufstieg und Fall der Stadt Mahagonny*, Brecht considers the different emphases of dramatic and epic theatre. In the latter, 'the great struggle for supremacy between words, music and production ... can simply be by-passed by radically separating the elements'. Bertolt Brecht, 'The Modern Theatre

is the Epic Theatre' (1930), in John Willett (ed. and trans.), *Brecht on Theatre: The Development of an Aesthetic* (London: Methuen, 1978), p. 37. For a reassessment of this notion, see Fredric Jameson, *Brecht and Method* (London and New York: Verso, 1998), pp. 70–8 and 144–5.

23 Heiner Müller, *Explosion of a Memory: Writings*, ed. and trans. Carl Weber (New York: PAJ Publications, 1989).

24 Müller and Bergemann (1990), n.p. I am using here Pound's version in English.

25 'SELBSTKRITIK', in Müller and Bergemann. I cite the English translation by Carl Weber: 'SELFCRITIQUE', in Heiner Müller, *The Battle: Plays, Prose, Poems* (New York: PAJ Publications, 1989), p. 176.

26 Bertolt Brecht, *Kriegsfibel* (Berlin, 1955) (Figure 3). An English-language version finally appeared over 40 years later: Bertolt Brecht, *War Primer*, ed. and trans. with an afterword and notes by John Willett (London: Libris, 1998) (Figure 4).

27 Ruth Berlau in Brecht (1955), n.p, my translation.

28 For an overview of this notion, including problems of translation, see Jameson, *Brecht and Method*, pp. 99–105.

29 'Tage der Saarrückgliederung' (Day of the Return of the Saar), in *Adolf Hitler: Bilder aus dem Leben des Führers* (Altona-Bahrenfeld: Cigaretten-Bilderdienst, 1936), p. 20.

30 This early 'photo-epigram', dated 15 October 1940, is in Bertolt Brecht, *Journals 1934–1955*, trans. Hugh Rorrison, ed. John Willett (London: Methuen, 1993), p. 106. It is not included in the 1955 edition of *Kriegsfibel*, but appears in the English-language edition of 1998 as 'photo-epigram' 27. See note 26 above.

31 See the discussion in Bertolt Brecht, 'A Short Organum for the Theatre' (1949), in Willett (1978), pp. 200–2.

32 For further discussion on the two Germanys and their rival historical '*fables*' see Gerd Knischewski and Ulla Spittler, 'Memories of the Second World War and National Identity in Germany', in Martin Evans and Ken Lunn (eds), *War and Memory in the Twentieth century* (Oxford and New York: Berg, 1997), pp. 239–54.

33 Walter Benjamin, 'The Author as Producer', *Understanding Brecht*, ed. and trans. Stanley Mitchell (London: NLB, 1973), p. 100.

34 See David Evans, 'Brecht's *War Primer*: The "Photo-epigram" as Poor Monument', *Afterimage* 30:5 (2003), pp. 8–9.

35 This broader frame is emphasized in Georges Didi-Huberman, 'Bertolt Brecht *ABC de la guerre*, 1955', *Un Numéro de Choix*, *artpress Trimestriel* 5 (2007), included in *Appropriation* (2009) as 'Modest Masterpiece: Bertolt Brecht's *War Primer* (1955)', pp. 32–4.

36 Brecht (1993), p. 207.

37 In Heinz Willmann, *Geschichte der Arbeiter-Illustrierte Zeitung 1921–1938* (Berlin: Dietz Verlag, 1975), p. 125.

38 In Marc Silberman (ed. and trans.), *Bertolt Brecht on Film and Radio* (London: Methuen, 2000), pp. 164–5.

39 Heiner Müller, 'Intelligence without Experience: Interview with Harun Farocki' (1981), in Heiner Müller, *Germania* (New York: Semiotext(e), 1990), p. 161.

40 Sylvère Lotringer and Heiner Müller, 'Introduction' (1989), in Müller (1990), p. 79.

41 Boris Groys and John-Paul Stonard, 'Boris Groys in Conversation', *Immediations* 4 (2007), p. 137.

THE PHOTOBOOK AS OBJECT OF MEMORY AND NOSTALGIA: *ALEXANDRIE L'ÉGYPTIENNE* (1998) BY CARLOS FREIRE AND ROBERT SOLÉ

Colette Wilson

Alexandrie l'Égyptienne is a photobook depicting Egypt's second city by the Brazilian-born, Paris-based photographer Carlos Freire, with an introduction and accompanying image commentaries by Robert Solé, the Egyptian-born, Francophone writer and *Le Monde* editor.[1] The modestly produced softback published by Stock (part of the Hachette empire), measures 21 x 27.5 centimetres and its 94 photographs of the city, all in black and white and taken between 1992 and 1995, vary in size from double page bleed spreads to black-bordered one and a half page, full page, half and quarter page images interspersed with Solé's short texts. The book accompanied an exhibition held at the Petit Palais in Paris in 1998 and at the Centre de Coopération Culturelle et Linguistique in Alexandria and the Centre Français de Culture et de Coopération in Cairo in 1999, under the auspices of the French Embassy as part of the celebrations for L'Année France-Égypte (France-Egypt Year).

Born in Rio de Janeiro in 1945, Freire initially worked as a journalist before moving to Paris in 1968 and becoming a professional photographer. Despite having photographed a number of famous people including, to name but a few, Francis Bacon, Samuel Becket, the Dalai Lama, Lawrence Durrell, Michel Foucault, Doris Lessing, Henry Moore, Iris Murdoch and Rudolf Nureyev, Freire is hardly known in the UK, whereas in France he has enjoyed considerable success. His first major show was in 1977 at the Pompidou Centre alongside Robert Doisneau. Since the 1990s Freire has focused less on photographing famous people and more on creating portraits of cities and places, for example London, Lisbon, Rome, Naples, Mount Athos, Rio de Janeiro, New York, Aleppo, Morocco, Calcutta and Bali. In addition to his collaboration with Solé, several other writers have contributed introductions to Freire's exhibition catalogues including Lawrence Durrell (*L'Esprit des lieux*, 1986), the French surrealist poet and art historian Alain Jouffroy (*Tout doit disparaître*, 2000), the Syrian poet Adonis (*Alep*, 2004), and the French historian Marc Fumaroli (*Carnets de route*, 2005).

Freire's decision to focus on modern Alexandria, rather than, say, Cairo, or Egypt's ancient Pharaonic wonders, may seem a little surprising, for a British audience at least. For in spite of Britain's long occupation of Egypt (1882–1952) and her continuing links with the country, outside academic and literary circles, Alexandria's past reputation as a cosmopolitan city is not much discussed. Post-colonial approaches to the study of Egypt's history and its representation following Edward Said have tended to concentrate on the inequalities of the East-West encounter and on Egyptian nationalism and resistance to colonialism and as a consequence have tended 'to overlook the cosmopolitan narrative'.[2] In this chapter I would thus like to focus on Freire and Solé's *Alexandrie l'Égyptienne* as an example of nostalgic discourse for that cosmopolitan past within the context of Egypt in the 1990s.

Founded by Alexander the Great in 331 BC, reconquered successively by the Romans, Arabs, Mamelukes, Ottomans and Napoleon, and then refounded and modernized along European lines by Mohammed Ali in the first part of the nineteenth century, the golden age of cosmopolitan Alexandria began in 1850. The inauguration of the Suez Canal in 1869 formed the high point of French intervention in Egypt, while the British occupation from 1882 until the military coup and revolution of 1952 resulted in the abdication of King Farouk finally brought an end to the old order.[3] The subsequent 'Crisis' and nationalization of the Suez Canal in 1956 resulted in the expulsion from Egypt of all British and French nationals, as well as Jews, Greeks, Italians, Maltese, Christian Levantines and Armenians, many of whose families had been in Egypt for generations.

When President Anwar Sadat reopened Egypt's relations with the West in the 1970s, both French and British technological and cultural interests in the country flourished once again. And in the first decade of the twenty-first century Alexandria is set to attract the world's attention as the Egyptian government, in collaboration with French architects, plans to turn the city into a major tourist destination with the construction of a giant underwater museum showcasing the ruins of Cleopatra's palace and, in the process, revitalize the city as a whole. Freire's photographs thus capture the city on the cusp of change in the mid-1990s.

In his preface to *Alexandrie l'Égyptienne* Freire states that his aim was to focus on the effects of light in his photographs of modern-day Alexandria (p. 5). He also stresses that as a visitor to the city he specifically did not want to follow the well-worn path of previous writers and travellers.

Instead, by setting out very early each morning by way of the Corniche, the city's famous seafront promenade, during the course of a number of visits, he gradually came to know Alexandria and her welcoming inhabitants for himself and to take the measure of the dangers to which the city is exposed. These said 'dangers' remain unspecified, but it is perhaps logical to assume that Freire is referring to the seemingly unstoppable construction projects that are wiping out parts of the old city, with bulldozers even being employed at night to clear away the rubble, a fact mentioned later by Solé. Freire undertook two or three visits to the city on his own but Louis Adem, an ex-Alexandrian of Lebanese descent he met in France, accompanied him on seven separate occasions. As a fluent Arabic speaker, Adem was able to act as interpreter and help smooth the photographer's path through the city, a particularly important role given that Egypt is not the sort of country where a professional photographer can wander around taking photographs as he chooses and remain unchallenged. Adem also introduced Freire to Mohammed Awad, an Egyptian of Greek and Arabic origin and at that time a local government adviser on urban development, who arranged for Freire and Solé to meet the Governor of Alexandria. Awad is currently Director of the Alexandria and Mediterranean Research Centre at the Biblioteca Alexandrina and also founder of the Alexandria Preservation Trust, a charity campaigning with the British Council to save and restore the Villa Ambron, where Durrell stayed while in Alexandria. Awad's photograph appears in the book alongside that of the Villa Ambron (p. 26).

Solé was in many ways an obvious choice for writing the introduction to *Alexandrie l'Égyptienne*. By the late 1990s he had published a number of histories and three popular novels set in Egypt.[4] Born in Cairo in 1946 and a Roman Catholic of Syro-Lebanese descent, Solé spent idyllic summers with his family in Alexandria before leaving Egypt for Paris in 1964 in order to complete his education and pursue a career as a writer and journalist. His decision to leave for Paris coincided with the mass exodus of 'foreigners' after 1956. When approached by Freire to write the introduction to *Alexandrie l'Égyptienne*, Solé says he agreed on condition that he accompanied the photographer back to the city in order for them to explore it together. Much moved by Freire's images, Solé had to confront his own demons on his return to the city of his youth.

Those who are not familiar with the history of Alexandria and the socio-political context in Egypt in the 1990s and who cannot read Solé's French text are free to focus their attention just on the form and technical aspects of Freire's images, and thus construct their own reading of *Alexandrie l'Égyptienne*. Left to themselves, Freire's images, like all photographs, would be ambiguous and open to all sorts of interpretations. As Susan Sontag famously declared, 'strictly speaking, one never understands anything from a photograph', hence the perceived need for photobooks to be accompanied by written introductions, captions and commentaries. [5] For those who can read French, however, it proves difficult to isolate Freire's images from Solé's textual frames, which invariably guide the reader/viewer towards an interpretation of *Alexandrie l'Égyptienne* coloured by the writer's own point of view. Consequently, *Alexandrie l'Égyptienne* is as much Solé's book as it is Freire's. The aim of this chapter, therefore, is to explore the relationship between word and image, and between private and public memory in *Alexandrie l'Égyptienne*. While at first there would appear to be a tension between Freire's stated aesthetic aim and Solé's own engagement with the city, ultimately word and image are seen to work together to create a coherent narrative about the city's past, present and future.

In contrast to Freire's perspective as an outsider getting to know Alexandria in the 1990s, Solé's introduction to the book immediately reveals itself to be a very personal, passionate response to the city. He begins by declaring that he loved Alexandria beyond all measure (p. 7). His use of the past tense is typical of the writings of Alexandrian exiles.[6] This is not the city at the time of writing in the late 1990s, but his own remembered Alexandria that is being described; an Alexandria of the emotions and the senses, of private memories and nostalgia for a lost time. As Janelle Wilson suggests, there is a strong link between memory, nostalgia and identity: 'memory, the actual recall of the past, and nostalgia, the emotional component of remembering and longing, are instrumental in one's quest to know who one is'.[7] Wilson also argues that 'being nostalgic is similar to being in love: in particular, to the feeling state experienced after a love relationship ends. That which is presently unattainable is not only valuable, but idealized'.[8] One might add, however, that it is not uncommon for love to turn to hate when a relationship ends, and this is precisely what happened in Solé's case. His strong attachment to the Alexandria of his youth meant that for a long time after he left Egypt he turned his back completely on the realities of the present-day city. On the brief occasions when he did return to Alexandria, he hated nearly everything that he saw there, such as the grey, rampart-like concrete blocks that were springing up everywhere, replacing the summer vacation villas of his childhood. The city was choked with traffic and pollution and once peaceful villages bordering the sea were now part of the urban sprawl. He could no longer find his bearings and even the smell of the sea seemed to have disappeared. He hated Alexandria with as much passion as he had previously loved it.

For Solé, Alexandria had for a long time been 'une ville à l'imparfait' (a city in the imperfect tense) (p. 8). In other words, Alexandria existed both in the past and the present simultaneously. This cliché neatly sums up Solé's own personal relationship with the city at a particular time in his life and which will always be an integral part of who he is. As Svetlana Boym contends:

> At first glance, nostalgia is a longing for a place, but actually it is a yearning for a different time – the time of our childhood, the slower rhythms of our dreams. In a broader sense, nostalgia is rebellion against the modern idea of time, the time of history and progress. The nostalgic desires to obliterate history and turn it into private or collective mythology, to revisit time like space, refusing to surrender to the irreversibility of time that plagues the human condition.[9]

The 'city in the imperfect tense', however, also references the wider perception of cosmopolitan Alexandria as a much *written* about and much *read* about city. Solé talks of the existence of multiple Alexandrias created by writers as diverse as the Greek poet Cavafy, the Egyptian novelist Naguib Mahfouz and the Italian poet Giuseppe Ungaretti, as well as E.M. Forster and Lawrence Durrell.

Looking at Freire's photographs of Alexandria, however, suddenly brought the city into the present tense for Solé, even if he could not fail to detect a trace of the past running through them. As Maurice Halbwachs points out, there is a close relationship between memory (personal and collective) and the city:

> In the modern city itself we can rediscover the characteristics of the old city because our eyes and thoughts [actively] seek [these] out. Thus when, within a society which has transformed itself [over time], there still remain traces of what that society had once been, those people who had known [the city] in its original state are able to focus their attention on those ancient traces or traits which provide them with access to another time and place.[10]

There is also, of course, a close association between memory, nostalgia and photographs. Photographs are good at capturing the old, the changing and the new. As Sontag suggests, photographs 'actively promote nostalgia' and can act as *memento mori* but can also show movement and change.[11] Elizabeth Edwards also argues for the importance of the *materiality* of the photograph itself as a physical object and carrier of memory and how that materiality is

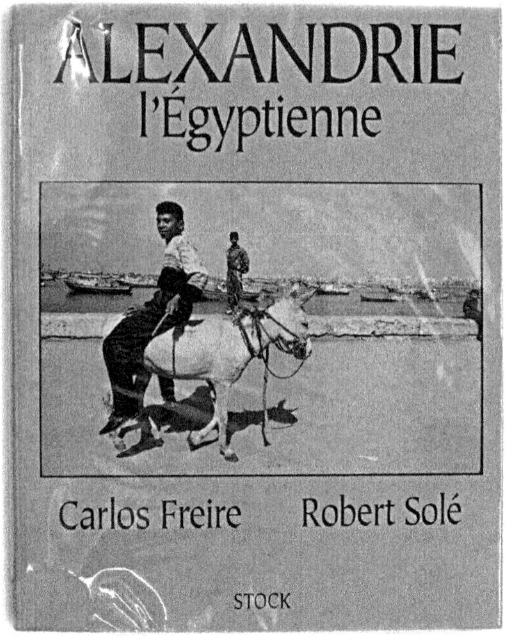

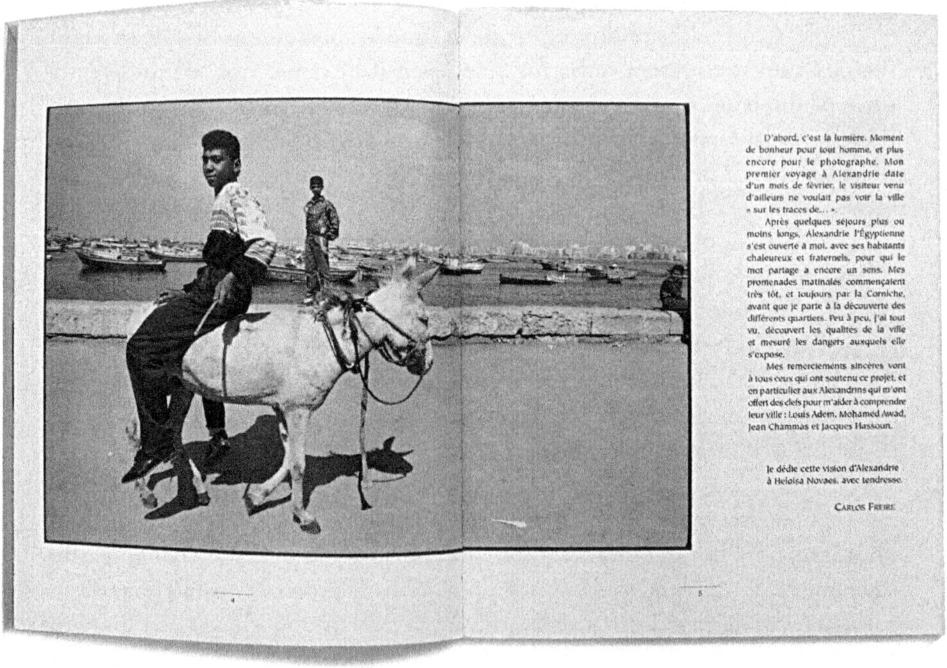

1. Carlos Freire and Robert Solé, *Alexandrie l'Égyptienne* (Paris, 1998).

'integral to its affective tone as an *image*' (her emphases).[12] The photograph as a material and cultural form of memory is central to 'the way in which people construct themselves and are constructed by others'; photographs have 'intrinsic and affective qualities which matter to people in terms of evocation, of making pasts'.[13] Once photographs are grouped together in a book, further dimensions come into play. There is the tactile quality of the book and the memories, sights, and even smells the photographs evoke,[14] as well as the 'journey' we as readers/viewers undertake as we wander at will from page to page, much as we would from street to street in the city itself, often subverting the pre-ordered 'itinerary' of the book's layout to suit our own interests.

Alexandrie l'Égyptienne cannot but function, therefore, as an object of memory and nostalgia for those who, like Solé, had a personal connection with the city in the past. Freire's photographs forced Solé to put his own emotions in order and the writer's return to the city, he says, satisfied his need to confront not time but physical space. This was not a pilgrimage into the past but an encounter with the flesh-and-blood city of today (in the 1990s) (p. 9). Or so he claims.

For Solé, the image of Alexandria that emerged during his visit with Freire was of an 'amnesiac city' that was slowly reconnecting with its past as well as regenerating itself (p. 11). Together, they met a wide range of people and in the process discovered a welcoming and seductive Mediterranean city which, according to one shopkeeper's wry observation, is of no interest to terrorists (p. 10). This is one of the rare oblique references to contemporary politics in the book and while Solé uses this reported comment to imply that Alexandria is now very much a backwater, the fact that terrorists are mentioned at all is telling in itself. Solé, however, points out that Alexandrians claim that there is nothing much to see because they do not realize the extent to which this mythical city continues to be the stuff of dreams for many people, or indeed how much the city would have to gain by opening itself up to the outside world, now that it no longer has anything to fear in terms of its own identity. This appeal for Alexandria to embrace the rest of the world, in other words be more like it was in the past, is a recurring theme for Solé and one to which we shall also return.

Among those photographed by Freire is a boy on a donkey with two other boys in the background. The image is privileged in that it appears both on the front cover and facing Feire's preface on page 5 (Figure 1). The boy sits, with adolescent perversity, on the donkey's rear, facing the wrong way. He stares at the lens (we can see his pupils) and there is a hint of a bemused, or perhaps even contemptuous smile about his face as he points the stick used to beat the poor emaciated animal directly at the intended Western viewer. The thin, dark shadow cast by the stick (a symbol of the boy's masculine dominance and power) cuts across the donkey's pale body. However, despite his apparent control over the donkey, and indeed the viewer, this young lad's position within the photograph, and no doubt in life, too, is thoroughly unstable. Perched as he is with his feet off the ground, he could topple over at any moment. Boy and donkey together, like Janus, represent the past and the present pulling in opposite directions: the boy in his Western clothes and smart shoes represents aspiration and the future (his own and his country's), while the donkey stubbornly pulls him back (or forward, depending on whether we read from left to right or vice versa) to the past. The image is certainly representative of an Egyptian Alexandria but the sense of unease it creates in the viewer is not typical of the rest of the photographs in the book.

More typical are the photographs taken in the streets and cafés around the city. We are presented with a cross-section of different ethnic groups: Fellahins, Bedouin Arabs and other nomadic tribesmen, middle-class Egyptians who may be of Syro-Lebanese or Greek origin, or Christian Copts, and a few old European Alexandrians. Freire is also fond of photographing people from the back on city trams and out in the streets. There are several head and shoulder shots which recall Rembrandt's turbaned oriental types, nineteenth-century anthropological illustrations, and Wilfred Thesiger's Arabians. There are a number of photographs of the many Fellahin *bowabs* (janitors), who are seen everywhere in the city, guarding even the most dilapidated of buildings. What all these photographs have in common is that the subjects are never named and sometimes not even referred to in Solé's accompanying texts. It is telling also that Freire never enters inside working-class living and working spaces. The subjects are thus in danger of being reduced to types. One is reminded of Susan Sontag's criticisms of August Sander's photographs of different social types: 'Laborers and derelicts are usually photographed in a setting (often outdoors) which locates them, which speaks for them – as if they could not be assumed to have the kinds of separate identities normally achieved in the middle and upper classes'. [15] Sontag identifies this form of photography as particularly 'European' (as typified by, amongst others, Henri Cartier-Bresson and Edward Steichen) as opposed to the American tradition, which she describes as grittier, partisan and confrontational.[16]

Tempting as it is to follow this line of argument, it is important to note in counterpoint that the so-called 'European' form of realist photography we find in Freire and which is now considered somewhat old-fashioned, is also practised by Yasser Alwan, an Iraqi who has lived in the USA and is now based in Cairo. His portraits of anonymous Egyptian working-class subjects from the late 1990s are similar to some of those by Freire.[17] This is not altogether surprising as there is an element of the typical in all portraiture; all faces to some extent bear the 'mask', as Roland Barthes would have it, of the particular society and history of which they are a product.[18] Alwan's aim, however, was specifically to photograph Egyptians at work while Freire's project with its emphasis on lighting effects and composition is more overtly aesthetic and more wide-ranging in scope with the inclusion of landscapes and dramatic panoramas. Nevertheless, both photographers do share the same poetic, humanist intent. In Freire's case, his attitude towards his subjects is, as Alain Jouffroy suggests, non-judgemental but at the same time neither neutral nor indifferent, thus achieving a delicate balance between sympathy and empathy.[19]

In contrast to the anonymous Fellahin, Bedouin Arabs and Berbers, Freire's *Alexandrie l'Égyptienne* also contains a number of portraits of well-known members of Alexandria's remaining cosmopolite intelligentsia, but interestingly there are no photographs of the Governor of the city or of any businessmen, financiers, local politicians or policemen – in other words, none of the Egyptians who are actually running the city. These sorts of people are clearly not part of Freire and Solé's circle. Thus in addition to the portrait of Mohammed Awad who, Solé informs us, studied at Victoria College, the renowned educational establishment modelled on the British public school system, and also in London,[20] we have photographs of the writers Edouard Al-Kharrat (p. 38) and Bernard de Zogheb (p. 64) and the controversial filmmakers Youssef Chahine (p. 33) and Asma El-Bakri (p. 70).

Al-Kharrat, a Christian Copt, was born in Alexandria in 1926 and is considered one of the most important writers in the Arab world today.[21] According to Solé, he is Alexandria's greatest poet (p. 39). At the time Solé was writing his commentary (1997) Al-Kharrat's latest novel, *Belles d'Alexandrie*, had just been translated into French. It was translated into English as *Girls of Alexandria* in 1993. An admirer of Cavafy whom he considers an 'authentic Egyptian', Al-Kharrat is critical of Durrell whose image of the city (in *The Alexandria Quartet*) is, he claims, 'tronqué' (truncated, incomplete).

The cineaste Youssef Chahine was also born in Alexandria in 1926. His father was a Lebanese Catholic, his mother a Greek Orthodox and his wife French. He studied at both of Alexandria's prestigious public schools, the English Victoria College and the French Collège Saint-Marc.[22]

Born in 1924, Bernard de Zogheb was the last descendant living in Alexandria of a Syro-Lebanese family who moved to Egypt following Napoleon's conquest in 1798, acquired titles, and became an important part of the social and cultural life of the city. Solé quotes him as saying: 'It's still the same city. I still take much pleasure in strolling along the Corniche. I look at the sea, which hasn't changed. I don't look at the other side.' (p. 64) This is a statement that, once again, highlights the nostalgic yearning for the city by those left behind and the tensions between their own and the city's past and present. Zogheb died in 1999, a few years after Freire photographed him, and Chahine died in July 2008. *Alexandrie l'Égyptienne* is, therefore, a memorial not just to the city but also to the fast disappearing cosmopolite generation.

Asma El-Bakri was born in Cairo in 1947 into an upper-bourgeois family. Her mother's family were Levantines who emigrated to Egypt at the beginning of the nineteenth century and her father's ancestors were the founders of the Sufi religious order. In Freire's double portrait of El-Bakri (p. 70), we see a strong, confident woman with unkempt greying hair, dressed in a thick sheepskin coat smiling at the camera and, provocatively for a woman in Arab society, sitting on her own in a café smoking a *shisha* (water pipe). We learn from Solé that while filming at Alexandria's Fort Qaitbay, El-Bakri discovered that the underwater ruins out in the bay would be irreparably damaged by the planned construction of a sea barrier. Thanks to her intervention the ruins were saved.

In keeping with the general 'life-cycle' sequencing of the photographs in *Alexandrie l'Égyptienne*, we find images of Jewish, Catholic and Greek Orthodox gravestones (p. 62) as well as a shot of a mausoleum belonging to the Suarès, a once-prominent Jewish family (p. 63). However, while there are external shots of the city's main mosque and a photograph of Muslim men at prayer, Muslim burial grounds and portraits of Muslim religious leaders are conspicuous by their absence.

Freire, however, did spend time in the company of Jo Harari, one of only 50 or so Jews left in Egypt at the time of his visit. Harari was responsible for the upkeep of one of Alexandria's main synagogues, Eliahou Hanabi, situated on the rue Nébi-Daniel, which, like all the other synagogues in Egypt, fell into disrepair in the 1960s. Two photographs of Harari appear in the book. The first (p. 66), small in format, shows him as a slight, frail, but still dapper old man, on the steps of the imposing entrance to the synagogue which bears the inscription 'Jewish Community. Grand Rabbinate' in both Hebrew and French. By his side is an Egyptian caretaker, who smiles broadly for the camera while gently supporting Harari by the arm. Harari also looks pleased but also a little surprised to be the object of Freire's lens. A woman, possibly Harari's wife, is seen in the background, between the two men. In his commentary, Solé recalls the great Jewish families of the past whose names are inscribed on the synagogue's pews. The facing page (p. 67) carries a full-page photograph of Harari, this time sitting at his office desk with another

Egyptian assistant standing beside him. This photograph is not so obviously posed as the first. The two men appear to be have been snapped while in animated discussion and the assistant's elevated hand, the desk and the objects on it in the foreground are slightly out of focus. Harari, in the centre of the shot, is the main focus and the viewer's eye is drawn particularly to the letter he brandishes above his desk, which is covered in photographs protected by a glass top. Behind Harari we see a number of framed photographs and religious texts. One of these, situated directly above his head, bears a Hebrew inscription. It is more prominent than the rest and sits alongside a large, wall-mounted, official portrait photograph of President Hosni Mubarak, which bears a corresponding Arabic inscription. That we should find Mubarak's portrait in a synagogue is by no means unusual. Egypt is a paternalistic society and the display of a photograph of the then current 'father of the nation' is *de rigueur* in all public buildings and institutions. Mubarak's arresting image on the wall and the small plastic mineral water bottle resting on Harari's cluttered desk are reminders that this is a recent photograph (Mubarak was president from 1981 to 2011) as everything else in this office, one imagines, has looked much the same for decades.

Another long-standing member of Alexandria's cosmopolitan community is Mademoiselle Anahide Meramedjian, an Armenian whose family came to Egypt in the 1860s and who has never learnt to speak Arabic. An octogenarian at the time of Freire's visit, Meramedjian is seen in a full-page photograph (p. 41) serving a fellow elderly cosmopolite woman in her French bookshop, Vient de paraître (literally 'just out' or 'just published'), which first opened in 1935 in a courtyard behind what is now a dilapidated block of bourgeois flats. Despite Britain's political influence on the country, French was Egypt's lingua franca prior to 1956 and Meramedjian's shop selling the latest French publications was an important focus for Alexandria's cultural life. Solé bemoans the loss of the 'brillante francophonie d'Alexandrie' (Alexandria's dazzling Francophone past) (p. 40). He tells us of the demise in 1994 of the Egyptian French-language newspaper *Le Journal d'Égypte*, which used to be published in Cairo and featured a regular editorial entitled 'Alexandrinades', recounting the comings and goings of the city's last cosmopolite survivors, and of *Le Progrès égyptien*, the last French-language daily which is no longer sold at Ramleh, the city's main tram station.

Three further shots of Meramedjian's bookshop are included. In the first of these, a half page image (p. 40), we see, among other curios and stacked books, an old poster portrait of King Farouk. The portrait sits incongruously alongside a half-hidden portrait of the French nineteenth-century female writer George Sand. Two other equally surreal shots show how the bookshop spills out on to the street (p. 42). In one of these, Farouk and Sand are now relegated to the background, and Mubarak's portrait sitting centrally in the foreground is again a reminder among the mouldering stacks of books and old magazines that we are in the 1990s.

On the page facing the photographs of Meramedjian's dusty and decaying outside display, there is a photograph of another bookshop frontage (p. 43). The signage, in Arabic and French, tells us that this is the Librairie des Amis des Lettres (The Friends of Literature Bookshop) and Solé's text informs us that the owner, Ibrahim, seen sitting outside his store, is a warm and friendly man who does not try to push his selection of books and magazines from all over the world. Solé suggests that many treasures surely lie among the three-metre-deep piles of books crammed inside the shop; but how might one ever find them? He also tells us that lovers of antiquarian and rare books will be horrified to learn that in November 1997 the University of Alexandria Library sold off some 10 million of their volumes at a knockdown price. There is a parallel to be drawn here with the selling-off of the city's architectural heritage to make way for the new.

If Solé takes some comfort in the fact that the French language still survives in the city's shop signs and that some streets still bear the old blue plaques with their names in both Arabic and French, Freire's Atget-inspired, surreal images of carefully arranged detritus, decaying walls and faded French shop signs are reminders by contrast of the inexorable march of time and that everywhere death haunts the old city. The title of another of Freire's photobooks, *Tout doit disparaître* (Everything must disappear [go]), is equally apt in relation to the images in *Alexandrie l'Égyptienne*, and leads us back again to Atget, who scrawled 'va disparaître' (will disappear) on the back of his photographs of condemned Parisian streets and buildings.

Further photographs recalling Atget's turn-of-the-twentieth-century Paris include a barber's shop called Salon Moderne, and a tailor's by the name of Manchester House, with a dummy in the window, a cardigan hanging on a pole outside the entrance, and signage that includes an overlarge pair of scissors (pp. 76–7). Between them, these two images recall Egypt's two old competing imperial powers. Britain is represented by Manchester, the chief cloth-manufacturing town of the nineteenth century, and France by the latest haircuts! The aspiration to quality and fashion stands in marked contrast to the shabbiness of the two buildings in which the shops are housed. Solé explains that the buildings are in such disrepair because they have not been maintained since rents were frozen in 1952 (p. 77). This was one of several measures put in place by the government to undermine the influence of 'foreign' property owners who were eventually forced to leave for economic if not for political reasons. All privately owned businesses were nationalized following the revolution. This included the city's two well-known department stores, Magasins Hannaux and Omar Effendi, both of which were originally founded by Jewish entrepreneurs.

Freire's close-angled shot of Omar Effendi (p. 20) emphasizes the apparently easy co-existence in the city of Muslim tradition and Western-style modernity. Western-style children's clothes are on display in the store window below a sign declaring 'Très Chic' alongside the Arabic translation. Two caricature European babies form part of the original signage while in the foreground below, at street level, five women are seen walking past the shop wearing their *hijabs* (headscarves). The young woman in the centre of the shot, however, is also wearing a Western-style knitted sweater emblazoned with a rabbit motif while a young girl aged about 10 and dressed completely in Western clothes stands at the shop entrance. In addition to department stores, the film industry, represented by a photograph of the historic Rio cinema (p. 34), was another European import.

Having discussed a selection of representative images and texts in *Alexandrie l'Égyptienne*, I would like to conclude by looking specifically at the last three photographs because between them I believe they sum up the social, political and memorialist issues raised by the book as a whole. The first of these is a full-page photograph of three generations of Fellahin women fruit and vegetable sellers (p. 91) (Figure 2a). Solé describes the timid young woman in the centre of the photograph as 'absolutely superb' and as the incarnation of Alexandrie l'Egyptienne – Egyptian Alexandria – and indeed of Egypt in general.[23] We should note that there is a play on words in the French title of the book, as *Alexandrie l'Égyptienne* can be translated as 'Alexandria, the Egyptian city' or as 'Alexandria, the Egyptian woman'. There is no disputing the fact of the young woman's beauty or that, as a working-class Fellah, she typifies her city and her country, but Solé's gallant compliment raises some uncomfortable issues. This timid young woman, who has her counterpart in countless similar nineteenth-century tourist postcards, represents a way of life that has hardly changed for thousands of years. She has little hope of ever breaking out of the cycle of poverty and lack of education that has condemned her and generations of her family to eking out a meagre living selling vegetables on the streets of a country that remains deeply divided between rich and poor. Furthermore, it is difficult to gauge whether Solé is being purposefully ironic when he points out that the slogan on the torn posters (coincidentally mounted beneath an Italianate sejant lion) on the wall behind the three women declares that 'Islam is the solution' (p. 90), given the notorious attacks by Islamist extremists that were taking place elsewhere in Egypt at the time the photograph was taken (p. 90). It is worth noting that between 1992 and 1997 more than 1,000 people were killed in these attacks, which unleashed a particularly violent and repressive backlash on behalf of the government.[24]

The image of the three women is followed by that of the statue of Saad Zaghloul, the anti-imperialist Fellahin prime minister of Egypt who stood up to the British in the 1920s and advocated an all-embracing form of Egyptian nationalism (pp. 92–3) (Figure 2b). Freire's photograph drastically reduces the monumental scale of the statue, made in Paris by the Egyptian sculptor Mahmoud Moukhtar, which is actually placed on an extremely high pedestal in the central square named after Zaghloul.[25] Spread over one and a half pages, the photograph is accompanied by a short text by Solé pointing out that Zaghloul wears the costume of a bygone age (frockcoat and fez) as he faces the open sea (p. 92). Solé adds that until the 1940s Alexandria was the gateway to Egypt but that nowadays one arrives by air, via Cairo. Alexandria, nevertheless, merits a detour.

The message to take away from this image and Solé's adjacent closing remarks is that Egypt in the 1990s has much to learn from Zaghloul's vision of an independent, progressive and forward-looking Egypt, free from imperialist intervention, puppet monarchs or undemocratic dictators, and that it would do well to model itself on Alexandria's past example as a successful multicultural, multi-ethnic and religiously diverse community. Such an interpretation acquires further resonance following the country's revolution in 2011. Nostalgia is usually associated with the past but it can also be a longing for a utopian state that was dreamed about and never really experienced.[26] Thus, silhouetted against the vast expanse of brooding evening sky, Zaghloul's statue has a powerful symbolic charge that exemplifies the utopian nostalgia that underpins the whole of *Alexandrie l'Égyptienne*.

As the companion piece to the double-page bleed photograph of the city at dawn which opens the book, Freire's stark, poetic image brings the metaphorical 'day in the life' of the city to a close. There is, however, a final image that merits our attention. This comes on an unnumbered page after the list of publications by Freire and Solé (p. 94) and could easily be overlooked. The half-page photograph depicts the upper part of a single palm tree, its fronds silhouetted against a pale, cloudless sky. At first sight one could read the image simply as a clichéd emblem of Egypt. The palm, however, is deeply symbolic. In the Christian tradition, the palms of Palm Sunday prefigure Christ's resurrection while in Assyrian art, the palm tree

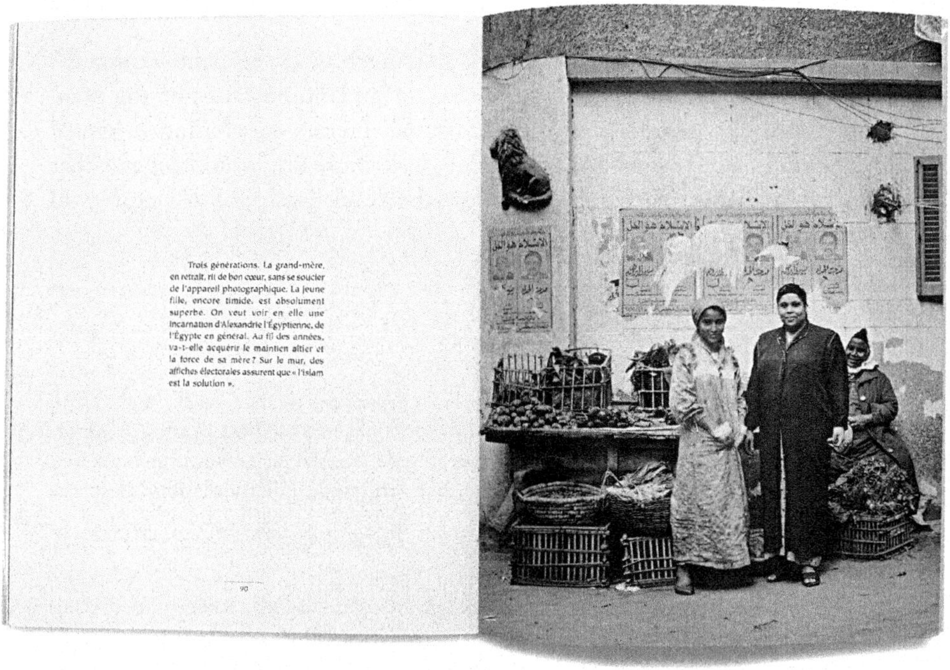

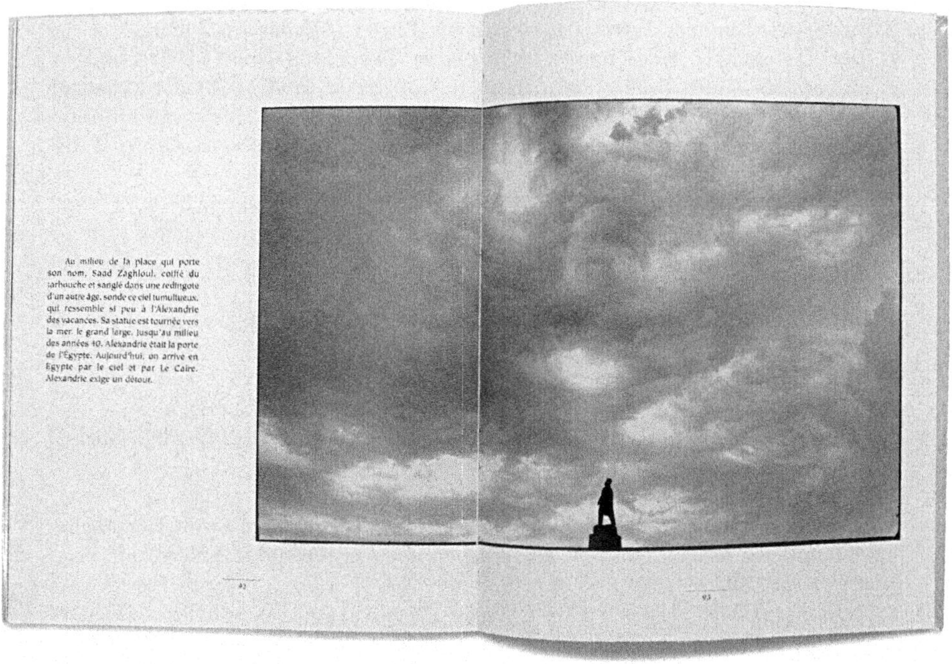

2. Carlos Freire and Robert Solé, *Alexandrie l'Égyptienne* (Paris, 1998).

symbolizes the Tree of Life. With its undying leaves, the palm represents everlasting life, fecundity and the ascension and immortality of the soul. Palm fronds also represent victory and fame. Freire's concluding image of an Egyptian palm tree is thus particularly well chosen. It would suggest that whatever challenges Alexandria may face, her soul lives on and victory will surely be hers.

Notes

1 Carlos Freire and Robert Solé, *Alexandrie l'Égyptienne* (Paris: Stock, 1998). All interpolated references are from this edition. I would like to thank Carlos Freire for granting his permission to include photographs of selected pages from the book and Louis Adem and Mohammed Awad for their assistance. All translations from the French are my own.

2 Deborah A. Starr, *Remembering Cosmopolitan Egypt: Culture, Society, and Empire* (London: Routledge, 2009), p. 9. See also, Robert Ilbert, *Alexandrie 1830–1930*, 2 vols (Cairo: Institut français d'archéologie orientale, 1996), Robert Ilbert, Ilios Yannakakis and Jacques Hassoun, *Alexandrie 1860–1960* (Paris: Autrement, 1992), and Michael Haag, *Alexandria: City of Memory* (New Haven, CT and London: Yale University Press, 2004).

3 See Sophie Pommier, *Égypte, l'envers du décor* (Paris: La Découverte, 2008).

4 See, for example, Solé's novels *Le Tarbouche* (Paris: Seuil Points, 1992), and *La Mamelouka* (Paris: Seuil, 1996), trans. respectively as *Birds of Paradise* (London: Harvill, 2000) and *The Photographer's Wife* (London: Harvill, 1999), and historical works *L'Égypte, passion française* (Paris, 1997), and *Les Savants de Bonaparte* (Paris: Seuil, 1998).

5 Susan Sontag, *On Photography* ([1977]; London: Penguin, 1986), pp. 23–4, 71.

6 See Veronica Della Dora, 'The Rhetoric of Nostalgia: Postcolonial Alexandria between Uncanny Memories and Global Geographies', *Cultural Geographies* 13 (2006), pp. 207–38 (p. 210).

7 Janelle L. Wilson, *Nostalgia: Sanctuary of Meaning* (Cranbury, NJ: Lewisburg Bucknell University Press, 2005), p. 35.

8 Wilson, p. 34.

9 Svetlana Boym, *The Future of Nostalgia* (New York: Basic Books, 2001), p. 56.

10 Maurice Halbwachs, *La Mémoire collective*, ed. Gérard Namer (Paris: Albin Michel, 1997), p. 188.

11 Sontag, p. 15.

12 Elizabeth Edwards, 'Photographs as Objects of Memory', in Marius Kwint, Christopher Breward and Jeremy Aynsley (eds), *Material Memories* (Oxford and New York: Berg, 1999), p. 223.

13 Edwards, p. 225.

14 See Serge Tisseron, *Le Mystère de la chambre claire: photographie et inconscient* (Paris: Flammarion, 1996), p. 138.

15 Sontag, p. 61.

16 Sontag, pp. 41–2, 63.

17 Yasser Alwan, *The Liberty of Appearing: Photographs of Egyptian Working People* (Portsmouth: Peacock Imprint, 2008).
18 Roland Barthes, *La Chambre claire: note sur la photographie* (Paris: Seuil, 1980), pp. 61–3. See also Ernst Van Alphen, *Art in Mind: How Contemporary Images Shape Thought* (Chicago: University of Chicago Press, 2005), pp. 21–47.
19 Alain Jouffroy in Carlos Freire, *Tout doit disparaître* (Paris: Hazan, 2000), p. 4.
20 Victoria College, founded in 1902, counts among its alumni King Hussein of Jordan, Omar Sharif and Edward Said, who gives his personal, bitter account of his experience as a pupil there in *Reflections on Exile and Other Literary and Cultural Essays* (London: Granta, 2001), pp. 271–2.
21 On Al-Kharrat see Starr, chapter 3. On the discrimination against Copts within Egyptian society see Pommier, pp. 130–1.
22 The Collège Saint-Marc, founded by the religious order Les Frères des Écoles chrétiennes in 1927, was inaugurated in 1928 by King Fouad I. Dodi Al-Fayed was a noted alumnus. On Chahine see Starr, chapter 5.
23 See Della Dora, p. 210.
24 Pommier, p. 72.
25 There is a similar statue of Zaghloul in Cairo.
26 Wilson, p. 37, drawing on Elihu. S. Howland.

THE EYE OF THE LENS AND THE FEET OF THE PHOTOGRAPHER: EDUARDO GAGEIRO'S *LISBOA NO CAIS DA MEMÓRIA* (2003)

Paul Melo e Castro

In 2003, Eduardo Gageiro, one of Portugal's foremost photojournalists, published *Lisboa no Cais da Memória 1957–1974* (Figure 1).[1] This work is an anthology of photographs taken in the period indicated and arranged so as to provide an encompassing picture of Portugal's capital in the latter half of the *Estado Novo* dictatorship.[2] The photobook, composed exclusively of monochrome images, comprises loose thematic chapters, each prefaced by a poem, or an extract from a poem, by well-known Portuguese writers that sets the tone for the images that follow. The chapters include one providing a geographical cross-section of the city (ranging from the traditional neighbourhoods to the new post-war suburbs), one focusing on the children of Lisbon, chapters concerning the working day of the city and working-class life in the streets, and chapters covering crucial public events of the period. There are times when the tone of these images is humorous, others when it strikes a nostalgic note, but in the photobook as a whole what we find are 'aspects of a city submitted to half a century of dictatorship, that underwent repression and lagged behind the other capitals of Europe'.[3] In all of these chapters, but especially the ones that represent the current affairs of the period, the focus shifts back and forth between the street photographic and the photojournalistic, or what Clive Scott describes as the 'indefinite article' of street photography, focusing on the artistic use of the randomness of urban life, and the 'definite article' of photojournalism, more interested in the identity and exact actions of those depicted.[4]

As a photographer crisscrossing the city in this period, and focusing on the ordinary people of Lisbon and current affairs as they impacted on their lives, Gageiro's work and practice can be seen as intimately bound up with the question of the everyday. In this chapter I mobilize some of the critical

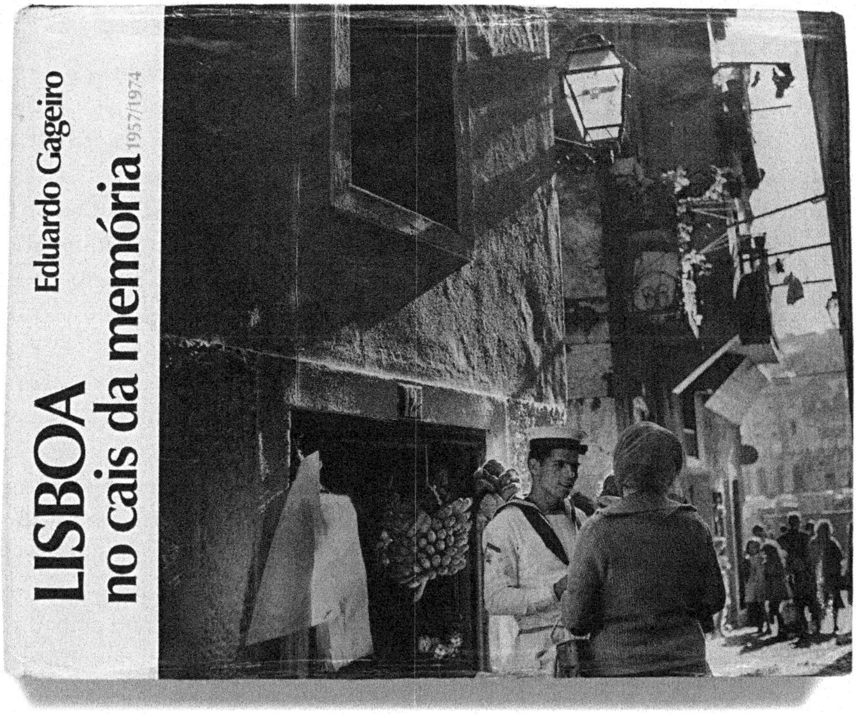

1. Eduardo Gageiro, *Lisboa no Cais da Memória 1957–1974* (Lisbon, 2003).

concepts outlined by Michel de Certeau in his work *The Practice of Everyday Life* in order to think through two aspects of Gageiro's work.[5] Firstly: the capture of the images contained in Gageiro's book, which took place within an everyday dominated by an authoritarian government that fostered a reductive and repressive vision of the city and the country. Secondly: the construction of the photobook as a representation of Lisbon 1957–74, one made by and for a form of walking, and which signifies in the same way as an urban trajectory constructed by this practice.

What I am attempting here is not an application but a metaphorization of certain aspects of Certeau's thought.[6] Following on from John Roberts's assertion that there exist 'anthropological links between photography and flâneuring' and that the indexical status of the photographic image makes it 'a record of visual experience',[7] we can understand photobooks dealing explicitly with the life of a city, such as *No Cais da Memória*, as the collated traces of various pedestrian trajectories through the city of Lisbon in the latter period of the Salazar dictatorship. If the sort of photographic activity recorded takes place in parallel with everyday practice, then Certeau's ideas on the constraints and significations of moving through the city can illuminate both street-based photography and the photobook explicitly conceived as a representation of a viewpoint traversing urban space. Certeau's ideas are intimately concerned with how we consume creatively, within structures and situations we do not create. Photography on the streets and the reading of a photobook of the city take place in a space created by others: Certeau's ideas can therefore be seen as relevant not just to the production of a photobook of the city, but also to its perusal.

To examine the field surrounding the capture of the images in Gageiro's photobook, I draw on Certeau's notions of the voyeur and the pedestrian, and more importantly the strategy and the tactic. For Certeau, the voyeur is the position taken by the centre of power. The pedestrian is an example of an individual negotiating the constraints of this power, not necessarily contesting it yet attempting to exercise a modicum of freedom within a situation beyond his or her control. If the sort of humanist street photography of the type we find in *No Cais da Memória* depends on proximity, ordinariness and empathy, then the act of image-making can be seen to place the photographer on the side of the pedestrian, rather than drawing him into the position of the voyeur. This taking of sides can be seen, for example, in the images concerning the 10 June commemorations of 1966, the height of the colonial war. One image, on page 277 of *No Cais da Memória*, shows in the background a line of almost anonymous individuals in suits and uniforms (although on closer inspection the faces of Prime Minister Salazar and President Thomaz are distinguishable). These shadowy figures are the people who control the nation and have made the abstract decision to send a country's youth to war in order to prevent the self-determination of Portugal's colonial possessions. In the foreground we see the people of Lisbon whom their decisions affect. Two ordinary soldiers with medals pinned to their chests stand stiffly. They appear to be aware that a camera is trained upon them and seem to be studiously trying to ignore it and to contain their emotions. Next to them, two women, one young, one old, dressed in mourning, weep and comfort each other. One can presume that their husband and son, like thousands of other victims of the conflict, have not made it home.

Voyeurism, on Certeau's terms, surveys ordinary people from above and occurs unilaterally in the silence of abstraction. If, as Roberts argues, photographic realism allows subjects to speak back from the concrete space of the everyday, to give an account of themselves, then such photography has a dialogic element that establishes a human-level connection, and therefore opposes, on Certalian terms, the silencing, controlling impulse of voyeurism. The image of the two women weeping, for instance, displays the human misery of war that the government tried to play down in favour of the pomp and ceremony of patriotism.

For Certeau, the operations of the voyeur take the form of strategies, whilst the 'creativity of groups or individuals already caught in the nets of "discipline" (p. xxii), of those marginalised or opposed by power' (p. xxii) take the shape of tactics. On Certeau's terms tactics and strategies are two entirely different orders of behaviour. Certeau describes strategies as 'the calculation or manipulation of power relationships that becomes possible as soon as a subject with will and power [he gives the examples of a business, an army, a city or a government] can be isolated. It postulates a *place* that can be delimited as its *own* and serve as a base from which relations with an exteriority composed of targets and threats can be managed' (p. 36). Strategies, amongst other embodiments, are the rational, economic, political and ideological frameworks imposed by bodies such as the state in order to police the meanings and manoeuvres possible in a place, such as to render it what Certeau terms a 'proper' (p. 40). These exist in different embodiments everywhere, but can be seen as having particular relevance for a photographer operating within an authoritarian regime that not only repressed the country through censorship and a secret police force, but also an ideological framework which manipulated certain popular forms of entertainment, music and religion to create a certain normative image of the country. Again, the photograph taken on 10 June 1966 serves as an example of how the ideological strategy of the dictatorship could be counteracted by the tactic of the photographer, even though the state had the power to see that the photograph in question would not at that time see the light of day.

What is argued here is that it is within 'the proper' of a subject with will and power – the networks of the regime dominating Portugal – that Gageiro as a photographer on the street creates images that express a freedom of consumption in a variety of ways. We can argue that street photography is always tactical, always 'in the swim of things' and always taking place in the space of strategies, though, of course, one of its favourite topics is the tactics of others.[8] The street photographer is not one of Certeau's *wandersmänner*, though passers-by are often the focus of his attention.

There are two places where my use of the concepts of the tactic and the strategy might be problematic. Now, for Certeau, a strategy is a 'mastery of a place through sight ..., a panoptic practice ... whence the eye can transform foreign forces into objects that can be observed and measured and thus control and include them within its field of vision', whilst tactics are described as 'blind' (p. 36). However, for Certeau the difference between sight and blindness is one of distance and instantaneousness. Perhaps proxemic street photography can be thought of as 'blind' in Certalian terms in that the product of the act of street photography is invisible at the moment of decision-making. Taking place in the split second, it is a way of experiencing a scene, not yet a way of examining it. This latency is particularly clear in the sequences dealing with some of the most politically charged incidents of this period shown in *No Cais da Memória*: pro-democracy demonstrations that were broken up by the police (such as we see on pp. 280–5), student protests that occupied university campuses (pp. 288–92), popular resentment spilling out at sports events (pp. 255–6). The full import of these situations can only be determined, or constructed, in retrospect, through such historiography as that performed by Gageiro in *No Cais de Memória*.

Another possible sticking point is that Certeau sees everyday practices as their own ephemeral product, a status that varies greatly from the archive the photographer can constitute. However, having said this, Certeau holds cooking and reading as everyday products, both of which yield, or can yield, a product for consumption that is not as momentarily transient as the word 'ephemeral' suggests. Cooking after all yields recipes and reading builds insights, and both activities can be used by the individual to build cultural capital. Nonetheless, we cannot take street photography and photojournalism as just other examples of an everyday practice. What we can do is see them as working in a similar fashion. What I want to argue, then, is that Gageiro's street photography and photojournalism constitute tactics taking place, like everyday practices, in the space of social strategies.

How can the format of the tactic be seen in the practice of street photography and photojournalism? For Certeau, the tactic is 'a calculated action determined by the absence of a proper locus' that takes place in 'the space of the other' (p. 37), a space conditioned, but never totally controlled, by strategies. The street photographic and the photojournalistic are tactics in so far as they 'result from combat at close quarters, limited by the possibilities of the moment' (p. 38). Certeau writes:

> [t]he place of the tactic belongs to the other. A tactic insinuates itself into the other's place, fragmentarily, without taking it over in its entirety ... it has at its disposal no base where it can capitalise on its advantages, prepare its expansions, and secure independence with respect to circumstances ... . [B]ecause a tactic does not have a place it is always on the watch for opportunities that must be seized 'on the wing'. The weak must continually turn to their own ends forces

> alien to them. This is achieved in the propitious moment when they are liable to combine heterogeneous elements .... [T]he intellectual synthesis of these given elements takes the form, however, not of a discourse, but of the decision itself, the act and the manner in which it is seized. (p. xix)

It is in this way that the tactic can be seen as the modus operandi of the photographer in the midst of larger strategies in which he and the people he takes as his subjects are enmeshed. 'The Decisive Moment' was of course the English-language title of Cartier-Bresson's book *Images à la sauvette*.[9] Certain photographs, which 'depend upon the possibilities offered by circumstances' (p. xix), or the transient conjunction of autonomous forces in an uncontrolled setting, must be taken 'on the wing' (p. xix), that is, tactically. The decisive moments these photographs represent are, as tactics, the intellectual synthesis of heterogeneous elements, split-second choices made within the space-time of ordinary life in the streets. Certeau writes: 'a tactic boldly juxtaposes diverse elements in order suddenly to produce a flash shedding a different light on the language of place and to strike the hearer', it makes 'a clever use of time', it is 'a hunter's trick' (p. 39). In this description of a practice that composes a disparate range of elements with an illuminating flash, avails itself of time and achieves its aims through stealth and stalking, the practice of the pedestrian can, I argue, be seen as the perfect metaphor for the street photographer's capacity to catch a decisive moment. Commentators on Certeau's ideas, such as Highmore and Buchanan, pointed out that no binary division between strategies and tactics can be made. One can shade into the other. In a similar way, the photographs that have been captured tactically in the street can find a strategic use within the bounds of a photobook, that is to say, to be used to construct a 'place' under the autocratic (or authorial) control of the compiler. In turn, of course, the photobook is liable to a tactical approach on the part of the reader in the same way that the pedestrian or the photographer approaches urban space. The photobook is as open to use as the streets of the city.

I would like to look at two examples of an attempt on the part of the state to control the city and to impose meaning, and how Gageiro's work subverts this strategic manoeuvring. The first example concerns the representation of a protest march in favour of democracy that took place in Lisbon on 5 October 1960. The first image in the sequence representing the evolution of the march on pages 280–5 (Figure 2a, verso) shows a group of protesters amassed before Lisbon town hall. There are two national flags. One is in the shade, hanging from the side of the building above the crowd; the other is

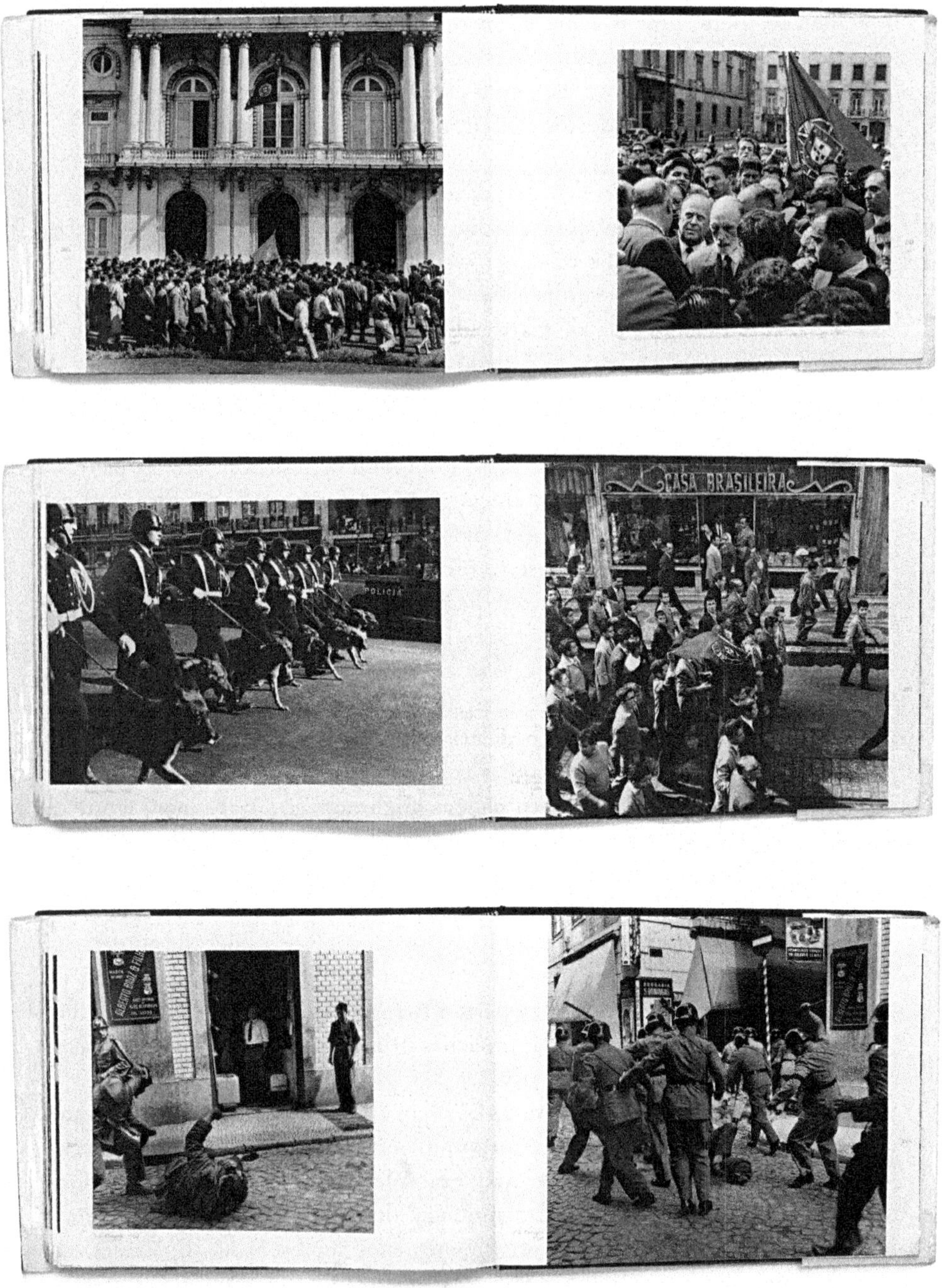

2. Eduardo Gageiro, *Lisboa no Cais da Memória 1957–1974* (Lisbon, 2003).

illuminated by the sun, held aloft by one of the protesters. The image makes use of the momentary alignment of the two flags to symbolize the clash of the two sections of the country: the repressive, voyeuristic state attempting to impose control from above, and the section of the public agitating in the street for freedom. The point of view here is also from pedestrian level. In almost cinematographic style, the next photograph (Figure 2a, recto) cuts in closer in order to identify the key protagonists taking part in the march. It takes advantage of the triangular arrangement of faces in the midst of the sea of people to pinpoint the best-known figures.

The linkage established between the following shots shows the manner in which the photographer can, in a sense, carry his tactical behaviour from the street into the archive. The following image, in the next double-page spread, dates not from 1960, but from 1966 (Figure 2b, verso). It depicts what appears to be a police parade through central Lisbon. In a strong diagonal line stretching from the bottom left upwards and inwards, a row of uniformed officers march with their police dogs walking along in front of them. The effect is intimidating, not least because, due to the harsh sunlight, the policemen's eyes are invisible in the shadows beneath the brims of their helmets. At the far end, hemmed in between a police vehicle and a prohibitive police sign, stand the public, looking on.

The next photograph, on the facing page (Figure 2b, recto) shows the protest in full flow. A couple of the figures towards the back of the group look back nervously over their shoulders. In contrast to the serried rank of policemen in the previous image, the protesters form a loose phalanx. One of the figures holds aloft a flag, illuminated as in the first image. The juxtaposition of these two images on opposite pages creates the effect that the stragglers are glancing back at the policemen on the previous page. There follows an image that shows how the hope embodied in the march was crushed, and provides a synthesis of the two previous images with their separate depictions of the police and the marchers (Figure 2c, verso). In the centre of the composition, a policeman swoops down on one of the protesters, caught at the moment where, instead of the banner of hope the marchers bear aloft on the preceding page, he holds a truncheon. The image is blurred, suggesting the tumult of state violence inflicted upon a peaceful protester. The contrast between the aggressive posture of the policeman and the supine protester figures in almost diagrammatic terms the relationship between state and population enacted in this incident. In the background, a group of bystanders watch on impotently. While the events of the protest might transform the lives of those protesting, for those looking on what they witness is part of an ongoing process of repression. Are they figures for the impotence of the photographer? Yes and no. By catching these images on the fly, the photographer has managed tactically to preserve the protesters' indictment of conditions that this state violence was supposed to silence.

The second example is the sequence documenting the burial of Salazar in 1970. The first images show the pomp and ceremony surrounding the event: the casket is borne aloft, mourners stand with eyes downcast, a procession files through the streets of Lisbon. State propaganda under the *Estado Novo* had encouraged the portrayal of Salazar as the father of the nation. In the final image in the series, Gageiro captures an image that undoes the rhetoric of state manipulation of the event and we see a damning metaphor for the damaging effect of Salazar's rule. Rather than concentrating on Salazar's lying in state, the photographer's gaze is displaced onto a boy limping past on crutches, composing the scene so that the mourners surrounding the casket are moved to the background. Even within special, even elite events, Gageiro's eye searches out the ordinary and the superficially unremarkable, the join between the historic and the historical. This image suggests metaphorically that Salazar's death has not so much left the Portuguese people orphaned, rather his life has left the Portuguese crippled, and struggling on into the future.

Here I move from the capture of the images in the city to the organization of the photographs to form a sort of virtual street or, in the case of the photobook, a virtual city. It is my argument that the photographs that compose *No Cais da Memória*, taken by a pedestrian moving through the city, are concatenated to create the possibility of a virtual trajectory through the time-space of Lisbon 1959–74. There is some slippage at this point in that here I am analysing the product of an action rather than the action itself. Nonetheless I see the sort of photographs I have been discussing as instances of a decisive act, as an act in themselves, albeit ones that live on as products of the decision that constitutes them. Certeau writes that '[t]he act of walking is to the urban system what the speech act is to language or to the statement uttered' (p. 97). Can we then say that the act of street photography is to urban life what the act of recording a speech act is to language? In any case, here I am going to use the way in which Certeau sees walking through the city functioning as a signifying practice as a way to examine how Gageiro's photographs can be seen to convey their meaning to a reader walking through the pages of his virtual city (the photobook), actualizing the potential of the space created through Gageiro's own acts of tactical pedestrian creativity.

I shall return here for a moment to the 'tempting analogy' that walking through the city is similar in procedure to a speech act.[10] Like a speech act, 'it establishes a *present* relative to a time and place, and it posits a contract with the other (the interlocutor) in a network of places and relations' (p. xiii). Drawing on French work on urban semantics, Certeau posits the idea that a walk tells a story, and does so through linguistic structures. I argue that the photobook sets up a space-time to be traversed, and that the elements perused in this traversal will tell a tale in similar manner. Certeau's ideas are interesting as they allow us to approach something that is not linguistic, yet which possesses properties of language and which, for sure, tells us something. Parallels between text and city, reading and walking are common, but Certeau's ideas allow us to see linguistic structures in acts which communicate without an apparent language.

For Certeau a pedestrian trajectory is a sequence of rhetorical forms possessing 'metaphorical drifts, elliptical condensations, metonymic miniaturizations' (p. 39). The pedestrian trajectory, for Certeau, signifies by a process of juxtaposing the disparate, cropping out the extraneous and enlarging the relevant, all eminently photographic actions. This spatial phrasing via elimination and connection is, I propose, a working definition of a photobook that, like *No Cais da Memória,* purports to represent a certain space and time.

Through the pedestrian trajectory of *No Cais da Memória*, a composite picture is constructed in which a multitude of times, places, situations and emotions co-exist, creating a powerful indication of the situation of the city of Lisbon in the second half of the Salazar dictatorship. There are images dealing with some of the most pernicious aspects of the time, pluralizing them and undercutting the univocal interpretation promulgated by the regime. There are images of hardship and poverty, which, although they did not prevent times of happiness as some of the more positive images show, certainly did not enable them. One image on page 176, taken in 1965, shows Cardinal Cerejeira, the patriarch of Lisbon and a long-time acquaintance and political ally of Salazar on a visit to a kitchen, presumably as part of some sort of official engagement. Two female cooks greet him, one with an exaggerated bow of welcome. The Cardinal is all smiles. The next image, on page 177, overturns this rosy picture. It shows two dirty, obviously impoverished people eating a meagre dinner on a street corner. Blurred in the foreground, a stray dog turns to look on hungrily. This juxtaposition serves to throw into relief the distance between both the gulf between the haves and the have-nots and the distance separating the reality of the times from the picture painted by the government. Other images show two of the central social facts of the period: emigration, and the colonial war. Between pages 269 and 271, there is a series of images of Portuguese 'voting with their feet', in a departure that was not just a new start but also an irreparable loss of home. One image on page

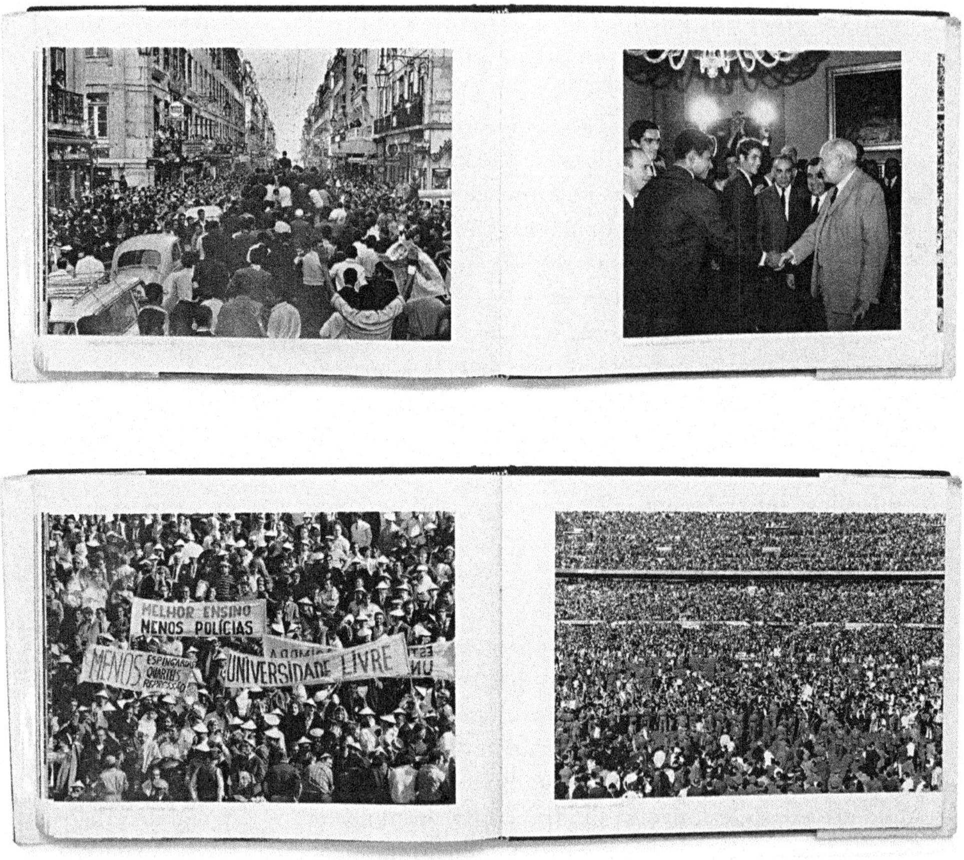

3. Eduardo Gageiro, *Lisboa no Cais da Memória 1957–1974* (Lisbon, 2003).

270 shows a family group waiting to take the train to France or Germany. There are two children present: an infant, who stares at the camera over her mother's shoulder, and an older girl, who looks uncertainly to the right, as if towards the unknown future. The following sequence of images, between pages 272 and 275, shows one of the main impetuses behind emigration: conscription to fight in the colonial war. These are not images depicting the send-off of valiant defenders of a transcontinental motherland, but photographs showing a rupture of family that often proved tragically final. One image shows an old man in what seems to be a sort of pedal wheelchair. He is looking up at the immense ship that is making ready to depart. He waves

tentatively and puts on a brave, but anxious smile. His disability forecasts that of the many men who would return handicapped like him, if they returned at all. Moreover, the man's condition echoes the social and financial incapacitation of the country caused by the conflict, and which created the conditions for the revolution in 1974. All of Gageiro's photographs on these themes gesture towards a lived reality that today risks becoming a historical abstraction or merely yet another statistic.

This process of condensing, linking and yet representing a wider scene, can be found in the series of photos in between pages 251 and 257 dealing with football. Portuguese historian Santos Lopes has this to say about the sport, which took on a special importance in the period with which *Cais da Memória* deals:

> In the 1950s, football in Portugal takes on a special importance. It is impossible to ignore its role in the imagination and the everyday of the Portuguese people, and the subtle dialectic that was generated between state attempts to instrumentalize the sport, in the interests of a politically and ideologically marked nationalism and the use on the part of the people of the experience of sporting events as a way to escape from an everyday that was so often frustrating and to expend a polemical energy that had no other outlet given the drastic limits placed on freedom of expression in the period.[11]

Gageiro's images again blur the distinctions between photojournalism and street photography, moving as they do between the official image of the sport, the spectacle itself, and the way in which the spectacle was used by the fans to break free from the constrictions of the everyday. In the short series of images, each element stands for a wider aspect of football under the *Estado Novo*, highlighting the ambiguous nature of Portugal's national sport.

The image on page 251 gestures towards how the game is experienced in the time-space of the everyday. It is a picture of the enthralled crowd absorbed in events on the pitch. It is both an image of the lived aspect of the game as working-class entertainment and a picture redolent of the extent to which the Portuguese population was distracted by sports events. The next image on page 252 shows the object of the crowd's adulation, Eusébio. In the context of the wider role of football, he can be seen here as an ambiguous national hero.

Eusébio and Portugal's greatest achievement was to reach third place in the World Cup of 1966. There follows on page 253 (Figure 3a, verso) an image of the streets of the *Baixa* lined with people. The hands of the adoring masses are raised as the players look down from an open-topped bus. Just how their prowess on the pitch is translated into propaganda is clear from the next image on page 254 (Figure 3a, recto). Apparently an official reception given of the team, a beaming Salazar shakes the hand of a proud-looking Eusébio, whilst striker Torres, half-turned, looks back with approval. Having been voted European footballer of the year in 1965, Eusébio returned top scorer from the World Cup. Two flashguns fire from the back of the room, representing the mass presence of the press corps. It is these two flashes that distance the image from straight sports reportage, as it indicates how the dazzle of the event affected the country. The year 1966 was the height of the colonial war, and conflict raged across the African provinces, including Eusébio's native Mozambique. It was a time when Portugal was under attack on the ground and in the UN. The regime's position was that Portugal was a multicontinental and pluriracial country. The Portuguese national team, given the ideological importance of football within Portugal and the Portuguese-administered overseas province, seemed the perfect embodiment of this 'lusotropicalist' discourse with its players drawn from both continental Portugal and the black African and white European communities of the overseas provinces. This image condenses the importance football had for the dictatorship and its propaganda machine.

The image on page 255 shows, however, the subversive potential of the game, the danger that football could pose to the regime with its ability to unite a mass of people in a city where assemblies for any other reason were closely controlled. One photograph (Figure 3b, verso) shows the fans of Académica, the team from the university town of Coimbra, staging a protest during the Portuguese Cup Final. The entire frame is filled with a sea of angry faces. Three banners are held aloft: one reads 'Better Teaching, Less Policing', one reads 'Less Guns, Barracks, Repression' and the last 'Free University'. Events such as the Cup Final were supposed to be strategic distractions to deflect Portuguese public attention away from the political situation of the everyday, yet we see here how the attention lavished upon such occasions could be used tactically, in order to subvert the regime.

Taken in 1971, one of the many years in which Benfica won the Portuguese championship, one photograph (Figure 3b, recto) shows the jubilant fans surging on to the pitch to celebrate the club's victory. In the middle of the surging crowd can be seen the remains of a cordon of police, some of whom seem to be singularly ineffective and the rest indifferent or complicit. Similar thongs of people, citizens and uniformed officers together, were soon to be seen not in the stadiums but in the streets of the city – three years later at the time of the Carnation Revolution that brought democracy to the country.

After all its images of Salazarist Lisbon, *No Cais da Memória* ends with a series of photographs depicting the immediate aftermath of the Carnation Revolution of 25 April 1974. The images with which the photobook closes document outpourings of joy and relief: the first May Day celebration after the revolution on pages 308 to 312. This point in time, however, is where Gageiro's assembly of the past into images (or the assembly of images into history) ends, with the continued use of tactics on the part of the photographer but in the face of a new strategic regime, that of the forces controlling post-revolutionary Portugal, an epoch that, for us to attempt to understand through photographic images, would require a photobook of its own.

Notes

1 The title can be translated as 'Lisbon at the Dockside of Memory'. Born in 1935, Eduardo Gageiro had his first photograph published on the front page of the *Diário de Notícias* newspaper in 1947 and went on to work for publications such as *O Século Ilustrado*, *Eva* and *Match Magazine*. He also edited the magazine *Sábado*.

2 The *Estado Novo*, or New State, period lasted from 1933 to 1968 (though in a sense it can be said to have started with the revolution of 1928 and to have ended with the Carnation Revolution of 1974). Headed by António de Oliveira Salazar, it was blindly nationalistic, deeply conservative and made extensive use of censorship and a repressive secret police force known as the PIDE (*Polícia Internacional e de Defesa do Estado*).

3 António Valdemar, 'A Lisboa de Gageiro e Nossa', *Diário de Notícias*. 20 November 2003, p. 11.

4 Clive Scott, *Street Photography from Atget to Cartier-Bresson* (London: I.B.Tauris, 2007), p. 85.

5 Michel de Certeau, *The Practice of Everyday Life*, trans. Stephen Rendall (London: University of California Press, 1984); subsequent references in brackets in the text.

6 'Michel de Certeau's work is nothing if not the refusal of the logic of application'. Ben Highmore, *Michel de Certeau: Analysing Culture* (London: Continuum, 2006), p. 6.

7 John Roberts, *The Art of Interruption: Realism, Photography and the Everyday* (Manchester and New York: Manchester University Press, 1998) pp. 16 and 79.

8 Ian Buchanan, *Michel de Certeau: Cultural Theorist* (London: Sage Publications, 2000), p. 89.

9 Henry Cartier-Bresson, *The Decisive Moment* (New York: Simon and Shuster, 1952).

10 Buchanan, *de Certeau*, p. 109.

11 Pedro Santos Lopes, 'Coimbra, Tradição e Desporto nos anos 50: A Questão do 40.900', *Ideologia, Cultura e Mentalidade do Estado Novo: Ensaios sobre a Universidade de Coimbra*, ed. with an introduction by Luís Reis Torgal (Coimbra, Portugal: Faculdade de Letras, 1992), pp. 130–45 (my translation).

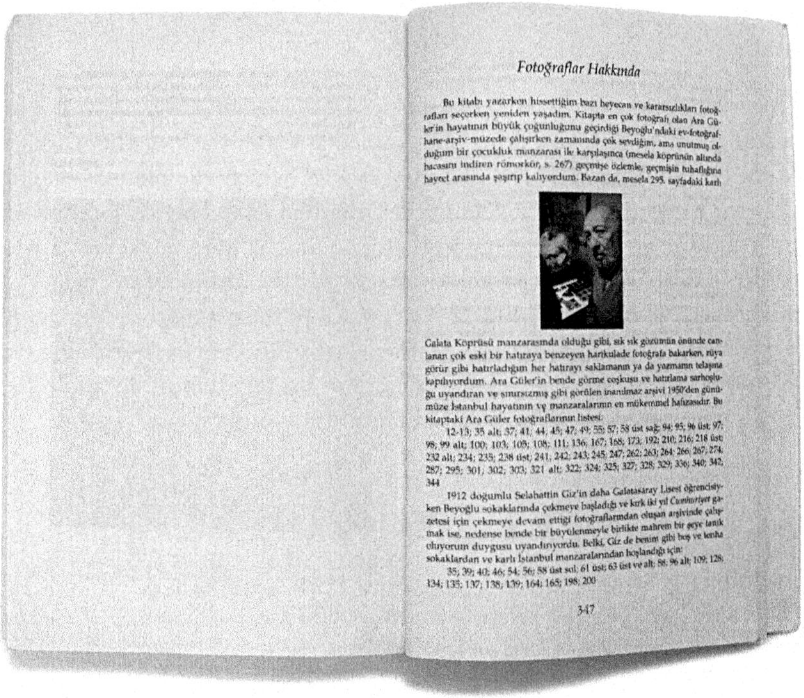

Fotoğraflar Hakkında

Bu kitabı yazarken hissettiğim bazı heyecan ve kararsızlıkları fotoğrafları seçerken yeniden yaşadım. Kitapta en çok fotoğrafı olan Ara Güler'in hayatının büyük çoğunluğunu geçirdiği Beyoğlu'ndaki ev-fotoğrafhane-arşiv-müzede çalışırken zamanında çok sevdiğim, ama unutmuş olduğum bir çocukluk manzarası ile karşılaşınca (mesela köprünün altında bacasını indiren römorkör, s. 267) geçmişe özlemle, geçmişin tuhaflığına hayret arasında şaşırıp kalıyordum. Bazan da, mesela 295. sayfadaki karlı Galata Köprüsü manzarasında olduğu gibi, sık sık gözümün önünde canlanan çok eski bir hatıraya benzeyen harikulade fotoğrafa bakarken, rüya görür gibi hatırladığım her hatırayı saklamanın ya da yazmanın telaşına kapılıyordum. Ara Güler'in bende görme coşkusu ve hatırlama sarhoşluğu uyandıran ve sınırsızmış gibi görülen inanılmaz arşivi 1950'den günümüze İstanbul hayatının ve manzaralarının en mükemmel hafızasıdır. Bu kitaptaki Ara Güler fotoğraflarının listesi:

12-13; 35 alt; 37; 41; 44; 45; 47; 49; 55; 57; 58 üst sağ; 94; 95; 96 üst; 97; 98; 99 alt; 100; 103; 105; 108; 111; 136; 167; 168; 173; 192; 210; 216; 218 üst; 232 alt; 234; 235; 238 üst; 241; 242; 243; 245; 247; 262; 263; 264; 266; 267; 274; 287; 295; 301; 302; 303; 321 alt; 322; 324; 325; 327; 328; 329; 336; 340; 342; 344

1912 doğumlu Selahattin Giz'in daha Galatasaray Lisesi öğrencisiyken Beyoğlu sokaklarında çekmeye başladığı ve kırk iki yıl *Cumhuriyet* gazetesi için çekmeye devam ettiği fotoğraflarından oluşan arşivinde çalışmak ise, nedense bende bir büyülenmeyle birlikte mahrem bir şeye tanık oluyorum duygusu uyandırıyordu. Belki, Giz de benim gibi boş ve tenha sokaklardan ve karlı İstanbul manzaralarından hoşlandığı için:

35; 39; 40; 46; 54; 56; 58 üst sol; 61 üst; 63 üst ve alt; 88; 96 alt; 109; 128; 134; 135; 137; 138; 139; 164; 165; 198; 200

347

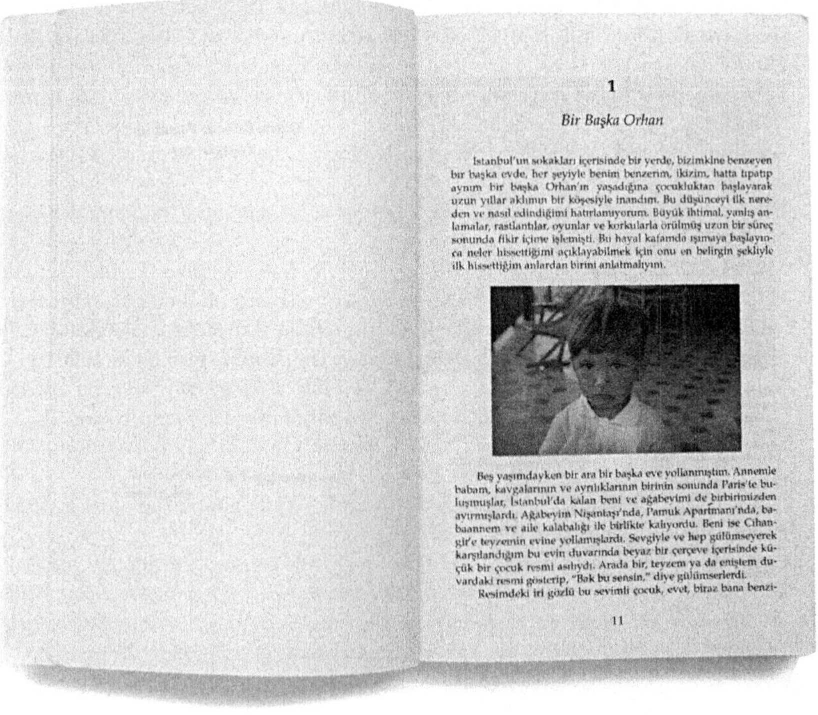

1

Bir Başka Orhan

İstanbul'un sokakları içerisinde bir yerde, bizimkine benzeyen bir başka evde, her şeyiyle benim benzerim, ikizim, hatta tıpatıp aynım bir başka Orhan'ın yaşadığına çocukluktan başlayarak uzun yıllar aklımın bir köşesiyle inandım. Bu düşünceyi ilk nereden ve nasıl edindiğimi hatırlamıyorum. Büyük ihtimal, yanlış anlamalar, rastlantılar, oyunlar ve korkularla örülmüş uzun bir süreç sonunda fikir içime işlemişti. Bu hayal kafamda ışımaya başlayınca neler hissettiğimi açıklayabilmek için onu en belirgin şekliyle ilk hissettiğim anlardan birini anlatmalıyım.

Beş yaşımdayken bir ara bir başka eve yollanmıştım. Annemle babam, kavgalarının ve ayrılıklarının birinin sonunda Paris'te buluşmuşlar, İstanbul'da kalan beni ve ağabeyimi de birbirimizden ayırmışlardı. Ağabeyim Nişantaşı'nda, Pamuk Apartmanı'nda, babaannem ve aile kalabalığı ile birlikte kalıyordu. Beni ise Cihangir'e teyzemin evine yollamışlardı. Sevgiyle ve hep gülümseyerek karşılandığım bu evin duvarında beyaz bir çerçeve içerisinde küçük bir çocuk resmi asılıydı. Arada bir, teyzem ya da eniştem duvardaki resmi gösterip, "Bak bu sensin," diye gülümserlerdi.

Resimdeki iri gözlü bu sevimli çocuk, evet, biraz bana benzi-

11

1. Last and first photographs in Orhan Pamuk, *Istanbul, Hatiralar Ve Sehir* (Istanbul, 2003).

ORHAN PAMUK'S MELANCHOLIC NARRATIVE AND FRAGMENTED PHOTOGRAPHIC FRAMING – *ISTANBUL: MEMORIES OF A CITY* (2005)

Gabriel Koureas

> The Nobel Prize in Literature for 2006 is awarded to the Turkish writer Orhan Pamuk who in the quest for the melancholic soul of his native city has discovered new symbols for the clash and interlacing of cultures.[1]

When Orhan Pamuk was awarded the Nobel Prize for literature in 2006 the Swedish Academy chose to announce the award by concentrating on Pamuk's memories of Istanbul in his autobiography, *Istanbul: Memories of a City* (2005).[2] The main concern of this chapter is to investigate the 'new symbols' that Pamuk uncovered in his pursuit of the melancholic soul of the city and the ways in which such symbols work in order to reveal the precariousness of cultural realignments. Geographically, Istanbul sits on the cusp between what is perceived as the East/West divide and provides the ideal space from which one can address such issues. What also distinguishes the book is its use of photography. Like the positioning of Istanbul at the intersection of two 'civilizations', the position of the book is on the cusp of what is usually described as a photobook – a bound collection of photographs and texts – and an illustrated memoir.

The format of the book is pocket-size paperback and the reproduction of the 200 photographs is on poor-quality paper that renders the photographs themselves as rather poor reproductions. By contrast, one expects a photobook to be printed on high-quality paper, usually in hardback and of 'coffee table' dimensions. However, the differences are not only in terms of the physicality of the publication but also in terms of the relationship between image and text. Whereas in a photobook the prominence of the photographer is evident, in *Istanbul,* the photographers are only acknowledged at the end of the book, at which point the relationship between photography and text starts to emerge.

The last photograph (Figure 1a) in the ultimate chapter/photographic acknowledgment section in the memoir shows Pamuk and the photographer Ara Güler, whose photographs of Istanbul constitute the majority of the photographs in the book. It is only at this point that we are partly informed of the relationship between the photographs and the author's narrative when Pamuk reveals that he relived the excitement and puzzlement of writing the book while choosing the photographs. This enthusiasm is evident in the smile on the face of Pamuk, who is seen sitting in front of a selection of slides and seems to be placing them in some kind of order the process of which made him 'drunk with memories' (p. 335).[3] For Pamuk the photographs represented a projection of his 'own memory onto a screen', a statement that reminds us of Freud's notion of screen memories, which according to Freud are not childhood memories as such but memories about childhood. Important facts are not retained; instead, their psychic significance is displaced on to closely associated but less important details.[4] Freud elaborated on this idea in another essay, where he compares screen memories with dreams, arguing that their common trait is visual representability similar to that of mnemic symbols and images.[5] This projection of screen memories would make Pamuk want to 'capture and preserve' the dreamscape that each photograph represented and 'write about it' (p. 335). The selection and ordering of the photographs, the intoxication that follows such a process and the memory/screen association provide some indication of the relationship between photography, memory, autobiography and the text in *Istanbul.*

My main concern here is to pose a number of questions that I hope will untangle what seems at first glance a very straightforward relationship. My first question is to what extent do the temporality and spatiality of the photographic image, and in particular the image of ruins, present a particular relationship to melancholia and memory that moves beyond the symbolic mode of the text? How does Pamuk use the two media in tandem in order to address questions of representation, mediation of private and public memory, and the possibility of an alternative model of cultural memory that departs from the cultural confines of borders?[6]

The use of photography in autobiographies became increasingly popular after the invention of photography, especially in a new kind of memoir/autobiography that Annette Kuhn terms 'revisionist autobiography'[7]. The mid-1980s saw the publication of a number of autobiographical books in which intellectuals and academics wrote of their own earlier lives, dwelling, in particular, on the broad contexts of class, education, culture and history. As Suzannah Radstone argues, these 'revisionist' autobiographies make explicit and reflect critically on subjectivity's relations with culture, time and history.[8] Kuhn also observes that photography has become one of the main characteristics of revisionist autobiographies, arguing that images are just as much productions of meaning as words.[9] The special relationship between photography and autobiography forms the main concern for Linda Haverty Rugg, who argues that photographs in autobiographies, or even a reference to photographs, cue the reader into a complex play of signifiers that indicates the presence of a person upon whom text and images rebound.[10]

Discussions of the relationship of photography to text have largely relied on a binary relationship that sees photographs as lacking intentionality, with language providing the framing of the photograph and the construction of its meaning. This is what Clive Scott terms as the 'narrative resources' of the photograph,[11] which he elaborates by concentrating on the grammatical and syntactical characteristics of titles and captions in photographic genres.[12] W.J.T. Mitchell provides a different framework by arguing for the dialectical nature of the relationship by focusing on what he terms 'textual pictures' and 'pictorial texts',[13] both of which concentrate on the interrelationship of the two media as mutually dependent and fully collaborative, a view that is shared by Marsha Bryant who argues for the acknowledgement of the multiple and competing ways in which the visual and verbal components interact.[14] Jay Prosser argues most convincingly that photography in autobiography functions as a memento mori that makes real a loss and helps one to apprehend it by capturing a reality that we would otherwise not see or, most importantly, 'we would choose not to see', and it is exactly this intentional oversight that cannot be recovered by the text.[15]

This chapter will discuss the use of photography in Pamuk's book and the ways in which one can become intoxicated with memories through the juxtaposition of text and image. The book, a melange of Pamuk's autobiography and the history of Istanbul while the author was growing up combined with flashbacks to the Ottoman past of the city, concentrates on the melancholy of the author and of the city, or to be more precise it focuses on the Turkish equivalent of the Western idea of melancholy, *hüzün*. There are around 200 photographs and illustrations in the text, from Orientalist images of the city to pictures by Turkish photographers and a collection of family photographs. However, the association between image and text does not stop here: chapters are given titles such as 'Black and White' (chapter 5) or Istanbul is described by Pamuk as a 'city that mourns over its loss of colour' (p. 39).

Despite the heavy use of photography and photographic language, the numerous reviews of the book that were published hardly touch on the subject. Usually, they just mention that it is illustrated, with the exception of a couple of reviewers who concentrate on this important relationship; David Flusfeder, for example, sees the photographs as serving a 'romantic purpose' in order to allow the 'foreign reader to experience the same pangs as the city's inhabitants'. However, the journey offered by Pamuk is, according to Flusfeder, a visual journey that the use of photography accentuates and 'as we are taken through the sites of ruins, as changes in the light are described to us, the other senses get hungrier'. [16] Alberto Manguel argues that the photographs produce 'double images' of the city, reflections that mirror its lost Ottoman past. These double images unfold according to Manguel 'like a series of Rorschach tests, multiplying its stained ghosts and tempting the reader with potentially infinite interpretations'.[17]

The idea of the 'double image' and of infinite interpretations is introduced in the very first page, where Pamuk reveals that at a very young age he feared that somewhere in Istanbul existed his twin or double. This fear arose from a photograph of a child that hung on the wall of his aunt's house where he stayed as a young child during one of the many turbulent separations endured by his parents. His aunt would point out the photograph to young Pamuk and say 'Look! That's you' (p. 3). Jacques Lacan in his exploration of the mirror stage, the phase in which the infant perceives itself as an 'I', argues that this phase depends upon a splitting between the 'I' which perceives and the 'I' which is perceived.[18] The implications of such recognition in terms of autobiography are, according to Suzannah Radstone, that autobiography is no longer a mirror of the author's soul and that there is a contradiction between the self that appears in autobiography and the self that speaks.[19] The photograph of that European child provides a shock to the child Pamuk, a 'shock of self-recognition and self-alienation'[20] that is inherent in autobiographical discourses and, according to Haverty Rugg, is exemplified by the inclusion of photographs, the role of which is to disrupt the singularity of the autobiographical pact by pointing to a plurality of selves; photographs in an autobiographical text also insist on something material, the embodied subject, the unification of author, name and body.[21]

Pamuk recognizes this inherent autobiographical contradiction when he realizes that this was not young Pamuk but instead 'a kitsch representation of a "cute child" that someone had brought back from Europe' (p. 3). This photograph had a profound impact on the child's mind: the picture of himself and the picture he resembled would all slide into a confusion that made him long to be at the family home surrounded by his family. He would even seek out this other child in the streets of the city, looking though people's windows in order to find this 'other' self. When he was older and whenever he was unhappy, he would imagine the comfort of this 'other' self that he felt had no need to visit other parts of the world. Istanbul, with its many histories, provided a cocoon where he would on the one hand feel protected and on the other hand feel claustrophobic and alienated from his surroundings. This rupture informs the narrative throughout the autobiography and it is photography that provides a realization of the loss of self and a rich cultural past.

I want to concentrate on the photograph that Pamuk chooses to have on the first page of the first chapter (Figure 1b) where he describes the memory of his interaction with the photograph of the other child: A snapshot of himself at about three years old that very much encapsulates that idea of shock. The photograph is taken on what looks like the veranda of the family home. The young Pamuk is captured from above, making the child look even smaller and by implication defenceless against the act of being photographed. He looks not only surprised but also concerned with the process of picture-taking. The narrative does not engage with this picture but instead engages with the picture of the other child that we the readers cannot see but have to rely solely on Pamuk's narrative for our understanding of the missing image. This absence/presence provides a simultaneous self-recognition and self-alienation. The shock of the other self is for Pamuk connected to the fact that for all his life he lived in the same area of Istanbul and for most of the time within the same apartment block where his extended family lived: 'I stayed in the same city on the same street, in the same houses, gazing at the same view. Istanbul's fate is my fate: I am attached to this city because it has made me who I am' (p. 6).

This statement immediately brings together the importance of place and memory in the construction of the self. It is here that the history of the city and Pamuk's life converge and become identified. Haverty Rugg argues that while the autobiographical act begins with a disassociation, which in the case of Pamuk is manifested in the opening chapter by the inclusion of the unseen photograph of the 'other' European child, the introduction of photographs into the autobiography not only represents that disassociation but also offers a possibility of reconciliation and reintegration.[22] The many photographs of the city in the book offer exactly that possibility of reconciliation, whereas the family portraits provide the anchoring through the body, the origin of language. However, in the case of Pamuk this reconciliation is not only one that involves the self alone but also the various communities that formed and still structure the city of Istanbul. Like the photograph of the European child through which he identifies himself, the city of Istanbul is remembered through the writings, lithographs and photographs of Orientalist writers, artists, architects and photographers such as Gustave Flaubert, Le Corbusier, Gérard de Nerval, Antoine Ignace Melling and Théophile Gautier who construct the identity and, most importantly, the memory of the city that Pamuk wants to remember. These European artists engaged with the city before the collapse of the Ottoman Empire and for Pamuk they offered the viewer/reader the variety of life that characterized the city before the Turkish republic was established and from which point onwards the 'world almost forgot that Istanbul existed' (p. 6). The Istanbul of the Turkish republic was 'poorer, shabbier and more isolated than it had ever been in its two-thousand-year history' (p. 6). For Pamuk the Istanbul in which he was born and lived all his life was a 'city in ruins' and most importantly, of 'end-of-empire melancholy', which he spent most of his life 'either battling' or 'making it my own' (p. 6). How is this melancholy constructed through photography and its relationship to the text?

For some preliminary considerations of this relationship I want to look at two other photographs that Pamuk uses in the first chapter (there are three in all including the one previously discussed). The first is a double-spread panoramic view of Istanbul by Ara Güler (Figure 2a) and the second is another family snapshot of baby Pamuk in the arms of his mother. Neither of these photographs is referred to in the text, as is the case with the majority of the images that punctuate and to a certain extent puncture the pages of the book and the flow of the narrative. The panoramic view is of the historical part of the city, the Sultanahmet area with Ayia Sophia in the foreground, the Blue Mosque and the Bosporus in the background. It is very much a picture postcard image of Istanbul with its two main tourist attractions. What the photograph also represents is the two civilizations that inform the construction of the identity of the city: the Byzantine and Ottoman Empires and the way these two civilizations clash in the spatiality and psychic of the city in the same way that young Pamuk fears and is attracted to the European boy whom we never see. The difference of this image from all subsequent images of the city is that this is a more positive image of Istanbul, whereas a certain melancholy characterizes the majority of the other images. Another complication is that the photographer of the image, Ara Güler (who is also the photographer of the majority of the images of Istanbul in the book), is of Armenian descent. This fact is not revealed to the reader. The importance of this association is related to the fact that Pamuk himself was prosecuted under the anti-Turkishness law (Article 301 of the Turkish Penal Code), by which anyone who expresses views contrary to those advocated by the government

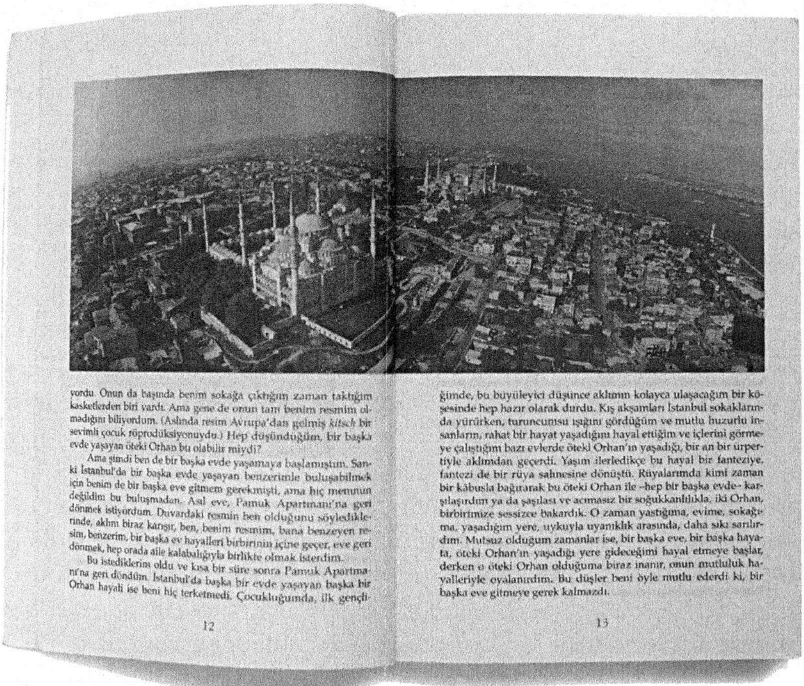

yordu. Onun da başında benim sokağa çıktığım zaman taktığım kasketlerden biri vardı. Ama gene de onun tam benim resmim olmadığını biliyordum. (Aslında resim Avrupa'dan gelmiş *kitsch* bir sevimli çocuk röprodüksiyonuydu.) Hep düşündüğüm, bir başka evde yaşayan öteki Orhan bu olabilir miydi?

Ama şimdi ben de bir başka evde yaşamaya başlamıştım. Sanki İstanbul'da bir başka evde yaşayan benzerimle buluşabilmek için benim de bir başka eve gitmem gerekmişti, ama hiç memnun değildim bu buluşmadan. Asıl eve, Pamuk Apartmanı'na geri dönmek istiyordum. Duvardaki resmin ben olduğunu söylediklerinde, aklım biraz karışır, ben, benim resmim, bana benzeyen resim, benzerim, bir başka ev hayalleri birbirinin içine geçer, eve geri dönmek, hep orada aile kalabalığıyla birlikte olmak isterdim.

Bu istediklerim oldu ve kısa bir süre sonra Pamuk Apartmanı'na geri döndüm. İstanbul'da başka bir evde yaşayan başka bir Orhan hayali ise beni hiç terketmedi. Çocukluğumda, ilk gençli-

12

ğimde, bu büyüleyici düşünce aklımın kolayca ulaşacağım bir köşesinde hep hazır olarak durdu. Kış akşamları İstanbul sokaklarında yürürken, turuncumsu ışığını gördüğüm ve mutlu huzurlu insanların, rahat bir hayat yaşadığını hayal ettiğim ve içlerini görmeye çalıştığım bazı evlerde öteki Orhan'ın yaşadığı, bir an bir ürpertiyle aklımdan geçerdi. Yaşım ilerledikçe bu hayal bir fanteziye, fantezi de bir rüya sahnesine dönüştü. Rüyalarımda kimi zaman bir kâbusla bağırarak bu öteki Orhan ile –hep bir başka evde– karşılaşırdım ya da şaşılası ve acımasız bir soğukkanlılıkla, iki Orhan, birbirimize sessizce bakardık. O zaman yastığıma, evime, sokağıma, yaşadığım yere, uykuyla uyanıklık arasında, daha sıkı sarılırdım. Mutsuz olduğum zamanlar ise, bir başka eve, bir başka hayata, öteki Orhan'ın yaşadığı yere gideceğimi hayal etmeye başlar, derken o öteki Orhan olduğuma biraz inanır, onun mutluluk hayalleriyle oyalanırdım. Bu düşler beni öyle mutlu ederdi ki, bir başka eve gitmeye gerek kalmazdı.

13

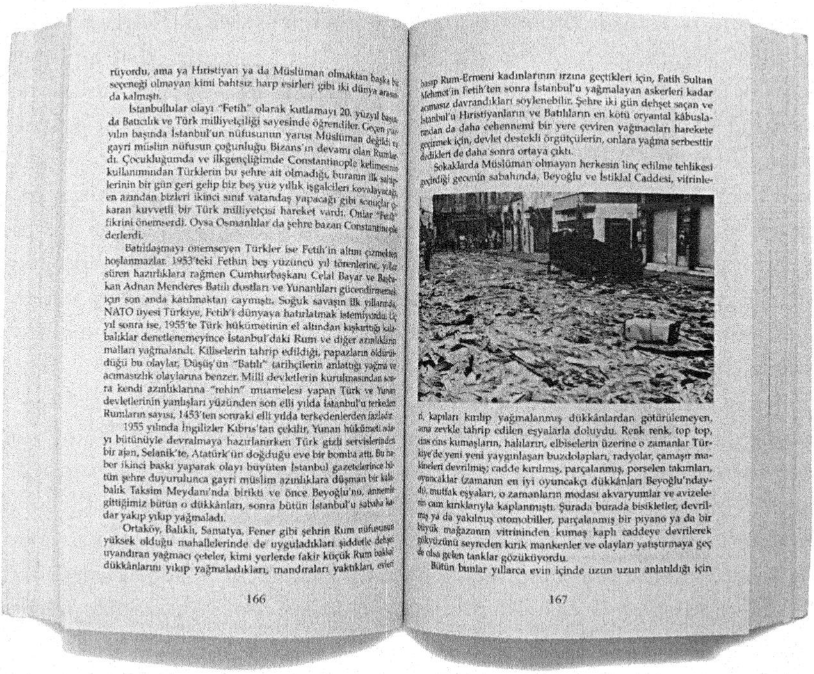

rüyordu, ama ya Hıristiyan ya da Müslüman olmaktan başka bir seçeneği olmayan kimi bahtsız harp esirleri gibi iki dünya arasında kalmıştı.

İstanbullular olayı "Fetih" olarak kutlamayı 20. yüzyıl başında Batıcılık ve Türk milliyetçiliği sayesinde öğrendiler. Geçen yüzyılın başında İstanbul'un nüfusunun yarısı Müslüman değildi ve gayri müslim nüfusun çoğunluğu Bizans'ın devamı olan Rumlardı. Çocukluğumda ve ilkgençliğimde Constantinople kelimesinin kullanımından Türklerin bu şehre ait olmadığı, buranın ilk sahiplerinin bir gün geri gelip biz beş yüz yıllık işgalcileri kovalayacağı, en azından bizleri ikinci sınıf vatandaş yapacağı gibi sonuçlar çıkaran kuvvetli bir Türk milliyetçisi hareket vardı. Onlar "Fetih" fikrini önemserdi. Oysa Osmanlılar da şehre bazan Constantinople derlerdi.

Batılılaşmayı önemseyen Türkler ise Fetih'in altını çizmekten hoşlanmazlar. 1953'teki Fethin beş yüzüncü yıl törenlerine, yıllar süren hazırlıklara rağmen Cumhurbaşkanı Celal Bayar ve Başbakan Adnan Menderes Batılı dostları ve Yunanlıları gücendirmemek için son anda katılmaktan caymıştı. Soğuk savaşın ilk yıllarında, NATO üyesi Türkiye, Fetih'i dünyaya hatırlatmak istemiyordu. Üç yıl sonra ise, 1955'te Türk hükümetinin el altından kışkırttığı kalabalıklar denetlenemeyince İstanbul'daki Rum ve diğer azınlıkların malları yağmalandı. Kiliselerin tahrip edildiği, papazların öldürüldüğü bu olaylar, Düşüş'ün "Batılı" tarihçilerin anlattığı yağma ve acımasızlık olaylarına benzer. Milli devletlerin kurulmasından sonra kendi azınlıklarına "rehin" muamelesi yapan Türk ve Yunan devletlerinin yanlışları yüzünden son elli yılda İstanbul'u terkeden Rumların sayısı, 1453'ten sonraki elli yılda terkedenlerden fazladır.

1955 yılında İngilizler Kıbrıs'tan çekilir, Yunan hükümeti adayı bütünüyle devralmaya hazırlanırken Türk gizli servislerinden bir ajan, Selanik'te, Atatürk'ün doğduğu eve bir bomba attı. Bu haber ikinci baskı yaparak olayı büyüten İstanbul gazetelerince bütün şehre duyurulunca gayri müslim azınlıklara düşman bir kalabalık Taksim Meydanı'nda birikti ve önce Beyoğlu'nu, annemle gittiğimiz bütün o dükkânları, sonra bütün İstanbul'u sabaha kadar yakıp yıkıp yağmaladı.

Ortaköy, Balıklı, Samatya, Fener gibi şehrin Rum nüfusunun yüksek olduğu mahallelerinde de uyguladıkları şiddetle dehşet uyandıran yağmacı çeteler, kimi yerlerde fakir küçük Rum bakkal dükkânlarını yıkıp yağmaladıkları, mandıraları yaktıkları, evlere

166

basıp Rum-Ermeni kadınlarının ırzına geçtikleri için, Fatih Sultan Mehmet'in Fetih'ten sonra İstanbul'u yağmalayan askerleri kadar acımasız davrandıkları söylenebilir. Şehre iki gün dehşet saçan ve İstanbul'u Hıristiyanların ve Batılıların en kötü oryantal kâbuslarından da daha cehennemi bir yere çeviren yağmacıları harekete geçirmek için, devlet destekli örgütçülerin, onlara yağma serbesttir dedikleri de daha sonra ortaya çıktı.

Sokaklarda Müslüman olmayan herkesin linç edilme tehlikesi geçirdiği gecenin sabahında, Beyoğlu ve İstiklal Caddesi, vitrinleri, kapıları kırılıp yağmalanmış dükkânlardan götürülemeyen, ama zevkle tahrip edilen eşyalarla doluydu. Renk renk, top top, ... cins kumaşların, halıların, elbiselerin üzerine o zamanlar Türkiye'de yeni yeni yaygınlaşan buzdolapları, radyolar, çamaşır makineleri devrilmiş; cadde kırılmış, parçalanmış, porselen takımları, oyuncaklar (zamanın en iyi oyuncakçı dükkânları Beyoğlu'ndaydı), mutfak eşyaları, o zamanların modası akvaryumlar ve avizelerin cam kırıklarıyla kaplanmıştı. Şurada burada bisikletler, devrilmiş ya da yakılmış otomobiller, parçalanmış bir piyano ya da bir büyük mağazanın vitrininden kumaş kaplı caddeye devrilerek gökyüzünü seyreden kırık mankenler ve olayları yatıştırmaya geç de olsa gelen tanklar gözüküyordu.

Bütün bunlar yıllarca evin içinde uzun uzun anlatıldığı için

167

2. Orhan Pamuk, *Istanbul, Hatiralar Ve Sehir* (Istanbul, 2003), photographs by Ara Güler.

is liable to prosecution. Pamuk was prosecuted under this law for mentioning the Armenian and Kurdish genocides during an interview with the Swiss newspaper *Tages Anzeiger* in February 2005. The publication of the interview resulted in a public outcry in Turkey which culminated in the burning of his books and of his photograph and with *Hurriyet*, Turkey's largest circulation newspaper, calling him an 'abject creature'.[23]

Let us take a closer look at the relationship between text and photography in the first chapter, where the above images are positioned, in order to look at the screen memories that Pamuk claims photographs of Istanbul create for him and his relationship to the city, which he describes as 'one of fate' (p. 7). He accepts the city in which he was born although it is an 'ageing' and 'impoverished' city 'buried under the ashes of a ruined empire' (p. 7). This conditional acceptance of the city provides the main connection to his relationship with the photographs. In the Turkish language, according to Pamuk, a special tense distinguishes 'hearsay from what we've seen with our own eyes' (p. 8). This tense is used when relating dreams, fairy tales, or past events that were not witnessed. The distinction is a useful one according to Pamuk, especially when one is narrating one's life because we cannot remember our earliest memories since these are told to us by somebody else, are 'imprinted in our minds' and 'end up mattering more than what we ourselves remember' (p. 8). The formation of the self through these memories that are handed down to us and in fact are what Freud described as 'screen memories' works in the same way that the identity of a city is formed through memories handed down through previous generations and according to Pamuk always depend on 'others' to tell the story: 'we let others shape our understanding of the city in which we live' (p. 8). What Pamuk is also engaging with at this point and throughout the book is the relationship of memory and photography and the argument put forward by Walter Benjamin and other commentators that photography creates a 'false' or 'counter' memory which results in what Sontag calls the replacement of memory by a photograph.[24] The relationship of the two photographs to the text can then provide a third reading: the two images if read in conjunction can provide an allegorical meaning to the text, the motherly protection that baby Pamuk receives in the arms of his mother offers protection and comfort to the smiling young child looking over the balcony of their apartment at the world below in the same way that the photograph of the city provides a pacified coherent image of Istanbul that like the motherly love can also produce a symbiosis between the two religions, East and West, as well as a number of ethnic groups.

This relationship of photography to memory also creates the main problem for representations of Istanbul. Because of the absence of such visual representations from Islamic artistic tradition, Istanbul's identity and memory are established only through the images produced by Western travellers mainly in the nineteenth century. The question that then arises is what kind of cultural memory is produced in relation to a city that relies exclusively on the Western gaze? The answer lies in chapter 2, 'The Photographs in the Dark Museum', and chapter 5, 'Black and White', which directly refer to photography and memory. In chapter 2, Pamuk engages with his memories of the interior of the family home and, in particular, concentrates on the sitting room. He grew up in an apartment block where two generations of Pamuks lived and where each family had their own apartment and each apartment had its own sitting room/mausoleum/museum. These rooms 'were furnished not for the living but for the dead' and were not places one could relax in but rather they were 'little museums designed to demonstrate to a hypothetical visitor that the householders were westernized' (p. 10). The locked cabinets housed collections of porcelain, crystal and silver, sets that 'no one ever touched' (p. 10) in the same way that the pianos in these rooms were never played but instead were 'places for exhibiting photographs' as well as every available surface being 'covered with frames of all sizes' (p. 11). The history of the family was captured through the rows of photographs that adorned the room, starting with the two 'imposing' and 'enormous' portraits that hang over the never-used fireplace. These were the retouched photographs of Pamuk's grandparents and their Westernized posing positioned them at the head of the family. What also characterized these collections and displays of family photographs was that once they were assigned their 'place in the museum' they were 'never moved' (p. 13).

For Pamuk the importance of these photographs in relation to memory was twofold: firstly, they exerted an influence in their daily lives by their sheer presence and immobility and the memories that were frozen in time could be weaved into the present. Secondly, the photographs pulled the author in two directions, 'wanting to get on with life but also longing to capture the moment of perfection, savouring the ordinary but still honouring the ideal' (p. 13). The chapter entitled 'Black and White' moves from the interior to the exterior in order to provide the same analogy in the relationship between photography and memory to the city where the interior of the 'bleak museum' and its melancholy is transferred to the cityscape of Istanbul and its psyche. The city is described in photographic terms: the dark surfaces of the buildings, their texture and shading and the black and white crowds in the darkening streets during wintertime. Pamuk favours the winter darkness because it offers protection from the inquisitive Western gaze since it veils the 'shameful poverty of our city' (p. 32). A photograph by Ara Güler is at this point intersected into the narrative referring not only to the literal poverty of the city but also to the shame of the nation in the eyes of the West regarding the Armenian genocide. The photograph, which is referred to in the text, captures, according to Pamuk, the back streets of his childhood where concrete apartment blocks stood next to old wooden houses. It is the chiaroscuro of the photograph, the 'chiaroscuro of twilight' (p. 32), that best encapsulates the photograph as a representation of the city. Pamuk writes that it is not what is represented in the photograph – the cobblestone streets and pavements, the iron grilles on the windows or the empty, ruined wooden houses – but the shadows that the two people form in the photograph that provide the punctum: 'these two people who are dragging long shadows behind them on their way home are actually pulling the blanket of night over the entire city', thus metaphorically pulling a blanket over the city's inconvenient history (p. 32). This blanket will bring the desired invisibility from the foreign gaze, thus creating an oxymoron: a photograph is supposed to throw light, to reproduce an instance, to enlighten a situation through its presumed representation of reality and not bring darkness and veiling. What the photograph and the oxymoron it creates achieves in this instance is to bring to the forefront the immensity of loss that Pamuk is feeling in relation to his city and the nation as a whole.

To see the city in black and white, as in a monochrome photograph, 'is to see it through the tarnish of history: the patina of what is old and faded and no longer matters to the rest of the world' (p. 38). The protection that the black and white offers can also be seen in the way the people dress; they all wear 'the same pale, drab, shadowy clothes', something that Pamuk interprets as a deliberate act in order to make a moral point: 'this is how you grieve for a city that has been in decline for a hundred and fifty years' (p. 39). At this point, another photograph is inserted, although there is no mention of it in the text. With the exception of the family photographs, this is one of the very few photographs with people in it. However, we only see the backs of the people crossing the bridge and the only person who is facing the viewer is bent under the load of a crate that he is carrying on his back. This faceless, sombre, dark crowd provides concrete evidence of the grieving city.

Through this grieving comes the idea of *hüzün* that Pamuk develops in chapter 10. He places importance on the distinction between the Western idea of Melancholia and its Turkish equivalent, *hüzün*. The word has its roots in the Arabic language and is meant to convey a feeling of deep spiritual loss. However, the word took two different meanings in Islamic history. The first meaning signifies the feelings that are associated with investing too much in worldly pleasures and material gain, whereas the second meaning, which arises out of Sufi mysticism, is the spiritual anguish one feels because one cannot be close enough to Allah. A true Sufi follower will pay no attention to worldly concerns, like death, and suffers from grief, emptiness and inadequacy because he can never be close enough to Allah (p. 81). What is important, according to Pamuk, is the absence rather than the presence of *hüzün*, which causes distress; it is the failure to experience *hüzün* that leads to feelings of *hüzün* and one suffers because one has not suffered enough. Hence, the melancholia that characterizes the life and culture of Istanbul can be attributed partly to this idea of honour that one feels in experiencing *hüzün* but for Pamuk this is not a complete explanation of the melancholy felt by the inhabitants of Istanbul. In order to understand this melancholy one needs to place it within the social and historical context of the city following the fall of the Ottoman Empire and the way in which this history 'is reflected in the city's "beautiful" landscapes and people' (p. 82). It is through this positioning that we can understand *hüzün* as a 'state of mind that is ultimately as life affirming as it is negating' (p. 82).

However, the word becomes even more ambiguous if we look at its use in order to describe an illness. Like Western thinkers (Robert Burton, Aristotle) Ottoman thinkers saw *hüzün* as the 'black bile', the 'black passion' that is an all-occluding pain. However, whereas for Western thinkers like Burton melancholy paved the way to happy, creative solitude, for Ottoman thinkers *hüzün* was at odds with the communal purpose. Hence, *hüzün* is not the melancholy of a solitary person, best encapsulated in the idea of Western individualism, but the 'black mood shared by millions of people together' (p. 83). According to Pamuk, to feel this *hüzün* is to 'see the scenes, evoke the memories in which the city itself becomes the very illustration, the very essence of *hüzün*' (p. 83).

It is exactly at this point that the relationship between the photographs and the narrative becomes clearer. The photographs convey to us the *hüzün* of the city by making us see the scenes and by making the city the actual illustration. What this visualization of the city through the photographic also achieves is a sensual encounter with the *hüzün*. One can 'sense it everywhere', almost 'touch it' (p. 89). The tactility of the photographic image is transformed into the tactility of the *hüzün* in the city. Photography, an imported Western medium, provides the evidence of the ruins of the Ottoman Empire which litter the city and which are 'reminders that the present city is so poor and confused that it can never again dream of rising to the same heights of wealth, power and culture' (p. 91). Memory, wrote

Walter Benjamin, is not an instrument for the exploration of the past but rather its theatre is the medium of what has been experienced, as the earth is the medium in which cities lie buried in debris. Most importantly, for Benjamin 'facts are only layers, which deliver ... the true assets hidden within inner earth: the images, which stand like ruins as the treasures in the prosaic chambers of our belated insights'.[25]

The *hüzün* is presented visually through the many photographs of ruins and decay (Figure 3a). They puncture the text in order to remind us of the loss that Pamuk feels in relation to the Ottoman past of the city. What is also conspicuous about these photographs is the absence of life. Any contemporary visitor to Istanbul will be struck by the intensity of life in the city, the noises, the smells, the crowds of people moving constantly day and night along its main streets. Pamuk himself stated in an interview for the BBC that:

> there is another thing, and that is the sounds – things that you hear in each city that are different. ... In Istanbul it's the 'vvvvoooot' – sirens of the boats, the 'chck' from the chimney waves of the Bosporus hitting the quays along with the seagulls and old fashioned little boats 'putu putu putu' kind of thing.[26]

Instead, the photographs Pamuk chose for his text are characterized by an eerie silence, the tranquillity of ruins and the melancholy of loss. Walter Benjamin commenting on Atget's photographs of empty Paris streets wrote that the 'city in these images is cleaned out like an apartment that has not yet found a new tenant'.[27] For Pamuk, like Atget, the empty streets of Istanbul stay empty after the expulsion of its multi-ethnic inhabitants following the demise of the Ottoman Empire in the early twentieth century and the establishment of the Turkish Republic, and it is photography that conveys this loss in a much stronger way than the text. In the photographs that Pamuk uses there is none of the regenerative energy that usually characterizes Atget's photography and enables the viewer to see the ordinary streets of Paris from a fresh angle and light, although for the Turkish reader the photographs might present an invitation to see their city in a different light – as haunted by the past.

One could accuse Pamuk of nostalgia for a past that no longer exists and for seeing the Ottoman Empire through a tinted lens that purifies its history of the wars and destructions that it instigated. Nostalgia has been seen by social commentators as a 'social disease'[28] or, as Svetlana Boym argues, the 'nostalgic desires to obliterate history and turn it into private or collective mythology, to revisit time like space, refusing to surrender to the irreversibility

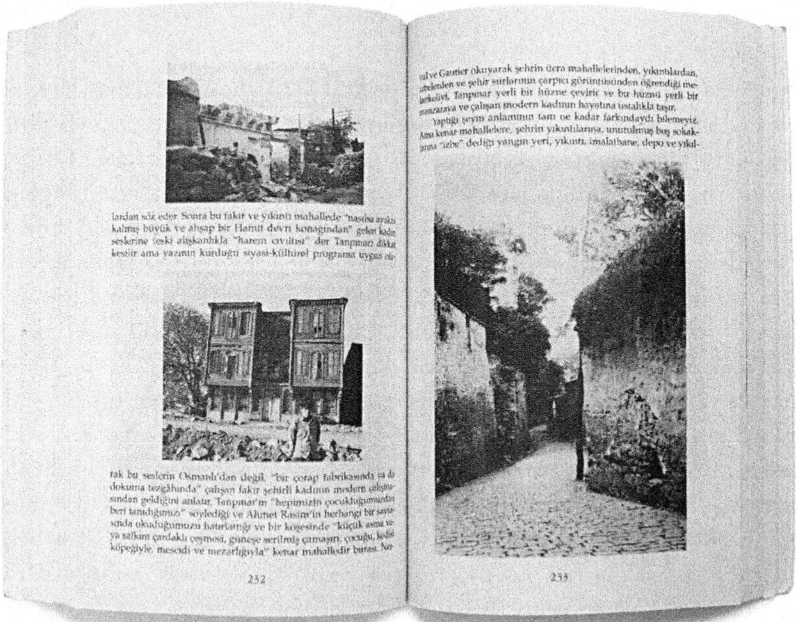

lardan söz eder. Sonra bu fakir ve yıkıntı mahallede "nasılsa ayakta kalmış büyük ve ahşap bir Hamit devri konağından" gelen kadın seslerine (eski alışkanlıkla "harem cıvıltısı" der Tanpınar) dikkat kesilir ama yazının kurduğu siyasi-kültürel programa uygun ol-

rak bu seslerin Osmanlı'dan değil, "bir çorap fabrikasında ya da dokuma tezgâhında" çalışan fakir şehirli kadının modern çalışmasından geldiğini anlatır. Tanpınar'ın "hepimizin çocukluğumuzdan beri tanıdığımız" söylediği ve Ahmet Rasim'in herhangi bir sayfasında okuduğumuzu hatırlattığı ve bir köşesinde "küçük asma veya salkım çardaklı çeşmesi, güneşe serilmiş çamaşırı, çocuğu, kedisi köpeğiyle, mescidi ve mezarlığıyla" kenar mahalledir burası. Ne-

252

val ve Gautier okuyarak şehrin ücra mahallelerinden, yıkıntılardan, izbelerden ve şehir surlarının çarpıcı görüntüsünden öğrendiği melankoliyi, Tanpınar yerli bir hüzne çevirir ve bu hüznü yerli bir manzaraya ve çalışan modern kadının hayatına ustalıkla taşır.

Yaptığı şeyin anlamının tam ne kadar farkındaydı bilemeyiz. Ama kenar mahallelere, şehrin yıkıntılarına, unutulmuş boş sokaklarına "izbe" dediği yangın yeri, yıkıntı, imalathane, depo ve yıkıl-

233

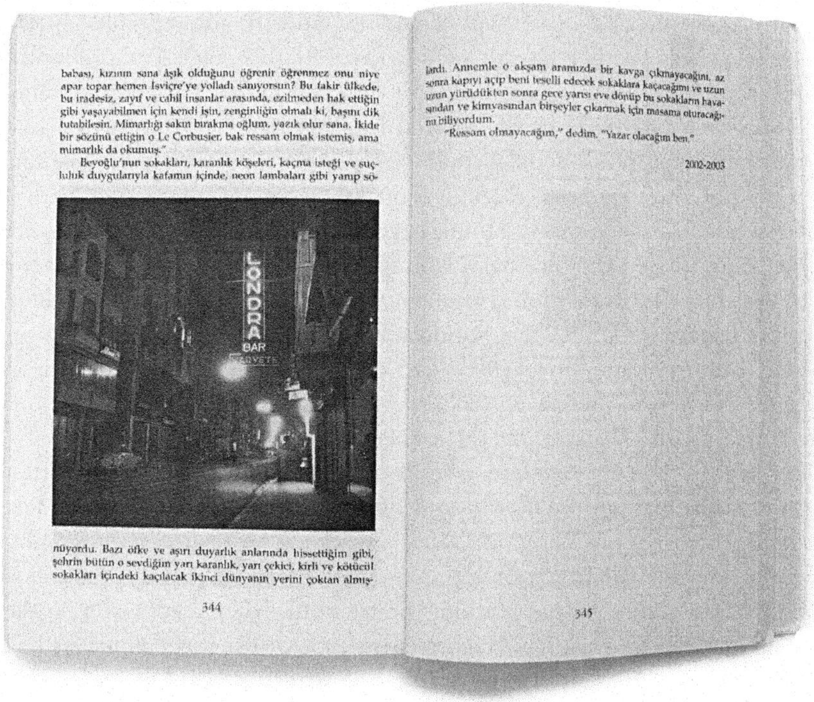

babası, kızının sana âşık olduğunu öğrenir öğrenmez onu niye apar topar hemen İsviçre'ye yolladı sanıyorsun? Bu fakir ülkede, bu iradesiz, zayıf ve cahil insanlar arasında, ezilmeden hak ettiğin gibi yaşayabilmen için kendi işin, zenginliğin olmalı ki, başını dik tutabilesin. Mimarlığı sakın bırakma oğlum, yazık olur sana. İkide bir sözünü ettiğin o Le Corbusier, bak ressam olmak istemiş, ama mimarlık da okumuş."

Beyoğlu'nun sokakları, karanlık köşeleri, kaçma isteği ve suçluluk duygularıyla kafamın içinde, neon lambaları gibi yanıp sö-

nüyordu. Bazı öfke ve aşırı duyarlık anlarında hissettiğim gibi, şehrin bütün o sevdiğim yarı karanlık, yarı çekici, kirli ve kötücül sokakları içindeki kaçılacak ikinci dünyanın yerini çoktan almış-

344

lardı. Annemle o akşam aramızda bir kavga çıkmayacağını, az sonra kapıyı açıp beni teselli edecek sokaklara kaçacağımı ve uzun uzun yürüdükten sonra gece yarısı eve dönüp bu sokakların havasından ve kimyasından birşeyler çıkarmak için masama oturacağını biliyordum.

"Ressam olmayacağım," dedim. "Yazar olacağım ben."

2002-2003

345

3. Orhan Pamuk, *Istanbul, Hatiralar Ve Sehir* (Istanbul, 2003), photographs by Ara Güler.

of time that plagues the human condition'.[29] It might appear that Pamuk is adopting this nostalgic mode with his insistence on revisiting time through the space of photography. However, as Boym continues to argue, 'nostalgia is about the relationship between individual biography and the biography of groups and nations, between personal and collective memory',[30] and she distinguishes between restorative nostalgia which attempts a transhistorical reconstruction of the lost home as evidence of truth and tradition. By contrast, reflective nostalgia is about the longing itself and concentrates on challenging the idea of absolute truth. Most importantly, for Boym, reflective nostalgia 'allows us to distinguish between national memory that is based on a single plot of national identity and social memory, which consists of collective frameworks that mark but do not define the individual memory'.[31] Reflective nostalgia does this by lingering 'on ruins, the patina of time and history, in the dreams of another time and place',[32] whereas 'restorative nostalgia has no use for the signs of historical time – patina, ruins, cracks, imperfections'.[33]

These ruins, cracks and imperfections form the subject matter of the photographs that Pamuk uses in his book in order to create, I would argue, an 'in-between space' in relation to the text and the photographs. In order to develop this further I want to introduce at this stage a photobook for which Pamuk wrote the foreword: *Ara Güler's Istanbul*.[34] The book contains 153 duotone photographs of Istanbul by Güler and it is presented in the more traditional photobook format with a short foreword at the beginning and the photographs printed on high-quality, gloss paper presented with just their titles. In the foreword Pamuk engages again with the idea of *hüzün* in order to argue that the black and white sorrow in Güler's photographs made him use them in his memoir. Pamuk also explains that he specifically looked for the 'backstreet scenes that would reflect the *hüzün*'[35] and going through Güler's archive made him realize that to write a memoir is not 'to review all of one's memories, preserving each in turn, but to forget almost all of them, creating instead a story from those memories that refuse to go away'.[36] In other words, the photographs provided the Freudian screen memories of the *hüzün* he wanted to describe and the embodiment of that loss he felt as he was growing up in Istanbul. What also characterizes the photographs in the photobook, which Pamuk discusses in the forward, is that the majority of them are about people working in Istanbul. They are mostly workers, labourers and street vendors (Figure 4a) who according to Pamuk evoke the fragility of their lives and the poverty of the streets of Istanbul. These images 'shed the heavy weight of the past and a hope in the future to concentrate instead in the present' and 'open our eyes to the city'.[37]

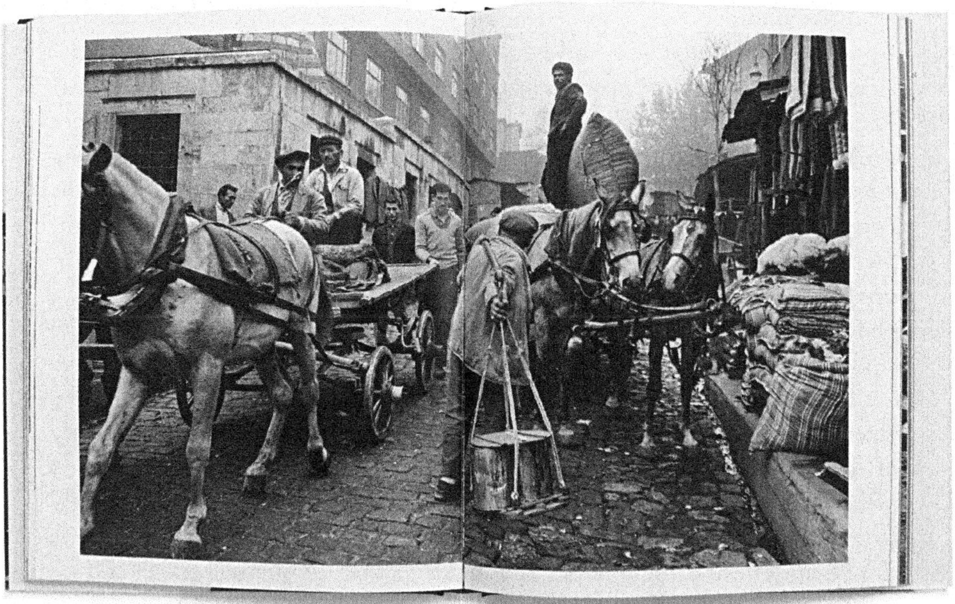

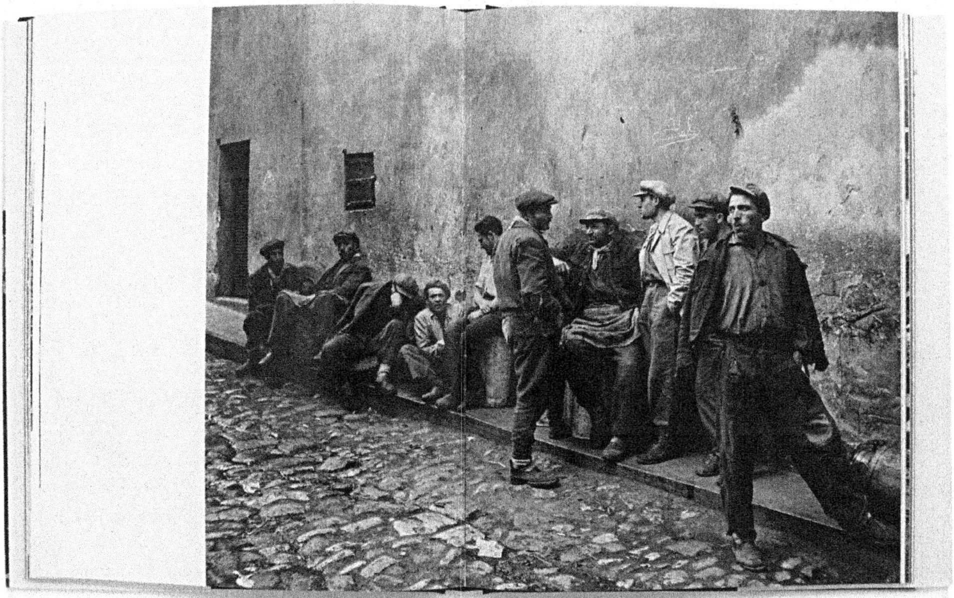

4. Ara Güler and Orhan Pamuk, *Ara Güler's Istanbul* (London, 2009).

In the photobook, the separation of the text from the photographs creates a boundary both physical and psychic between the two. In the case of the memoir, the in-between space is at the intersection of photography and text. The memories that Pamuk chooses to represent are aligned in order to create a plane of coexistence. Each of his screen memories is a process of becoming that transubstantiates memories through their encounters with photographs around them. This metamorphosis allows the memories to be released from the systems they belong in order to work for the whole rather than function singularly. The process that Pamuk instigates between text, memories and photographs endows them with transforming possibilities in relation to the landscape that surrounds them.

This is a space without boundaries which receives its form from the abject space of the ruins and whose form is the outside of the identity of the others that constitute the enemy or the friend, in order to provide possibilities, realignments and openness as opposed to cohesion and unity so much favoured by the Turkish Republic. This space is where identities can be undone and the binaries and dualisms that dominate Turkish culture can be rethought and contested. This space also allows the reconstitution of identities and the re-evaluation of what constitutes the other. As Elizabeth Grosz argues, 'any identity is always riven with forces, with processes, connections, movements that exceed and transform identity and that connect individuals to each other and to worlds, in ways unforeseen by consciousness and unconnected to identity'.[38] The in-between space that photography/text creates provides the fertile ground for the establishment of a subjectivity relational to the city space, its history and its lost cultures, whether Armenian, Jewish, Turkish or Greek, that characterized the cosmopolitanism of the city's past.

Notes

1 The Swedish Academy, press release, 12 October 2006, online at: http://nobelprize.org/nobel_prizes/literature/laureates/2006/press.html (accessed 7 November 2011).
2 Orhan Pamuk, *Istanbul: Memories of a City* (London: Faber, 2005), p. 335. All interpolated page references refer to this edition.
3 The book photographed here is the Turkish edition: Orhan Pamuk, *Istanbul, Hatiralar Ve Sehir* (Istanbul: YKY, 2003).
4 Sigmund Freud, 'Screen Memories', in *The Standard Edition of the Complete Psychological Works of Sigmund Freud*, trans. James Strachey (London: Hogarth Press, 1974), vol. 3, pp. 47–69.
5 Sigmund Freud, 'Remembering, Repeating and Working-Through', in *The Standard Edition of the Complete Psychological Works of Sigmund Freud*, vol. 12, pp. 147–56.

6 Authors tend to concentrate on W.G. Sebald; see, for example, Garloff Katja, 'The Emigrant as Witness: W.G. Sebald's "Die Ausgewanderten"', *The German Quarterly* 77:1 (2004), pp. 76–93; Harris Stefanie, 'The Return of the Dead: Memory and Photography in W.G. Sebald's "Die Ausgewanderten"', *The German Quarterly* 74:4 (2001), pp. 379–91; J.J. Long, 'History, Narrative, and Photography in W.G. Sebald's "Die Ausgewanderten"', *The Modern Language Review* 98:1 (2003), pp. 117–37.
7 Anette Kuhn, 'A Journey Through Memory', in Suzannah Radstone, *Memory and Methodology* (Oxford: Berg, 2000), pp. 179–96.
8 Suzannah Radstone, *The Sexual Politics of Time: Confession, Nostalgia, Memory* (London: Routledge, 2007), p. 198.
9 Kuhn, p. 182.
10 Linda Haverty Rugg, *Picturing Ourselves: Photography and Autobiography* (Chicago and London: University of Chicago Press, 1997), p. 21.
11 Clive Scott, *The Spoken Image: Photography and Language* (London: Reaktion, 1999), p. 62.
12 Scott, p. 11.
13 W.J.T. Mitchell, *Picture Theory: Essays on Verbal and Visual Representation* (Chicago and London: University of Chicago Press, 1994), p. 109.
14 Marsha Bryant, *Photo-textualities: Reading Photographs and Literature* (Newark, NJ: University of Delaware Press, 1996), p. 11.
15 Jay Prosser, *Light in the Dark Room: Photography and Loss* (Minneapolis: University of Minnesota Press, 2005), pp. 2 and 9.
16 David Flusfeder, *Daily Telegraph* (13 May 2005), online at: http://www.orhanpamuk.net/popuppage.aspx?id=48&lng=eng (accessed 26 August 2009).
17 Alberto Manguel, 'My City in Ruins', *Washington Post* (26 June 2005), online at: http://www.orhanpamuk.net/interviews.aspx (accessed 26 August 2009).
18 Lacan Jacques, *Ecrits: A Selection*, trans. Alan Sheridan (London and New York: Tavistock Publications and Norton, 1977), pp. 3–9.
19 Radstone, *The Sexual Politics of Time*, p. 30.
20 Haverty Rugg, p. 136.
21 Haverty Rugg, p. 13.
22 Haverty Rugg, p. 14.
23 See Pamuk's interview with *Die Zeit* (14 May 2005).
24 Susan Sontag, *On Photography* (London: Allen Lane, 1978). See also, Roland Barthes, *Camera Lucida: Reflections on Photography* (New York: Hill and Wang, 1981) and Walter Benjamin, 'Short History of Photography', in Alan Trachtenberg (ed.), *Classic Essays on Photography* (New Haven, CT: Leete's Island Books, 1980), pp. 199–216.
25 Walter Benjamin, *Berlin Childhood Around 1900* (Cambridge, MA and London: Belknap Press, 2006), p. 40.
26 Orhan Pamuk, 'Sense of the City: Istanbul', BBC interview (7 August 2003), online at: http://news.bbc.co.uk/1/hi/world/europe/3131585.stm (accessed 26 August 2009).
27 Benjamin, 'Short History of Photography', p. 209.
28 Susan Stewart, *On Longing: Narratives of the Miniature, the Gigantic, the Souvenir, the Collection* (Durham, NC and London: Duke University Press, 1993), p. ix.
29 Svetlana Boym, *The Future of Nostalgia* (New York: Basic Books, 2001), p. xv.

30 Boym, p. xvi.
31 Boym, p. xvii.
32 Boym, p. 41.
33 Boym, p. 45.
34 Ara Güler and Orhan Pamuk, *Ara Güler's Istanbul* (London: Thames & Hudson, 2009).
35 Güler and Pamuk, p. 13.
36 Güler and Pamuk, p. 14.
37 Güler and Pamuk, p. 13.
38 Elizabeth Grosz, *Architecture from the Outside: Essay on Virtual and Real Space* (Cambridge, MA and London: MIT), p. 95.

A SELECT BIBLIOGRAPHY OF SECONDARY SOURCES

(For more on the individual photobooks, see the notes in each chapter)

Armstrong, Carol, *Scenes in a Library: Reading the Photograph in the Book, 1843–1875* (Cambridge, MA: MIT, 1998).

Barclay, Clare, *The Exhibition of Japanese Artefacts in Britain Historically and Now: Exhibition Catalogues and Their Functions* (MA dissertation, University of Plymouth, unpublished, 2007).

Barthes, Roland, *Mythologies*, ed. and trans. Annette Lavers (London: Paladin, 1973).

——, 'The Rhetoric of the Image' (1964), in Stephen Heath (ed. and trans.), *Image-Music-Text* (London: Fontana, 1977).

——, *Camera Lucida: Reflections on Photography*, trans. Richard Howard (London: Cape, 1982).

Benjamin, Walter, 'Unpacking My Library: A Talk about Book Collecting' (1931), in Hannah Arendt (ed.) and Harry Zhon (trans.), *Illuminations* (Bungay, Suffolk: Fontana/Collins, 1983), pp. 59–67.

——, *The Work of Art in the Age of Its Technological Reproducibility and Other Writings on Media*, ed. Michael W. Jennings, Brigit Doherty and Thomas Y. Levin (Cambridge, MA and London: The Belknap Press of Harvard University, 2008).

Bolton, Richard (ed.), *The Contest of Meaning: Critical Histories of Photography* (Cambridge, MA: MIT Press, 1989).

Boym, Svetlana, *The Future of Nostalgia* (New York: Basic Books, 2001).

Brewster, David, 'Photogenic Drawing, or Drawing by the Agency of Light', *Edinburgh Review* 76 (1843), pp. 309–44.

Bryant, Marsha, *Photo-textualities: Reading Photographs and Literature* (Newark: University of Delaware Press, 1996).

Büchler, Pavel (ed.), *Books: Turning Over the Pages* (Cambridge: Kettle's Yard Gallery, 1986).

Bury, Stephen (ed.), *Breaking the Rules: The Printed Face of the European Avant Garde 1900–1937* (London: The British Library, 2007).

Carroll, Noël, *A Philosophy of Mass Art* (Oxford: Clarendon Press, 1998).

Chalfen, Richard, *Snapshot Versions of Life* (Ohio: Bowling Green University Press, 1987).

Classen, Constance, *The Book of Touch* (Oxford and New York: Berg, 2005).

Coleman, A.D., *Depth of Field: Essays on Photography, Mass Media, and Lens Culture* (Albuquerque: University of New Mexico Press, 1998).

Crimp, Douglas, *On the Museum's Ruins* (Cambridge, MA: MIT Press, 1993).

De Certeau, Michel, *The Practice of Everyday Life*, trans. Stephen Rendall (London: University of California Press, 1984).

Dexter, Emma, and Weski, Thomas (eds), *Cruel and Tender: The Real in the Twentieth-Century Photograph* (London: Tate Publishing, 2003).

Di Bello, Patrizia, *Women's Albums and Photography in Victorian England: Ladies, Mothers and Flirts* (Aldershot, UK and Burlington, VT: Ashgate, 2007).

Edwards, Elizabeth, 'Photographs as Objects of Memory', in Marius Kwint, Christopher Breward and Jeremy Aynsley (eds), *Material Memories* (Oxford and New York: Berg, 1999), pp. 221–36.

Edwards, Elizabeth, and Hart, Janice (eds), *Photographs, Objects, Histories: On the Materiality of Images* (London and New York: Routledge, 2004).

Eisenstein, Sergei, *The Film Sense*, ed. and trans. Jay Leyda (London: Faber and Faber, 1968).

Evans, David, 'Brecht's *War Primer*: The "Photo-Epigram" as Poor Monument', *Afterimage* 30:5 (2003).

Fusco, Maria, and Hunt, Ian (eds), *Put About: A Critical Anthology of Independent Publishing* (London: Book Works, 2004).

Gidley, Mick (ed.), *Writing with Light; Words and Photographs in American Texts* (Oxford: Peter Lang, 2010).

Gidley, Mick, and Lawson-Peebles, Robert (eds), *Modern American Landscapes* (Amsterdam: VU University Press, 1995).

Goldschmidt, Lucien, and Naef, Weston J., *The Truthful Lens: A Survey of the Photographically Illustrated Book 1844–1914* (New York: Grolier Club, 1980).

Grosz, Elizabeth, *Architecture from the Outside: Essay on Virtual and Real Space* (Cambridge MA and London: MIT).

Halbwachs, Maurice, *On Collective Memory*, ed. and trans. Lewis A. Coser (Chicago and London: Chicago University Press, 1985).

——, *The Collective Memory*, trans. Francis J. Ditter Jr and Vida Yazdi Ditter, introduction by Mary Douglas (New York: Harper & Row, 1980).

Hatt, Michael, '"The Book Beautiful": Reading, Vision, and the Homosexual Imagination in Late Victorian Britain', in Luisa Calé and Patrizia Di Bello (eds), *Illustrations, Optics and Objects in Nineteenth-Century Literary and Visual Cultures* (Basingstoke: Palgrave Macmillan, 2010), pp. 167–84.

Haworth-Booth, Mark, *Photography: An Independent Art* (Princeton: Princeton University Press, 1997).

Holman, Valerie, *Printing for Victory: Book Publishing in England 1939–1945* (London: British Library, 2008).

Holmes, Oliver Wendell, 'The Stereoscope and the Stereograph' (1859), in Alan Trachtenberg (ed.), *Classic Essays on Photography* (New Haven: Leete's Island Books, 1980).

Hoskins, Janet, *Biographical Objects: How Things Tell the Stories of People's Lives* (New York: Routledge, 1998).

Hughes, Alex, and Noble, Andrea (eds), *Phototextualities: Intersections of Photography and Narrative* (Albuquerque: University of New Mexico Press, 2003).

Hunter, Jefferson, *Image and Word: The Interaction of Twentieth-Century Photographs and Texts* (Cambridge: Harvard University Press, 1987).

Kelly, Mary, 'Reviewing Modernist Criticism', *Screen* 22:3 (London: British Film Institute, 1981).

Kozloff, Max, *Lone Visions, Crowded Frames: Essays on Photography* (Albuquerque: University of New Mexico Press, 1994).

Langford, Martha, *Suspended Conversations: The Afterlife of Memory in Photographic Albums* (Montreal and Kingston: McGill-Queen University Press, 2001).

Levinas, Emmanuel, *Totality and Infinity: An Essay on Exteriority*, trans. Alphonso Lingis (Pittsburgh: Duquesne University Press, 1969).

Lippard, Lucy, *Six Years: The Dematerialization of the Art Object from 1966 to 1972* (New York and London: Praeger/Studio Vista, 1973).

Mariño, Melanie, 'Almost Not Photography', in Michael Corris (ed.), *Conceptual Art* (Cambridge: Cambridge University Press, 2004), pp. 63–74.

McDonald, Peter D., 'Ideas of the Book and Histories of Literature: After Theory?', *PMLA* 21:1 (2006), pp. 214–28.

McKenzie, Donald F., *Making Meaning: 'Printers of the Mind' and Other Essays* (Amherst, MA: University of Massachusetts Press, 2002).

Mitchell, W.J.T., *Picture Theory: Essays on Verbal and Visual Representation* (Chicago and London: University of Chicago Press, 1994).

Nora, Pierre 'Between Memory and History: Les Lieux de Mémoire', *Représentations* 26 (1989), pp. 7–24.

—— (ed.), *Les Lieux de mémoire* (Paris: Gallimard, 1984–93).

Parr, Martin, and Badger, Gerry, *The Photobook: A History*, 2 vols (London: Phaidon, 2004, 2006).

Perrée, Robe, *Cover to Cover: The Artist's Book in Perspective* (Rotterdam: NAi Publishers, 2002).

Prosser, Jay, *Light in the Dark Room: Photography and Loss* (Minneapolis: University of Minnesota Press, 2005).

Rancière, Jacques, *The Politics of Aesthetics* (Paris, 2000; London: Continuum, 2004).

Roberts, John (ed.), *The Impossible Document: Photography and Conceptual Art in Britain 1966–1976* (London: Camerawork, 1997).

——, *The Art of Interruption: Realism, Photography and the Everyday* (Manchester and New York: Manchester University Press, 1998).

Rose, Gillian, *Mourning Becomes the Law: Philosophy and Representation* (Cambridge: Cambridge University Press, 1996).

Roth, Andrew, et al., *The Book of 101 Books: Seminal Photographic Books of the Twentieth Century* (New York: PPP Editions in association with Roth Horowitz LLC, 2001).

—— (ed.), *The Open Book: A History of the Photographic Book from 1878 to the Present* (Göteborg: Hasselblad Center, 2004).

Rugg, Linda Haverty, *Picturing Ourselves: Photography and Autobiography* (Chicago and London: University of Chicago Press, 1997).

Schwarz, Hillel, *The Culture of the Copy: Striking Likenesses, Unreasonable Facsimiles* (New York: Zone Books, 1996).

Scott, Clive, *The Spoken Image: Photography and Language* (London: Reaktion, 1999).

——, *Street Photography from Atget to Cartier-Bresson* (London: I.B.Tauris, 2007).

Sekula, Allan, 'On the Invention of Photographic Meaning' (1975), in Victor Burgin (ed.), *Thinking Photography* (London: Macmillan, 1982), pp. 84–109.

Sontag, Susan, *On Photography* (1977; London: Penguin, 1986)

Stewart, Susan, 'Prologue: From the Museum of Touch', in M. Kwint, C. Breward and J. Aynsley (eds), *Material Memories: Design and Evocation* (Oxford and New York: Berg, 1999) pp. 17–36.

——, *On Longing: Narratives of the Miniature, the Gigantic, the Souvenir, the Collection* (Durham, NC and London: Duke University Press, 1993).

Stimson, Blake, *The Pivot of the World: Photography and Its Nation* (Cambridge, MA: MIT, 2006).

Tagg, John, *The Disciplinary Frame: Photographic Truths and the Capture of Meaning* (Minneapolis and London: University of Minnesota Press, 2009).

Tisseron, Serge, *Le Mystère de la chambre claire: photographie et inconscient* (Paris: Flammarion, 1996).

Trachtenberg, Alan, *Reading American Photographs: Images as History, Matthew Brady to Walker Evans* (New York: Hill and Wang, 1990).

Twyman, Michael, *Printing 1770–1970: An Illustrated History of Its Development and Uses in England* (1970; London: The British Library, 1998).

Van Alphen, Ernst, *Art in Mind: How Contemporary Images Shape Thought* (Chicago: University of Chicago Press, 2005).

Wainwright, Loudon, *The Great American Magazine* (New York: Alfred A. Knopf, 1986).

INDEX